DAILY LIFE DURING

The American Revolution

The Greenwood Press "Daily Life Through History" Series

DAILY LIFE DURING

The American Revolution

DOROTHY DENNEEN VOLO AND JAMES M. VOLO

The Greenwood Press "Daily Life Through History" Series

GREENWOOD PRESS
Westport, Connecticut • London

Library of Congress Cataloging-in-Publication Data

Volo, Dorothy Denneen, 1949–
    Daily life during the American Revolution / Dorothy Denneen Volo and James M. Volo.
        p. cm.—(The Greenwood Press "Daily life through history" series, ISSN 1080–4749)
        Includes bibliographical references (p.   ) and index.
        ISBN 0–313–31844–1 (alk. paper)
        1. United States—History—Revolution, 1775–1783—Social aspects.   2. United States—Social life and customs—1775–1783.   3. United States—Social conditions—To 1865.
        I. Volo, James M., 1947–   II. Title.   III. Series.
E209.V65   2003
973.3'1—dc21   2002044842

British Library Cataloguing in Publication Data is available.

Library of Congress Catalog Card Number: 2002044842
ISBN: 0–313–31844–1
ISSN: 1080–4749

First published in 2003

Greenwood Press, 88 Post Road West, Westport, CT 06881
An imprint of Greenwood Publishing Group, Inc.
www.greenwood.com

Printed in the United States of America

The paper used in this book complies with the Permanent Paper Standard issued by the National Information Standards Organization (Z39.48–1984).

10 9 8 7 6 5 4 3 2 1

Contents

Chronology

1766	Rockingham becomes prime minister
	The Declaratory Act is passed by Parliament
1767	The first Townshend Duties become law
1768	John Dickinson publishes *Letters from a Farmer in Pennsylvania*
1769	Townshend Duties reissued
1770	The Boston Massacre
	The regulars are withdrawn to Castle William in Boston Harbor
	The Townshend Duties are revoked
	Lord North becomes prime minister
1771	Boston seethes with unrest, but Anglo-American commerce increases
1772	The revenue cutter *Gaspee* is burned by irate colonials in Rhode Island
	The *Boston Pamphlet* is released
1773	Committees of Correspondence formed in many colonies
	Boston Tea Party
1774	The Coercive Acts, including the Boston Port Bill, the Quebec Act, and those known as the Intolerable Acts
	Virginia House of Burgesses is dissolved by Lord Dunmore
	The First Continental Congress adopts the Continental Association
	Lt. Gen. Thomas Gage becomes the military governor of Massachusetts
	The Powder Alarm
1775	Royal governor Josiah Martin dissolves the assembly in North Carolina
	Battle of Lexington, Massachusetts
	Battle of Concord Bridge and the retreat to Boston
	Battle of Great Bridge, Virginia
	Lord Dunmore of Virginia retreats to the ships of the Royal Navy

The Second Continental Congress meets in Philadelphia

Fort Ticonderoga, New York, taken by Ethan Allen and Benedict Arnold

First U.S. flag approved by Congress (Margaret Manny's Flag of Union)

Generals Burgoyne, Clinton, and Howe arrive in America

George Washington takes command of the patriot army at Boston

The capture of the British store ships *Nancy* and *Concord*, and the troop ships *Anne, George, Lord Howe,* and *Annabella*

Battle of Breed's Hill (Bunker Hill) and shelling of Charlestown, Massachusetts

Montreal taken by Richard Montgomery

Battle of Quebec

Encampment of the patriot army at Boston (winter 1775–1776)

1776   The first cruise of the Continental Navy

The first landing of the Marines (New Providence, Bahamas)

British evacuate Boston

Royal Navy shells New York

Battle of Moore's Creek Bridge, North Carolina

Battle of Long Island (Brooklyn Heights), New York

Patriots retreat to Manhattan over the East River

Battle of Harlem Heights, New York

Nathan Hale hanged as a spy

Battle of Pell's Point (Pelham Bay), New York

Patriots escape Manhattan by way of Kingsbridge

Battle of White Plains, New York

Falmouth (Portland, Maine) bombarded by the Royal Navy

Attack on Charleston, South Carolina

Battle of Valcour Island, New York

Fort Washington, New York, falls

The flag of the United States recognized by the Dutch governor of St. Eustasius, West Indies

Fort Lee, New Jersey, abandoned.

Patriots retreat across New Jersey

The great New York fire

Washington crosses the Delaware River and attacks the Hessians at Trenton, New Jersey

First encampment of the patriot army at Morristown, New Jersey (winter 1776–1777)

1777   Battle of Princeton, New Jersey

Burning of Danbury, Connecticut

Battle of Ridgefield, Connecticut

Patriots abandon Fort Ticonderoga, New York

Betsy Ross's stars and stripes flag approved by Congress

Siege of Fort Stanwix, New York

Battle of Oriskany, New York

Action at Hubbardton, Vermont

Battle of Bennington, Vermont

Congress flees Philadelphia

Howe captures Philadelphia

Saratoga campaign (Freeman's Farm and Bemis Heights), New York

Battle of Brandywine (Chadd's Ford), Pennsylvania

Battle of Germantown, Pennsylvania

Burgoyne surrenders

Action at Thomas Swamp, Florida

Encampment of the patriot army at Valley Forge, Pennsylvania (winter 1777–1778)

1778   The Conway Cabal

Ranger battles *Drake*

Battle of Monmouth, New Jersey. Charles Lee removed from the army

Wyoming Valley, Pennsylvania, massacre

Cherry Valley, Pennsylvania, massacre

The French alliance

Kaskaskia, Illinois, and Vincennes, Indiana, fall to the patriots

French attack on Newport, Rhode Island

British take Savannah, Georgia

Second encampment of the patriot army at Morristown, New Jersey (winter 1778–1779)

1779   Raid on Greenwich, Connecticut

Burning of Norwalk, Fairfield, and Westport, Connecticut

Battle of Stony Point, New York

Sullivan-Clinton campaign against Iroquois

Attack on Paulus Hook, New Jersey

Bonhomme Richard battles *Serapis*

Attack on Lloyd's Neck, New York

Battle of Fort Morris, Georgia

Battle of Port Royal, South Carolina

Battle of Kettle Creek, Georgia

French attack Savannah, Georgia

Encampment of the patriot army at Redding, Connecticut (winter 1779–1780)

1780   Fall of Charleston, South Carolina

Action at Waxhaw, South Carolina

Battle of Camden, South Carolina

The Burning of the Valleys, New York

Benedict Arnold's treason is discovered

Major John Andre hanged as a spy

Battle of King's Mountain, South Carolina

The southern campaign continues as the northern army winters in the Hudson Highlands, New York

Third encampment of the patriot army at Morristown, New Jersey (winter 1780–1781)

1781   Several regiments of the Pennsylvania Line mutiny at Morristown, New Jersey. The ringleaders are executed

Battle of Cowpens, South Carolina

Action at Haw River, North Carolina

Battle of Guilford Courthouse, North Carolina

Action at Hobkirks Hill, South Carolina

Attack at Ninety-six, South Carolina

Action at Green Spring (Hot Water), Virginia

Action at Eutaw Springs, South Carolina

Battle of the Chesapeake (Virginia) Capes

Battle of Yorktown, Virginia

1782   Battle of the Saintes (in the West Indies)

Shawnee villages on the Great Miami River, Ohio, are destroyed

Peace negotiations commence in Paris

Final encampment of the patriot army at Newburgh, New York (winter 1782–1783)

1783–January   The Peace of Paris ends the war

The independence of the United States is recognized

Introduction

In all the wars against the French the Americans never showed so
much conduct, attention, and perseverance as they do now.
                                        —Lt. General Thomas Gage, 1775[1]

The Peace of Paris of 1763, which ended the French and Indian War
(1754–1763), left Britain with a worldwide trading empire. The ministry
in London had never before attempted to rule an overseas empire of
such size and complexity as the one it had just acquired from France.
Although the British had an established military, naval, and colonial administration, it was under great pressure, for the empire had almost instantly outgrown the structure of government.[2]

The struggle with France for North America had required the cooperation of the colonials and the British Army to a degree never before
experienced. However, the effort was marred by ill feelings created during the initial tactical phases of the conflict. The Crown officials felt that
they should have been met with gratitude for defending the colonies.
Instead, the provincial legislatures resisted their propositions and treated
the British military with disdain, ridicule, and even contempt. In this
regard the French wars, and the French and Indian War in particular,
represent formative episodes in the history and culture of the United
States.[3]

British army officers "never tired of reminding one another that the
American colonists made the world's worst soldiers."[4] They viewed the

colonials as "the dirtiest, most contemptible, cowardly dogs" that could be conceived, who needed to learn "how a war should be fought."[5] Yet many of the initial military successes against the French were directly attributable to the ceaseless determination of the provincial forces raised by the New England colonies.[6] Provincial forces also stopped an army of French regulars from splitting the British colonies in half in 1755 at the battle of Lake George. This victory served to counter the severe psychological impact of the concurrent defeat of Gen. Edward Braddock and his regulars on the Monongahela River, where only the cool response of the Virginia militia and the decisive actions taken by George Washington saved the majority of the survivors from total annihilation. Each success on the battlefield by colonial forces increased their sense of self-importance and lowered the prestige of the royal government and the British military in their eyes.

The Crown found the colonials shortsighted, selfish, and even maliciously insubordinate. A British officer wrote, "I have been greatly disappointed by the neglect and supineness of the assemblies of those provinces, with which I am concerned. They promised great matters and have done nothing whereby, instead of forwarding, they have obstructed the service."[7] The citizens of Massachusetts were particularly incensed by critical comments like these because they had answered every call by the Crown to assault the French with a laudable immediacy. Their frontier settlements bordering Canada had borne the brunt of Indian attacks, abductions, and scalpings. In the final years of the struggle one-third of all the able-bodied males in Massachusetts were in the army, and a large portion of these men died in service of wounds, neglect, or exposure. Public debt in the colony skyrocketed, and local taxes almost doubled.[8]

Although colonial enthusiasm for fighting the French made the failure of British arms seem less disastrous, it would be an error to claim, as many Americans did, that the provincials alone had won North America for the empire. By 1763 both the regulars and the provincials had gained knowledge, discipline, and experience in warfare. However, their mutual antagonism caused respect for royal authority in the colonies to shrink to such a small measure in the interim that Parliament felt the need to exert its full authority to keep the colonists in subjection.

Meanwhile, young King George III allied himself to Prime Minister George Grenville and First Lord of Trade Charles Townshend. Grenville was openly hostile to the colonial governments in America, especially with regard to the strict enforcement of the trade statutes, including the full range of duties and taxes envisioned by Townshend. A "growing interest in colonies as markets rather than as sources of raw materials . . . implied that the colonies would be constrained permanently to buy more than they sold—an economic grievance which did a great deal to link colonial planters and merchants to colonial politicians." Many

Anglo-Americans came to fear that they would become perpetual debtors to the financial interests in England, living and dying in poverty regardless of their personal resolve to labor, invest, and save.[9]

The Grenville program for America astounded the governing classes on both sides of the Atlantic. Yet the ministry believed that the colonials would not seriously resist these changes to their traditional political and economic status. The architects of public change rarely understand beforehand the extent of the economic, social, or political innovations their actions have turned loose. In this case the Crown grossly underestimated the reaction of the American people. Nonetheless, Grenville intended that the laws regulating trade and revenue be enforced to the letter. To that end, he sent British army officers to command the frontier outposts, Royal Navy warships to patrol the American coastline, and an army of petty bureaucrats to collect the revenue and man the government offices. In each of these acts the colonials perceived that they were the targets of imperial condescension, distrust, and animosity.

In this manner the American Revolution, like other civil upheavals before and since, began as a conservative movement calling for a return to former times. The colonials had a powerful case on their side, rooted in the British constitution and established by the precedent of more than a century of colonial self-government. They also had numerous proponents of their position—mostly moderate Whigs—to speak for them in Parliament. However, revolutions often begin by sounding orthodox, traditional, or nostalgic in their rhetoric. Handbills, broadsides, editorials, letters, and petitions circulated throughout the colonies. Speeches were made; sermons were preached; and enthusiastic crowds harangued public officials. In this way an essentially economic dispute between two factions of the same empire evolved into a political and military confrontation that would rip it apart.

Because the American Revolution gave birth to the nation, it has received the attention of uncounted historians. Many of these, particularly those writing during the chaotic period surrounding the American Civil War, took liberties with the facts in order to firm up the traditional foundations of an America in peril. The authors of the present history have tried to separate the facts from the propaganda, and the politics from the policies. We have incorporated the words of persons contemporary to the period wherever possible, and have attempted a meaningful analysis of the implications of what they wrote or said.

However, most ordinary Americans, whether patriots, redcoats, or loyalists, put few of their thoughts on paper. Private Joseph Plumb Martin and Sgt. Benjamin Gilbert are notable exceptions. American, British, French, and Hessian officers, being educated men, tended to write of contemporary events in journals and letters, and to produce memoirs in their retirement, as did Henry Lee, Banastre Tarleton, John von Krafft,

James Thacher, Charles Cornwallis, and Molyneux Shuldham. Some published blistering attacks and counterattacks, as did Thomas Graves and Henry Clinton, blaming each other for the loss of America. The writings and correspondence of George Washington and the journals of the Continental Congress have proved eminently useful.

We have utilized several excellent collections of personal letters, diaries, and journals of less prominent persons who lived through the war. The personal correspondence of Capt. Nathan Peters and Lois Peters, his wife, is particularly useful in documenting the day-to-day matters of maintaining a family of small children and a business in wartime. The journals of Christopher Hawkins and Thomas Dring, held prisoners during the war, give a unique insight into this particular area of Revolutionary history. The diaries of Elizabeth Drinker, Dorothy Dudley, and Baroness von Riedesel are invaluable in bringing forward the female perspective on the war.

Recently published studies concerning the Revolution from the British and loyalist points of view have been used extensively. Additionally, we have mined the collections of several state historical societies for the thoughts of militiamen, local politicians, and native Americans. We have tapped the wealth of material in the records of the British Admiralty, the Colonial Office, the United States Army Center of Military Studies, and the United States Naval War College.

In 1775 all of the residents of the Atlantic-facing colonies were British subjects endowed with the rights of Englishmen, and both those loyal to the king and those determined to be independent of him considered themselves "patriotic Americans." We are mindful of the need to differentiate between these two thoughtful and devoted groups of Americans, but we do not want to strip the Loyalist population of the colonies of their nationality by pitting them grammatically against those who rebelled against their rightful monarch. Both groups were decidedly *American* in their character, *patriotic* with regard to their country, and *loyal*, each in their own way, to their beliefs. We decided to defer to a common contemporary designation given to the *patriot party* and *loyalist party* by certain journalists. The term *patriot* is used when referring to those Americans in rebellion, and *loyalist* is used for those who remained devoted to the king. The terms *regulars* and *redcoats* are used when referring to British troops from overseas, and *militia*, *provincials*, or *Continentals* for those forces raised in America.

NOTES

1. Jonathan Gregory Rossie, *The Politics of Command in the American Revolution* (Syracuse, NY: Syracuse University Press, 1975), 19.

2. James Truslow Adams and Charles Garrett Vannest, *The Record of America*

(New York: Charles Scribner's Sons, 1935), 77; Michael Pearson, *Those Damned Rebels: The American Revolution as Seen Through British Eyes* (New York: DaCapo Press, 1972), 7.

3. See James M. Volo and Dorothy Denneen Volo, *Daily Life on the Old Colonial Frontier* (Westport, CT: Greenwood Press, 2002).

4. Fred W. Anderson, "Why Did Colonial New Englanders Make Bad Soldiers? Contractual Principles and Military Conduct During the Seven Years' War." *William and Mary Quarterly* 3rd ser., 38 (1981), 395.

5. Reported in Charles A. Beard and Mary R. Beard, *The Rise of American Civilization* (New York: Macmillan, 1927), 227; General St. Clair to General Braddock, April 10, 1775, in Andrew J. Wahll, ed., *The Braddock Road Chronicles, 1755* (Bowie, MD: Heritage Books, 1999), 124.

6. New England then included Massachusetts (which claimed all of Maine), Connecticut, Rhode Island, and New Hampshire. Vermont was a disputed area claimed by both New York and New Hampshire. It was sometimes called the "Grants."

7. A letter to Sir Robert Napier from Braddock, April 19, 1755, in Andrew J. Wahll, ed., *The Braddock Road Chronicles, 1755* (Bowie, MD: Heritage Books, 1999), 354.

8. Richard Koebner, *Empire* (New York: Grosset and Dunlap, 1965), 94. See also Douglas E. Leach, *Roots of Conflict: British Armed Forces and Colonial Americans, 1677–1775* (Chapel Hill: University of North Carolina Press, 1986), 25–30.

9. Eric Robson, *The American Revolution in Its Political and Military Aspects, 1763–1783* (New York: Norton, 1966), 8.

1

Anglo-America in the Eighteenth Century

We cannot but observe with sorrow that [the regulars] . . . afforded us but little assistance during this and the last war. The[y] . . . neither helped our distressed inhabitants to save their crops, nor did they attack our enemies in their towns, or patrol on our frontiers.[1]
—James Otis, on the British role during Pontiac's Rebellion, 1764

MIGRATIONS OF COLONIAL AMERICANS

Among the diverse groups of Europeans to immigrate to America before 1775, there were at least four distinct waves of English-speaking colonists. This was no random flood of migrating people, but rather a sequential movement of four separate and distinct sets of Britons, each with unique political, religious, and social characteristics. While all four waves shared a common language and adherence to the Protestant faith, they spoke different dialects, sometimes belonged to mutually belligerent religious sects, built their houses differently, held diverse views on business and farming, and had different conceptions of public order, political power, and personal freedom.[2]

The first mass migration consisted of Puritans who came as religious dissenters from the east of England to Massachusetts. The first of these, the Pilgrims, decided to abandon England in the belief that only by separating themselves from the established Anglican Church could they live "in the presence of God" and advance the "gospel of the kingdom of Christ in those remote parts of the world."[3] The second wave was composed of a small royalist elite, supporters of Anglicanism from southern England, and a number of indentures whom they brought along to serve them. These settled mainly in Virginia during the Republican period of Puritan rule in England. The third movement was composed of persons from the northern midlands of England and Wales—Quakers and other religious dissenters who settled the Delaware Valley in an attempt to found a "Holy Experiment" in the wilderness of Pennsylvania. The fourth wave—composed mostly of Scotch-Irish Presbyterians—was from the borders of northern Britain and northern Ireland. While the majority of the English clung to the coastal towns and cities, the Scoth-Irish moved through the established settlements into the backcountry that formed the frontier.[4]

Language

The English-speaking colonials were joined by diverse people from many other cultures during the eighteenth century. A contemporary observer in New York City[5] noted that he heard English, High Dutch, Low Dutch (Flemish), French, and several native American languages spoken on a daily basis in his business. In Pennsylvania the sounds of English, German, and Dutch were mixed with the accents of Welsh, Gaelic, and Swedish. In this regard the Germans achieved a far greater social solidarity than any other linguistic group by maintaining their tongue and by separating themselves into distinct communities based on religion and place of origin. Joshua Gilpin, traveling through eastern Pennsylvania, noted, "I never knew before the total want of a language for in this respect we might as well have been in the middle of Germany."[6] In some regions the influence of the Dutch was so strong that several families with English roots were speaking the Dutch language as their own within two decades of their arrival. Nonetheless, English remained the predominant language of almost all colonial Americans.[7]

Religion

The distinctive folkways of the colonists created an expansive pluralism in America, which may help explain the rapid onset of political polarization and upheaval. In particular, the Scotch-Irish Presbyterians, who settled in the Appalachian backcountry of the southern colonies with their dreams of a Jacobite restoration, crushed at Culloden in 1746, "came from the Celtic fringes of the British Isles, propelled by failed rebellion, a decaying clan system, agrarian transformation and sheep enclosures, high rents, poverty, and famine." With the crest of their migration less than a decade old at the time of the Revolution, the tough-minded

Scotch-Irish held to their contrary political views on the frontier. Having only recently been in open rebellion against the Crown, they remained actively anti-English or unwilling to work cooperatively with English authorities.[8]

The English-Welsh Quakers, who dominated the political life of Pennsylvania, carefully avoided the appearance of political or religious disharmony. By 1760, they had become a minority in the colony they had founded. Protestant pietists from Germany, Switzerland, and Alsace made up 42 percent of the population of the colony by midcentury, and the Presbyterian Scotch-Irish an additional 30 percent. The non-Quaker immigrants were hurried on their way west to the frontiers, however, and English-speaking Quakers maintained their political control of the government, holding 75 percent of the seats in the colonial legislature on the eve of the war.

New York, taken from the Netherlands in the late seventeenth century, was the most socially and religiously diverse colony. In the former Dutch colony, the Church of England (Anglican) had become the established religion, replacing the Dutch Reformed Church, but only in New York City was a state religion recognized. A small population of Sephardic Jews had established itself in the city before the English takeover of the colony, and small groups of Spaniards, Portuguese, and Italians had arrived during the Dutch regime. Each had proclaimed an adherence to the official Calvinist doctrine required by the Dutch Reformed Church. The remainder of the colony was remarkably diverse with regard to religion; pockets of French Huguenots, Flemish Walloons, German Lutherans, Dutch Reformed Hollanders, and Anglicans scattered about the river valleys of the colony.

Puritan thinking, which had traded royal authority for a dogmatic and intolerant theocracy in Massachusetts in the 1620s, dominated New England in the form of an overwhelming allegiance to the Congregational Church. The Congregationalists had turned out all other minor Protestant sects from New England and had resisted the authority of the established Anglican Church. Puritan intolerance had been overcome only by an influx of Anglicans supported by the Crown, but the Congregational Church remained the majority religion in all of New England.

Only in the tidewater South were the followers of the established church in a majority. The great planters of Virginia and Maryland had initially been either Anglicans or Catholics, but the former had supplanted the latter almost everywhere, including in Catholic-founded Maryland. The frontier regions of the Carolinas were largely populated by Presbyterians or pietists, whose religions were rooted in orthodox Calvinist thinking. "They had no sympathy with state support of the Established Church or with the ceremonies of Anglicanism and resented the payment of taxes to support the Established Church."[9]

Old Stone Fort. Used as a place of refuge from Indian attack, this fine stone building was a Dutch Reformed church situated in Schoharie, New York. Today it houses a Revolutionary period museum and bookstore.

In 1702, Queen Anne had granted liberty of religion to all the colonies as long as they paid their tithe to the established church, but she deprived Catholics of the right to hold office or to vote. Similar legislation prevented Catholics from settling in New York and Georgia. These laws were partially a reaction to French aggression from Canada, but they were not repealed until 1774, as part of the Quebec Act.

On the eve of the Revolution, it has been estimated that there were almost 3000 churches or meeting houses in the American colonies. Of these, 22 percent were Congregational; 20 percent were Presbyterian; 16 percent were Baptist; 10 percent were Quaker; and 5 percent were Lutheran and Dutch Reformed. The Catholic religion, which had once predominated in Maryland, now made up a mere 2 percent of the congregations, a number surpassed even by the nascent Methodist following. Notably, the established religion (Episcopalian or Anglican) represented only 16 percent of the churches in the colonies, even with the support of the Crown. The vast majority of the Congregational churches were in New England, and those of the Presbyterian faith dominated the frontier regions.[10]

That the Revolution was to take root most strongly among the religious dissenters of New England and the western frontiers, while loyalism remained the strongest characteristic of the south and of urban New

York, can be attributed in no small measure to the part played by these religious affiliations. The dissenting clergy generally sided with the revolution and were described by a British officer as "the most canting, hypocritical, lying scoundrels . . . the descendants of Oliver Cromwell's army, who truly inherit the spirit which was the occasion of so much bloodshed . . . from the year 1642 till the Restoration."[11]

Literacy

One measure of literacy in a society is the extent to which writing and reading replace oral communications. "Literacy . . . makes practical the maintenance of a communication network wider than one's locality."[12] If only the ability to write one's name is used as the standard for literacy, documentary evidence suggests that most Americans in the eighteenth century were probably literate. If the ability to read is added, drawing a valid conclusion as to the literacy of the general population becomes more difficult. The difference between signing one's name and a true literacy, where concepts and strategies are being shared or modified in written or printed form, has enormous implications. Without a true literacy, fomenting a widespread revolution is almost impossible.

It is almost certain that most Americans, belonging to nonconforming religions that valued personal Bible reading, possessed a basic reading literacy. However, simple comprehension of the Bible is a great deal different from the sophisticated skills required to read difficult prose, political and philosophical treatises, theoretical works in languages other than English, or the Greek and Roman classics. All of these modes were referenced by the patriots in newspapers, pamphlets, plays, and letters to further their political agenda. This suggests they believed that their audience was a fairly literate and sophisticated one.

Moreover, an analysis of legal documents, letters, and journals of the period suggests that as much as 90 percent of free white men in New England were literate. This proportion shrinks to 70 percent among the Scotch-Irish males on the frontier, where there were few books available beyond the Bible. The planters of the aristocratic South seem to have mirrored the high literacy rates found among their social and economic peers in England, and they probably owned the most extensive personal libraries.

Education

In an era before public schools, only those who were wealthy could afford extensive formal educations. Most educated persons learned their letters from tutors or itinerant teachers. By their early teens—much younger than students today—young men might receive a college education in law, science, or theology at Princeton, Yale, Harvard, Dartmouth, or William and Mary. Most colonial youngsters learned their letters from their parents, their minister, or a local learned gentleman. For the vast majority, there was a practical education as an apprentice to a tradesman or artisan. This did not mean that they were not taught to read and write. Reading and writing were an important part of any business enterprise.

Women's education with respect to reading and writing was far more limited than that of men, and there was a great disparity of education between the genders in all regions of the colonies. Most women outside the lowest classes of society would not be thought uneducated, but they were generally not as well versed as their husbands or brothers. In 1780 it was estimated by anecdotal means that literate men outnumbered literate women by two to one, yet by 1850, when the federal census first measured literacy, there was little difference between the genders. Only in the South had women's education lagged behind.[13]

Abigail Adams, herself an excellent writer and reader, regretted "the trifling narrow, contracted education of females" available in the colonies.[14] Elizabeth Lucas Pinckney received a fashionable education in England that stressed "female topics," but she thought it inexcusable for women "who have had an education above that of a chambermaid" to voluntarily remain "greatly deficient" in more serious matters. As a young woman, the poised and confident Pinckney managed her father's several plantations in South Carolina, and in the 1740s she experimented with means of increasing the production of indigo with stunning success.[15]

Books and Publishing

Almost all of the books read by colonials came from England. There was a good-sized printing industry in the colonies, but it made its profits from newspapers, broadsides, and government printing jobs. There were more English texts than American ones because they were simply less expensive even though they were imported. There were few American authors. Colonial gentlemen "loved their books and often acquired a polished literary style, but they seldom ventured into print." To write a treatise on surveying, mining, or husbandry and share it with one's social equals was one thing, but to publish such a work for the common people to read offended their "sense of propriety."[16] In this regard, New Englanders were somewhat an exception. Cotton Mather, for instance, published no fewer than 450 books and religious pamphlets. Dozens of captivity narratives of life among the Indians were published in New England before the revolution. These served the purpose of escapist literature for a population too conservative to appreciate the developing literary form known as the adventure novel.

Most Americans owned a Bible. It is listed in almost all the available inventories of books from the period. The *Book of Common Prayer* was also widely available, but other works dealing solely with theology are notably lacking. This may be because of the overarching nature of religion in eighteenth century life. Texts dealing with politics, law, and even science were filled with references to religion and God. Political works by Locke, Hobbes, Milton, Swift, and Montesquieu were often founded, in the style of the times, on premises carefully extracted from biblical quotations.

A large number of practical texts on agriculture, botany, husbandry, the care and breeding of livestock, surveying, mathematics, architecture, pharmacy, and basic medical care were available. Books containing specific legal statutes were reserved for those who practiced the law, but many gentlemen included in their libraries generic texts and law dictionaries such as Blackstone's *Commentaries*. Plays and collections of poetry could be found in the larger libraries of the social elite. These were the basis for a great deal of entertainment, especially on isolated southern plantations. Shakespeare's plays appear almost everywhere, and the works of Dryden, Addison, Sheridan, and Moliere (often in English translation) were common. Many histories pepper the surviving inventories; they include those of ancient Greece and Rome, as well as more modern works concerning the English Civil Wars, the Republican period, and the Restoration.

A modern researcher has noted, "Through their use of [personal] libraries . . . the colonists were intellectually well prepared for the struggle for independence . . . [and] had read widely and thought deeply about the principles of freedom and government."[17] However, there is evidence of an unexpected amount of current literature among the libraries of men whose affairs probably left them little time for recreational reading. Jefferson noted in 1771 that through popular literature, "The spacious field of imagination is thus laid open to our use, and lessons may be formed to illustrate and carry home to the mind every moral rule of life."[18]

COLONIAL GOVERNMENT

There were three types of colony in Anglo-America: royal, proprietary, and corporate. Pennsylvania, Delaware, and Maryland had been virtually self-governing fiefdoms under the jurisdiction of proprietors or trustees. Others were created under charters or maintained by the Crown. The government had tried to bring all the colonies of the Northeast, including New York, under the Dominion of New England as royal entities, but Connecticut and Rhode Island had maintained their status as

Table 1.1

The Population of the Colonies in 1775

Colony	Population
Virginia	504,000
Massachusetts*	337,000
Connecticut	298,000
Pennsylvania	270,000
Maryland	255,000
North Carolina	247,000
New York**	193,000
South Carolina	170,000
New Jersey	122,000
New Hampshire	81,000
Rhode Island	58,000
Delaware	37,000

*Includes Maine, then a part of Massachusetts.
**Includes Vermont, known as the New York Grants.

corporate colonies by refusing to submit to the revocation of their charters. Connecticut legislators went so far as to secure the parchment document against confiscation in the hollow of an oak tree. Massachusetts continued to operate under a separate constitution granted in 1691. All the rest had been made royal colonies before the revolution began.[19]

No two colonies were alike in their governance, but all who inhabited them considered themselves "Englishmen" with the same set of political rights. A modern historian of the period has noted, "The colonists were and felt themselves to be thoroughly British; their political institutions were modelled on the British pattern: each colony had a governor, representing the King, an elected Assembly or legislature on the lines of the House of Commons, and an appointed upper chamber known as the Council." The real power, as in Britain, rested with the legislatures, and the colonials had grown accustomed to determining their own affairs.[20] Another historian has noted, "Except for the regulation of trade by Parliament, the colonies had been left largely to themselves, had raised their own taxes, and had defended themselves on land with the occasional cooperation of the British fleet and army."[21]

The resulting decentralization of authority and myriad incoherent policy positions, residing in the nearly autonomous colonial legislatures and asemblies, made the governance of North America difficult. Benjamin Franklin's plan for a union of all the colonies in the face of French aggression, made at Albany in 1754, failed to resolve the morass of intercolonial grievances and suspicions. A concerted response to the problem of uniform governance was then made by the Crown, which tried to put the administration of the colonies on a more firm imperial footing.

The Board of Trade

In 1696, a regular body known as the Board of Trade and Plantations was organized for the purpose of "drawing under one high authority every branch of colonial economy and every transaction of consequence effected by His Majesty's governments beyond the seas." Until the eve of the revolution, this body controlled American affairs. "If an English merchant or manufacturer had a complaint or suggestion to make about acts of any colonial assembly, about the doings of any colonial authority, or about methods of controlling American industry, he could find a sympathetic hearing before the Board of Trade. . . . If, on the other hand, a colony had a grievance to air, it could instruct its agents in London to appear before the Board to present the case." Benjamin Franklin sometimes served as such an agent for the colony of Pennsylvania. When the Board failed to render satisfaction, a hearing could be held before the appellate courts. The secretary of state for colonial affairs, who was usually a political appointee of the ruling party, could insinuate himself into this procedure at any point. "In this way issues could be carried into politics and, if necessary, made the subject of action in Parliament."[22]

A number of other agencies of government in London also had some authority over the colonies. These included the Treasury, the Admiralty Board, the Attorney General, the Solicitor General, and any naval or military officer given authority over a particular station or post. Finally, the bishop of London exercised a good deal of power in supervising matters affecting the established church, including those forbidding or curtailing the actions of the nonconforming religions.[23]

The Proclamation of 1763

During the French and Indian War, Gen. Edward Braddock built a wagon road from Virginia to the forks of the Ohio River, and Gen. James Forbes built a road across the southern tier of Pennsylvania in 1758. These two roads were the greatest public works projects attempted in the British colonies during the period, and they provided improved access into the wilderness. In Pennsylvania, large cargo wagons known as Conestogas were developed to take advantage of these roads, and they quickly became the principal means of transportation beyond the Appalachian Mountains, into what was then considered Indian land.

English traders, land speculators, and settlers began to pour into the Indian territory not only along the roads but also on every Indian trail and through every available mountain gap. This resulted in a breakdown of relations with the frontier tribes. "Indian people from Quebec and Maine to Georgia and the Floridas were complaining in vain to colonial authorities about trespasses on their land, and about schemes to get it." The British had spent seven decades wresting away the allegiance of the tribes from the French. The flood of settlers crossing the mountains, if undiminished, threatened to undo all the work of untold negotiations with the tribes and to make renewed warfare more likely.[24]

In order to limit friction with the Indian nations, George III signed the Proclamation of 1763, which prohibited any white settlement west of the Appalachians and required those who were already settled there to immediately return east of the mountains. The line between the Indian lands and the colonies was "so hastily adopted" that it took no account of the settlements already made, nor of the lands granted to certain colonies and land companies in their charters. The colonial assemblies had invested large sums of money "in raising men, building forts, and supporting the King's civil government" in the frontier regions, and the people had responded to the call for fighting men and had joined the "King's service and common cause." The proclamation offered not a single shilling of indemnification to the colonials for the losses they would now sustain.[25]

The settlers who had taken the earliest steps on the frontiers were now those most disadvantaged. A contemporary observer noted that the frontiers had been "repeatedly attacked and ravaged by skulking parties of the Indians, who have with the most savage cruelty murdered men, women, and children without distinction, and have reduced near a thousand families to the most extreme distress."[26] Many Anglo-Americans had invested both their labor and their scant capital in recently cleared fields, unharvested crops, and newly erected homes, barns, and fences. The economic hardship that they faced if they obeyed the proclamation and abandoned these holdings was staggering.[27]

In 1764 Matthew Smith and James Gibson responded to the proclamation in an open letter to Parliament. Called *A Remonstrance from the Pennsylvania Frontier*, the letter was published and widely read in the colonies. It stated in part, "It grieves us to the very heart to see such of our frontier inhabitants as have escaped savage fury with the loss of their parents, their children, their wives or relatives, left destitute by the public, and exposed to the most cruel poverty and wretchedness [by the government]."[28]

The real problem illustrated by the Proclamation of 1763 was that, given the reality of the colonial frontier at the time, the gradual elimination of the Native American population was as inevitable in the trans-Appalachian country as it had been in the east a century and a half earlier. It was all but impossible for the Crown to regulate trade with the Indians and to maintain its political alliances among the tribes without some military authority, whether imperial or local, appearing to impinge on the rights of the frontier population. British policies that aspired to control the Indians were doomed to fail because of their inability to control the settlers. Increased regulation "only aggravated the tensions, alienated backcountry settlers and ensured that many of them would throw in their lot with the rebels once the Revolution began."[29]

Pontiac's Rebellion

In 1764 a serious Indian uprising in the interior was undertaken by a coalition of tribal nations under the leadership of the Ottawa warrior Pontiac. The effect of this uprising on colonial relations with London can not be underestimated. The Grenville ministry had assured the colonials that the regulars in garrison on the frontier would be "a thin red line between kidnap, scalping, and massacre," and security for the white settlements now that the French were gone. However, Pontiac's uprising seemed to validate many of the negative convictions held by the colonials with regard to the regulars. Every British garrison in the Great Lakes region was taken by the Indians save two, Fort Pitt and Fort Detroit. Although the back of the uprising was broken by the regulars of the Black Watch under Col. Henry Bouquet at the battle of Bushy Run in Pennsylvania, the British army seems to have been unable to fully secure the frontiers until 1766. Colonial confidence in British arms was severely shaken. The British regulars were humiliated, and the bureaucracy in London was embarrassed by the effectiveness of the Native American attacks.[30]

Colonial sensitivities were further assaulted when the line of frontier settlement proposed by the Proclamation of 1763 was "deliberately distorted" by Parliament into a permanent barrier. The "undeniable primary principle" of this line was to foster a market for British manufactures along the coastline and to prevent the development of any colonial industry in the interior.[31] Americans soon began to realize that their own best interests were not always those of the Crown. James Otis, writing from the perspective of the colonials, noted, "The late acquisitions in America, as glorious as they have been, and as beneficial as they are to Great Britain, are only a security to these colonies against the ravages of the French and Indians. Our trade upon the whole is not, I believe, benefited by them one groat."[32]

NOTES

1. Samuel Eliot Morison, *Sources and Documents Illustrating the American Revolution 1764–1788 and the Formation of the Federal Constitution* (New York: Oxford University Press, 1965), 14.

2. David Hackett Fischer, *Albion's Seed: Four British Folkways in America* (New York: Oxford University Press, 1989), 6.

3. Louis B. Wright, *The Atlantic Frontier: Colonial American Civilization, 1607–1763* (New York: Alfred A. Knopf, 1951), 106–107.

4. Fischer, *Albion's Seed*, 6–11.

5. In order to prevent confusion, we have used "New York" to refer to the province, and "New York City" or "the city of New York" when dealing with the town on the island of Manhattan. The city of New York was not incorporated until the nineteenth century, and eighteenth-century sources usually referred to it as New York Town.

6. Peter O. Wacker, *The Musconetcong Valley of New Jersey, A Historical Geography* (New Brunswick, NJ: Rutgers University Press, 1968), 50–51; Joshua Gilpin, "Journey to Bethlehem," *Pennsylvania Magazine of History and Biography* 46 (1922), 25.

7. Wacker, *Musconetcong Valley*, 42; George W. Cummins, *History of Warren County* (New York: Lewis Historical Publishing Co., 1922), 73.

8. Colin G. Calloway, *The American Revolution in Indian Country: Crisis and Diversity in Native American Communities* (Cambridge: Cambridge University Press, 1999), 19.

9. Wright, *Atlantic Frontier*, 96–97.

10. Fischer, *Albion's Seed*, 423.

11. Henry Steele Commager and Richard B. Morris, *The Spirit of Seventy-six: The Story of the American Revolution as Told by Participants* (New York: Harper & Row, 1975), 152–153.

12. Linda K. Kerber, *Women of the Republic: Intellect and Ideology in Revolutionary America* (Chapel Hill: University of North Carolina Press, 1980), 192–193.

13. The disparities between women and men with regard to literacy prior to the nineteenth century are not well documented, and may require reappraisal.

14. Letter from Abigail Adams to John Adams, June 30, 1778, quoted in Kerber, *Women of the Republic*, 191.

15. Ibid., 191–192. In the 1740s indigo production rose from 5000 tons to 130,000 in the Charleston, South Carolina, area because of her activities.

16. Arthur Pierce Middleton, *A Virginia Gentleman's Library* (Williamsburg, VA: Colonial Williamsburg Foundation, 1952), 7.

17. Ibid., 6.

18. Ibid., 10.

19. Citizens of Great Britain were all considered Englishmen, though they may have been from Old England, Wales, or Scotland. The name Great Britain was officially adopted as the title of the triune kingdom in 1707, when the crowns of England and Wales (united in the thirteenth century) were formally added to that of Scotland, although all three crowns had been worn by one monarch since the reign of James Stuart (simultaneously James I of England and James VI of Scotland).

20. Peter Padfield, *Maritime Supremacy and the Opening of the Western Mind* (New York: Overlook Press, 2002), 222.

21. James Truslow Adams and Charles Garrett Vannest, *The Record of America* (New York: Charles Scribner's Sons, 1935), 77.

22. Charles A. Beard and Mary R. Beard, *The Rise of American Civilization* (New York: Macmillan, 1927), 197–199.

23. Ibid., 202–203.

24. Calloway, *The American Revolution*, 23.

25. Morison, *Sources and Documents*, 8.

26. Ibid., 14.

27. Ibid., Morison, 10–11.

28. Ibid., 11.

29. Calloway, *The American Revolution*, 21.

30. John Keegan, *Fields of Battle: The Wars for North America* (New York: Vintage Press, 1997), 135.

31. Morison, *Sources and Documents*, xx.

32. Ibid., 7.

2

The Anglo-American Economy and Trade

One fact is undoubted—under Parliament the state of America has been kept in continual agitation. Everything administered as a remedy to the public complaint . . . is followed by an heightening of distemper.[1]

—Edmund Burke, Minister to Parliament

FOUNDATIONS OF EMPIRE

The British trading empire was founded on the principle of mercantilism. Formulated in the seventeenth century, mercantilism theorized that colonies existed chiefly to benefit the parent state. This benefit was realized in two ways. Real wealth was to be measured by the store of precious metals a nation held, and the state that accumulated the greatest store of silver and gold was thought to be the richest. Second, any nation that could maintain a favorable trade balance with its neighbors could always settle the difference by demanding payments in gold. Freedom from foreign trade deficits, therefore, was considered a measure of commercial strength and economic health.

The vitality of the British economy and the empire itself had initially been founded upon the monopolies granted to chartered trading companies, which brought wealth into the empire through their operations. The Honourable East India Company was unquestionably the most successful of these being valued at £21 million in 1775. However, as the Industrial Revolution dawned in Britain, a highly self-contained and independent manufacturing economy evolved, and this came to better characterize the quintessential mercantile state of the eighteenth century. Both the raw materials and the markets for all of the finished products of a robust manufacturing economy had to remain inside the empire for the state to be successful. Accordingly, Britain sought to remain the center of manufactures, banking, and military resources, while the colonials were confined to the dual role of providers of raw materials and consumers of manufactured goods.[2]

The profits from colonies could be precarious. The most lucrative profits realized by the empire proved to come from the genial addictions, "a quiet smoke, a nice cup of tea, a sweet tooth . . . exotic rarities converted into cravings."[3] When Thomas Garway began offering tea in his coffeehouse in 1657, it quickly became the quintessential British beverage. Tea, like the more "aggressively bitter" coffee or chocolate, was thought to require sugar "to make it palatable." Moreover, the thick sap of the sugarcane plant could be heated and distilled into a very satisfying rum. The British, therefore, highly valued their possessions in the East and West Indies because of their output of tea and sugar, and they stationed troops and warships to defend them long before a single redcoat was stationed in the Anglo-American colonies. The defense of the tobacco plantations of North America was left to the colonials.[4]

The list of important raw materials from continental North America grew with its economy. Besides furs from the forests of the Northeast, timber, barrel staves, wooden shingles, masts, turpentine, rope, wool and leather, pig iron, copper ore, and potash were being exported. The southern and middle American colonies were a source of tobacco, lumber, deerskins, and rice, cotton, and other agricultural produce; and New England was a source of naval stores, whales, and cod and other fish, as well as a defensive outpost "having many great rivers, bays, and harbors fit for the reception of ships of war."[5]

ANGLO-AMERICAN TRADE

As the English colonies in America grew, so did their volume of trade. Between 1720 and 1750 the colonial plantation economy of the early decades changed to a trading economy, and the volume of colonial imports from and exports to Britain doubled. While this circumstance should have been greeted as evidence of a growing and prosperous British trading empire, the colonies were trading with other countries as much as they were with England. South Carolina traded as much as one-ninth of all its rice production directly with the countries of the Mediterranean for wine, fruit, and salt. In like manner Connecticut traded its vegetables; Maryland traded its wheat; and Pennsylvania traded its corn. Massachusetts, and much of coastal New England, clandestinely traded cod with the French islands in the Caribbean in return for salt and molasses. Moreover, colonial merchants and shipowners were becoming active everywhere, being "fully in command of the coastwise commerce" in America and extending their operations into the transatlantic and East Indian trade. It soon became obvious to the Crown that its North American colonies were slowly approaching economic independence.[6]

The Triangular Trade

Parliament, under George II, had attempted to reassert its authority over trade practices in Anglo-America with the Molasses Act of 1733. The heavy import duties on molasses imported from non-British Caribbean islands should have eliminated the trade. Instead, they seemingly made both the colonials and their foreign suppliers more eager to work together, and the contraband rum industry flourished. This patently illegal trade was extremely lucrative, surviving even the outbreak of war between France and Britain. The importance of the rum was in its use in trading for African slaves.

While many historians remain fascinated by the three-way traffic in molasses, rum, and slaves, the Triangular Trade was fundamentally supported by the fisheries of the Grand Banks that provided the dried cod used to feed the slaves on the sugar plantations. Without the cod, the islands would have been unable to support the large number of slaves needed to produce sugar and molasses. Nonetheless, profits were to be had with every exchange made on the trading triangle. Englishmen who never saw their sugar plantations in the Caribbean, made great fortunes during the eighteenth century. Rum distillers in New England made tidy profits changing the molasses into liquor, and the indigenous slave traders of Africa used the rum as both a consumable and an item for further trade. The ubiquitous New England skippers and shipowners took their share of the profits by carrying the cargoes, including human ones, on each leg of the trading triangle. Profits from this business helped New England to offset its considerable deficit in commodity trading with Britain, that amounted to nearly £1.5 million in the decade before the outbreak of the Revolution.[7]

Reorganizing the Empire

While the peace treaty of 1763 was being negotiated, a bitter debate arose in Parliament over whether France should be made to cede to Britain all of Canada or the single sugar island of Guadeloupe in the Caribbean. Under mercantile theory, Britain should have valued the wealth-producing sugar of the tiny island much higher than all the vast plains and forests of Canada. Guadeloupe would have been an immediate and valuable asset. However, the Crown wished to rid itself of the French presence in North America that was interferring with the normal flow of commerce (ships, tobacco, sugar, and slaves) with its Atlantic-facing colonies.

There was never a thought in London of dividing this vast region into an assortment of new English colonies in the interior. The existing set of English provinces had proved frustrating enough. It seemed easier to administer Canada as a single entity unhampered by the activities of white settlers. London would simply reaffirm the mercantile role of the coastal colonies as a source of raw materials and a market for manufactures. The opinion of the Board of Trade was that opening the interior to further settlement might "divert [his] Majesty's subjects in America from the pursuit of these important objects."[8] The Board further noted that its policy was "to confine [the] settlements as much as possible to the sea coast and not to extend them to places inaccessible to shipping and consequently more out of the reach of commerce."[9]

There is little doubt that London intended to prohibit the colonials from following the natural pathways of geographical expansion and economic growth that lay before them. The consumption of British goods would not be promoted by new colonies in the interior, "which being proposed to be established at the distance of fifteen hundred miles from the sea . . . [will] probably lead [the colonials] to manufacture for themselves."[10] Moreover, the Crown wanted all the trade regulations and prohibitions enforced to the letter, and promised the colonials peace, security, and stability in return.

A Changing Economy

London had made few prohibitions against the development of colonial maritime industries because it was thought that they strengthened the empire. Soon after the Peace of Paris, Americans began to revitalize their natural interests in the sea. No longer needing the protection of the Royal Navy at sea, American trading vessels, whalers, and slavers inundated the ports of the world. Of the twenty largest cities in Anglo-America, only one (Lancaster, Pennsylvania) was not a port. New England was soon providing almost half of British shipbuilding capacity worldwide. In Maine and New Hampshire there were more people engaged in shipbuilding than in agriculture, and in Massachusetts it was estimated that there was one ship for every hundred inhabitants. Colonial shippers and merchants made their profits by moving raw materials to England and returning finished goods to the colonial markets. The government took its part of the wealth generated by this activity in the form of taxes, port fees, and customs duties.[11]

The nature of colonial trade in North America had changed more than

Table 2.1

The Twenty Largest Colonial Cities in 1775

Rank	City and Province	Population
1	Philadelphia, PA	40,000
2	New York, NY	21,000
3	Boston, MA	17,000
4	Charleston, SC	12,000
5	Newport, RI	11,000
6	New Haven, CT	8,300
7	Norwich, CT	7,000
8	Norfolk, VA	6,300
9	Baltimore, MD	6,000
10	New London, CT	5,300
11	Salem, MA	5,300
12	Lancaster, PA*	5,000
13	Hartford, CT	4,900
14	Middletown, CT	4,700
15	Portsmouth, NH	4,600
16	Marblehead, MA	4,400
17	Providence, RI	4,300
18	Albany, NY	4,000
19	Annapolis, MD	3,700
20	Savannah, GA	3,200

*Lancaster was the only one of these cities that was not a port.

anywhere else in the British global trading empire. North America had evolved a more modern form of industrial economy than any other region under British control. Americans were increasingly employed as tradesmen, artisans, and skilled manufacturing workers. The populous coastal cities quickly became the focus of colonial wealth and talent. In the two largest, Philadelphia and New York, technology, science, and industry had become so well entrenched that the population did not practice the self-sufficiency characteristic of their rural cousins.[12]

Nonetheless, most Americans lived on the land. The agricultural nature of the southern plantation economy and the subsistence farming of the frontiers were still highly visible. In the 1780s, Benjamin Franklin noted that the "great business" of America was farming, and that "historians down to the present have kept the notion alive." However, skilled trades, craftsmanship, and shipbuilding had actually overtaken agriculture as the leading commercial activities in terms of the value of their annual production. Skilled tradesmen like shipwrights, joiners, metalsmiths, metal founders, furniture makers and cabinetmakers, cartwrights, saddlers and shoemakers, stonemasons and brick masons, wigmakers,

and printers—known collectively as mechanics and artisans—were ascending the economic ladder to prosperity and financial security in a manner undreamed of by their equals in Britain before the Revolution.[13]

Financially fortunate Americans desired many of the luxury items
available in Europe, but they did not want to pay the duties and taxes
levied on all imports by the government. The unceasing demand for
these items engendered the internal development of a number of colonial
manufactures that were not evisioned under the concept of mercantilism,
such as glassmaking and ceramic making, iron and brass founding, printing and book publishing, and other colonial industries. The establishment of some of these industries in the colonies was considered illegal,
and many craftsmen, actually producing new manufactures, resorted to
the fiction of serving as repairmen or of reworking finished items imported from Britain.[14]

Farming

Almost all white colonials involved in agriculture worked their own
land and planned their lives around rural activities and seasonal chores.
On small farms in the northeastern and middle colonies, family members
usually cooperated in completing the chores, and parents worked beside
their children and grandchildren in an idyllic, if not mechanically efficient, simplicity. They raised a variety of food crops, including several
types of grains and vegetables. Much of their land was in pasturage or
in the production of hay. If the climate and soil allowed, they might put
in a few acres of low-grade tobacco as a cash crop. Their livestock commonly included chickens, hogs, oxen, sheep, goats, milk cows, and a
horse or two.

Those colonials practicing subsistence farming on the frontiers rarely
experienced a lack of the basic necessities of life because a man wielding
an ax could turn trees into lumber or firewood, and a single well-aimed
musket ball could bring down a month's meat in the forest. Pastures and
fields were enclosed with the rooted ends of tree stumps or split rail
fences to control the livestock, but the hogs and chickens were generally
allowed to run free in the brush, to be harvested as the need arose. Hogs
proved particularly capable of fending for themselves against wolves
and other predators, and other livestock could overwinter on a diet of
corn, hay, and turnips.

An enterprising farmer might make a few shillings each season by
selling deerskins and furs at the trading post or by splitting out roofing
shingles and cutting firewood for sale in the towns. From this he could
clothe his family in something other than animal skins. But the common
residents of frontier communities, scraping a living from among the
stumps of the newly cleared forests, would not realize a surplus of ag-

ricultural produce for decades. Thereafter, almost all of the wealth accumulated by years of labor resided in their livestock, the land, and the improvements that they made upon it, such as barns and fences.

Southern agriculture in the tidewater regions revolved around the largely autonomous plantation economy, which came to depend on race-based slavery. Tobacco and rice were the most important export crops in pre-Revolutionary America. The production of lumber and indigo helped to supplement plantation income. Very little of the valuable variety of long staple cotton was grown in this period except in the Sea Islands of South Carolina, and the more common short-staple variety was used domestically. Sugar production was reserved almost entirely for the islands of the Caribbean. The largest crop grown in the South in terms of its volume was corn.

Southern planters generally lacked true aristocratic bloodlines, but they formed an aristocracy of their own devising by applying their wealth and social status to the wheels of colonial government. Yet most plantation owners were cash-poor and constantly in debt. They could, however, support themselves through the annual agricultural cycle with the products of their own plantations. When their crops were sold, they experienced a glut of money with which to pay their debts or buy luxury goods. Thus the agricultural cycle drove much of the business cycle in the southern colonies.

WEALTH AND MONEY

The wealth generated by mercantilism was not evenly distributed among all Americans. It has been estimated that the average free white person in British America in 1770 had a net wealth of £74 (sterling). This represented only an average distribution of a total wealth (buildings, farmlands, slaves, livestock, cash, and personal belongings) in all the colonies estimated at £150 million. New England residents averaged a mere £33 in personal wealth; those of the middle colonies, £51; and those on the agricultural plantations of the South, £132. By comparison, the far less numerous whites living on the fabulously wealthy sugar plantations of the West Indies averaged £1200 each.[15]

More important, the total wealth of the southern plantations (estimated at £86 million) was four times greater than that of New England (£19 million) and two and half times that of the middle colonies (£30 million). While most of the labor force of the South was composed of slaves, whose value was added as wealth, a much greater proportion of the labor force in the North was composed of free whites. Moreover, much of the wealth in the northern colonies came to reside in the hands of just a few fortunate colonial merchants, tradesmen, and shippers. The slow pace of wealth accumulation may have contributed to the general dissatisfaction with the mercantile economy expressed by many working-class colonials in New England.[16]

Wages

In the British trading empire wages varied between 9 shillings and 12s per week, with 10s being one of the most common rates found in business records from the period. The wages of textile workers were generally below those of other laborers, and they were often charged for the use of the employer's looms or stocking frames. This may help to account for the large number of patriot recruits who identified themselves as weavers. Workers with special skills, such as masons, or those who provided their own specialized tools, such as leather workers, may have made as much as 15s per week.

Evidence submitted to British authorities in London suggests that an average day laborer could expect to earn between £25 and £40 annually if fully employed. However, determined and skillful employees doing piecework might briefly increase their weekly earnings to £1 or even £2. These wages were difficult to sustain in a colonial economy driven by seasonal spurts of agricultural productivity. By way of comparison, an unmarried clerk had a reasonable expectation of earning a steady wage amounting to £50 annually without regard to the season of the year. Particularly well-to-do artisans—the makers of jewelry, of optical and musical instruments, of clocks and carriages, or of fine furniture—might increase their annual earnings to over £100 by the employment of apprentices and journeymen.[17]

Households

The colonial family of parents and children usually numbered five or six, but almost all colonial households contained members of an extended family living together. A widowed grandparent or an unmarried aunt or uncle might reside in the same home with a nuclear family. In the absence of public orphanages, many children were made the wards of relatives or reputable families. Apprentices and jouneymen were often considered part of the houshold, and servants or slaves might live under the same roof as the family.[18]

Women throughout the colonies were expected to work and contribute to the family income. Mainstream Puritan thinking, the basis of New England society, was particularly devoted to "an especially draconian hierarchy of the sexes in which the woman's role was that of obedient, quietly devoted helpmate." Sole authority in matters economic, religious, and political resided in the male head of the household. Women were responsible only within the bounds of "huswifery." On the other extreme, the Pennsylvania society dominated by the Quaker religion, founded by Margaret Fell and George Fox, was one in which women were given greater authority in child rearing, in women's matters, and even in the church.[19] The aristocratic mistresses of royalist plantations in the South were charged with managing the entire household. They budgeted the family income, dealt with merchants, and supervised a number of household servants and slaves. Frontier women everywhere were not generally confined to gender-specific roles, doing any task that furthered the subsistence and survival of their families.[20]

Many laboring-class women hired out for charing, washing, cooking, sewing, and nursing services. They often manned market stalls in the town square or hawked wares in the streets from carts or baskets. The work of dispensing food and drink often fell to younger females who tended customers as serving girls or tavern wenches. The widows of tavern keepers and shopkeepers often continued the business long after the death of their husbands, and a remarkable number of licensed establishments seemingly had no male proprietor that anyone could remember. The wives of these men were also their business partners, helping to run the establishment, providing food and clean clothing for the workmen or boarders, and sometimes maintaining the accounts. A mid-eighteenth-century source noted, "None but a fool will take a wife whose bread must be earned solely by his labor and who will contribute nothing towards it herself."[21]

Contrary to common perceptions, the woman and girls who served as "wenches" and waitresses in taverns and alehouses rarely provided illicit entertainment of a sexual nature. This business was reserved for the bordellos and alleyways of the town "set apart for dance-houses, doxies, and tapsters." Nonetheless, street prostitutes could be brought into a tavern by patrons for a few pence and the promise of a tankard of ale. The owners of these businesses, however, commonly frowned upon this practice because they could be fined by the authorities for running a disorderly establishment.[22]

Cost of Living

The real value of the weekly wage in terms of the purchasing power it brought to the wage earner is difficult to pin down largely due to the paucity of records, the bartering of goods and services, swings of deflation and inflation, and the wide variety of currencies and exchange rates characteristic of the American colonial economy. The reported expenses for the family of a married man with two or three children vary widely in the available estimates from 8 shillings, 3 pence (8s 3d) to over £1 weekly. They include the cost of food and drink, clothing, rental housing, and fuel. These estimates are viewed with some suspicion by students of the period as being "miscellaneous and incidental" in nature. However, it is clear that the income of most colonial laborers was barely enough to sustain their families, and the common wage did not allow for the accummulation of much in the way of personal wealth or possessions.[23]

The Coin Shortage

The colonies had always suffered a severe shortage of hard currency that affected the daily lives of the people in many ways. It would be an error to underestimate the importance of this circumstance. Even the simplest of everyday commercial transactions was made difficult by the shortage of coins. Individuals and families with good credit could run up annual accounts with local merchants, but most laborers, farmworkers, and travelers were required to pay in cash.

To help relieve the coin shortage, bar silver was sometimes chopped into small wafers called cobs, which were weighed on a scale to determine their value. Silver coins were literally cut into pieces in order to create smaller denominations. The silver Spanish dollar, worth 8 reales, was conveniently sliced into eight wedges like pieces of a pie. Half-coin pieces, quarter-pieces, and one-eighth "bits" were commonly used in trade, passing at full value with little regard to any irregularities in their shape. Many shopkeepers resorted to producing wooden tokens and paper coupons, which were given in lieu of change to their customers. Cash was so scarce that the colonial legislatures regularly accepted for the payment of taxes tobacco bonds and other promises to pay, based on future agricultural production. Furs, tobacco, potash, cattle, corn, and wool became the equivalent of legal tender, known as "country money." Even the lead musket ball passed in Massachusetts for a time as the legal equivalent of a farthing (1/4 penny) "providing that no man be compelled to take more than 12 pence of them at a time."[24]

The Crown was conscious of the chronic shortage of metal coins, and allowed the colonies to mint their own. Massachusetts produced two remarkable issues, one marked with "NE" and one known as the pine tree Shilling. Maryland issued many quality coins, including shillings, sixpence, groats, and pennies. Most other colonial coins were poorly wrought, of limited issue, and so easily counterfeited that they circulated under a cloud of suspicion.

In 1749 Parliament tried to relieve the cash shortage by granting Massachsetts a payment of more than £175,000 in coins for its expenses in capturing Louisburg (on Cape Breton Island) four years earlier. The payment came in the form of 650,000 ounces of Spanish silver coins and nine tons of copper half-penny and two-farthing pieces. The Colonial Office in London also introduced thousands of copper coins into the middle and southern colonies in 1754. These were sacked, boxed, and shipped at a cost to the government of 6 percent of their face value. This excessive expense prohibited further shipments.

SPOON SILVER

The colonials themselves were largely at fault for removing hard currency from circulation. Coins from England were hoarded, hidden behind wallboards, or buried in gardens by apprehensive and economically unsophisticated colonials. Metal coins meant to facilitate commerce were equally well-suited for the casting of heavily taxed household items and could be melted down to provide metal for flatware, tea services, candlesticks, and ornaments. Craftsmen, utilizing the fiction that they were recasting scrap, charged their customers a weight of coins to be used as a raw material in manufacturing an item, keeping the excess as compensation for their labor and skill. So common was this practice that the term "spoon silver" was used to describe certain specie coins. Copper coins melted down and alloyed with zinc were recast as brass candlesticks, door knockers, and other ornaments that would have required the payment of a duty if imported from Britain.

Silver coins were sometimes shaved, clipped, or otherwise debased. The practice of scraping precious metal from the face and reverse of specie coins was called shaving; removing metal from the edge was called clipping. Some coins, like the Spanish dollar, had a complex face pattern in high relief and minute ridges milled on their edge to prevent shaving and clipping. The ridges also made couterfeiting particularly difficult. Nonetheless, many genuine coins were melted down, debased by adding tin or lead to the molten metal, and restruck by counterfeiters. Not all of the counterfeit coins were discernible from true currency. Many Americans, especially those in the frontier regions, rarely handled hard money and had difficultly detecting fakes especially among unfamiliar foreign coins.[25]

Money Matters

The metallic currency of many countries circulated in the colonies. To the standard English shillings (s) in silver, and copper pence (d), halfpence (1/2d), and farthings (1/4d) were added Irish coins of similar denominations and composition. The foreign coins in circulation included French guineas and sous, Dutch gulden, Swedish rixdalers, Venetian sequins, and Spanish dollars (pieces of eight). Silver was the standard, but coins made of gold were available. These included English sovereigns, crowns, and lion dollars; French louis d'or and double louis d'or (doubloons); Spanish pistoles; and Portuguese johannes. "Each gold piece was weighed separately and no two of the same nominal value were [ever] rated alike."[26] The nominal value of these coins in English money varied. The approximate values were English sovereigns, 20s, crowns, 10s, and lion dollars, 120s; French louis d'or, 24s, double louis d'or, 48s; Spanish pistoles, 12s, 3d; and Portuguese johannes, 36s.

As long as silver circulated freely, most other metal coins maintained their value regardless of their origin. Ironically, the value of the English shilling seems to have varied more from province to province in America than that of the Spanish dollar. Thus the exquisitely minted silver Spanish dollar, produced in Mexico and Central America, quickly became the standard for colonial currency. The Spanish dollar was available through trade with the West Indies, and it was freely spent by pirates and privateers in New York and New England, where the merchants were all too glad to receive hard cash with no questions asked about its source.[27]

LAWFUL MONEY

In all the colonies, monetary accounts, debts, and public finances were kept in the standard English pounds (£) of 20 shillings (s) of 12 pence (d) each. Because there was no £1 coin, it remained a simple accounting unit. The constantly changing value of silver made bookkeeping difficult, and it also rewarded colonists with an increasing wealth if they hoarded silver shillings and dollars rather than spending them. The desire to accumulate silver caused the specie coins to increase in value with respect to the paper accounts. The government in London tried to solve this problem by fixing the value of silver by law. Sterling silver dollars could pass at no more than 6 s, and accounts based on this value were known as "lawful money"—a term that appears in many contracts, indentures, wills, and commercial documents from the period.

Nonetheless, the value of the silver dollar continued to fluctuate in the colonies until midcentury when it leveled off for several years at the equivalent of 4s, 6d English sterling. By 1750 New England and the southern colonies were valuing their own accounts at 6s per Spanish dollar; the middle colonies of Maryland, Pennsylvania, Delaware, and New Jersey, at 7s, 6d; and New York at 8s. These exchange rates for the Spanish dollar continued in force until the eve of the Revolution.[28]

Merchants, shippers, lenders, and tax officials constantly referred to vast tables of equivalents to calculate the exchange value of commercial and public accounts in English currency. These exchange tables were usually available to the public in annual almanacs. The value of cargoes, contracts, insurance, and such were thereby made subject to the most recent tables available, and could change from port to port. A contemporary observer noted of the monetary system, "You will not wonder that there was confusion worse confounded."[29]

Paper Money

The colonial governments substituted paper currency, each of their own devising, in an attempt to solve the problems caused by a lack of coins. Maryland produced the best form of paper currency before the Revolution. The sterling silver conversions for a Maryland dollar were clearly printed on its reverse, using symbols for crowns, shillings, and pence that aided in its circulation and helped to maintain its value. The 1767 Maryland issue, designed with the help of Benjamin Franklin, became the basis for the new Continental currency of the American Revolutionary government in 1776.

Historians have noted that "the evils of paper money inflation were common in the colonies long before the war of independence." The value of paper currency varied from colony to colony. As long as the specie coins circulated freely, the paper maintained its value. As the coins disappeared from circulation, as they did during the war, the paper currency depreciated. The value of the paper usually reflected that of the Spanish dollar. In mid-century, £100 sterling silver in London was worth £160 in local paper in New York and New Jersey, £170 in Pennsylvania, £200 in Maryland, £800 in South Carolina and Georgia, and £1400 in North Carolina.[30]

Counterfeiting

Compared to coins, paper issues were easy to counterfeit. A particularly good counterfeit issue in Virginia almost brought the economy of the colony to a complete halt as apprehensive colonials refused all currency for a time and accepted only bartered items. The laws against counterfeiting varied from province to province, and there was even a question of whether counterfeiting a colony's money outside its borders was actually a crime. In New York counterfeiting was punishable by death, while in neighboring Connecticut the crime drew only a fine. The British authorities in London, believing that control and regulation could solve the currency problem, declared all paper currency illegal in New England in 1751, and all further paper issues in America were prohibited in 1756. This prohibition did not remove the paper currency then circulating in the colonies, however.

Cash Crisis

The Sugar Act of 1764 required the payment in coin of all public debts. This effectively made all paper money then in circulation worthless. All of the colonies except Massachusetts, which had redeemed most of its paper obligations, faced financial ruin as the value of their outstanding paper evaporated.[31] Americans like Benjamin Franklin believed that a free flow of capital in the provinces would keep interest rates low and help facilitate trade. However, the natural flow of hard currency under the system of mercantilism was purposely tilted toward the parent country, and the resulting balance of payments continually removed cash from the colonies. Although Parliament was actually attempting to formally stablize the monetary systems of all the colonies, the colonists assumed, incorrectly, that the coins paid in duties and taxes would be shipped to England, leaving them nothing in which to make the payments of trade balances. In fact, the British ministry intended to keep the coins in the colonies to help pay for the thousands of troops that it had authorized for colonial protection.

A fear of the resultant drain of hard currency from North America gripped all the colonies, but it particularly affected the cash-dependent and currency-starved merchants of New England. Colonials foresaw a future of perpetual debt that would be unpayable regardless of how hard they labored or how successful were their businesses. Some imaginative Bostonians calculated that if all the silver coins needed to pay the duties were beaten into thin sheets, they "would entirely cover the main road from [Boston] to the border of New York." The genius of this propaganda was in its disarming simplicity, which obscured the much deeper economic realities of colonial life. The fundamental problems surrounding the colonial monetary system were never rectified, and the cash provisions of the Sugar Act remained in effect until the eve of the Revolution, serving as an undercurrent to the general discontent that the colonials had formed against British trade regulation.[32]

In 1775 Alexander Hamilton estimated that there was close to £7 million in genuine currency in the colonies. This represented about £2.70 per free white person. This might seem an adequate stock of currency when a single shilling commonly bought a meal at an inn, a room for the night, and stabling and feed for a horse.[33] However, adequate quantities of money did not necessarily translate into a stock of currency capable of sustaining normal business transactions. Many coins and paper issues were not "denominated" in terms that allowed them to "circulate as freely and easily as they might have," making it easier to pay a year's rent with a single gold coin than to purchase a side of bacon once a week.[34]

SMUGGLING

Americans began evidencing a general dissatisfaction with the intrusive nature of British rule in their daily lives as early as 1764. There were many areas of contention prominent at the time, but the one point that struck sparks with the Crown was the colonial passion for avoiding customs duties by smuggling. Although smuggling was an old and wide-spread activity practiced throughout the empire, American smugglers proved particularly adept at evading the customs, especially with respect to trade with the West Indies, southern Europe, and the west coast of Africa.

Smugglers were criminals, but they enjoyed a certain prominence in colonial society largely because they provided manufactured goods and luxuries at much lower prices than could legitimate sources. Many highly born and well respected men in America dabbled in contraband wines, brandies and rum, tea and coffee, fine fabrics, glass and dinner-ware, alloyed metals such as brass and bronze, finished metal objects, tools and machines, printer's type, and other goods manufactured out-side of Britain. John Hancock, a respected merchant and member of the colonial social elite, was held to be one of the most notorious smugglers in colonial America. When his sloop *Liberty* was seized with a cargo of smuggled Madeira wine, a riot broke out among the people of Boston in his support.[35]

The port of Boston was constantly abuzz over the landing of smuggled goods. Respectable citizens were horrified at the flagrant and unashamed manner of the smugglers. Yet, informers to the customs agents, if found out, were beaten, dragged through the streets, or tarred and feathered. Similar occurrences were recorded in New York, Newport, and Phila-delphia. Two royal customs officers in Philadelphia, who had seized a shipment of wine, were set upon by a mob that assaulted them and then stole the wine. A schoolchild was mistakenly killed by an informer in Boston who was trying to avoid the retribution of the mob. "The Boston people are run mad," reported Governor Thomas Hutchinson. "The frenzy was not higher when they . . . hanged the poor witches."[36]

Smuggling, taken together with illegal manufactures and a determined and unrelenting resistance to properly constituted authority, disrupted the well-founded underpinnings of the British trading empire. The stock-holders of legitimate trading companies, apprehending the loss of a large proportion of their profits to the colonials, complained bitterly to London about the lack of enforcement of legitimate trade regulations. The loss of revenue for the government was also considerable. The Exchequer esti-mated the losses due to smuggling alone at almost £40,000 each year. In response, the customs officials were ordered to fit out a number of lightly armed sloops and schooners to patrol the American coastal waters and halt the smuggling. These vessels were generally known as revenue cut-ters.[37]

It should be noted that contemporary reports of widespread evasion of the customs among Americans may be overstated. From 1765 to 1767 only six seizures of contraband were made in New England waters by customs officials, and only one of the cases brought against the supposed

smugglers was won by the Crown.[38] On the other hand, Americans simply may have been expert at avoiding detection by customs officials.
Colonial smugglers became adept at darting in and out of the innumer-
able coves and inlets that characterized the American coastline in whaleboats, launches, and canoes. Many created large fortunes for themselves
by nosing these craft into the coastal shallows and small rivers where
the revenue cutters could not follow.[39]

THE NAVIGATION ACTS

To better maintain its economic strategy, the British trading empire
was ruled by a series of maritime regulations called Navigation Acts.
Such regulations had long been characteristic of the trade relations between Britain and its colonies, the first having been passed in 1660, during the reign of Charles II. Initially the Crown allowed a good deal of
trade to take place between the individual colonies and foreign markets
under the watchful eyes of colonial governors and the Board of Trade.
However, beginning with the reorganization of the empire initiated by
George III in 1760, there developed a decided change in attitude toward
colonial trade and economic regulation by the British ministry and its
officials.

It seems that the vigorous enforcement of the regulations, rather than
the actual financial burden of the taxes, was the cause of much of the
colonial alienation. The colonials viewed the new measures as violations
of fundamental constitutional principles rather than as the simple enforcement of established trade practices by government bureaucrats. Colonial customs officials in particular seem to have become "tactless,
arbitrary, and mercenary" in the performance of their duties.[40]

Admitting that any system poised to control economic affairs would
inevitably be highly complicated, the colonies were actually affected by
only a handful of regulations. In the seventeenth century the basic Navigation Acts were designed to protect British shipping from competition.
Additional policies were adopted to funnel enumerated colonial products through British ports; to encourage specific industries by the use of
bounties; to promote the production of certain raw materials; and, finally, to directly prohibit new industrial endeavors that would compete
with those already established or promoted by other legislation.[41]

Initially, the Navigation Acts were "not a source of serious complaint
by the Americans."[42] In most cases the regulations had neither a positive
nor a negative effect on colonial prosperity. Rather than being oppres-
sive, certain aspects of the acts were actually an important source of
colonial wealth.[43] Colonial planters could accumulate large fortunes in
only a few years by growing enumerated crops, such as rice, tobacco,

and indigo. Moreover, restrictions placed on the colonial iron, hat, and shipping industries did "not materially hamper" their development.[44]

In *The Wealth of Nations* (1776) the political economist Adam Smith wrote, "Though North America is not yet as rich as England, it is much more thriving, and advancing with much greater rapidity to the further acquisition of riches." Americans with their rugged self-sufficiency were poised to leap forward economically, but only in a manner most profitable to themselves. A comtemporary observer noted of the Americans that "the same individual tills his fields, builds his dwelling, contrives his tools, makes his shoes, and weaves the coarse stuff of which his dress is composed." Such people could not be held back by old ideas, restrictive legislation, or slow-moving bureaucracies.[45]

It must be remembered, however, that the idea that basic mercantile practices were "wrong" was not a part of American thinking in the 1760s, "but was a concept developed by a later generation of writers."[46] Prohibitions, restrictions, and the granting of monopolies were the common stuff of eighteenth-century economic policy, and the free trade theories of writers like Adam Smith had just begun to find traction in the organization of economic life.[47]

THE SUGAR ACT

The Sugar Act of 1764 was the first of the new measures designed to reorganize the empire and raise revenue from America. The act put a small 6 penny (6d) tax on each gallon of molasses, but it contained more than forty provisions for changes in the customs and commerce regulations, thereby effecting an unprecedented change in the status of the colonies "amount[ing] to a constitutional revolution."[48]

Documentation and regulatory paperwork was vastly increased, and enforcement was extended to almost all coastwise traders, including the smallest intercolony shippers who might move cargoes only a few miles along the shoreline. The skippers of vessels greater than ten tons were required to obtain documentation of their cargoes before they were shipped out and to do likewise when they were landed, even if going from one colony to another. "If any goods are shipped without such sufferance . . . the officers of the customs are empowered to stop all vessels . . . which shall be discovered within two leagues of the shore of any such British colonies or plantations, and to seize all goods on board."[49]

The Townshend Acts

In 1766 Charles Townshend became Lord of the Exchequer, the department of government that levied and collected taxes and duties.

Townshend was directly opposed to any policy of caution or moderation with respect to the colonies. He proposed a series of revenue measures to help pay for the administration and security of the colonies and thereby relieve the burden on the British taxpayer in England. The demands made on America might not have been as great had London extended these measures to the entire empire and tapped its resources in India. However, Townshend was a champion of the charter rights of the Honourable East India Company and a friend to many of the directors of the company who also served on the Board of Trade. He declared all revenues derived from India to be the property of the company and free from taxation. He further materially reduced the tax burden on landlords in Britain, whom he considered "harassed country gentlemen." These decisions further increased the portion of the revenues to be derived from America.[50]

There was a good deal of resistance to the passage of the bill, and although Townshend died suddenly in 1767, the Townshend Revenue Act "stole through the House; no man knew how."[51] The duties were reissued and expanded in 1769. They set taxes on a vast number of "goods and commodities of growth, produce, or manufacture of the British Colonies." These fell into two groups distinguished as *enumerated* and *non-enumerated*. Enumerated items of colonial production included:

Tobacco, cotton, wool, indigo, ginger, fustick, or other dying [*sic*] woods; pitch, tar, turpentine, hemp, masts, yards, and bowsprits; sugar, molasses, rice, coffee, pimento, cocoa nuts, and raw silk; beaver skins, hides, deerskins, and leather; copper ore, whale fins, and potash.[52]

The list of enumerated items encompassed almost all the yield of colonial production on the North American continent and in the islands of the Caribbean. A number of the articles—tobacco, indigo, ginger, dyeing woods, and cocoa—were subject to duties even when they were shipped between colonies. In other words, a shipment of tobacco moving between Norfolk in Virginia and Baltimore in neighboring Maryland would be taxed.

There were also enumerated items that were subject to duties when imported directly from Britain. These included Spanish, Portuguese, and all other wines except French; all teas; red and white lead; white, red, and green glass; all sorts of paper; and painter's colors. The non-enumerated items—mostly iron and builder's lumber—could be shipped to Britain without a duty. However, the shipper had to post a cash bond of twice the value of the cargo, and he was subject to forfeiture of the bond, his vessel, and the cargo if he landed them in any part of Europe except Britain and specified parts of Ireland.[53]

London expected the duties to raise £40,000 per year. The Townshend

Acts also created writs of assistance (general search warrants), which were widely regarded as unconstitutional and damaging to personal liberty. Vessels and cargoes could be condemned on the most technical grounds, and the regulations were to be enforced in the admiralty courts operating under a system of law different from that used in the local colonial court system. This was a particularly offensive part of the act to the colonials, somewhat like having a present-day parking ticket judged by a military tribunal.[54]

No course of action by the government in London could have been calculated to more greatly arouse colonial resentment. Many Americans claimed that the customs officials tried "to use the revenue laws as a cloak to set up in America a centralized authority over domestic and foreign commerce."[55] Hostility toward "a plundering revenue service" was especially strong in localities in which enforcement of the regulations was most vigorously prosecuted in terms of harassment by bureaucrats, excessive fees by the courts, and the seizure of vessels and cargoes by the Royal Navy.[56]

It would be an error to consider these attitudes concerning the customs a mere expression of colonial pique. Simple adherence to the old shipping practices was no longer acceptable, and the new rules were so burdensome that they could feasibly be followed only in the large ports, where the docks and customs facilities were physically near each other. Many seaside towns had no customs facilities. Gloucester, Massachusetts, for example, was a trading port of some size, but it did not have a single customs office. Obeying the new law required that a trading vessel from Gloucester stop at Salem or Boston to clear the customs before beginning its voyage.[57] Localities like these became the natural centers of the revolutionary movement as disgruntled skippers stood in long lines to have their paperwork processed and signed by petty bureaucrats.[58]

As hostility grew, spontaneous demonstrations erupted at the sight of a revenue cutter. Customs officials were mocked as they passed in the street, and Royal Navy recruiters looking for men for a short-handed vessel met with unprecedented levels of noncooperation and even violence. As relations deteriorated between New England and Britain, the Crown repeatedly responded with "the worst possible moves," further restricting trade to English ports and inexplicably barring New England fishermen from the Grand Banks, which produced more than £300,000 of colonial export trade each year.[59]

It is unlikely that the regulations alone imposed so serious a burden on the colonial economy that it caused the Americans to disrupt one of the greatest trading empires of the eighteenth century simply to redress trival inconveniences.[60] Nonetheless, it must be admitted that the Sugar Act and the Townshend Revenue Acts produced considerable organized opposition in New England and the middle colonies. The linkage between these acts and revolution is unmistakable.[61] The representative attitudes of Americans—merchants, gentry, clergy, and their political supporters—as presented in journals, sermons, newspapers, broadsides, pamphlets and other contemporary literature supports the idea that the regulations were enforced in such a manner as to erode the historic loyalty to the Crown of a great number of Americans.[62]

Finally, the ill feelings engendered by the regulation of trade and the enforcement of the customs quickly evolved into a wholly new ideological argument, which denied the right of Parliament to legislate for the colonies. Edmund Burke, one of the most vociferous advocates for America in Parliament, noted:

When experience and the nature of things are brought to prove, and do prove, the utter impossibility of obtaining an effective revenue from the colonies . . . so as to drive the advocates of colon[ial] taxes to a clear admission of the futility of the scheme, then, Sir, the sleeping trade laws revive from their trance, and this useless taxation is to be kept sacred, not for its own sake, but as a counterguard and security of the laws of trade. Then, Sir, you keep up the revenue laws, which are mischievous, in order to preserve trade laws that are useless. Such is the wisdom of our plan in both its members. They are separately given up as of no value; and yet one is always defended for the sake of the other.[63]

NOTES

1. Hammond Lamont, ed., *Burke's Speech on Conciliation with America* (Boston: Ginn, 1897), 5.

2. Lucy M. Salmon, *The Dutch West India Company on the Hudson* (Poughkeepsie, NY: Published privately, 1915), 15–20.

3. Simon Schama, *A History of Britain: The Wars of the British, 1603–1776*, vol. 2 (New York: Hyperion, 2001), 409.

4. Ibid.

5. Samuel Eliot Morison, *Sources and Documents Illustrating the American Revolution 1764–1788 and the Formation of the Federal Constitution* (New York: Oxford University Press, 1965), 72.

6. John J. McCusker and Russell R. Menard, *The Economy of British America, 1607–1789* (Chapel Hill: University of North Carolina Press, 1991), 80.

7. Ibid., 82.

8. Morison, *Sources and Documents*, 72.

9. Ibid., 70.

10. Ibid., 72.

11. Marjorie Hubbell Gibson, *H.M.S. Somerset, 1746–1778: The Life and Times of an Eighteenth Century British Man-o-War and Her Impact on North America* (Cotuit, MA: Abbey Gate House, 1992), 2.

12. William Peirce Randel, *The American Revolution: Mirror of a People* (Maplewood, NJ: Hamond Books, 1973), 157.

13. Ibid., 108–109.

14. McCusker and Menard, *Economy of British America*, 179, 315.

15. Ibid., 61.

16. Ibid.

17. M. Dorothy George, *London Life in the Eighteenth Century* (Chicago: Academy Chicago Publishers, 1999), 167.

18. See James M. Volo, "Slavery in Connecticut: A Study of Our Hometown," an unpublished study available through the Norwalk, Connecticut, school system, funded by the National Endowment for the Humanities and the Connecticut Humanities Council in 1991.

19. Schama, *A History of Britain*, vol. 2, 186.

20. See James M. Volo and Dorothy Denneen Volo, *Daily Life on the Old Colonial Frontier* (Westport, CT: Greenwood, 2002).

21. George, *London Life*, 171.

22. Herman Melville, *Billy Budd* (New York: Literary Classics, 1983), 1361.

23. George, *London Life*, 103.

24. Beth Gilgun, "Money in the Colonies," in *Tidings from the Eighteenth Century* (Texarkana, TX: Surlock Publishing, 1993), 216.

25. Ibid., 218–219.

26. Helen Evertson Smith, *Colonial Days and Ways: As Gathered from Family Papers* (New York: Century, 1901), 343.

27. The Spanish dollar remained legal tender in the United States until 1857. The dollar sign ($), an "S" crossing two parallel vertical lines, may symbolize the two vine-covered columns that appear on the Spanish milled dollar.

28. The British pound (£) was not actually a coin; it was an accounting unit. Expressed in terms of pounds sterling, the exchange rates of colonial money would be: £1 (240d) Br. = £1 6s 8d (320d) MA = £1 13s 4d (400d) PA = £1 15s 7d (427d) NY.

29. Gilgun, "Money in the Colonies," 217.

30. Eric Robson, *The American Revolution in Its Political and Military Aspects*, 1763–1783 (New York: Norton, 1966), 7.

31. All of Massachusetts' paper was redeemed by 1773.

32. John C. Miller, *Origins of the American Revolution* (Boston: Little, Brown, 1943), 269.

33. The reader might want to compute the present-day equivalent of a one night stay at a motel chain with free parking and a buffet breakfast, and compare it to an average person's wage in order to better visualize the value of a shilling.

34. McCusker and Menard, *The Economy of British America*, 339.

35. See Dorothy Denneen Volo and James M. Volo, *Daily Life in the Age of Sail* (Westport, CT: Greenwood Press, 2002), 266–267.

36. Charles A. Beard and Mary R. Beard, *The Rise of American Civilization* (New York: Macmillan, 1927), 220–221.

37. Samuel W. Bryant, *The Sea and the States: A Maritime History of the American People* (New York: T.Y. Crowell, 1967), 34. See also James Truslow Adams and Charles Garrett Vannest, *The Record of America* (New York: Charles Scribner's Sons, 1935), 80.

38. Oliver M. Dickerson, *The Navigation Acts and the American Revolution* (New York: A. S. Barnes, 1963), 63–102.

39. Ibid., 122–125.

40. Ibid., 208.

41. Ibid., 6–7.

42. Ibid., 296–297.

43. Ibid., 32.

44. Ibid., 48.

45. Quoted in Peter Padfield, *Maritime Supremacy and the Opening of the Western Mind* (New York: Overlook Press, 2002), 217.

46. Dickerson, *The Navigation Acts*, 140.

47. Ibid., 157.

48. Ibid., 179.

49. Morison, *Sources and Documents*, 77.

50. Beard and Beard, *Rise of American Civilization*, 216; also see John C. Miller, *Origins of the American Revolution* (Boston: Little, Brown, 1943), 244–246.

51. Adams and Vannest, *Record of America*, 250.

52. Morison, *Sources and Documents*, 78.

53. Ibid., 79.

54. Dickerson, *The Navigation Acts*, 172–183.

55. Ibid., 298.

56. Ibid., 299.

57. Mark Kurlansky, *Cod: A Biography of the Fish That Changed the World* (New York: Penguin, 1997), 94.

58. Dickerson, *The Navigation Acts*, 299–300.

59. Ibid., 172–183, 295–300; Kurlansky, *Cod*, 96–97.

60. Dickerson, *The Navigation Acts*, 4.

61. Ibid., 295.

62. Ibid., xiv.

63. Lamont, *Burke's Speech*, 39–40.

3

Taxation Without Representation

I am sincerely one of those . . . who would rather be in dependence on Great Britain, properly limited, than on any other nation on earth, or than on no nation. But I am also one of those, too, who, rather than submit to the rights of legislating for us, assumed by the British Parliament, and which late experience has shown they will so cruelly exercise, would lend my hand to sink the whole island in the ocean.[1]
—Thomas Jefferson

UNSTABLE LEADERSHIP

From 1760 to 1782 the British government went through seven prime ministers. The almost constant change in leadership disappointed and polarized Parliament, and the apparent weakness of each prime minister left them subject to political challenge. The earl of Bute was the only Tory, and he remained in office less than two years. Party designations with regard to policy in Britain often proved complex and ambiguous because the Whigs were divided into two warring camps. Only their mutual hatred of the Tories allowed Whig government to proceed.

Lord North, a Whig, was prime minister longer than his six predecessors combined, and he inherited all the problems created during the previous decade of confused leadership in Parliament. Yet he was so little troubled by the events taking place in America that only the destruction of £18,000 worth of tea belonging to the most powerful corporation operating in the British empire moved him to action.

Table 3.1

Parliamentary Governments of Britain, 1760–1782

Dates in Office	Prime Minister
1757–1762	Thomas Pelham, duke of Newcastle
1762–1763	John Stuart, earl of Bute*
1763–1765	George Lord Grenville
1765–1766	Charles Watson-Wentworth, marquis of Rockingham
1766–1768	William Pitt (the Elder), earl of Chatham
1768–1770	Augustus Henry Fitzroy, duke of Grafton
1770–1782	Frederick Lord North
1782–1782	Marquis of Rockingham**

*The only Tory administration of the period.
**Rockingham's second administration lasted six months and was replaced by a coalition government.

THE STAMP ACT CRISIS

The French and Indian War created a vast debt estimated by the British Exchequer at an unprecedented £150 million. An additional annual appropriation of almost £2 million was needed to provide for an army and navy to secure an empire that stretched from Hudson's Bay in Canada to Bombay in India, half the globe away. Almost £350,000 of the annual expense was due to the administration of the American colonies. Although the Parliament expected to pay the lion's share of future expenditures, the Grenville ministry decided to extract at least some of the money—estimated at about £60,000 in 1765—from the colonies in the form of a stamp tax on all legal and business papers, newspapers, printed forms, playing cards, wallpaper, and licenses.

Although Americans were familiar with paying taxes, the legislation laying *internal taxes* had always come from the colonial assemblies. The stamp tax was clearly the first attempt to levy an internal tax from outside the colonies. "[L]ooking back it is clear that such a tax, being internal instead of external, might raise a storm of protest." Along with the passage of the Stamp Act, Parliament renewed the Mutiny Act, which required the colonial assemblies to house and support the troops sent to America. These provisions of the Mutiny Act were known as *quartering*.[2]

The Grenville ministry sought to minimize the potential reaction to the stamp tax by appointing American stamp agents rather than English ones. The insignificant size of the tax assured many in Britain that any protests would be minimal. A voyage could not possibly be worthwhile if the cost of a stamp caused a ship not to sail; and if a few pennies for a stamp on a marriage license prevented the ceremony, "a man might

The hated stamp. Stamps like this one, in red on the front pages of the
London Gazette, welded the colonials into a single mass of protesters against
the government.

forfeit such a poor wife" and remain a bachelor. Moreover, the Stamp
Act was calculated to fall heaviest upon the wealthy and to divide the
population along the lines of social class or sectional interests.[3]

This plan misfired badly. It seems that the Grenville ministry miscal-
culated both the effect of the tax and the breadth of the reaction to it.
Unlike the frontier farmers, who rarely dealt with public papers, colonial
shippers and merchants were required to take out numerous public documents while conducting business—including bills of lading, clearance
permits, insurance policies, rental agreements, mortagages, attachments
of property, and all kinds of contracts. The Stamp Act also affected lawyers, newspaper editors, printers, and an army of municipal employees
who signed indentures, produced public documents, or ran a licensed
business. As many as 70 percent of colonials read newspapers with the
stamp prominently in view,[4] and in an economy as regulated as was that
of Anglo-America, almost every businessman, craftsman, street vendor,
innkeeper, and shopkeeper was required to obtain an annual license and
pay the tax. The tax on playing cards was particularly irksome because
almost everyone played cards. New decks with the king's tax stamp on
the package screamed *taxation* to every person who played whist or cribbage in a tavern or in a parlour.

The Virginia Resolves

Contrary to the hopes of Parliament, the whole of Anglo-America seemed to unite in opposition to the Stamp Act. In May 1765, seven anti-stamp tax resolutions were proposed in the Virginia House of Burgesses. The Virginia Resolutions claimed that only the colonial legislature had the right to tax Virginians. "Taxation of the people by themselves, or by persons chosen by themselves to represent them . . . is the only security against a burthensome taxation, and the distinguishing characteristic of British freedom." Among the resolves was firmly lodged the concept of consensual government found in the political writings of Thomas Hobbes, John Milton, and John Locke, a foundation stone of American political theory. "His Majesty's liege people . . . have without interruption enjoyed the inestimatable right of being governed by such laws, respecting their internal polity and taxation, as are derived from their own consent."⁵

The first reaction in the colonies to the unprecedented Virginia Resolves was one of shock, yet many Americans found themselves in accord with their primary thrust. Although three of the seven resolves were defeated, the acceptance of the remaining resolutions was cheered throughout the colonies. All seven were published in the colonial newspapers as if they had been passed unanimously. Soon even the common people began to denounce taxation without representation, and they spoke openly of supporting the rights of Englishmen, of defending American liberties, and of government by the consent of the governed. The argument over specific regulations and taxes had quickly evolved into an all-out battle concerning constitutional principles.

The Stamp Act Congress

In October 1765, a Stamp Act Congress met in the city of New York with representatives from nine colonies in attendance. The congress prepared a resolution, which it sent to King George III and Parliament, requesting the repeal of the Stamp Act and the revenue acts of 1764. The petition also asserted that the basic rights of the colonials had been violated by Parliament's attempt to tax them without their consent. Many merchants pledged not to import English goods until the laws were repealed, and those who did not pledge faced open intimidation by the mob.

Nonetheless, one month later, the Stamp Act took effect. In some colonies business was suspended. In others the law was ignored. Almost everywhere colonists refused to use the stamps. Those Stamp Act agents who had not already resigned, hid in their homes and refused to appear in public. In Massachusetts, many fled to the protection of British troops in Boston. In New York, violence broke out when a mob gathered to burn the royal governor in effigy and harassed the troops with a surprising lack of regard for their own safety. Several homes were invaded and looted. Windows were broken and fires were set in the streets. Only the restraint practiced by the regulars and their officers prevented an exchange of gunfire.

Sons of Liberty

Popular organizations, called Sons of Liberty by British Colonel Isaac Barre in a speech before Parliament, had been formed almost everywhere in the colonies by 1765. Each town had a Liberty Tree under which the Liberty Boys met and from which certain discreetly chosen personages were periodically burned in effigy.[6] In Boston, Sons of Liberty formed the nucleus of the mobs who intimidated royal officials charged with making the Stamp Act work. The home of Lt. Gov. Thomas Hutchinson was ransacked by a mob, his furniture stacked in a pile in the street, and the pile burned.

Many in the upper social classes in the city of New York, including the powerful and wealthy Delancey and Livingston families, were openly friendly to the local Sons of Liberty. While the DeLanceys used the uproar to better consolidate their own power in the Assembly, their political rivals, the Livingstons, held the true support of the mob. Many in the New York Assembly were more interested in winning power from the colonial governor in the short term than in maintaining the rights of the people. Nonetheless, the Sons of Liberty influenced many legislators to refuse much of what the British requested for their troops under the quartering provisions of the Mutiny Act.

SEEDS OF DISCONTENT

Grenville had gotten the Stamp Act passed in Parliament, but the Rockingham administration inherited all the troubles that it caused. In March 1766, after being warned of a possible armed revolt, Parliament repealed the Stamp Act. This was greeted with great rejoicing in the colonies. Both spontaneous and deliberate celebrations were initiated, and nighttime illuminations and bonfires were held in many cities. The *New York Mercury* reported that more than 1000 Liberty Boys met in New Jersey at the Sussex County courthouse.[7] However, the vigor with which the colonials had responded to the stamp tax caused an unfortunate reaction by the Rockingham ministry.[8]

On the same day that the Stamp Act was repealed, Rockingham secured passage of the Declaratory Act, which stated that Parliament had the absolute right to legislate any laws governing the American colonies in all cases whatsoever. Seen as a face-saving device, the Declaratory Act seems to have produced little colonial reaction at the time, and the boycott of English goods was generally relaxed. However, at least some of the more radical thinkers in the colonies saw the Declaratory Act as "a statute, laid up for future use, like a sword in a scabbard."[9]

Quartering

The provisions of the quartering bill, part of the Mutiny Act, which established a standing army for the protection of the empire, were to cause a great deal of trouble in the colonies. Quartering placed additional stress on the already strained finances of the provincial legislatures, but it had little direct effect on individual citizens. Under the quartering provisions, the Parliament could extract a great part of the expense of "defending, protecting, and securing" the colonies without seeming to violate the constitutional principle of taxation without representation by simply obliging the provinces to pay the bills that the regulars accumulated while in America.[10]

Opposition to the Mutiny Act—which was a minor grievance during the Stamp Act crisis—now began to surface. The center of the storm was New York City, where the British army maintained its American headquarters. During the summer of 1766, violence broke out in the town between the mob, including the Sons of Liberty, and British regulars over the legislature's continued refusal to comply with the quartering provisions. After noting the growing groundswell of disquieting events and fearing a repetition of the Stamp Act resistance, the Crown, with William Pitt now serving as prime minister, suspended the New York legislature for its continued refusal to comply with the law.

Understanding that this time London would not be intimidated, most of the colonies refused to follow New York's lead. Yet only Pennsylvania executed the quartering provisions to the letter of the law. The other provinces granted provisions to the troops through acts and bills of their own devising, thereby preserving the appearances of consitutional principles and their own freedom of action. South Carolina accorded the British all that they asked except salt and beer, and New Jersey evaded the growing political dilemma without acknowledging the law by authorizing a special commission with instructions simply to follow the traditional practices in providing for the quartering of British troops. Massachusetts initially attemped to nullify the law, but when the British troops at Castle William in Boston Harbor claimed the existence of an emergency, the city council relented and sent them food, fuel, and candles. This raised a cry of outrage among the Boston radicals, which prevented any more supplies from being voted. Thereafter, much of New

England followed Massachusetts' example and ignored the authority of the law.[11]

Colonial opposition to the Mutiny Act created a series of strange alliances in Parliament that joined Whigs and Tories in an effort to punish the colonies for their bad behavior. This reaction was exacerbated by the illness of Pitt, who failed to control the House of Commons from his seat among the Lords. It is here that the continued effect of instability in the post of prime minister can most clearly be seen. Without a strong political head, Parliament seems to have taken an unwise course regarding America, with little regard for its possible consequences.

The colonials were perfectly serious in their belief that taxation by Parliament without their consent was a violation of their constitutional rights. However, many in London considered these arguments to be simple fabrications designed to avoid paying taxes. Using the idea that the Americans would trump up arguments against external taxes as easily as they had against internal ones, Tories in Parliament pressed for new bills with unfortunate similarities to the Stamp Act. It seems certain, however, that everyone in Parliament understood the need to exercise the right to tax America at this time, and many foresaw the colonial ambition to become a nation of independent states creeping over the horizon.

The greatly enlarged customs bureaucracy imposed by Parliament was the feature of these policies that most annoyed the colonials. A patriot pamphlet referred to the customs officials as "miscreants, blood suckers, whores, and Cossacks." Subsequently, Ebenezer Richardson, a customs official and friend of Governor Thomas Hutchinson of Massachusetts, killed a young Bostonian during a protest in 1767. Hutchinson allowed Richardson to avoid prosecution by claiming self-defense. The Boston radicals were outraged. They vowed to prosecute the official for murder and robbery, and to wipe out the entire system of customhouses and customs officials.[12]

By the winter of 1767, colonials everywhere were searching for new methods to oppose and confound Parliament. Taxation without representation now became a test of political wills. More than any other issue of the period, this one served to "radicalized such key [American] figures as Henry Laurens and John Hancock." Governor Hutchinson went so far as to suggest the "abridgement" of the "rights of Englishmen" for all colonials who continued to dispute the power of Parliament to legislate for the colonies.[13] It was becoming obvious that the Anglo-Americans would either completely throw off Parliament's right to tax them or submit to the total sovereignty of the Crown. The middle ground of continued compromise was quickly disappearing.[14]

The Circular Letters

In February 1768 the radical faction in the Massachusetts General Court sent a message to the assemblies of the other colonies that urged a united resistance to the Townshend duties. This message was called the Circular Letter. It was designed to throw up an impregnable defense against taxation by Parliament in every colony and to make certain that colonial liberties were not undermined in the guise of imposing mere trade duties. The Virginia House of Burgesses followed with a circular letter of its own in March. Most Americans saw no fault with the circular letters as simple attempts to redress grievances with the Parliament, but by June the Sons of Liberty in Boston, at the instigation of Sam Adams, James Otis, and John Hancock, had mobbed royal officials and rioted in the streets. Many conservative colonials viewed the riots and the harrassment of royal officals as intemperate, disrespectful, and disloyal, and the circular letters were widely blamed for inciting the violence. British officials in London were keenly aware of the renewed colonial unrest brought on by the Townshend legislation, and many members of Parliament considered the circular letters "little better than an incentive to rebellion."[15]

Lord Hillborough, who had become colonial secretary at Townshend's death, decided to take a more firm stand with the colonies by ordering the governor of Massachusetts to dissolve the General Court. He also dispatched four regiments of British regulars to Boston. Their presence was intended to intimidate the colonists into submission and to suppress dissent. They accomplished neither of these desired effects. After landing in the colony in October 1768, two of the four regiments were immediately detached for service in Halifax, Nova Scotia, leaving the remaining units woefully undermanned and generally incapable of effectively dealing with the Boston mobs.

A warship of fifty guns, *Preston*, was summoned by the customs officials in Boston to enter the harbor to add psychological support to the presence of the regulars, but it had little effect, largely because almost no one in Boston thought the Royal Navy would actually fire on the city. Additional warships were added to the harbor fleet with equal lack of success. Some of these—particularly *Asia* (sixty-four guns), *Somerset* (sixty-eight guns), and *Boyne* (seventy guns)—requiring deeper waters than those of the generally shallow harbor, were confined to the deeper shipping channels. They could, therefore, neither maneuver among the marshlands nor get into position to effectively bombard the shore.[16]

The unremitting upheaval in Boston spread to the other colonies. In March 1769, the merchants of Philadelphia joined the boycott of British goods, and in May, the Virginia House of Burgesses was dissolved by the royal governor for its continued opposition to taxation without representation. The burgesses met the next day at the Raleigh Tavern in Williamsburg and agreed to a boycott of British goods, luxury items, and even slaves. In New York in January 1770, the Sons of Liberty clashed with forty British soldiers over the public posting of anti-government broadsheets. Several men on both sides were seriously injured. Parliament retaliated by ordering that all Americans accused of agitating on the topic of taxation be sent to England for trial.

The Boston Massacre

Throughout the winter of 1769–1770, daily life in Boston was marked by numerous clashes in the streets between soldiers and civilians. Both sides waited for the one incident that would spill over into irreconcilable violence. Early in the winter a group of soldiers was accosted by a mob armed with clubs. One soldier received a significant wound from a blow served up with a bit of iron bar, and the mob was driven away only by the discharge of a musket into the air. Mobs of colonists and Liberty Boys, egged on by radical leaders, roamed the streets, spoiling for a fight. "The soldiers nerves were frayed to a ragged edge" as singly and in pairs they were set upon in alleys or along the darkened wharfs. By spring, Colonel Dalrymple, the British regimental commander in Boston, noted, "I don't suppose my men are without fault but twenty of them have been knocked down in the streets . . . and no more has been heard of it, whereas if one of the inhabitants meets with no more than just a kick for an insult to a soldier, the town is immediately in an alarm."[17]

Unfortunately, the colonists were mistaking British restraint for undisputable license, and they came to believe that they could harass the troops with impunity. In March a group of radicals headed by a free African-American named Crispus Attucks confronted a squad of soldiers near the customhouse. Many in the crowd were carrying clubs. The British soldiers, frightened by the threats and taunts of the mob, opened fire on the crowd at point-blank range. Attucks and two others were killed instantly, and two more were mortally wounded. The colonials spread the rumor that a group of small boys hurling snowballs had brought on the resulting clash, and Paul Revere made a particularly effective, if inaccurate, engraving of the incident that served to inflame many throughout the colonies.

The political leaders of the Boston mob labeled the incident a massacre, and demanded the arrest and trial for murder of the soldiers and their commander, Capt. Thomas Preston. Consequently, the soldiers were confined, but no one could be found to act in their defense. Finally, John Adams and Josiah Quincy of Braintree, Massachusetts, volunteered to act as their attorneys. They provided a defense sufficient to acquit Preston and all of his men of murder, save two, who were convicted of manslaughter and branded upon the thumb as a punishment. Thereafter, Governor Hutchinson prudently withdrew the troops from the city streets to an island garrison in the harbor.

The Tea Tax

In April 1770, under the new ministry of Lord Frederick North, the Mutiny Act failed to be renewed and the Townshend Acts were repealed by Parliament. That is, all of the duties were repealed except that on tea, which Parliament, once again, retained as a symbol of its right to tax the colonies. Moreover, the customs facilities, regulations, and the royal officials needed to enforce them were left in place. The warships and troops sent to intimidate the colonials also remained on station. Subsequently, with the repeal of the bulk of the Townshend duties, "all except the most radical [of colonials] withdrew from the protest movement."[18]

Ironically, very little English tea had been imported into the American colonies in the decade before the passage of the Tea Act. The populous colony of Pennsylvania imported only 2000 chests of tea annually, and New York used about the same. The southern colonies used tea in like proportion to their smaller populations. This was partially because Dutch smugglers swarmed in and out of most colonial ports with their own East Indian tea, thereby filling much of the demand for the warm amber liquid. Only in Boston had the customs officials effectively succeeded in surpressing the illicit trade in tea. However, tea became a symbol for deeper grievances.[19]

The dedication of Americans to drinking tea was overestimated by the ministry at the time, and it has been somewhat overstated by historians since. Benjamin Franklin noted, "The British Ministry have no idea that any people can act from any other principle but that of interest, and they believe that three pence in a pound of tea, of which one does perhaps drink ten pounds in a year is sufficient to overcome all the patriotism of an American."[20]

The Burning of *Gaspee*

For little more than a year thereafter the colonies were marked by a general lack of cooperation among colonials. In 1772, the uneasy quiet was suddenly changed into overt violence. The Royal Navy cutter *Gaspee*, commanded by Lt. William Dudingston, intercepted the colonial packet *Hannah*, commanded by Benjamin Lindsay, in Narragansett Bay. The master of the *Hannah*, inbound to Providence from New York City, refused to heave to and have his papers examined. Lindsay, annoyed by Dudingston's arrogant and officious manner, had taken advantage of a fresh wind, an ebb tide, and a shallow draft to avoid the cutter, which ran aground on a sandbar. A frustrated Dudingston sat aboard the stranded cutter, waiting for the flood tide to float it off.[21]

Hannah continued on to Providence, where word spread of the revenue cutter's predicament. Eight longboats under the direction of Capt. Abraham Whipple were launched, each filled with vengeful colonists armed with staves, stones, and a few firearms. In the dead of night, the colonials overwhelmed the crew of the lightly armed *Gaspee* and burned the vessel to the waterline. Dudingston, who was wounded during the encounter, was arrested on a specious charge and fined by the local sherriff. This almost inexplicable turn of events, wrought upon the hapless Dudingston in the performance of his duty, ended when his admiral paid the lieutenant's fine.

The British government was outraged by the burning of its vessel and the detention of its officer, but a Royal Navy investigation failed to make any recommendations for avoiding similar events in the future. The colonial government of Rhode Island expressed its regret and sympathy over the incident, and a reward of £500 was posted for information leading to the arrest of the attackers. However, no one could be found to identify the assailants even though the pledged amount represented several years' income for a common laborer.

The burning of *Gaspee* serves to highlight the deteriorated state of central control and the unambiguous nature of authority that came to characterize colonial government in this period. However, it still remains unclear why so many colonials should have so quickly taken advantage of this particular opportunity to express their resentment toward the Royal Navy, which had patrolled the same waters without a remarkable incident for several months.

Committees of Correspondence

During 1772 and 1773 many colonials formed themselves into committees whose purpose was to maintain communications with other towns and cities. The first such *committee of correspondence* was formed at a Boston town meeting called by Samuel Adams. The committee had twenty-one members. Similar groups were formed in Virginia, New Hampshire, Rhode Island, Connecticut, and South Carolina. Many persons who would come to lead the Revolution were among the initial members. These included Thomas Jefferson, Patrick Henry, and Richard Henry Lee. The committees were important because they served as the first mechanism for welding the separate colonies into a unified body.

In November 1772 the committee in Boston, under the leadership of Samuel Adams, issued an anti-British publication known as the *Boston Pamphlet*. Bound with a simple thread stitch, as were many such inexpensive publications, the pamphlet categorically attacked the British positions on taxation, standing armies, admiralty courts, jury trials, and support for the established church. The *Boston Pamphlet* was widely circulated through the efforts of the individual committees of correspondence.

The Boston Tea Party

Parliament renewed the Tea Act in 1773, which maintained the 3 penny tax on every pound that had been in effect for almost six years. Although the government had rescinded all duties except the tax on tea, it now gave the East India Company a virtual monopoly on its sale. By allowing the company to sell directly to its colonial agents, Parliament bypassed any middlemen, including the colonial merchants, in the resulting transactions. So low was the resulting price of tea that even smugglers could not sell it as cheaply as the company. By this ruse the Crown hoped to reaffirm the right of Parliament to tax the colonies as Americans submitted to the payment of the duty on the tea for the sake of their pocketbooks.

Parliament authorized the shipment of half a million pounds of tea to the colonies and demanded that the tax be paid when the cargo was landed. The main object of colonial anger in this instance was a shipment belonging to the Honorable East India Company sitting aboard three ships at the dock in Boston. Additional ships loaded with tea were turned away in other colonies, but the cargoes arriving in Boston were allowed to dock. They were not allowed to unload, however. On the night of December 16, 1773, as many as 8,000 people massed to listen to a speech given by Samuel Adams, which targeted the tea in the harbor as a symbol of British tyranny. After the speech a group of Bostonians, loosely disguised as Mohawk Indians beforehand and joined by torch-carrying rabble-rousers, boarded one of the three East Indiamen in the harbor and threw 350 chests of tea into the water. The demonstration, which was anything but spontaneous, has come to be known as the Boston Tea Party.

Once again London was outraged and rewards were posted, but no one would identify the guilty parties. This time, however, the ministry responded with a series of retaliatory bills. The first that passed Parliament was the Boston Port Act, which closed the entire port as a punishment and as a warning to the other colonies. The bill also required that Massachusetts reimburse the East India Company for the loss of the tea and the Exchequer for the lost tax revenues. This circumstance led directly to an enhanced support for the Bostonians throughout the colonies. One supporter ridiculed the idea of paying for the lost tea. "If a man draws a sword on me to deprive me of life or liberty, and I break his sword, ought I to pay for the sword?"[22]

The Boston Tea Party was the most notable protest undertaken by the American radicals. The North ministry would not tolerate the destruction, and closed the port.

From town meetings and provincial congresses throughout America came words of support for the actions of the Bostonians. "Future ages will hardly believe that we were descended from the British, when they read of our having borne so long and resented so feebly these outrages," wrote one radical. From every quarter came resolves to scorn the British claims. Besides moral support, aid in the form of money and food flooded into Boston, and a call went out for a great congress of colonial representatives to be held. Many colonists loyal to the Crown declared the country to be in a state of rebellion from this time.[23]

The Coercive Acts

The closing of the port of Boston was followed by a series of acts known in Britain as the Coercive Acts of 1774. These were called the Intolerable Acts by the Americans. The Massachusetts Regulating Act put the colony under martial law. The Government Act and the Administration of Justice Act virtually ended colonial self-government in the province and freed the army commanders from being sued in colonial courts. Governor Hutchinson was replaced by Lt. Gen. Thomas Gage as the chief administrative officer of the colony. Under these acts it was the most highly specialized colonial tradesmen and artisans who suffered the most, and they tended to unite in open opposition to the actions of London.

Among the Coercive Acts were two that tended to unite the colonies. The first was a renewed Quartering Act that flew in the face of continuing legislative opposition in almost every colony. The second was the Quebec Act, which placed the trans-Appalachian lands under the administration of the province of Quebec and which "from political considerations" recognized throughout Canada and the French communities to the west "the free exercise of the religion of the Church of Rome." This raised fears of a Catholic conspiracy against the Protestant population of New England and threatened to further deny the Atlantic-facing colonies the right to expand to the west. The First Continental Congress formally protested against it, and "in New York and New England still greater hostility to the measure was shown."[24]

The Continental Association

In September 1774 a meeting was held in Philadelphia that was attended by representatives of every colony save Georgia, which was dealing with a serious Indian uprising at the time. This First Continental Congress adopted a formal agreement known as the Continental Association. Its chief provisions revolved about a renewed boycott of British goods, but it also established permanent committees to report on violations of the boycott. The nonconsumption agreement would leave any merchant ill-disposed to the American cause with no market for the proscribed wares. The Association also promoted the expansion of local militia units and quickly evolved into a structure for armed resistance that would provide a nucleus for the Continental Army.

Along with English items such as finished cloth and metal goods, no tea was to be used, and Americans who supported the Association made a great show of serving alternative beverages such as rose hips tea, herb teas, and drinks made from the roots of sassafras and chicory. Many colonials found it more difficult to forgo the consumption of imported wine, and the enjoyment of horse racing, plays, and "other expensive diversions and entertainments" enumerated by the association. The latter sacrifices, born of traditional Puritan ethics, might help to prepare the people for the impending civil crisis.[25]

The enforcement of the nonimportation and nonconsumption provisions of the boycott was ruthless. Those who violated the spirit of the Association were accused of disaffection and betrayal of the liberties of America. The names of those reported to be in violation were printed in newspapers, and merchants who refused to take the associator's oath were threatened with tar and feathers. Associators pledged to break off all dealings with offenders. It was from this point that many of the political lines between the patriots (Whigs) and loyalists (Tories) were drawn.[26]

If the Association was strictly enforced, it might bring Parliament to its knees by threatening a British economy that needed the cooperation of its colonies to function. "We want nothing but self-denial, to triumph," opined a writer to the colonial press. Thus, without firing a shot, America hoped to bring Britain to recognize the futility of contending with a people so dedicated to its economic ruin. Nonetheless, as the situation in Boston worsened, many colonials took the stance that open warfare was necessary and that conciliation was impossible.[27]

NOTES

1. George F. Scheer and Hugh F. Rankin, *Rebels and Redcoats* (Cleveland, OH: World Publishing, 1957), 149.

2. James Truslow Adams and Charles Garrett Vannest, *The Record of America* (New York: Charles Scribner's Sons, 1935), 83.

3. Ibid., 111.

4. In Dedham, Massachusetts, in 1765, on a petition to the government every man signed with his signature rather than using a mark.

5. Samuel Eliot Morison, *Sources and Documents Illustrating the American Revolution 1764–1788 and the Formation of the Federal Constitution* (New York: Oxford University Press, 1965), 17.

6. The Sons of Liberty were officially organized in January 1766.

7. Roger Champagne, "The Military Association of the Sons of Liberty," in *Narratives of the Revolution in New York* (New York: New York Historical Society, 1975), p. 2.

8. Adams and Vannest, *Record of America*, 82–83.

9. Richard N. Current and John A. Garraty, *Words That Made American History: Colonial Times to the 1870's* (Boston: Little, Brown, 1965), 111.

10. Adams and Vannest, *Record of America*, 238.

11. Ibid., 238–239.

12. John C. Miller, *Origins of the American Revolution* (Boston: Little, Brown, 1943), 266–267.

13. Michael Pearson, *Those Damned Rebels: The American Revolution as Seen Through British Eyes* (New York: DaCapo Press, 1972), 26.

14. John J. McCusker and Russell R. Menard, *The Economy of British America* (Chapel Hill: University of North Carolina Press, 1981), 356.

15. Miller, *Origins of the American Revolution*, 261.

16. The expectation that the Royal Navy would not fire on colonial cities proved false in other cases. *Asia* opened a broadside on New York City in 1776, and a number of coastal towns underwent naval bombardment from warships during the course of the war.

17. Miller, *Origins of the American Revolution*, 294–295.

18. McCusker and Menard, *Economy of British America*, 356.

19. Miller, *Origins of the American Revolution*, 267.

20. Claude Halstead van Tyne, *The Loyalists in the American Revolution* (Ganesvoort, NY: Corner House Historical Publications, 1999), 11–12

21. The spelling of the name of this vessel is given in various sources as *Gaspé* and *Gaspee*. There was in 1775 a warship on station in Maine named *Gaspee* that was armed with six guns and a crew of thirty men, but this was not the small revenue cutter commanded by Dudingston in 1772. As *Gaspee* was the more common spelling of the name, we have decided to use it.

22. Van Tyne, *Loyalists in the American Revolution*, 23.

23. Ibid.

24. William H. Sadler, *History of the United States* (New York: Smith and McDougal, 1879), 176.

25. Miller, *Origins of the American Revolution*, 385. Identical language had been used by the Puritans during the English Civil Wars of the mid-seventeenth century.

26. Ibid., 379.

27. Ibid., 391.

4

Agitators and Radicals

Will you suffer your liberties to be torn from you by your own representatives?

— Alexander McDougall, New York radical leader

WHIGS AND TORIES

Prior to 1764 American colonists had generally accepted the doctrine that Parliament could pass acts regulating trade and imposing duties on imports. They had nullified any act that proved too irritating by smuggling, by producing enumerated goods clandestinely, or by simply ignoring the law. The importance of the reaction to the Stamp Act and Townshend Acts was that they raised to prominence a group of extraordinary radical leaders from within the provinces. After 1764 the voices of this new, more radical group were raised above the normal background of discontent common to the colonial middle classes.

During the 1760s colonial newspapers began to identify particular persons or groups as Whigs and Tories based on their positions on the political issues of the day. These appellations were extended from similar ones used in Britain, but they generally failed to describe the true political philosophy of either the patriots or the loyalists in America. A colonial newspaper explained that the term *Whig* was first given to the Presbyterians in Scotland who were forced to survive on buttermilk whig, or whey, when they were persecuted by the established church in the seventeenth century. The term *Tory*, applied to the Anglican church-men, originally refered to Irish highwaymen who lived by plundering innocent travelers. "Whig and Tory, then, are used only with allusion to the originals," claimed the editor. "Such as trust to our common diction-aries for an explanation, will only deceive themselves."[1]

COLONIAL AGITATORS

The most influential agitators were those whose activities led directly to the Revolution, and they can be divided into two relatively distinct groups—one in the political arena and the other physically active in the streets. The first group attempted to radicalize the political process in the colonies by launching opposition campaigns in the legislatures and by influencing that fraction of the press that was friendly to the American cause. These men manipulated provincial legislation or cast votes meant to confound the ministry in London. Their stock in trade was logical arguments, dignified resolutions, and politely worded petitions. They were generally outspoken and wrote letters, pamphlets, and editorials about the American point of view in order to marshal political support for the movement among the middle and upper classes of the popula-tion. They attacked George III by disparaging his ministers in their speeches and pamphlets—"a time-honored way of making the Crown reverse course while still preserving intact the dignity and independence of its sovereignty." Prominent among this group were James Otis, John Dickinson, and Patrick Henry.[2]

Other radicals took a more physically active role in the conflict by inciting street demonstrations among the working classes or taking to the streets themselves at the head of groups of ruffians known as "the mob." They attempted to hijack the political dispute between the colonies and the parent state for their own ideological or social purposes. Their stock in trade consisted of the rabble and ruffians of the streets, a liberal coat of tar and feathers, and the threat of the torch. The active arm of their efforts was the Sons of Liberty. Notable among these radicals were Samuel Adams and John Hancock in Boston, and Isaac Sears and Alex-ander McDougall in New York City.

Although the political radicals are portrayed and remembered by his-torians as "founding fathers," the influence on the Revolution of those persons who were willing to "take to the streets" and openly confront the British authorities at the tip of a bayonet cannot be underestimated. The shift from speaking and writing to shouting and shoving was "a startling violation of decorum in an age when body language spoke vol-umes about authority and its vulnerability." By going beyond humble supplication, the insurgents gave an effective spur to the American cause by evoking a cry of anguish from their intended targets that was heard all the way in London.[3]

James Otis

At a Boston town meeting early in 1764, James Otis publicly launched the idea that Parliament had no authority to tax the colonies without their consent. In a pamphlet which followed that summer, *The Rights of the British Colonies Asserted and Proved*, Otis suggested that the colonies be given representatives in Parliament in order to solve the growing impasse. This was a logical solution, but it was unlikely that such a proposal would be met with agreement. Many classes of people in the empire lacked direct representation in Parliament, including most of the population of Britain's largest cities.

From 1764 to 1769 Otis produced a succession of speeches, pamphlets, and letters that gained him a reputation as a colonial agitator. His first crusade was against the Writs of Assistance. He also made arguments that utilized the ideals of "social contracts" and "natural rights" proposed by political philosophers such as Thomas Hobbes and John Locke. Otis did not intend to foment a revolution. Like many colonials in the early years of agitation, his ideas were politically conservative. His proposal for colonial representation in Parliament, which might have prevented or shortened the war, was largely lost in the euphoria that accompanied the passage of the *Declaration of Independence*.[4]

John Dickinson

John Dickinson of Pennsylvania is known as "the penman of the Revolution." He wrote several of the important papers and petitions produced by the Stamp Act Congress and the First and Second Continental Congresses. Dickinson probably would have been chosen to write the Declaration of Independence, but he found it impossible to support such a radical move at the time. He continued to support the American cause, however, and wrote the first draft of the Articles of Confederation, which served as the structure of the infant United States.

In 1768 Dickinson published a series of documents called *Letters from a Farmer in Pennsylvania*. The writing of letters to newspapers under a pseudonym was a favored means of communicating political ideas to the population. Letters to the editor, both real and fabricated for effect, were published in local papers and reprinted in the press of other colonies. They were read by the literate and reread to the illiterate. Dickinson's letters were some of the most widely circulated and influential of all American writings during the Revolutionary period.[5]

Patrick Henry

While arguing a pivotal legal case against the Crown in the Virginia courts, Patrick Henry seems to have formulated the concept that if the Crown broke the social contract between the king and his subjects, that action could free the people of their allegiance. Immediately thereafter, he became a member of the House of Burgesses, where he championed American rights during the Stamp Act crisis. Henry gained widespread renown throughout the colonies with his impassioned pleas "Give me liberty or give me death!" and "If this be treason, make the most of it!"

Henry's "Liberty or Death" was widely adopted by patriots throughout the colonies, but he was generally opposed to complete independence from the British. Although he served in the First and Second Continental Congresses, helped to draft the Virginia constitution, and briefly served as the state's governor, Henry was never comfortable with the new form of American government. He and Thomas Jefferson, once close, drifted apart politically, and ultimately became quite hostile to one another. During the constitutional controversies of 1788, Henry expressed the essence of his hostility to a strongly federalized government for the United States in another, less quoted statement of opposition to unrestrained political power, "I smell a rat!"[6]

Samuel Adams

For reasons that are not particularly clear, Samuel Adams harbored a bitter hostility toward England that consumed almost all of his energies. Yet he seems to have been a skilled political intellectual. As the head of a radical political club in Boston and a clerk of the General Court, he wrote "scathingly bitter articles in the Boston press, castigating the Massachusetts power structure and warning people of a secret conspiracy to enslave them." Adams may have been the first American radical to conceive of a completely independent America.[7]

Adams possessed an extraordinary ability to manipulate public opinion, and he devoted himself to inflaming the people of Boston against the authorities on every possible occasion. He controlled two Boston mobs—one more radical than the other—and it was thought that he could organize a riot or other civil disturbance at a moment's notice. No single person was more responsible for the outbreak of the American Revolution than Samuel Adams.

John Hancock

John Hancock was a Boston merchant who had inherited both money and position from his father. He was noted for his immaculate attire and his fine carriages, numerous servants, and elaborate home. He was most likely deeply involved in smuggling, and was considered a creature of Sam Adams by the British. However, in contrast to Adams, Hancock's youthful appearance and social standing in the community insulated him from accusations of rabble-rousing, while his politics bound him to the radicals. Hancock's activities quickly caught the attention of the ministry in London, and he became a major object of British ridicule and scorn. By 1775 Hancock and Adams headed the list of the colonials to be arrested and brought to trial for treason.

Isaac Sears

The struggle for political dominance in New York was no unevenly matched contest between mobs of citizens and a few soldiers, as it was in Boston. No place in America was so evenly split in its loyalties. From first to last, patriots and loyalists in and around the city were in constant conflict and turmoil.[8] Isaac Sears, a former privateer and shopkeeper, became a leader of the Liberty Boys. He controlled the mob in New York much as Samuel Adams did in Boston. Sears insisted that the socially prominent had no right to call themselves Sons of Liberty, and seems to have seen the coming civil strife in terms of a struggle between social classes.

Moderates in the city formed a committee of fifty-one men, mostly political moderates who subsequently became loyalists, to direct the actions of the people against Parliament. This committee rudely jostled Sears from his position of leadership, but in 1775 Sears led a raid on a British supply depot that once again raised his political capital. He was imprisoned by the committee but was rescued by the mob. In 1776, he was chosen by the Committee of Safety to surpress the Tories on Long Island who he noted swallowed the oath of allegiance to America like it was "a four pound shot, that they were trying to get down."[9]

Alexander McDougall

Alexander McDougall was initially an undistinguished figure on the New York waterfront, but during the quartering controversy he emerged as "a first-rate agitator." After the New York Assembly voted to provide supplies to the British, he published an anonymous pamphlet titled *To the Betrayed Inhabitants of the City and Colony of New York*, in which he blasted the Assembly for violating the trust of the people. At a public meeting he asked, "Will you suffer your liberties to be torn from you by your own represenatives?"[10] Fearing that McDougall might bring down the Assembly, partisan members led by James De Lancey accused him of sedition, and had him arrested and indicted. While imprisoned to await trial, McDougall announced from jail, "I rejoice. . . . The cause for which I suffer is capable of converting chains into laurels and a gaol [jail] into a paradise."[11]

While spending three months under arrest, McDougall received delagations of radicals who showered him with donations of food and furniture that made his cell more comfortable. He commonly entertained large parties including many women. His persecution by the Delancey family turned the mob against them. The members of the Livingston family—always opposed to the designs of the De Lanceys—took up McDougall's cause, and they were embraced by the radical population of the city. Fearful that McDougall and his followers posed a clear danger to their businesses, the merchants of the city persuaded the Assembly to release him on bail. He was never brought to trial.

Resistance to the Boycott

The power of the New York radicals was broken in May 1770 when the majority of the city's merchants began to openly sell British goods in defiance of the boycott. The Sons of Liberty—massed to threaten the offenders—were beaten off by crowds recruited for that purpose and armed with walking sticks. So formidable was the conservative reaction that many among New York's radicals, including Sears and McDougall, removed to New Jersey. With the financial assistance of Boston radicals, they set up a trading company in Perth Amboy to compete with the New York merchants. This attempt was doomed to failure because the entire structure of the colonial boycott collapsed with the withdrawal of New York. One loyalist reported at the time that the colonial associations "tumbled one after another like Nine-pins."[12]

THE LOYALIST PARTY

While companies of armed patriots were rallying from every part of the country to repel the regulars, thousands of Americans of a more dignified character were practicing their own form of obstinate loyalty to the king. The formation of a loyalist party, or Tory resistance, has been largely dismissed by generations of American historians as reactionary. Early writers, devoted to portraying the activities of the patriots as necessary and appropriate in light of the democratic institutions that followed in the wake of the Revolution, simply ignored the existence of widespread support for royal authority among many Americans.

In the absence of dynastic disputes, loyalty was the normal and expected condition of colonial society, exhibited by the vast majority of Americans throughout the eighteenth century. As the patriot radicals strove to convert men's opinions to suit a new order of society, loyalists tended to pursue their lives and business with a quiet but determined allegiance to the continuance of the existing order. Supporting the loyalist cause was the natural conservatism of those who found prosperity under the king. That same conservative spirit undoubtedly dissuaded many loyalists from taking action against the unbridled mobs that formed about them, and they shuddered at the thought of speaking out too forcefully, lest the "gathering storm . . . should burst on their own heads." It was obvious that the vocal patriot mob would show no mercy to any person who spoke for the king or against the American cause. As a result, the majority of loyalists "preserved for the most part an arrogant silence toward the arguments of the opposition" and kept their political opinions to themselves.[13]

Loyalists generally came from those elements of colonial society considered to be Tories before 1775. Among these were the colonial office-holders, whose own incomes, and those of their relations and friends, depended on the continuance of the old order. Most of the Anglican clergy had loyalties similar to those of the Crown officials. There were also those persons who were naturally conservative in their views, or who were honestly convinced that Parliament had a right to tax the colonies. Finally, there were the factional Tories like the De Lancey family, whose position was simply a reaction to that of their traditional political enemies, the Livingstons, who took the patriot side.

Tory Radicals

It was not in the nature of the most conservative among the loyalists to act as radicals and agitators. Not until the outbreak of hostilities did a whole new cadre of activists, fearful of being ruled by the mob, arise in support of the Crown. As the siege of Boston progressed through the summer and fall of 1775, many persons who wished to remain neutral were driven from their homes in the countryside by the more radical elements among the rebel patriots. Timothy Ruggles, chosen as a counselor to Lt. Gen. Thomas Gage, was attacked in the night, and his horse had its tail cropped and was painted over its entire body. Israel Williams, an elderly Tory, was tied in a chair by a mob. With the doors and chimney of his house closed, a fire was set in the fireplace, and the poor old man was smoked for several hours before being released. Daniel Leonard, another Tory adviser, avoided the mobs but had several musket balls shot through the windows of his sleeping chamber in the night.

Milder methods were also used to display the crowd's displeasure with those deemed loyalists. The lieutenant governor of Massachusetts, Thomas Oliver, was forced to submit to a public haranguing by a mob of 4000 people who surrounded his house. The Reverend Edson was ignored by his congregation when he stood to read a psalm, and they refused to sing with him during the service. Even Sir William Pepperell, son-in-law of the colonial hero from the days of the French and Indian War, was denounced by his neighbors, who vowed to "withdraw all connection, commerce and dealings with him." The judges of the King's Court in Great Barrington were ordered by the patriots to leave the district, which they immediately did. Persons chosen to serve as jurors in the King's Court refused to appear lest their names be published in the American press as enemies of the patriot cause.[14]

Against all of this violence and intimidation, Gen. Thomas Gage issued a proclamation that promised the arrest and prosecution of those found to have participated in anti-government activities. Yet those persons loyal to the Crown who resided outside the town of Boston soon found themselves also outside Gage's protection, their situation quickly becoming intolerable. Consequently, the city of Boston was soon filled to overflowing with civilians seeking the protection of the army and navy. Here Tory activists canvassed for support up and down King Street, in the homes of well-disposed merchants, or along the wharves.

Many of the merchants of Boston had supported the patriots, opposing the duties imposed by Parliament, because they hoped to increase commercial intercourse within the colonies, and very few refused to sign the boycott agreements. However, after the imposition of the Boston Port Act, this same body of merchants generally refused to join the Continental Association. Moderates among the Bostonians attempted, at a meeting at Faneuil Hall, to have the Committee of Correspondence censured or dismissed, but their proposals failed to be carried by those assembled there.[15]

There followed a campaign of broadsides containing the names of 123 disaffected persons, published by the patriots, along with the loyalists' occupations and places of business. Stars were placed near the names of those who were not born in America. Tax collectors, treasurers, and government clerks were distinguished by exclamation points. Fourteen of the names were of Crown officers, and sixty-three were merchants and traders. The remainder were portrait painters, lapidaries, coachmakers, jewelers, bookbinders, and other craftsmen who owed their livelihood to the aristocracy. The prominence given to these persons was quite unwelcome.[16]

The majority of Boston loyalists assembled in the coffeehouses of the town, where their numbers were large enough to protect them if they spoke their minds. Nonetheless, they limited their public declarations to tavern talk and anonymous letters in the Tory press. British officals in London gave speeches and made positive statements about the determination of the government to support those who remained loyal to the king. These also appeared in the press. "This encouragement was welcomed by the Tories who as a rule either received no encouragement or, if they did, it was not sufficiently backed up by the British government." When Washington forced the British army to evacuate Boston in 1776, many of the most loyal colonials and their families took ship with them. These loyalists were deposited in Halifax, Nova Scotia, where they either found transportation to England or remained as residents.[17]

Determined Allegiance

With Boston secured to the patriots after the departure of the regulars, the focus of the war switched to the city of New York. Unlike Massachusetts, where open support of the Crown was all but eradicated, loyalism was never completely surpressed in the area around New York. The majority of the residents remained loyal even through the patriot occupation in the summer of 1776. The city of New York, Queens and Brooklyn counties on Long Island, Richmond county on Staten Island, and the mainland areas known as the Bronx and Westchester counties were witness to an ongoing struggle between patriots and loyalists that focused on food, military supplies and weapons, and recruits for the opposing factions.

While the New York provincial congress was trying to secure powder and muskets for the patriots from Europe and the West Indies, loyalists were receiving arms from Royal Navy ships in New York harbor. These were *Asia*, a 64-gun warship; *Phoenix, Kingfisher*, and *Savage* (all of 20 guns), and a small naval cutter, *Viper*. These vessels abandoned the harbor in April 1776 after arming a number of loyalists and firing a broadside into the town.

Almost all of Staten Island and much of Long Island was populated by devoted loyalists. It is possible that Gen. William Howe chose Staten Island as the base for his troops in the summer of 1776 for this reason. A manifesto detailing the loyalty of the Tories from Queens County was signed by 788 men immediately after the disappearance of the Royal Navy from the harbor. A leading Whig newspaper noted of these men, "Every fool is not a Tory but every Tory is a fool. The man who maintains the divine right of kings to govern wrong is a fool and also a genuine Tory."[18] The Long Islanders openly defied the rebels: "Impelled by the most powerful arguments of self-defense, we have at last been driven to procure a supply of those means of protecting ourselves."[19]

Richard Hewlett of Rockaway, along with Jacob Norstrant, Isaac Denton, Jr., and John Smith, were reported to have munitions enough for an army hidden in the marshy areas of Long Island. Joseph Robinson, a Whig informant, warned that these men had organized several dozen loyalist companies, and had distributed powder and arms to them in preparation for a unified resistance to the patriot army. This report was substantiated by loyalists arrested and brought to testify before the Conspiracy Committee of the provincial congress.

Sabotage

The Conspiracy Committee was formed after a store of several hundred patriot weapons had been sabotaged in the Bronx. The provincial congress had accumulated about 300 cannon. Although many were small, old, and mounted on wooden garrison trucks, they were still serviceable. The cannon stood in three artilery parks overlooking the East River near Kingsbridge. During the night the guns in the park on Valentine Hill had been spiked, clogging the touch holes, and large cobbles had been jammed into the muzzles. The Conspiracy Committee met and took evidence concerning the case from informants, but the identity of the saboteurs was never definitely established.

The integrity of informants was always questionable. Many were simply taking an opportunity to even old scores against their neighbors even when there was no validity to the claims. Plots and counterplots, most of them false, were uncovered through this means, and many persons were dragged before questioning tribunals for the most trivial statements suggesting loyalty to the king. A widespread atmosphere of distrust seems to have seized the population of the entire region. Moderation on any topic even loosely connected with the rebellion quickly disappeared as the politics of the situation became so highly charged that only on the extremes could the average person find support. This circumstance became a characteristic of the entire Revolutionary period thereafter.

Rooting Out the Tories

James Jauncey, a member of the New York Assembly, was an especially active Tory. He was forced to leave his home in the city when a mob of patriot radicals broke in for the purpose of riding him out of town on a rail. He escaped to the Bronx, but he and his sons were soon arrested and taken to prison in Connecticut. His family was stripped of its property, and Jauncey estimated his loss at £100,000. Samuel Tilley of Westchester was imprisoned for selling provisions to the British, but he escaped to serve with a loyalist regiment. His house was plundered, and his wife and children were forced to flee. Isaac Low, a member of the First Continental Congress, was the president of the New York Chamber of Commerce, but he decided to support the British when Washington evacuated the city. Judge Jonathan Fowles and Rev. Samuel Seabury of Eastchester (in the Bronx) were placed under arrest and had their belongings confiscated or destroyed. Both men were sent off as prisoners to Connecticut under a strong guard.[20]

A coat of tar and feathers awaited any person who refused to follow the dictates of the Continental Association. This period illustration, which appeared in the British press, showed the Americans in an unfavorable light.

The list of Tories in New York was almost inexhaustible. Many Tories paid for their loyalty with a coat of tar and feathers. Yet "the Tories in New York were given comparatively moderate treatment . . . much to the disgust of patriots elsewhere." As the tensions and violence grew, however, so did the plight of the Tories. The rough treatment suffered during the "carting" of Doctor Kearsley, a leading Tory of Philadelphia, was described in the memoirs of Alexander Graydon, who witnessed it in August 1775:

He was seized at his own door by a party of the militia, and, in the attempt to resist them, received a wound in his hand from a bayonet. Being overpowered, he was placed in a cart . . . [and] paraded amidst a multitude of boys and idlers. . . . The Doctor, foaming with rage and indignation, without his hat, his wig disheveled and bloody from his wounded hand, stood up in the cart. . . . Tar and feathers were dispensed with, and excepting the injury he had received in his hand, no sort of violence was offered by the mob to the victim. But to a man of high spirit, as the Doctor was, the indignity in its lightest form was sufficient to madden him. It probably had this effect, since his conduct became [thereafter] so extremely outrageous that it was thought necessary to confine him [in jail]. From the city he was soon after removed to Carlisle, where he died.[21]

It was not so easy to dispense with all Tory resistance by cartings, jailings, and threats of tar and feathers. Justus Sherwood, for instance, was taken by a mob from his home and forced to watch as his household belongings were torched. Sherwood was imprisoned, but he escaped. He then led forty other loyalists to Canada, where they formed one of the first loyalist contingents to join the British army.

James De Lancey

James De Lancey was probably the best-known American Tory. The grandson of the judge of the same name, who had presided over the freedom of the press trial of John Peter Zenger, James was the county sherriff of Westchester under the British regime. Driven from the city of New York in 1776, he formed a group of like-minded loyalists known as De Lancey's Refugee Corps. These men formed one of the most effective loyalist militia units to serve during the rebellion, and he was made a lieutenant colonel. The unit was headquartered at Morrisannia, where many displaced loyalist families "subsisted upon the spoils of raids undertaken by the Refugee Corps." De Lancey increased the size of his corps until it reached 450 by recruiting among the refugee families.[22]

The Hickey Plot

David Matthews was the Tory mayor of New York during the patriot occupation of the city by Washington's army. He became a suspect in a plot against Washington's life when Isaac Ketcham, a counterfeiter trying to help his own case, reported that he had overheard two of Washington's Life Guard, Sergeant Thomas Hickey and Private Michael Lynch, talking of taking British money to destroy the king's bridge near the northern end of Manhattan. Coincidentally, information about a man in the pay of Mayor Matthews, named James Mason, also included a reference to Hickey. When Mason was questioned, he involved a number of people, including the mayor; a gunsmith named Gilbert Forbes; and a young drummer in the Life Guard named William Greene. Testimony suggested that Mayor Matthews "had contributed 100 pounds for the expense of the plotters."[23]

Although warned by the arrest of the mayor, most of the conspirators were seized. Greene and Forbes proved more than happy to supply details about the plot, including some that probably were not true. Washington's housekeeper, Lorenda Holmes, was implicated in an attempt to poison his food, but under torture—she had her right foot burned with hot coals—she refused to admit any part it. The men also suggested the involvement of a number of Indians and black slaves in an improbable and complicated conspiracy to assassinate or kidnap all of Washington's staff. It seems certain, however, that Hickey had indeed been instructed to stab Washington with a knife. He was found guilty by a court-martial and hanged. There was no direct evidence against Mayor Matthews, who was imprisoned for the rest of the war in Connecticut for "treasonable practices against the states of America." The uncovering of the Hickey Plot was used to blacken the reputations of all Tories, and it generally "retarded their cause."[24]

Joseph Galloway

The most active Tory leader was a successful lawyer and merchant from Pennsylvania named Joseph Galloway. He initially suggested that the problems between the colonies and Britain could be resolved by establishing a constitutional federal government for Anglo-America. Galloway, like his mentor Benjamin Franklin, visualized a better-defined, and thereby more solid, union between the two countries. Like Franklin's Albany Plan of Union of 1754 and James Otis's proposal for colonial representation in Parliament, Galloway's plan appeared to be a reasonable compromise between the needs of the British Empire and the rights of Englishmen living in the colonies. Just why Franklin and Galloway found themselves on opposite sides in the Revolution is hard to determine. Franklin was a moderate during the earliest days of the Revolution and came to be one of its most radical political leaders, while Galloway drifted farther and farther from the Revolution, toward support for the authority of the king.[25]

Galloway's plan of union was rooted in the simple idea that the colonists had rights, but only as "members of the British state [who] owed obedience to its legislative authority." He was an open opponent of violence, and the battles of Lexington, Concord, and Breed's Hill drove him from the patriot cause. His open disaffection forced him to move from Philadelphia to rural Bucks County. Here he remained for some time, but he was in "the utmost danger" from the mobs of patriots that threatened "to hang him at his own door." In 1776, Galloway fled to the British Army in New Jersey for protection.[26]

Thereafter, Galloway became an active adviser to Gen. William Howe. In 1777, he was appointed superintendent of police in British-held Philadelphia. From here Galloway made contact with known loyalists in the region, secured supplies and horses for the British army, and helped to run an intelligence-gathering organization of up to eighty spies and informants. When the British abandoned Philadelphia, Galloway became dispirited, and he left the city for New York with over a thousand other loyalist families. Ultimately Galloway retired to England, where he took up an argument in the press with Howe over the nature and extent of Tory atrocities in New Jersey during the war.[27]

NOTES

1. Quoted in North Callahan, *Royal Raiders: The Tories of the American Revolution* (New York: Bobbs-Merrill, 1963), 68.

2. Simon Schama, *A History of Britain: The Wars of the British: 1603–1776* (New York: Hyperion, 2001), 108.

3. Ibid., 76.

4. In this regard both the American Revolution and the American Civil War had similar politically conservative roots. See Dorothy Denneen Volo and James M. Volo, *Daily Life in Civil War America* (Westport, CT: Grennwood, 1998), 55.

5. Richard N. Current and John A. Garraty, *Words That Made American History: Colonial Times to the 1870's* (Boston: Little, Brown, 1965), 97–101.

6. Dorothy Denneen Volo and James M. Volo, *Daily Life in CWA*, 7.

7. Michael Pearson, *Those Damned Rebels: The American Revolution as Seen Through British Eyes* (New York: DaCapo Press, 1972), 32.

8. See Thomas Jefferson Wertenbaker, *Father Knickerbocker Rebels* (New York: Charles Scribner's Sons, 1948).

9. John C. Miller, *Origins of the American Revolution* (Boston: Little, Brown, 1943), 485–486.

10. Ibid., 304.

11. Ibid., 305.

12. Ibid., 311.

13. Claude Halstead van Tyne, *The Loyalists in the American Revolution* (Ganesvoort, NY: Corner House Historical Publications, 1999), 7.

14. Ibid., 39.

15. Ibid., 32–33.

16. Ibid., 33–34.

17. Callahan, *Royal Raiders*, 69.

18. Ibid., 68.

19. James M. Volo, "The Acquisition and Use of Warlike Stores During the American Revolution," *Living History Journal* (Fall 1986), 12.

20. Callahan, *Royal Raiders*, 65.

21. Richard B. Morris and James Woodress, eds., *Voices from America's Past:*

The Times That Tried Men's Souls, 1770–1783 (New York: McGraw-Hill, 1961), 30–31.

    22. Callahan, *Royal Raiders*, 72.
    23. Ibid., 73.
    24. Ibid., 75.
    25. Ibid., 95.
    26. Ibid., 97–98.
    27. Ibid., 100.

5

A Whole Country in Arms

Keep a strict guard over the remainder of your powder; for that must
be the great means under God, of the salvation of our country.
                                                    —Maj. Gen. Israel Putnam

Thy sturdy blood secure remained,
And, when its patient cup was drained . . .
Or stamps and teas denounced and broke,
And with the land in union woke.[1]
                                    —A nineteenth-century epic poem

BOSTON

In May 1774, Thomas Gage undertook the administration of Boston with
a dedication to be firm, but he initially tied his policies to the precepts
of calm restraint and impartiality. Although he exhibited considerable
personal qualities in so doing, Gage proved to be inadequately prepared
for the task before him. His lack of immediate military action against the
mobs was seen as vacillation, and he was continually assaulted by editorials in the Whig press. Even London sensed that he would be ineffective, and began searching for a replacement.

In 1774 the colony may have been ungovernable in a practical sense.
The Americans continually circumvented Gage's best efforts at both conciliation and enforcement. The general attempted to appoint council
members, judges, and sheriffs who were loyal to the Crown, but these

men were either persuaded by the radicals to resign their positions or to refuse the appointments. Former colonial legislators frustrated Gage's administration of the colony by forming their own provincial congress in Concord, some twenty miles outside of Boston. John Hancock was the president of this body, which effectively assumed control of all the hinterland, leaving Gage in control of only Boston.

With 17,000 inhabitants, Boston was the third largest city in America. The city was confined to the end of a peninsula attached to the mainland by a long and extremely narrow neck of land. It would seem at first that the British, whose control of the local waters was ensured by the presence of the Royal Navy, might find a base surrounded by the sea to be an advantage. However, the harbor proved shallow, and the approach was narrow and difficult for warships to navigate. Even experienced naval officers were constantly in danger of running their vessels aground on the awkwardly placed mudflats and sandbars. Moreover, it was nearly impossible, because of the pattern of tidal channels, to anchor the ships in positions that favored the bombardment of the city.

Gage commanded three battalions of infantry, a company of marines, and five companies of artillery. He found that most of his possible strategic objectives lay in the countryside. To effect a simple reconnaissance by any means other than the Boston-Charlestown neck, he required a large number of boats. Vice Admiral Samuel Graves's fleet already suffered from a shortage of ship's boats to do all the ordinary work demanded of a fleet in harbor, including the mounting of nightly patrols to prevent sabotage and desertion.

In enforcing the Boston Port Act, Gage allowed himself considerable latitude. His vigorous enforcement of these regulations added to his problems with the residents. He completely cut off the city from any goods that might be loaded or unloaded at the wharfs, and the local ferries to the mainland were closed each night. British troops patrolled the streets at all hours, and only by the greatest of good fortune was a repeat of some violence like the Boston Massacre avoided. Disease and desertions carried away more than a hundred of his garrison, and he was required to support a growing number of persons loyal to the government who were "daily resorting to this town for protection, for there is no security to any person deemed a friend to government in any part of the country."[2]

The Powder Alarm

In September 1774, Gage sent a force by way of Boston neck to secure the king's munitions on the mainland in Charlestown and Cambridge. This mission was accomplished before the colonials could respond. However, a rumor was broadcast that six Americans had been killed during

the removal of the munitions and that the fleet had opened a bombardment of Boston. Neither of these reports was true. Word of the supposed
violence spread all over Massachusetts and to Israel Putnam in nearby
Connecticut. In charge of the regional militia, Putnam left his plowing
like the legendary Cincinnatus of Rome, placed half the colony under
arms, and began to march to the aid of Boston:

> But plough and oxen left to stand,
> While, mounting horse, he rode away
> To Boston in a single day,
> A journey three score miles and ten.[3]

Word spread all the way across Connecticut before it was found to be
a false alarm, and a contemporary observer in Litchfield, on the western
border of the colony, reported:

All along were armed men rushing forward—some on foot, some on horseback.
At every house, women and children making cartridges, running [molding] bullets, making wallets [linen traveling bags], baking biscuits, crying and bemoaning
and at the same time animating their husbands and sons to fight for their liberties, though not knowing whether they would ever see them again.[4]

By the next day more than 4000 armed colonials assembled in Cambridge, where they seized all the remaining cannon. Two days later an
amazing 6000 massed in Worcester. One of Gage's officers estimated that
the colonials would muster as many as 30,000 armed men if given the
time. With fewer than 3000 regulars, Gage had no hope of opposing such
a number, and he shut himself up in Boston.

Meanwhile, the patriots used their presence in Cambridge to force the
resignation of several royal officeholders who were "in haste to resign
their seats as neither Graves with his fleet, nor Gage with his army . . .
[could] insure them protection from the fury of their injured countrymen." One man, a hated customs agent named Benjamin Hallowell,
having ridden his horse to exhaustion in flight, was fired upon by his
pursuers as he ran through the picket guard to enter Boston afoot.[5]

The militia also chased into the British lines the elderly keeper of the
king's storehouse, Gen. William Brattle. Brattle had scrupulously delivered to the selectmen of all the towns those stocks of public powder
entrusted to his keeping, but he had maintained those of the Crown with
equal honesty and care. He later wrote, "Every soldier will say I did but
my duty." Brattle's case illustrates the plight of those who sought moderation in this crisis.[6]

The false alarm had all the markings of a skilled propagandist like
Samuel Adams, a perennial favorite for historians seeking out colonial

schemers, but Adams was in Philadelphia at the time. No other notable person has been definitely identified with initiating the rumors. Dire reports concerning the seizure reached Philadelphia several days after the event; John Adams heard of it there, and he was not informed of the true circumstances for two days more.

The militia leaders in Massachusetts may have allowed the false alarm to proceed, once given, as an inspired opportunity to demonstrate American military strength and resolve. Dr. Joseph Warren noted, "Had the [British] troops marched only five miles out of Boston, I doubt whether a man would have been saved of their whole number." Another contemporary observer wrote, "It was estimated to me . . . that on this occasion there were twenty thousand men in arms in Connecticut marching or equipt for marching towards Boston . . . [and] that forty thousand in Massachusetts province and New Hampshire also took arms."[7]

Minutemen

The powder alarm had far-reaching effects that pointed to a stiffening of American attitudes and a willingness to provide a military response if pressed by the regulars. Shocked by Gage's move to seize their weapon and munitions, and a similar operation by Governor Dunmore in Williamsburg, Virginia, the provincial council in Concord immediately set up a system of alarm riders to raise the "minutemen" units of the local militias. The minutemen were elite members of the local militia companies who were designated for a period of time to respond to an alarm at a minute's notice. This designation revolved through the members of the local company, with about one-quarter of their number pledged to have their guns, ammunition, and a few days rations close at hand.[8]

Focus of Discontent

The response to the powder alarm stripped Gage of any optimism. "Conciliating, moderation, reasoning is over. Nothing can be done but by forceable means. Tho' the people are not held in high estimation by the troops, yet they are numerous, worked up to a fury."[9] Gage saw his mission as changing from the pacification of a few malcontents in Boston to "making a conquest" of all of New England and beyond.[10] "It is somewhat surprising that so many in the other provinces interest themselves so much in behalf of this. I find that they have some warm friends in New York and Philadelphia, and I learn by an officer who left Carolina the latter end of August, that the people of Charlestown are as mad as they are here."[11]

Gage was clearly overwhelmed, and he took on the mind-set of a man besieged. His fortification of Boston Neck served as testimony to his overall apprehension of being overwhelmed by thousands of militiamen swarming through his lines. A contemporary observer noted that the general ordered "a number of field pieces up to the neck . . . and has got a number of workmen there, to build blockhouses and otherways repair the fortification." Patriots in the town attempted to sabotage the fortifications by smashing bricks and burning straw and lumber in the night, but the construction proceded apace.[12] Gage toyed with the idea of cutting a canal across the neck, but the selectmen of the town refused to allow it. He planned to erect artillery batteries "on the skirts of the town; more particularly that part opposite the country shore," and he was seen surveying the ground with his engineering officers.[13]

As September 1774 ended, the increasingly distraught Gage wrote to Lord Dartmouth, the Colonial Secretary:

Your Lordship will know from various accounts, the extremities to which affairs are brought, and how this province is supported and abetted by others beyond the conception of most people, and forseen [*sic*] by none. The disease was believed to have been confined to the town of Boston, from whence it might have been eradicated no doubt without a great deal of trouble, and it might have been the case some time ago; but now it's so universal there is no knowledge where to apply the remedy.[14]

Dartmouth followed the events in the colonies closely, and still believed that an accommodation could be reached should the colonials moderate their tone. Nonetheless, reports that the colonies were importing munitions made him apprehensive. Meanwhile the king's opinion of the situation had largely tied the hands of the ministry. "[T]he colonies must either submit or triumph," wrote the king. "I do not wish to come to severer measures, but we must not retreat."[15]

A GAME OF BRINKSMANSHIP

In January 1775, two British officers went into the countryside to map the surrounding region. They returned under the cover of a snowstorm to report that any advance would be extremely difficult because the terrain favored the militia: many hills, ravines, and marshes. Moreover, there were few good roads and fewer river crossings. Gage sent his troops—one battalion at a time—on short marches during the remaining winter months in order to familiarize them with the ground outside the city and provide them with a break from the boredom of garrison life. These excursions, kept small in order to avoid a massive American counterdemonstration, suggest that Gage was a competent commander.

In late February 1774, the 64th Foot under Lt. Col. Alexander Leslie, attempted to seize some cannon reported to be near the town of Salem.

Leslie was met by the Essex County militia under Col. Thomas Pickering. The quick response and a determined stand by Pickering, blocking the road with scores of minutemen, forced the 64th to return to Boston empty-handed. In late March an entire brigade of over 1200 men under Hugh Lord Percy, colonel of the 5th Foot, attempted a march to Cambridge. Percy met with insults and harassment along his route of march, and found that the militia had dismantled the nearby bridge over the Charles River and had set two cannon to guard another at Watertown. Under strict orders not to fire upon the populace, Percy faced about and returned to the city.

Gage felt that any operation which went further than a mere show of force would throw the country into open rebellion. Although bloodshed was avoided, these encounters were nonetheless unfortunate. They left the regulars and their officers feeling impotent and embarrassed, and they left the patriots with an unwarranted belief that any resolute stand would cause the redcoats to withdraw. In April 1775, Gage received authorization from Lord Dartmouth to take stronger measures. He was to arrest the colonial ringleaders, particularly John Hancock and Samuel Adams. Gage understood from the colonial secretary that the king wanted something done to end the standoff, and this would be deemed the most appropriate first step.

On April 15, Gage ordered all the flank companies of his regiments, those agile and active young men practiced in irregular tactics, to be taken from their regular duties. These 700 men began preparations for a march to Concord, where a store of patriot munitions was reported to be. The light companies of all the separate regiments were detached to serve together as a battalion, and the grenadiers were added to form an elite command. Admiral Graves prepared all of his small boats and ancillary craft to transport these troops directly to the mainland so that they might sidestep Boston Neck and the march over the Charles River. This expedition would not be turned back by any dismantled bridges or blocked roads.

Gage hoped to launch this operation in secrecy. Unfortunately, the preparations could not be made without notice. Officers of the various regiments, forced into a hastily amalgamated corps, needed to meet to organize the expedition. The sudden frequency of these unusual assemblies and the anxiety that surrounded them could not be hidden. Moreover, the preparation of the boats and their collection in the bay could not be concealed. The absence of various small craft from their normal duties indicated that something was up. By the evening of April 18, 1775, all the pieces of the operation were ready. Gage dispatched several small patrols to intercept any riders who might carry warnings from Boston, but these also were observed. The British were about to launch a covert

The patriots developed an excellent system for turning out the militia any-time the redcoats marched forth from Boston. The system used alarm riders, ringing church bells, and cannon firings as signals.

operation, but all of Boston knew about it before a single soldier left his barracks!

Alarm Riders

The provincial congress in Concord instituted an early warning system composed of horsemen known as alarm riders. The system was loosely organized, and many persons served as alarm riders. If any sizable contingent of British troops left Boston, the alarmed residents could remove their munitions and quickly raise up the minutemen to confront the passage of the regulars.

The best-known of the alarm riders was Paul Revere, a colonial silversmith, engraver, and political radical. He wrote in a letter to Dr. Jeremy Belknap in 1798:

In the fall of 1774 and winter of 1775, I was one of upwards of thirty, chiefly mechanics [artisans], who formed ourselves into a committee for the purpose of watching the movements of the British soldiers, and gaining intelligence of the movements of the Tories. We held our meetings at the Green Dragon tavern. We were so careful that our meetings should be kept secret that every time we met, every person swore upon the Bible that they would not discover any of our transactions but to Messrs. Hancock, Adams, Doctors Warren, Church[16] and one or two more.[17]

On April 16, Revere responded to a request made by Dr. Joseph War-ren, a young physician who headed the Committee of Safety, to ride to Lexington to warn Hancock and Adams that Gage might send troops to arrest them. Revere completed the trip and then returned to Boston on April 18, to determine the route to be taken by the regulars when leaving the city, which would determine the colonial response. One lantern was to be raised in the steeple of the Old North Church by John Pulling to inform agents on the Charlestown shore that the troops would leave by way of Boston Neck, as they had in the past. Two lanterns would indi-cate that they would indeed cross to the mainland by boat.

> One if by land, and two if by sea;
> And I on the opposite shore will be
> Ready to ride and spread the alarm
> To every Middlesex village and farm
> For the countryfolk to be up and to arm.[18]

Although Gage made every effort to conceal his plans, Dr. Warren was given credible information about the operation before the regulars left their barracks. William Dawes, an alarm rider, was sent out imme-diately by way of Boston Neck to make for Lexington. Revere, who de-spaired of passing the British guards on the neck twice in so short a period, determined to go to the mainland by boat. He arranged for two men to row him across the bay to a spot where he would be met by others with a horse.

Within a half-hour of the formation of Gage's troops in the lantern-lit streets before their barracks, Revere was on his way to Lexington. Ac-cording to his own account, he was almost immediately accosted by British pickets near the wharfside as he left his boat, and had to flee on horseback through the towns of Medford and Menotomy. Although Dawes had left first, Revere arrived in Lexington before him, at about midnight. He went straight to Rev. Jonas Clark's home, where Hancock and Adams were residing. Here he awaited Dawes, and the two set off toward Concord, joined by Dr. Samuel Prescott, a third alarm rider.

En route to Concord all three—inexplicably riding together—were in-tercepted by four British soldiers with drawn pistols. The alarm riders tried to escape. Dawes reined about and fled toward Lexington. Prescott made his escape by jumping his horse over a stone wall in one direction while Revere took to the woods in another. To Revere's surprise the woods contained a half-dozen more redcoats who were acting as scouts for the column of regulars. He was captured, questioned, and taken toward Lexington. He was left outside the town without his horse, having convinced his captors that more than five hundred militia were expected to assemble there by dawn. He then joined Adams and Hancock in their flight to Burlington.

The Redcoats Are Out!

Alarm riders sped along the roads to spread the word of the advance of the British troops toward Lexington and Concord. Besides the prearranged system of couriers, church bells, and beating drums, numerous persons took it upon themselves to spread the word that the British were out. Many of these remain unknown or uncelebrated, but several of their names have surfaced in the historic record. Thaddeus Bowman rode into Lexington at 4:30 A.M. on April 19 to bring news to the local militia, assembled at Buckman's Tavern near the town green, that the British column was half an hour away. Dr. Prescott, still active after a full night's service, reached Concord during the late morning, and a volunteer rider, Reuben Brown, rode to Lexington and returned with word of the skirmish there.

Notwithstanding his own account of the outing of the alarm riders on the night of April 18, Revere's ride, and that of his fellow couriers that night and thereafter, remained uncelebrated until a largely inaccurate and romanticized version of his tale was written in 1860 by Henry Wadsworth Longfellow. This poem became popular during America's Civil War, but it ignored the capture of Revere and the contributions of Dawes, Prescott, and the other alarm riders.

A SHOT HEARD 'ROUND THE WORLD

Lexington

On the morning of April 19, 1775, the war began. At about 10 o'clock the previous night, the regulars had left their barracks in Boston and marched to the boats waiting at the water's edge. After a relatively short row across Back Bay, a landing was made at Lechmere Point in East Cambridge, where a good road wound inland through Lexington.

The officers chosen to command the British expedition were Col. Francis Smith, the regimental commander of the 10th Foot, and Maj. John Pitcairn, the officer of Royal Marines, who would command the leading element of the advance. The marines had received specific training in making amphibious landings under much harsher conditions than those

The Lexington militia exchanging musket fire with the redcoats on the town green. The patriot lines were probably less ordered than they appear here, in the foreground.

posed by the Massachusetts mainland. However, the entire operation of loading the boats and crossing the bay took much more time than expected. The water's edge near Lechmere Point proved so shallow due to the receding tide that the overloaded boats grounded some distance from dry land. The troops had to wade ashore through the tidal mudflats, getting wet to the knees. They then had to stand about in the cold until two in the morning, in muddy shoes and wet canvas gaiters, while the rest of the contingent disembarked.

Although the march was meant to be noiseless, there was no possibility of masking the movement of 700 fully armed and uniformed men along the roads of a rural countryside. An advanced group of the 5th Foot was seen passing through Menotomy within a half-hour of their landing. Alarm guns could be heard in the distance by the regulars as they marched inland, knowing that every militia company for fifty miles had been alerted.

Capt. John Parker of Lexington had assembled his militia company by midnight, but most of the men had retired to Buckman's Tavern at the end of the green for warmth and a few drinks well before dawn. Nonetheless, when Pitcairn's men appeared through the early morning mists, the patriots—about seventy in all—were lined up two deep across the road. The leading elements of the British column, two companies, quietly deployed into a double line, and Pitcairn ordered the militia to lay down their arms and disperse. Parker had ordered his men to hold their fire regardless of provocation, hoping that intransigence alone would win the day. However, as more regulars filled the green, it became clear that the Americans were heavily outnumbered. Finding discretion a wiser course than obstinacy, Parker ordered his men to disperse. As the colonials slowly backed away, however, Pitcairn demanded that they leave behind their arms. The militia were unwilling to do this, but before Pitcairn's demand could become an issue, a shot rang out from somewhere on the edge of the green.

Known as the "shot heard 'round the world," this is considered by most historians to have been the first fire of the American Revolution. The identity of the person who fired the shot remains unknown, and it is equally uncertain which side fired it. Nonetheless, the British regulars almost instantaneously let go with a volley of musketry. Although British apologists deny it, it is incomprehensible that the regulars would have fired without an order to do so being given. Pitcairn apparently made some attempt to stay the fire, but a second volley rang out from a separate company. Some of the militia returned a sporadic fusillade, but most immediately fled, leaving eight Americans dead or dying on Lexington green.

Concord Bridge

Word of the fighting at Lexington spread rapidly throughout the region. Since it was known that the British objective was Concord, the militia responded to the general area of that town. Even distant militia companies that had begun their march at dawn were arriving by midday. As the leading elements of the British column reached the Concord town green, thousands of militiamen were also converging there.

The British commander sent his light infantry toward Concord bridge, which crossed a brook a small distance beyond the town center, so that they might search some houses in the vicinity for arms. At the bridge, the detachment encountered hundreds of patriots occupying the high ground surrounding the brook. The British formed a column of ranks on the bridge as the Americans opened fire. The first rank of regulars fired and then peeled off to the right and left to free the next rank to fire. The tactic, known as *street fighting*, was very effective in directing a continuous volume of fire from the narrow confines of the bridge. As the ranks of regulars fired, they fell to the rear, fighting a slow retreat to the center of the town. The patriots did not follow immediately. Two British soldiers were killed on the bridge. These were the first casualties suffered by the British that day, but they would not be the last.

Throughout the remainder of the day and into the early evening the

British column marched back toward Boston. With almost every step, they were peppered with musket and rifle shot from the patriots who scurried along the line of march in leapfrog fashion to fire at the redcoats. The British commanders attempted countermeasures by detaching flanking parties, but these were generally ineffective due to the broken nature of the ground. By the time Pitcairn and Smith reached the vicinity of Boston, and the support of a relief column, they had suffered enormous casualties.

After experiencing the humiliation of having his troops hounded back to Boston under galling fire, General Gage utterly failed to attempt to drive the patriots from the heights surrounding the city. Instead, he chose to sit behind his fortifications under the protective guns of the Royal Navy. Consequently, as the Americans massed outside the city, it became obvious that these heights should be fortified. The patriots were more active in this regard than the regulars, and almost overnight they built substantial earthworks on both Bunker Hill and Breed's Hill. The more extensive works were completed on the latter, and it was against Breed's Hill that the British opened the next phase of the Revolution.

Breed's Hill

The average soldier involved in the battle of Breed's (or Bunker) Hill used a smoothbore musket, which was wildly inaccurate at anything beyond 100 yards. Nonetheless, within that range a deliberate shooter had a good chance of hitting a man-sized target. The tactical error committed by the British generals[19] on the day of the battle was to attempt to carry the fortified positions of the rebels by repeated assaults that brought the regulars within lethal range. Hence, the caution given by Col. John Stark to his regiment to hold their fire "until you see the whites of their eyes" was more than mere bravado. It was a tactical imperative.[20]

The regulars, marching uphill, quickly met with added resistance from the terrain itself. "Stumbling in the tall grass and over low stone walls, bumping into wooden fences, sweating under their heavy packs, the British regulars pushed up the hill closer to the American lines. When only fifty yards away, they met a blaze of musketfire that mowed them down." A British officer who advanced with the troops noted, "An incessant stream of fire poured from the rebel lines. It seemed a continued sheet of fire for nearly thirty minutes."[21]

Owing largely to the expert marksmanship of the militia during this first pitched battle of the Revolution, the loss to the British in terms of men and officers was almost incomprehensible, and throughout the entire war the battle remained one of the worst bloodlettings in a single day of fighting. Of a British force of 2400 men engaged, 226 were killed and 828 wounded (44 percent), as compared to 140 killed and 271

Historians still have not resolved the problem of naming the bloodiest battle of the Revolution. It is certain that most of the conflict took place on Breed's Hill, but generations of Americans have called it the battle of Bunker Hill.

wounded of the more numerous Americans. The absolute number of patriots actively involved in the fighting is open to speculation, but their casualties were far fewer. A fifteen-year-old American who observed the battle wrote that the road leading down from Breed's Hill was "filled with chairs and wagons, bearing the wounded and the dead . . . [and] groups of men were employed in assisting others, not badly injured, to walk. Never having beheld such a sight before, I felt very much frightened and would have given the world if I had not enlisted as a soldier."[22]

News of a British victory in which more than 1100 regulars were killed or wounded led one London politician to note, "If we have eight more such victories there'll be not a soldier left alive to bring back the report!"[23] Ironically, there were many British officers who felt after the battle that taking the field to destroy the patriots was futile because their army would melt away of its own accord if not faced by an immediate danger to keep it together. General William Howe wrote to Lord George Germaine that it might be a "better policy to withdraw the troops entirely" and "leave the colonists to war with each other for sovereignty," as this was "the certain consequence" of their determination to separate from Britain.[24]

FIRST FIRE IN THE SOUTH

Word of the fighting at Lexington and Concord led to a series of en-counters in Virginia and North Carolina between the regional militias and their respective colonial governors, Lord Dunmore and Governor Martin. The number of men involved in Virginia at Great Bridge was much smaller than those engaged about Boston, and the American troops were not as well organized. The numbers engaged in North Carolina at Moore's Creek were larger. More than 2,500 men, mostly provincials, were distributed fairly equally on each side. Both of these southern bat-tles were undisputed victories for the patriots, but they have failed to find the same significance in history textbooks as those fought in New England.

Early in the summer of 1776, a British fleet appeared off Charleston Harbor and opened fire on the patriot fortifications on Sullivan's Island, commanded by Gen. William Moultrie. The British, under Sir Henry Clinton, attempted a reduction of the fort by bombardment from the sea and a land attack from the rear. However, the palmetto logs that formed the fort were so soft that the cannonballs sank into them without splitting the wood, and the fire of the southern militia, particularly the riflemen, proved too severe for the regulars. The British fleet was badly scattered by the cannon fire from the patriot fort, and Clinton withdrew his troops and sailed for New York.

> But Moultrie fearless, pipe in hand,
> Stood ready with his brave command,
> And hulled the Royal craft with shells.[25]

Independence

During the summer session of the Second Continental Congress, Rich-ard Henry Lee of Virginia proposed that the united colonies declare themselves independent states. The proposal was accepted by twelve of the thirteen delagations, New York abstaining. A committee composed of Thomas Jefferson, John Adams, Roger Sherman, Robert Livingston, and Benjamin Franklin was appointed to draw up a document setting forth the reasons for such a step. Each man provided political insights into the document's provisions, but Jefferson is commonly given sole credit for the authorship of the Declaration of Independence.

On July 4, 1776, the declaration was signed by 54 delegates from the various states.[26] The decision to take up the cause of independence rather than that of mere representation, proclaimed by the ringing of the Lib-erty bell in the steeple of the old state house in Philadelphia, was greeted by shouts of joy, illuminations, and the booming of cannon.

A dignified illustration of the signing of the Declaration of Independence. Some of the delegates signed many days after July 4, 1776, and Ben Franklin may have signed for several absent colleagues so that the document could be sent to the printer.

> How they shouted! What rejoicing!
> How the old bell shook the air,
> Till the clang of freedom ruffled
> The calm, gliding Delaware!
> How the bonfires and the torches
> Illumed the night's repose,
> And from the flames, like Phoenix,
> Fair Liberty arose![27]

MARTIAL MYTHOLOGY

The initial encounters between patriots and regulars cemented several false impressions in the minds of both that affected the prosecution of the war thereafter. The first was that militia would turn out in the tens of thousands to defeat regulars who attempted incursions into the interior. Certainly this was true of the battles at Lexington and Concord, but the actual number organized to fight the British in Boston is hard to determine. Nonetheless, the British army in America at the time was certainly not equipped to deal with an uprising of this size without considerable reinforcement.

The announcement of the Declaration of Independence was greeted with great joy by colonial patriots. Loyalists and moderates may not have been so joyous.

The second impression was that Americans would stand before trained troops only if they remained within their fortifications and the regulars attempted repeated frontal assaults. The reality was that it was virtually impossible for ill-disciplined and poorly supplied part-time soldiers to defeat a professional army in the open field. The militia were barely capable of maintaining a decent line of fire, and found it impossible to make complicated maneuvers like obliques and flanking movements. That British generals chose to make repeated frontal assaults on patriot positions is an indication of the low regard in which they held Americans as military opponents. In this regard General Putnam is reputed to have said, "Americans are not at all afraid of the heads, though very much afraid of their legs; if you cover these, they will fight forever."[28] General Charles Lee also noted that the patriots were "accustomed from their infancy to firearms, and experts in the use of them."[29] After the battle of Breed's Hill, General Gage was forced to admit that whenever the patriots could "find cover they make a good stand."[30]

The third impression left by the early encounters between the militia and the regulars was that the colonials would not stand before a determined bayonet charge. This impression was first created at Breed's Hill, where the militia broke before the third advance of the regulars. The idea was reinforced in the summer of 1776 at the battle of Long Island when the Americans fled from their forward positions and stopped their retreat only when they reached the safety of their entrenchments. A British officer noted, "Thus repulsed on every quarter, they appear to have been easy prey. . . . It requires better troops than even the Virginia riflemen . . . when they know their retreat is cut off."[31] The Americans broke again before the bayonets at Kip's Bay, where "those who were to have defended [the position] were happy to escape as quick as possible through the neighboring ravines."[32]

It should be remembered, however, that few Americans had bayonets, and it was difficult to withstand a charge at close quarters with nothing other than a "clubbed" musket or a tomahawk. The only logical recourse, should gunfire fail to stem the advance, was to retreat. Washington was sensible to the fact that bayonets were needed by his men, and that they needed to be trained in their use. By 1779, when Americans had bayonets, patriot regulars were able to successfully attack the British position at Stony Point, New York, with bayonets only, in a display of American discipline, training, and espirit de corps.

Finally, there was the impression that American riflemen were capable of remarkable accuracy on the battlefield and could pick off British officers up to 400 yards away. A British officer noted after the battle of Great Bridge, "[I]n less than ten minutes that we were exposed to the enemy's fire, upwards of seventy of our little detachment were killed and wounded."[33] Janet Schaw, a visitor to North Carolina from England, was impressed by the quality of patriot marksmanship. "Their exercise was that of bush-fighting . . . [and] the worst figure there can shoot from behind a bush and kill even a general."[34] A Hessian officer noted, "In their ability to hit an object . . . their riflemen are terrible."[35]

The concept of precise fire applied at longer ranges than that of the standard military musket had been demonstrated both in Europe, principally by German jaegers, and by American backwoodsmen during the French and Indian War. Yet it was not until the Revolution that such large numbers of riflemen were present on the battlefield, nor was their use ever before so ruthlessly applied. Captain William Congreve of the Royal Artillery noted that at the battle of Brooklyn Heights, "The riflemen being covered by trees and large stones had very much the advantage of us, who were upon open ground."[36]

General John Burgoyne described the tactics used by the patriot riflemen during the Saratoga campaign:

The enemy had with their army a great many marksmen, armed with rifle-barrel pieces: these during an engagement, hovered upon the flanks in small detachments, and were very expert in securing themselves and in shifting their ground.

In this action, many placed themselves in high trees in the rear of their own line, and there was seldom a minute's interval of smoke in any part of our line without officers being taken off by a single shot.[37]

THE BATTLE FOR THE BRONX

Colonel John Glover of Massachusetts is one of the "almost overlooked" heroes of the revolution. In command of a regiment of seafaring men from Marblehead, Glover played a pivotal role "in two brilliant amphibious operations" and an action in the Pelham Bay area of the Bronx that was critical to saving Washington's army from encirclement on the island of Manhattan in 1776. Glover's "sound grasp of tactics, his coolness under fire, and his keen insight into the psychology of the American fighting man" made him a candidate for a larger command.

When Washington found his army with the East River at its back on the evening after the battle of Brooklyn Heights, he almost despaired of continuing the war. However, Glover's Marblehead men, familiar with boats and the movement of cargo, were able to ferry the entire patriot force on Long Island across the river in a single night without alerting the British as to their movement. He repeated this feat in December 1776, ferrying the entire attacking force across the ice-filled Delaware River at Trenton to surprise the Hessians stationed there.

With the patriots temporarily secured on Harlem Heights in October 1776, William Alexander (Lord Stirling) was sent by way of the King's Bridge with a brigade to secure a new position for the patriots on the heights at White Plains. Meanwhile, Howe was seen to embark a sizable force on Royal Navy transports to make a wide sweep by way of the Hell's Gate in the East River into Long Island Sound. By this flanking maneuver Howe hoped to land his troops behind Washington's left and cut off his line of retreat.

Glover was sent to Throg's (Frog's) Neck in the Bronx with a brigade of four understrength regiments to head off Howe's landing. Here Howe found his advance hampered by a few score well-placed riflemen who found the ground "strong and defensible, being full of stone fences, both along the [Eastchester] road and across the adjacent fields."[38] Reembarking 3000 of his men under Sir Henry Clinton and Charles Lord Cornwallis, Howe had them make a landing at Pell's Point, three miles farther north, at the mouth of the Hutchinson River. Here the landing force composed of four regiments of Von Stirn's Hessians, the light and grenadier companies of the 4th and 16th Foot, and elements of the 16th Light Dragoons serving afoot were met by Glover's 750 men on the day of Washington's retreat to White Plains (October 18).

By placing his men behind the many stone walls and instructing each successive unit to hold the enemy in check as long as possible before falling back to a similar position in the rear, Glover showed an instinctive understanding of the American fighting man. "Since the first regiment was on the left side of the road it was expected these troops would be able to retire unmolested because the next unit in reserve was on the right and thus would distract the attention of the enemy away from the direction of the retreat." These tactics worked as expected. With three artillery pieces on the high ground, and his men firing by platoons from behind double stone walls, Glover reported, "The enemy halted, and played their artillery at us, and we at them, till night."[39]

With almost 4000 men engaged, the battle at Pelham Bay ranks with "such better-known engagements as Trenton, Bennington, Stony Point, King's Mountain, or the Cowpens." The total of British and Hessian casualties may have reached a thousand men (mostly Germans). Glover's men killed more members of the Crown forces at Pelham Bay than the acknowledged dead at the battles of Long Island, Harlem Heights, White Plains, and Princeton. In comparison Glover lost 6 killed and 13 wounded, and he "gave Washington time to form a line of temporary redoubts behind the Bronx River to shield the retreating Americans from further attack." The battle for the Bronx was a "crucial engagement fraught with strategic significance" and a prominent example of American tactical thinking.[40]

It was inconceivable to most Britons that a group of colonial farmers, laborers, and mechanics commanded by "pettifogging attorneys, bankrupt shopkeepers, and outlawed smugglers" could defeat the greatest military force in the world at the time.[41] Yet James Murray, an old friend and supporter of the Marquis of Rockingham, noted, "The notion of the provincials not fighting is very erroneous, and . . . they have pretty good planners among them."[42] Indeed, Gen. Thomas Gage may have been correct when he noted that the patriots were "not the dispicable [sic] rabble too many have supposed them to be."[43]

NOTES

1. Edward Johnson Runk, *Washington: A National Epic in Six Cantos* (New York: G. P. Putnam's Sons, 1897), 12.

2. Letter of Lt. Gen. Thomas Gage to Willian Legge, earl of Dartmouth, September 12, 1774, in Robert P. Richmond, *Powder Alarm, 1774* (New York: Auerbach, 1971), 35.

3. Runk, *Washington*, 36.

4. Richmond, *Powder Alarm*, 20–21.

5. Ibid., 30.

6. Brattle's letter to Gage was dated August 27, 1774. It was printed in the *Boston Gazette* on September 5, 1774. Brattle admitted writing the letter, but denied that it suggested an operation to remove the powder.

7. Richmond, *Powder Alarm*, 23, 26.

8. See John R. Gavin, *The Minute Men, the First Fight: Myths and Realities of the American Revolution* (Washington, DC: Brassey's, 1996).

9. Letter of Lt. Gen. Thomas Gage to William Legge, earl of Dartmouth, September 2, 1774, in Richmond, *Powder Alarm*, 33.

10. Letter of Lt. Gen. Thomas Gage to Willian Legge, earl of Dartmouth, September 25, 1774, in Richmond, *Powder Alarm*, 35.

11. Letter of Lt. Gen. Thomas Gage to William Legge, earl of Dartmouth, September 12, 1774, in Richmond, *Powder Alarm*, 35.

12. Robert Middlekauff, *The Glorious Cause: The American Revolution, 1763–1789* (New York: Oxford University Press, 1982), 265.

13. From a letter written by John Andrews, a merchant, dated September 6, 1774, in Richmond, *Powder Alarm*, 81.

14. Letter of Lt. Gen. Thomas Gage to Willian Legge, earl of Dartmouth, September 25, 1774, in Richmond, *Powder Alarm*, 35–36.

15. Ibid., 36.

16. Dr. Benjamin Church was later found to be a British spy and informer.

17. Richard B. Morris and James Woodress, eds., *Voices from America's Past: The Times That Tried Men's Souls, 1770–1783* (New York: McGraw-Hill, 1961), 9.

18. Henry Wadsworth Longfellow, "The Midnight Ride of Paul Revere," written in 1860 and first published in 1863 as part of *Tales of the Wayside Inn*.

19. See chapter 8 in this book, on the British commanders.

20. L. Edward Purcell and David F. Burg, eds., *The World Almanac of the American Revolution* (New York: Pharos Books, 1992), 47. Colonel William Prescott and Gen. Israel Putnam have also been credited with the remark.

21. Jack Coggins, ed., *Boys in the Revolution: Young Americans Tell Their Part in the War for Independence* (Harrisburg, PA: Stackpole Books, 1967), 23–24.

22. Ibid., 20–21.

23. Ibid., 9.

24. Eric Robson, *The American Revolution in Its Political and Military Aspects, 1763–1783* (New York: Norton, 1966), 124.

25. Runk, *Washington*, 23.

26. Some delagates signed several days later.

27. William H. Sadler, *History of the United States* (New York: Smith and McDougal, 1879), 184.

28. Quoted in Brendan Morrissey, *Boston 1775: The Shot Heard Around the World* (London: Osprey, 1995), 22.

29. Robson, *American Revolution*, 153–154.

30. Jonathan Gregory Rossie, *The Politics of Command in the American Revolution* (Syracuse, NY: Syracuse University Press, 1975), 19.

31. William P. Cumming and Hugh Rankin, eds., *The Fate of a Nation: The American Revolution Through Contemporary Eyes* (London: Phaidon Press, 1975), 106.

32. Ibid., 111.

33. Ibid., 84.

34. Ibid., 86.

35. Ibid., 145.

36. Charles Townshend, ed., *The Oxford Illustrated History of Modern War* (New York: Oxford University Press, 1997), 46.

37. Ibid.

38. George A. Billias, "Pelham Bay: A Forgotten Battle," In *Narratives of the Revolution in New York* (New York: New York Historical Society, 1975), 108.

39. Ibid., 116.

40. Ibid., 119.

41. Richard M. Ketchum, ed., *The American Heritage Book of the Revolution* (New York: Simon and Schuster, 1958), 248.

42. J. E. Tyler, "A British Whig's Report from New York on the American Situation, 1775," in *Narratives of the Revolution in New York* (New York: New York Historical Society, 1975), 19.

43. Rossie, *Politics of Command*, 19.

6

Redcoats

There are the redcoats; we must beat them today, or Molly Stark is
a widow.

—Gen. John Stark at Bennington, 1777[1]

A snake with rattles, twelve miles long,
The British army, thousands strong,
Reached Allentown; by noise in front
Of opposition scared, the burnt
Of battle they avoid, and borne
Toward Monmouth, on a Sabbath morn
Await the onset of the foe.

—Edward Johnson Runk, nineteenth-century poet[2]

THE BRITISH ARMY IN AMERICA

Regimental Structure

In 1775 the British army in America was composed of 18 regiments of
foot, and it numbered about 8600 men. By 1782 more than 60 regiments
and 50,000 men had done service in North America and the West Indies.
Generally, each regiment of foot in the British army was composed of a
single active battalion. The second battalion was usually used as a re-
pository for excess recruits. Notable exceptions to this were the 60th
Royal Americans with four battalions, and the 42nd (Black Watch) and

Chart 6.1

Organization of a British Regiment

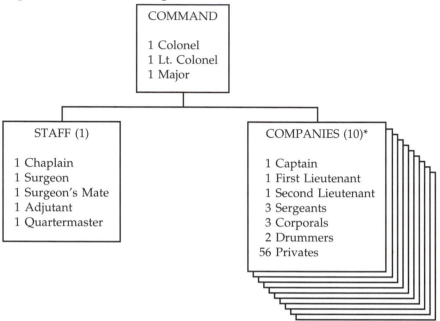

*Two of the ten companies were designated as light infantry and grenadiers, respectively, but they retained the same company structure as the infantry.

71st Highlanders with two battalions each. Mounted units were generally organized around 6 troops of 30 horsemen each, and the artillery was arranged in companies whose size varied depending on the task at hand.

Each line battalion was composed of ten companies on active service. Two companies of each regiment were composed of elite soldiers, one each of light infantry and grenadiers, designated as flank companies. The elite troops generally wore distinctive leather helmets or elaborate miter caps, while the remaining companies, known as "hat" companies, were issued military-style felt hats with turned-up brims. During the American war each company mustered 56 privates and 24 NCOs. The paper strength of an average infantry regiment was about 800, but this was greatly reduced by sickness, detachments, and lack of recruitment. Very little was done to ensure that regiments, or the companies that composed them, were equalized. However, there was some attempt to keep the elite flank companies up to strength. This was often accomplished by transferring men from the hat companies.

At the beginning of the Revolution there were almost 40,000 infantry-men in the British army. Additionally there were almost 7,000 cavalry and dragoons, and 2500 artillerists. Among the regulars were Dutch and German artillerists, Scottish Highlanders, and Swiss, German, and American infantry. Due largely to a lack of available horses, only two regiments of mounted men were dispatched to America, the 16th and 17th Light Dragoons.

Redcoats

All regular British infantry regiments incorporated some form of the basic color red in their uniforms. The colonials, who had served with the British in the French and Indian War, generally referred to the regulars as "redcoats" even though some units wore green or blue. Many myths have survived about the choice of red as a uniform color, including one which states that red would mask the the blood seen flowing from wounds. Such popular anecdotes take no note of the white smallclothes worn by almost every British soldier. Equally ridiculous are stories of red dye being cheaper than other colors. The use of red had evolved from the time of the English Civil Wars as a color chosen for "royal" regiments. In like manner the French infantry came to be suited mostly in gray-white, the Russians in green, and the Prussians in dark blue. Yet all used other colors. There was simply no attempt in the organization of European warfare to identify individual units or armies by color, nor was there any effort to provide camouflage for line troops, who were expected to stand in the open and exchange fire at intervals of less than 100 yards.

The British Clothing Board had the responsibility to inspect the pattern and quality of any uniform used by the army, but it was left to the colonels and regimental agents of each organization to determine the details of uniform color or decoration. There was, therefore, no hard-and-fast rule as to the use of colors. Red, scarlet, and crimson were common variations. Brick red seems to have been reserved for provincial units. This tended to separate the "redcoat" of the line infantry from the blues, greens, or browns of the artillery units, cavalry, provincial troops, or mercenary units. The fact that the British continued to use red uniforms for their infantry into the nineteenth century has helped to cement the image of "redcoats" into the fabric of history.

Enlistments

British regulars were generally drawn from the poorest of Britain's citizenry. Although military life was harsh and the pay poor (6s per day), the professional soldier rarely wanted for accommodations, clothing, or food. Enlistments in the army were essentially for life, meaning that a man would serve until he became too old, too worn, or too disabled to

"Poor Old Soldier." This contemporary illustration of a British soldier emphasizes his poverty with his wife and children in tatters—and the well-fed citizen to the left for contrast. Note the American rifleman firing from concealment at the right.

continue. It was mostly young men between 20 and 25 who volunteered for service. Most had failed to settled down to a trade or calling, were without strong family ties, or had no expectations that their condition would change. Although records show that some men as old as forty volunteered for service, few old men survived in the rank and file, and senior NCOs were generally in their late thirties and early forties.

In 1745, during the Jacobite crisis, the government established guidelines for army recruiting parties that discouraged the enrollment of any men who exercised "any lawful calling or employment." Rather, recruiters were encouraged to enlist "all such able-bodied, idle and disorderly persons who cannot upon examination prove themselves to exercise and industriously follow some lawful trade or employment, or to have some substance sufficient for their support and maintainance." A contemporary observer ungraciously claimed that the redcoats were "too stupid or too infamous to learn or carry on a trade." These guidelines were renewed during the enlistment crises of 1755 and 1778. Ironically, in the eighteenth century the redcoat, who generally volunteered for service— unlike the respected Jack Tar of the Royal Navy, who was often pressed into service—was disliked and looked down upon by the general population. Not until the nineteenth century did the heroic stand of the "thin

A squad of British grenadiers, thought to be among the best of British troops.

red line" during the Napoleonic Wars, and the inspiring stories of Rudyard Kipling's India, help to change this negative public perception.[3]

As with other laborers and craftsmen, British soldiers after some short period of service came to share a number of attitudes, quirks of language, and a store of common knowledge that brought them together in a rough camaraderie. This fellowship largely lacked the wholesome elements of a true esprit de corps and took on many of the unfortunate characteristics of its more unrefined and coarser members. This further separated the soldier from the more affluent and refined persons found among American shopkeepers, craftsmen, and politicians.

Nonetheless, the redcoats serving in America were hardly all the vagabonds, drunkards, and rogues that partisan American propagandists claimed. Rather, there remains some indication that they were somewhat reluctant heroes willing enough to go into the face of danger in a foreign war, but despised in the colonies for doing their duty with regard to an ill-founded and unpopular economic policy.

Highlanders

It was almost impossible to draw large numbers of volunteers from any part of Britain except Scotland. The English and Welsh showed little enthusiasm for the military life, and the Irish were mistrusted because of their Catholicism. Lowland Scots had long supported the Crown, and certain clans were considered foundations of the British army. However, if there was a prevailing negative stereotype of British soldiers in general, the image of the ferocious, wild, and clannish Highland Scots only served to reinforce it.

The highland clans rose against British rule several times in support of the royal house of Stuart, and the British had exacted a deadly toll in executions and reprisals against them as recently as 1746. But the Scots fought valiantly, and the Crown persuaded them to enter military service as the manpower pool of the empire dried up. These men formed Scottish regiments that rivaled any in the British army for steadfastness in the face of danger and devotion to duty. Moreover, a remarkable number of British general officers were Scots, and they seem to have wielded considerable powers of patronage in favor of their countrymen.[4]

Hessians

The German troops hired by Britain to fight in America were known as Hessians, but they were actually from the states of Hesse-Kassel, Hesse-Hanau, Brunswick, Waldeck, Anhalt-Zerbst, and Anspach-Bayreuth. The 30,000 Hessians who served in America were not true mercenaries because they received only their regular wages from their respective princes, who in turn were paid more than £4.5 million from Britain for their services. It is not surprising that the British hired German troops to help in their fight with the colonials. King George III's great-grandfather, George I, was the ruler of nearby Hanover and spoke no English at all, and his grandfather, George II, spoke English with a decided German accent.

The first Hessian regiments to arrive were quite the best of the German troops to serve in America. They were generally well-disciplined and highly trained men who had been brought up in the military traditions of Frederick the Great of Prussia. They were commanded by General Leopold von Heister, who led them at the battles of Brooklyn and White Plains. His subordinate, Col. Johann Rall, was caught completely unaware on the morning after Christmas 1776 at the battle of Trenton. Washington had deliberately cut off all outside contact with Trenton, and his surprise attack hit the Hessians in their barracks from two sides with perfect synchronization. Knox's artillery cut down the Germans as they exited the buildings and prevented them from developing an adequate defense. Over a thousand Hessians were killed or captured, while the patriots had only four men wounded.

Because of the Trenton disaster Von Heister was recalled in 1777 and replaced by Baron Wilhelm von Knyphausen, a tough and competent professional soldier. Von Knyphausen played important roles in the New York and New Jersey campaigns and figured prominently in the battle of Brandywine, where he broke the patriot center and captured some of their artillery. He assumed command of New York during Sir Henry Clinton's campaign against Charleston, and directed a number of operations against the Hudson Highlands and New Jersey. These were moderately successful, but filled with controversy. The British had convinced the Hessians that the rebels had resolved to give them no quarter in battle, "which made them fight desperately, and put all to death who fell into their hands."[5] A British officer noted the vigor with which the Hessians came to grips with patriot troops: "The Hessians . . . gave not quarter, and it was a fine sight to see with what alacrity they dispatched the rebels with their bayonets after we surrounded them so that they could not resist."[6]

The Hessians were widely feared and hated by the Americans, who generally accepted all the propaganda that was spread about them. The stories surrounding the Hessians included the burning of homes and the killing of prisoners, women, and children. A favored image spread by the patriot propagandists was that of babies spitted on the tips of Hessian bayonets. This powerful image was resurrected during both world wars of the twentieth century. Yet a British officer, Lord Francis Rawdon, noted a particular human frailty among these most feared monsters as they were landing on Long Island from the boats of the Royal Navy: "The Hessians, who were not used to this water business and . . . [were] exceedingly uncomfortable to be shot at whilst they were quite defenseless and jammed so close together. [They] began to sing hymns immediately."[7]

Although the elite element of German troops was known as the *Erbprinz*, or Prince Hereditaire regiment, most Hessian units were referred to by the names of their commanding colonels—Von Donop, Von Trumbach, or Von Bose, for example. The regiments initially served separately in New York, Canada, and Virginia with their own officers, artillery support, and small contingents of European riflemen known as jaegers. The Anspach and Bayreuth troops—Von Voigt and Von Seybothen—having only one grenadier and four line companies each, served together in a brigaded formation, while the Hessian jaegers were amalgamated into a separate rifle contingent.

In 1776 more than four thousand Hessians, actually the troops of the duke of Brunswick, landed in Quebec under the command of Lt. Gen. Baron von Riedesel. Many of these men accompanied General Burgoyne during the Saratoga campaign of 1777, making up almost half of his troops. A detachment of several hundred Germans were victorious against the patriot militia at Hubbardton in Vermont. However, a body of Hessians under Lieutenant Colonels Frederich Baum and Heinrich Breymann was severely whipped at the battle of Bennington by militia general John Stark and Lt. Col. Seth Warner. Two hundred Hessians dead, including Baum, were buried on the battlefield, and seven hundred became prisoners. Among these were the Brunswick Dragoons, sent to America without horses, who were captured at this battle, steadfastly protecting Baum's final position while serving on foot.

The remaining Hessians under Von Riedesel were pivotal in supporting Burgoyne during the battle of Freeman's Farm, and Breymann commanded a major strategic position (the Breymann redoubt) during the battle of Bemis Height. It was against the Breymann redoubt that Benedict Arnold joined the attack which broke the British will to resist. Arnold was wounded in his leg, and a monument, to his leg only, stands near the position today. Breymann and almost two hundred of his Hessians were killed.

Of the 5000 troops who surrendered at Saratoga, fewer than 2000 were Germans. These were added to almost 1000 Germans captured during the Trenton and Philadelphia campaigns. Many of the Hessian prisoners were allowed by their American captors to escape over the next four years, to melt into the farm populations of Pennsylvania, Virginia, and New York, where they mingled seamlessly with the established German-speaking residents. Estimates of desertions by Hessian soldiers as high as 5000 have been established by historians. Nearly 8000 died in battle or as a result of sickness.

NOTES

1. William H. Saddler, *History of the United States* (New York: Smith and McDougal, 1879), 191.

2. Edward Johnson Runk, *Washington: A National Epic in Six Cantos* (New York: G. P. Putnam's Sons, 1897), 58.

3. Quoted in Stuart Reid, *King George's Army, 1740–93.* Vol. 1, *Infantry* (London: Osprey, 1995), 18, 20.

4. Ibid., 12.

5. William P. Cumming and Hugh Rankin, eds., *The Fate of a Nation: The American Revolution Through Contemporary Eyes* (London: Phaidon Press, 1975), 110–111.

6. Ibid., 110.

7. Ibid., 110–111.

7

Of Patriots and Rebels

Among other things which will prevent a conciliation, the contempt every soldier has for an American is not the smallest. They cannot possibly believe that any good quality can exist among them.

—A British soldier, 1779

These people show a spirit and conduct against us they never showed against the French, and everyone has judged of them from their former appearance and behavior . . . which has led many into great mistakes.

—A British officer[1]

THE PATRIOT ARMY

The Militia

For most Englishmen and Americans, "the most noxious tool of impending tyranny" was a standing army. Throughout British history, standing armies had brought increased levels of taxation, repression, or civil strife. By comparison, reliance on a militia for defense was considered a sign of a healthy and vigorous society in which citizens took on the responsibilities of actively safeguarding "property, liberty, and life itself."[2]

In America, independent companies of riflemen and rangers patrolled the backwoods areas of the colonies, but a well-regulated and trained militia provided the most practical solution to the defense needs of most settlements. There remains the cherished romantic concept of the militia as a mythical army of self-trained and self-armed warriors springing from the colonial soil in times of trouble. This picture hardly aligns with the facts. The colonial militia system was a carefully constituted organization, established in all the colonies by the middle of the century, and tested in the French and Indian Wars. While less than adequate to substitute for a regular army, the militia was able to defend the settlements, drive back the Indians, and hold open the newly abandoned lands for European acquisition.[3] Such a force might have served before Lexington and Concord, but after 1775 the Revolution changed from a popular uprising into a very real war. The reality of continuing to rely on the militia for the prosecution of a political and social revolution quickly proved a disastrous illusion.[4]

A British surgeon at Boston in 1775 wrote of the patriot militia assembled there: "This army . . . is truly nothing but a drunken, canting, lying, praying, hypocritical rabble, without order, subjection, discipline, or cleanliness; and must fall to pieces of itself in the course of three months."[5] An optimistic French spy reported, however, that the militia were "stronger than others thought. It surpasses one's imagination. . . . Nothing frightens them."[6] The young men from the backcountry "were proud of their Indian-like dress and even wore leggings and breechclouts to church."[7] A Tory minister, Jonathan Odell, wrote a poem describing the patriot militia that he saw gathering in New Jersey in 1775.

> From the back woods, half savages came down
> And awkward troops paraded every town.
> Committees and conventions met by scores:
> Justice was banished, Law turned out of doors;
> Disorder seemed to overset the land;
> Those who appeared to rule, the tumult fanned.[8]

The weaknesses of the militia were obvious when it was used as a regional defense. John Adams wrote disparagingly of the militia raised to defend against Governor Tryon's raid on Connecticut in 1777. "[T]he stupid, sordid, cowardly, terrified country people let them [the British] pass without opposition."[9]

Ironically, even as the patriots relied less on the militia and more on Continental regulars, the fighting became "more of a partisan war for which the militia's style of fighting was better suited."[10] A Hessian officer wrote, "In the open field the rebels are not of much count, but in the woods they are redoubtable."[11] A British officer also noted their "agility in running from fence to fence and thence keeping up an irregular, but galling fire on our troops."[12] The constant string of raids and skirmishes

The local militia company turning out in their civilian clothes to defend American liberty. The flag at the left is the Flag of Union, the first national flag adopted by Congress.

that came to characterize the war in New Jersey, in particular, forced the British to maintain their combat readiness at all times in the face of small groups of militia. Outpost duty became continuous for the regulars, and the British could not quietly enjoy their winter quarters even in the cities. A regular noted that "being out almost every day harassed the garrison much."[13] No small group of soldiers or train of provisions was safe outside the British lines. A Scottish officer wrote, "As the rascals are skulking about the whole country, it is impossible to move with any degree of safety without a pretty large escort, and even then you are exposed to a dirty kind of tiraillerie [skirmishing]."[14]

The Local Militia Company

The heart of the militia was the local company.[15] Company strengths from province to province varied from 70 to 200 men. The companies were in some measure bound by kinship ties, but it was mostly neighbors who served in the same unit. Local command was invested in a captain, subalterns, and sergeants. The officers were usually elected by the men—a facet of the patriot army that seemingly frustrated many professional army officers. The overall command structure and the level of authority of individual militia leaders generally lacked clear definition, but their authority came from the provincial congress. Traditionally the militia was prohibited from serving for long periods far from home or outside the colony, and the men remained reluctant to leave their homes in time of danger to fight in other localities. These characteristics of the militia caused great difficulties for Congress when it attempted to establish the authority of the Continental Army.[16]

Provincial Forces

Most of the colonies had formal provincial units, recruited into regiments, paid by the colony, and established to replace the less formal militia units in major operations. By 1775, provincial forces had become permanent organizations with their own cadre of officers and a fixed chain of command. During the Revolution these provincial forces slowly evolved into state troops and the officers were numbered prominently among those given authority by Congress. However, the changing, patchwork organization of the patriot army, with its overlapping chains of command, competing systems of supply, and confusing terms of enlistment, posed severe problems for the patriots throughout the war.

Washington actually commanded three different army organizations during his tenure as commander in chief. The first was the Army of Observation, composed of the militia companies that besieged the British in Boston. The second was the Army of the United Colonies with its one year enlistments, which was soundly defeated by the British in New York in 1776. Its remnants, pursued through New Jersey, were nonetheless able to rout the Hessians at Trenton and the British regulars at Princeton. Finally there was the Continental Army established by the Congress in 1777, with its better organized departments, means of transportation, and ancillary units.

Throughout the war the armed forces of the United States would retain components from among the militia, the state forces, and the Continental regulars. Added to these were many local volunteers that turned out as the spirit moved them to be brigaded into temporary formations. Washington decried the reliance on well-disposed, but generally undisciplined and untrained, volunteers considering them no more dependable than "a broken staff."[17]

THE ARMY OF OBSERVATION

During the emergency of 1775, all the colonies except Pennsylvania put some militia units into the field. General William Heath was not impressed by these men. "As to the ability of this body of men I cannot fully determine. The greater part that I saw appeared able, but it is more probable that there are some advanced in life, and some lads, and a large number of negroes."[18] When Washington arrived in Boston, he was shocked by the army he saw stationed among the heights surrounding the city. He immediately called a conference of his officers to initiate changes in the structure of the patriot forces. The decisions reached at this meeting framed the structure of the patriot army for the rest of the war. The army was divided into 26 line regiments with separate formations of riflemen and artillery. Line regiments were to have a paper strength of 728 officers and men. Washington assigned quotas to the states in proportion to their troops who were present at Boston.

The Continental Army

In the fall of 1776, Congress decided to formalize the army structure in an act known as the 88 Battalion Resolves. This number of battalions (actually regiments) was arrived at by estimating the male population of the colonies. The provincial manpower quotas and regimental organization were little changed from those devised by Washington, but the number of regiments established in each state was modified somewhat. The details surrounding the organization of the Continental Army thereafter changed constantly, but the basic regimental structure remained throughout the war.

In 1777 the organization was increased to 110 infantry regiments. The four regiments of light dragoons authorized in 1776 were retained, but the artillery was reorganized into just four regiments and a single regiment of artillery artificers to provide prepared charges and repair the carriages. The several independent companies of riflemen and rangers from the frontier regions remained active. A corps of engineers was cobbled together, and wagoners, teamsters, provisioners, and a small hospital staff were placed under the Quartermaster's Department. The resulting organization of infantry, dragoons, riflemen, artillery, and ancillary units was to be known as the Continental Army.[19]

Infantry

Each line regiment had 8 companies of 76 privates, instead of the 10 companies of 56 privates that characterized the British foot regiments. Each company was divided into two platoons commanded by lieutenants. Washington also proposed the creation of 32 field officers and 64 NCOs per regiment, which would give the men a greater density of leadership than their British counterparts, who had 21 field officers and 48 NCOs per unit. This was thought to improve the deployment and maneuver of the less highly drilled American infantry. Moreover, the regimental commanding officers would remain with their units, while the general officers would act independently. This was not the case in

Table 7.1

The Organization of the Patriot Army, 88 Battalion Resolves, 1777

State	Infantry	Horse	Artillery	Militia/Rifles*
Massachusetts	15 Regts.	———	1 Regt.	3 Btns.
Connecticut	8 Regts.	1 Regt.	½ Regt.	1½ Btns.
New Hampshire	3 Regts.	———	———	———
Rhode Island	2 Regts.	———	———	½ Btn.
New York	4 Regts.	———	½ Regt.	½ Btn.
Maryland	8 Regts.	———	———	———
Virginia	15 Regts.	2 Regts.	1 Regt.	3 Btns.
North Carolina	9 Regts.	———	———	1 Btn.
South Carolina	6 Regts.	———	1 Regt.	———
Delaware	1 Regt.	———	———	———
Georgia	1 Regt.	———	———	———
New Jersey**	4 Regts.	———	———	2 Btns.
Pennsylvania***	12 Regts.	1 Regt.	1 Regt.	2½ Btns.
Unassigned	———	———	———	3 Btns.
Totals	88 Regts	4 Regts.	5 Regts.	17 Btns.

*Units of different sizes and organization formed into additional battalions of infantry, rifles, etc.

**New Jersey, with its patchwork of patriot and loyalist supporters, had each well-disposed township raise a company of 80 men.

***Pennsylvania, with its Quaker-controlled assembly, formed its troops as units of associators in order to maintain the fiction of not supporting war.

British units, where colonels were often absent and where lieutenant colonels, or majors, were sometimes detached to command brigades. This sometimes left an entire British regiment commanded by a senior captain.

On the field, American units were deliberately arranged in two ranks in order to present a longer front to the British, who generally took the field in three ranks (one kneeling and two standing). Although a third rank offered only an inaccurate fire at best, it was thought to carry more weight in a bayonet charge. British light infantry, relying on speed of deployment and maneuver, generally formed in two ranks. The two-rank formation brought all of its muskets into positions where a more precise fire might be expected. By the end of the war, the entire British command in North America had adopted the two-rank formation.

Artillery

The Continental artillery was under the overall command of Col. Henry Knox. His ability and foresight in organizing the artillery was

Chart 7.1

Organization of a Continental Regiment

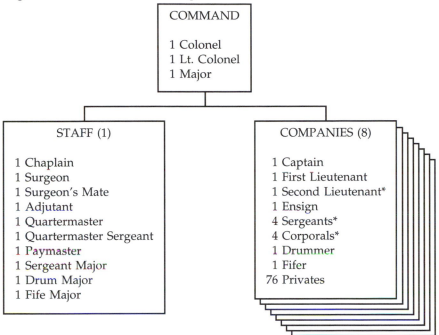

*The position of second lieutenant was eliminated under Baron von Steuben's reorganization, and the sergeants and corporals were decreased from four to three. These changes may have reflected the better training and discipline of the soldiers of the army after 1778.

remarkable. With only the knowledge acquired by his reading, Knox recommended a basic train of mobile artillery consistent with that used in Europe. He envisioned an entire train of artillery composed of brass pieces, including 100 3-pounders, 50 6-pounders, and 50 12-pounders, plus a smaller number of 18- and 24-pounders for general support and siege work. This was not possible before France entered the war.

Trained artillery crews were difficult to find. The greatest deficiency in the Continental artillery during the war was in *bombardiers* and *matrosses*. While any group of infantrymen could be drafted to move a piece, working a gun safely required the cooperation of a knowledgeable and qualified team. Shells had to have their fuses carefully timed, and the guns themselves were unforgiving; they could explode if improperly loaded, killing the men nearest them. The gunner needed to know how to vary the angle of the barrel and charge of powder in order to hit targets at great range. Many gunners were detached from the ships of

The use of linear tactics required the men to maintain a straight line in the face of the enemy.

the navy, where experienced men were more likely to be found. Moreover, artillerymen were a prime target for sharpshooters because of their value to the opposing army.

During the eighteenth century there was a shift from a battlefield dominated by cavalry to a battlefield dominated by infantry drawn up in massed formations and supported by artillery. The tactic of supporting these infantry with mobile artillery was devised by Gustavus Adolphus of Sweden and was refined by Frederick the Great of Prussia. There was little doubt that the offensive firepower of the infantry supported by improved and more mobile artillery was going to severely inhibit the tactics available to horsemen in the Revolution.[20]

Dragoons

In March 1776, Congress authorized 3000 horsemen formed into four regiments of Continental Light Dragoons, one each in Pennsylvania and Connecticut, and two in Virginia. The actual number of dragoons raised was not half that envisioned. Each regiment was composed of 6 troops of only 30 men. In a letter to Lafayette, Nathanael Greene, who was uncomfortable with an understrength mounted arm, warned, "Enlarge

This unit of dismounted light dragoons is undergoing inspection before taking post for guard duty.

your cavalry or you are inevitably ruined." His warning was validated when the British suddenly fell upon Washington's flanks at both Jamaica Pass (Long Island) and Chadd's Ford (Brandywine), although in both cases a few mounted vedettes were detailed specifically for this purpose.[21]

Considered elite troops, light dragoons were armed, equipped and trained to be equally effective as light cavalry and as light infantry. To this end they were issued swords, pistols, and carbines. Light dragoons wore uniforms typical of the rest of the army, or short coatees, to which were added leather helmets to protect the head from sword blows, and leather breeches and knee-high boots to protect their legs from chafing on their horse furniture and stirrups. They wore none of the armor common to heavy cavalry, but they still required remounts, saddles, bridles, holsters, and other equipment unique to horsemen. The dragoons were continually plagued by deficiencies in equipment, and the troopers often provided their own horses, horse furniture, and pistols. They sometimes carried tomahawks in lieu of swords.[22]

Dragoons were assigned as mounted vedettes, scouts, raiders, escorts, and couriers; but the bulk of their work was as foragers, advance or rear guards in the column of march, or as skirmishers on the battlefield. General Washington's life guard initially included a troop of dragoons and a company of light infantry drawn from the army on a rotational basis.

It was later organized into a permanent establishment of sixty men, half of whom were dragoons. Von Herr's *Marechaussee* (military police) served as provost guards and executioners. These dragoons were widely feared and hated by the troops of their own army, and served on the flanks and rear of the battle line to prevent desertions.

There were no significant mounted charges during the revolution and few hand-to-hand combats from the saddle. Some historians subscribe to the theory that the topography of America was simply unfriendly to sweeping maneuvers and charges by horsemen. However, this circumstance does not seem to have inhibited the cavalry during the American Civil War. In 1778, Polish Count Kasimir Pulaski was made a major general and commander of all cavalry. Pulaski attempted to make the dragoons into a more traditional mounted force, training them with lances and brigading small units into larger formations. The American dragoon officers resented this imposition. One challenged a Polish comrade of Pulaski to a duel after being unhorsed in practice. Pulaski was killed in action in October 1779, in an ill-advised mounted charge against the British entrenchments at Savannah. The organization that he envisioned for the Continental cavalry died with him.

Many southern militia companies and volunteers, such as those led by Francis Marion and Andrew Pickens, came to war mounted and could not be made to give up their horses to serve on foot. These volunteers laid claim to the traditional status of mounted aristocrats while avoiding the less desirable duties of infantrymen. Although they were not used as cavalry in the classical sense, these "mounted troops were indispensable" in the southern campaigns of 1780–1781.[23] They raided British supplies, cut off isolated units, and strangled communications. Their manner was undisciplined, their tactics with respect to loyalists were heavy-handed, and their equipment was largely improvised. Nineteenth-century historians may have exaggerated and distorted their contributions to the war, but it is certain that these mounted irregulars were effective in galling the British to distraction.[24]

The Legion

An entirely new formation, known as the legion, was developed during the American war. This structure teamed dragoons with light infantry, who would sometimes ride double in order to cover great distances. The light infantry provided defense and firepower, while the dragoons provided flexibility and speed in the attack. Before his death, Pulaski formed a legion recruited from among British deserters and prisoners of war, but afteward it reverted to the role of light infantry. The Pulaski Legion proved to be more of a hazard to its friends than to the enemy, due to "its routinely destructive behavior . . . [and] it enjoyed little success at any of its assigned tasks."[25]

The most effective legions were the Partisan Legion of Light Horse Harry Lee and that of William Washington, the commander in chief's cousin. Lee had three troops of horse (one composed of Oneida Indians) and two companies of light infantry; Washington's Legion was similarly composed from the 1st Dragoons and the remnants of the 3rd Dragoons, which had been massacred at Tappan, New York. The British Legion of Banastre Tarleton, a green-clad unit composed mostly of loyalists, seems to have been the equal of all the American organizations.[26]

The legions of Lee and Tarleton both wore dark green uniforms, and the leaders took care to make use of any mistaken identification. At Haw River, North Carolina, Lee was able to convince four hundred mounted loyalists under Col. John Pyles that he was Tarleton! When the loyalists dropped their guard and formed on parade to honor him, Lee's men fell upon them, killing ninety men and wounding or capturing the rest. Not one American was hurt. Tarleton, on the other hand, boldly rode into a patriot supply depot, identified himself as Lee, drew provisions for his horses and men, and signed a receipt before he quietly rode away.

Lee's and Tarleton's troopers clashed almost daily in small affairs, occasionally killing or wounding a man or horse. Such duty was tedious, nerve-wracking, and very hard on both men and horses. Cavalrymen faced this form of small war, or *petite guerre*, more often than their comrades in the infantry or artillery. Hours spent sitting picket duty on a horse in the dark, on a lonely road waiting to be attacked by a lurking enemy, fell short of the gallant cavalry charges portrayed in the schoolbooks and novels of the next century.

Lee and Tarleton never came face to face. However, at Cowpens in South Carolina, the horsemen of William Washington and those of Tarleton came together with saber-clashing bravado in a brief but indecisive clash. They hacked at one another for a short time like medieval champions amid their entangled comrades, but were separated in the heat of battle. The clash was not rejoined because Tarleton's men fled the field.

Tarleton had a similar experience in 1781 at Gloucester Point while escorting a foraging party with the 16th Dragoons. He observed a squadron of French horsemen (hussars) of the legion of the Duc de Lauzen pursuing them. He charged the leading elements of the French in a narrow lane, sword in hand, but the confines of the pathway prevented any sword-to-sword action. Just as the two leaders were about to come into contact, Tarleton fell from his horse. Only the quick action of his men saved him from being captured. The arrival of American infantry forced the British to withdraw.[27]

RECRUITS AND VOLUNTEERS

Only men between the ages of 16 and 60 were formed into units for training. This range of ages may leave the reader with an inaccurate picture of what the Revolutionary army looked like. Provincial armies were composed of adult males in the prime of life rather than of old men and young boys. Studies suggest that the average age of men serving in the army was just under 26, with 80 percent under 35 and less than 2 percent, many of them officers, over 55. Almost all of these men were true volunteers, unlike the soldiers of European armies, who may have been impressed or conscripted.[28]

Black Soldiers

Free blacks and black slaves from the southern plantations were welcomed into the British army in 1775 by Lord Dunmore, the governor of Virginia. They were formed into the governor's Ethiopian Regiment for service against their former masters. Dunmore hoped to attract 2000 black slaves to military service with the promise of freedom at the conclusion of hostilities. Although the northern colonies, particularly Rhode Island and Connecticut, made similar proposals to blacks willing to serve in the patriot army, southern landowners were horrified by Dunmore's action.

In the North most blacks were free men, but in the South most were slaves. The enlistment of slaves "violated the property rights of their masters," and there was a fear that the army might become a "refuge for runaway slaves." Georgia and South Carolina were the only states to refuse to enlist blacks. Elsewhere, any blacks wishing to volunteer for the patriot army were required to present evidence that they free men, a requirement knowingly overlooked by many manpower-hungry recruiters. Those blacks found to have served "while a fugitive" were routinely denied pensions after the war.[29]

There is little evidence that either loyalists or patriots refused to serve with black soldiers in battle. Several small groups of former slaves were reported to have raided patriot plantations in Virginia while under the command of white officers. At the battle of Great Bridge, one-third of the 400 British troops involved were of African heritage, and they were observed to serve with distinction, bravely attacking the fortified positions of their former masters even in defeat. Runaways captured in arms against the patriots were sent to the lead mines of southwestern Virginia or were sold in the West Indies.[30]

Many black soldiers and their families were taken aboard ship at Norfolk when Dunmore abandoned the mainland, but they were poorly treated and forced to serve as drudges aboard ship. Many enlisted as sailors, far from a unique experience for the manpower-hungry Royal Navy, which recruited among many races and nationalities around the world. The remains of a young British seaman, buried in his uniform coat, that was unearthed in an all-black cemetery in Manhattan in the 1980s is a silent testiment to the extent of their service.[31]

Most of the former slaves who volunteered to serve with the British simply disappeared into history. Hundreds may have died of a fever, possibly smallpox, reported to have swept the confines of the ships in the weeks before Dunmore burned Norfolk and sailed north. Thomas Jefferson claimed that 27 of the 30 slaves who fled his plantation to fight for the British died of smallpox or "putride fever." It has been estimated that the number of fatalities among blacks who fled to the British was approximately equal to the total incurred by white patriots during the course of the war.[32]

New England enrolled more men of African descent than any other region of the country because there was a good-sized population of free blacks in the seaport towns. Seamen of many races and ethnic backgrounds were a common sight in New England, and a good number of blacks served as sailors aboard American privateers. A contemporary observer noted that there were no regiments from New England that did not have some black soldiers. Estimates of blacks in New England regiments run as high as 8 percent.[33] Rhode Island had the largest proportion of blacks among its soldiers, and Connecticut had the greatest absolute number. The First Rhode Island Regiment enrolled almost two hundred black light infantrymen, and the members of the 2nd Company of the 4th Connecticut Regiment of the Continental Line were all of African descent. The state outside New England with the largest enrollment of blacks was Virginia.[34]

Dorothy Dudley noted in the journal of her stay with the patriot army, "There is an element in our camp life not to be overlooked—I mean the negroes, many of them slaves, who, heart and soul, enter into the interests of our country and render valuable service both in tent and field. It was a colored soldier, you know, who shot Major Pitcairn at Bunker Hill. Many of them are scattered through the ranks of the army, and in the hospitals and camp faithfully fill offices of many kinds."[35] The contemporary painter Johnathan Trumbull included two blacks in his famous painting of the death of Dr. Joseph Warren at Bunker Hill, and it is known that Salem Poor, Cuff Whitemore, and fourteen other unnamed black soldiers fought there.

The typical black enlistee served as a private in a patriot infantry regiment. A small number served with the artillery, and only rarely was one found in the elite mounted service, usually as a servant. Former slaves fought in every major engagement of the war. Many of the black soldiers served as orderlies, or were assigned to noncombatant functions

Three Revolutionary War reenactors. Folks like these try to bring the period alive for students and visitors to historic sites.

such as wagoners, farriers, guards for the stores, ditch diggers, or artillery dragropemen. Blacks who served in the patriot army were due the same wages, enlistment bounties, clothing allowances, food, and pensions given to white soldiers.

Many black soldiers received postwar pensions under legislation passed late in the century, but others remain unknown to history because they enlisted without surnames. Petitions to the state or federal government for emancipation or pension benefits included the names of James LaFayette and Saul Matthews, who served as spies; Caesar Tarrant, who served as a harbor pilot; and Richard Pointer, who fought off Indians on the frontier. Jeru Grant served as a teamster. Ned Griffin claimed emancipation for having served in the place of his master, William Kitchen, at the battle of Guilford Courthouse; and Lambo Latham and Jordan Freeman died defending Fort Griswold in Connecticut. Men like these were just as much heroes in the cause of freedom as Crispus Attucks, who died in the Boston Massacre; Salem Poor, who shot Major Pitcairn, or Prince Whipple, who crossed the Delaware with Washington at Trenton.[36]

The acceptance of black soldiers in the army was not universal, and "a pattern of exclusion" quickly developed.[37] General William Heath of New England noted, "For my own part I must confess I am never pleased to see them [blacks] mixed with white men."[38] After the first flush of the war, Congress encouraged all soldiers to reenlist at the end of their terms, "Negroes excepted, which the Congress do not incline to enlist again." New Hampshire refused to accept black reenlistments, and New Jersey required all black soldiers in its regiments to turn in their weapons and continue service as noncombatants, or not at all. Furthermore, Congress ordered all blacks found loitering near the camps to be seized and confined. The fate of such persons is absent from the record.[39]

Men of African heritage seem to have fought well on the battlefield. Historian Benjamin Quarles has noted, "Since Negro soldiers fought side by side with whites, rather than in separate organizations, there was no battle in which black Americans were conspicuous as a racial group." Nathanael Greene's regiment of black soldiers from Rhode Island came closest to being distinct as a race-based unit. A French officer described them as "most neatly dressed, the best under arms, and the most precise in [their] maneuvers."[40] They were one of six units of predominantly white light infantry that served with great skill at Newport in August 1778. Greene's black regiment was specifically commended for holding its position against three determined assaults by the British and the Hessians.[41]

Black troops also made up part of the French forces that came as American allies from the West Indies. The Count d'Estaing's army of 3600 had more than 500 blacks, recruited largely in Santo Domingo. Designated Volunteer Chasseurs, they served under white officers during the siege of Savannah and prevented the success of a British counterattack at a pivotal point in the operation. When the French fleet abandoned the siege of the city, the Volunteer Chasseurs went with them, and they played no further role in the Revolution on the mainland.

Boys at War

Those under the age of 16 played an important part in the revolution. Most served as fifers and drummers in the army, trumpeters in the cavalry, and powder boys in the artillery. Lieutenant Colonel Harry Lee was greatly moved when the unarmed teenage trumpeter of his dragoon regiment was shot down in a road by one of Tarleton's riders. Nonetheless, even youngsters of 10 or 12 who had lived on the frontier might be experienced enough with firearms not to waste a shot in haste at an enemy. Hunting for food and defending against Indian attack made a knowledge of firearms and their use imperative. At a time when most European armies pointed their muskets in the general direction of the enemy rather than aiming directly at them, some American youngsters might be considered "expert marksmen" by comparison.[42]

Many boys enlisted and fought on board privateers or on the ships of the Continental or Royal Navy as cabin boys, cook's helpers, or powder monkeys. Many more boys went to sea than served on land simply because it was common practice in coastal towns to apprentice as a seaman at an early age. Powder monkeys of ten or twelve years were particularly important on warships, where they brought ammunition from the powder magazines below the waterline to the gun decks during battle.

THE SIZE OF ARMIES

Modern researchers estimate that about half the military-age men in the population, 100,000 individuals, served in the Continental Army, provincial forces, or militias during the war.[43] It is certain that General Washington never personally commanded more than 25,000 troops. Only eight times during the war did the Continental Army as a whole show more than 20,000 men. Army strength varied with the seasons. As winter approached, many men would wander away from the camps to sit before the warm hearths of their own homes, and spring planting kept many men from returning to the army until late in the season. This was frowned upon by the officers, but the army was always happy to see the men return. The fighting force may have been augmented during some campaigns by volunteers who turned out in ad hoc formations. This was certainly true during the Saratoga campaign, where the appearance of Burgoyne's army of invasion drew patriot volunteers with great enthusiasm.

The best estimate of the average size of the army under Washington is less than 10,000. He may have had 25,000 to defend New York City, but he certainly had fewer than 7000 for the Trenton/Princeton campaign of December 1776. A return from July 1778 showed 16,782 rank and file fit for duty in White Plains, New York. This is the largest absolute number under Washington's direct command for which there is hard evidence, but these troops were actually arranged in six divisions spread in an arc that swept across parts of New Jersey, Westchester County, and Connecticut with a radius of 42 miles from New York City. No division was actually strong enough to prevent a determined outbreak by the British, nor were they close enough to each other to provide meaningful support. Washington has been criticized by students of military strategy for dispersing his troops so widely.

The Americans were successful in driving the British from New England, but throughout the war detachments of various size were required to maintain their authority. Patriot forces became somewhat scattered by the need to stem the aggressive moves of the Royal Navy along the New England coastline and to contain the operations undertaken by the loyalists regiments in Westchester. Moreover, in 1780 many units in the army were dispatched to the southern campaign, leaving Washington with a considerably smaller command. In 1781 he was able to field fewer than 8500 men, and at Yorktown his immediate command was only about 5000 Americans.

The combined armies of Richard Montgomery and Benedict Arnold that attacked Montreal and Quebec in the winter of 1775–1776 were estimated at 2500 men. At Camden and Charleston, the patriots lost two complete armies documented to contain almost 5000 men each, one under Horatio Gates and the other under Benjamin Lincoln. The patriot forces in the South, under Nathanael Greene, were thereby devastated, but continued to recover by the timely arrival of detachments from the North and by the operations of the militia that appeared from the back-country, foothills, and swamps of the Carolinas.

Among these were the irregular forces of Thomas Sumter, Francis Marion (the Swamp Fox), and Andrew Pickens, which harassed the British in Georgia and South Carolina after the fall of Savannah and Charleston. All three local leaders were daring, creative, and skillful, and they understood that those practicing partisan warfare must attack, avoid being pinned down, and quickly melt back into the countryside when faced with overwhelming strength. The volatile nature of these organizations makes estimating their number difficult.

The actual strength of the patriot army, therefore, is almost impossible to measure accurately, leaving the student with only an estimate of its numbers based on its effective strength. It is safe to say that the patriots were able to maintain an army big enough to oppose the operations of the British at most points. It is one of the failures of British strategy that their military strength was never again overwhelmingly focused on just one part of the colonies as it was at New York in 1776.

Recruiting Rebellion

The initial outpouring of patriot volunteers in 1775 and early 1776 quickly slowed as it became obvious that the war would drag on for some time. The recruits to the Continental Army of 1777 were at first asked to enlist for the duration of the war. Colonial laws regarding enlistments in previous wars had traditionally limited enlistments to one year. Washington understood that he could not effectively campaign with his troops on the verge of leaving the army each winter. Yet he warned Congress that long enlistments would hamper recruitment. A three-year term, or the duration of the war, should it prove shorter, was therefore considered an acceptable compromise for Continental service.

THE ARTICLES OF WAR

The rules that controlled military life were known as the Articles of War. All recruits signed them when they enlisted and pledged to live by them while in service. In signing, the recruit voluntarily gave up some of his civil liberties for the sake of military order and discipline. The initial articles of the Continental Army were based on earlier versions common to provincial service, but they were found deficient in deterring misbehavior among the men. In an attempt to improve discipline Congress strengthened them. The new version had seventy-six clauses that defined the soldier's rights and obligations under military law and provided a uniform structure to the courts of military justice. Congress raised a number of minor acts, such as looting, to capital crimes and increased the maximum corporal punishment from the biblical limit of 39 lashes to a full 100.

Many enlistees initially refused to sign the congressional version of the articles because they considered themselves provincial troops governed only by the militia regulations of their states. This was particularly true of the troops from Connecticut, who were supported in their refusal by Gen. David Wooster. Washington would have none of this, sending one regiment of Connecticut cavalry home at a critical moment in the New York campaign because they refused to do fatigue duties. He wrote, "Men accustomed to unbounded freedom, and no control, cannot brook the restraint which is indispensible [sic] to the good order and government of an army; without which licentiousness, and every kind of disorder triumphantly reigns." However, with time, this peculiarity of Continental service seems to have worked itself out, and free uniforms, bounties, and increased pay for Continental soldiers seem to have overcome any lingering objections to signing the Articles of War.[44]

Only once did any of the patriot forces refuse to serve while under arms. This was because their three-year enlistments had run out in Jan-

The tall man in the center is the subject of a court-martial. His judges are the officers seated at the right. This proceeding is being reenacted at Fort Ticonderoga, New York.

uary 1781. Several regiments of Pennsylvania infantry, having suffered from cold and hunger at the Morristown encampment, began an orderly march home. General Anthony Wayne initially charged them with mutiny, but the troops had not been paid for months and had indeed served out their terms. The mutiny briefly threatened the existence of the Main Army as two British agents among the men tried to spread the disagreement to other units. Nonetheless, cooler heads prevailed, and the troops were furloughed until the terms of their enlistments were worked out. The British agents, Ogden and Mason, were hanged as spies. Ironically, most of the Pennsylvania men reenlisted.

Punishments

The Articles of War were read periodically to all the troops at mass formations so that no man could claim ignorance of them. Regimental courts-martial were held almost weekly, and those charged with infractions were judged by a panel of officers drawn from the companies. Punishments were publicly inflicted before the entire regiment or brigade as a deterrent to further violations. Gambling, fighting between the men, bad language, petty theft, and discourteous behavior to officers were considered offenses warranting the lash, hanging by the thumbs, standing upon a wooden peg with the bare foot, or straddling a rail for some hours. Each punishment was designed to chastise, but not to permanently debilitate, the miscreant.

Desertion, cowardice, treason, murder, disobedience of direct orders, mutiny, sleeping on watch, looting, rape, and homosexuality could bring death, usually by hanging. James Thacher, a surgeon with the patriot army, noted, "Five soldiers were conducted to the gallows, according to their sentence, for the crimes of desertion and robbing the inhabitants. A detachment of troops and a concourse of people formed a circle round the gallows, and the criminals were brought in a cart, sitting on their coffins, and halter [*sic*] about their necks. While in this awful situation, trembling on the verge of eternity, three of them received a pardon from the commander-in-chief.... The other two were obliged to submit to their fate."[45]

NOTES

1. Richard M. Ketchum, ed., *The American Heritage Book of the Revolution* (New York: Simon and Schuster, 1958), 330.

2. James Kirby Martin and Mark Edward Lender, *A Respectable Army: The Military Origins of the Republic, 1763–1789* (Arlington Heights, IL: Harlan Davidson, 1982), 8–9.

3. The discussion of the militia and provincial force that follows is largely taken from the authors' earlier work. See James M. Volo and Dorothy Denneen Volo, *Daily Life on the Old Colonial Frontier* (Westport, CT: Greenwood, 2002).

4. See John R. Gavin, *The Minute Men, The First Fight: Myths and Realities of the American Revolution* (Washington, DC: Brassey's, 1996); John K. Mahon, "Anglo-American Methods of Indian Warfare, 1676–1794," *Mississippi Valley Historical Review* 45 (1958), 254.

5. Henry Steele Commager and Richard B. Morris, *The Spirit of Seventy-six: The Story of the American Revolution as Told by Participants* (New York: Harper & Row, 1975), 152–153.

6. Martin and Lender, *A Respectable Army*, 32–33.

7. Colin G. Calloway, *The American Revolution in Indian Country: Crisis and Diversity in Native American Communities* (Cambridge: Cambridge University Press, 1999), 18.

8. Quoted in North Callahan, *Royal Raiders: The Tories of the American Revolution* (New York: Bobbs-Merrill, 1963), 127.

9. Mark V. Kwasny, *Washington's Partisan War, 1775–1783* (Kent, OH: Kent State University Press, 1996), 125.

10. Ibid., 225–226.

11. William P. Cumming and Hugh Rankin, eds., *The Fate of a Nation: The American Revolution Through Contemporary Eyes* (London: Phaidon Press, 1975), 145.

12. Eric Robson, *The American Revolution in Its Political and Military Aspects, 1763–1783* (New York: Norton, 1966), 153.

13. George Inman, quoted in Kwasny, *Washington's Partisan War*, 126.

14. Sir James Murray, quoted in ibid.

15. See Fred W. Anderson, *A People's Army: Massachusetts Soldiers and Society in the Seven Years' War* (Chapel Hill: University of North Carolina Press, 1984); and "Why Did Colonial New Englanders Make Bad Soldiers? Contractual Principles and Military Conduct During the Seven Years' War," *William and Mary Quarterly* 3rd ser., 38 (1981), 395–417; Adam J. Hirsch. "The Collision of Military Cultures in Seventeenth-Century New England," *Journal of American History* 26 (March 1988) 1187–1212; Mahon, "Anglo-American Methods of Indian Warfare"; Louis Morton, "The Origins of American Military Policy," *Military Affairs* 22 (1958), 75–82; Jack Radabaugh, "The Militia of Colonial Massachusetts," *Military Affairs* 18 (1954), 1–18; and John W. Shy, "A New Look at Colonial Militia," *William and Mary Quarterly* 35 (1963), 175–185.

16. Radabaugh, "Militia of Colonial Massachusetts," 2.

17. Christopher Ward, *The War of the Revolution* (New York: Macmillian, 1952), 253.

18. Cumming and Rankin, *Fate of a Nation*, 158.

19. See A. N. Schultz, *Illustrated Drill Manual and Regulations for the American Soldier of the Revolutionary War* (Union City, TN: Pioneer Press, 1982).

20. Charles Townshend, ed., *The Oxford Illustrated History of Modern War* (New York: Oxford University Press, 1997), 23–24.

21. John K. Herr and Edward S. Wallace, *The Story of the U.S. Cavalry, 1775–1942* (New York: Bonanza Books, 1984), 18.

22. See Burt Garfield Loescher, *Washington's Eyes: The Continental Light Dragoons* (Fort Collins, CO: Old Army Press, 1977); and John T. Hayes, *Connecticut's Revolutionary Cavalry: Sheldon's Horse* (Chester, CT: Pequot Press, 1975).

23. L. Edward Purcell and David F. Burg, eds., *The World Almanac of the American Revolution* (New York: Pharos Books, 1992), 141.

24. See Noel Gerson, *The Swamp Fox, Francis Marion* (New York: Doubleday, 1967), 272.

25. Purcell and Burg, eds., *World Almanac of the American Revolution*, 363.

26. See Noel B. Gerson, *Light Horse Harry: A Biography of Washington's Great Cavalryman* (Garden City, NY: Doubleday, 1966).

27. Brendan Morrissey, *Boston 1775* (London: Osprey), 41–42.

28. Anderson, *A People's Army*, 231, 44.

29. See under the Pension Act of 1832 in Benjamin Quarles, *The Negro in the American Revolution* (Chapel Hill: University of North Carolina Press, 1996), 13; and Ray Raphael, *A People's History of the American Revolution: How Common People Shaped the Fight for Independence* (New York: New Press, 1991), 288–289.

30. See Quarles, *Negro in the American Revolution*, 19–32.

31. Dorothy Denneen Volo and James M. Volo, *Daily Life in the Age of Sail* (Westport, CT: Greenwood, 2002), 103, 110–111.

32. Raphael, *A People's History*, 298.

33. Ibid., 284.

34. Quarles, *Negro in the American Revolution*, 73–74.

35. Dorothy Dudley, *Theatrum Majorum: The Diary of Dorothy Dudley* (New York: Arno Press, 1971), 36.

36. Raphael, *A People's History*, 282–285.

37. Quarles, *Negro in the American Revolution*, 13.

38. Cumming and Rankin, *Fate of a Nation*, 158.

39. Quarles, *Negro in the American Revolution*, 15.

40. Raphael, *A People's History*, 287. See also 284.

41. Quarles, *Negro in the American Revolution*, 79–80.

42. Jack Coggins, ed., *Boys in the Revolution: Young Americans Tell Their Part in the War for Independence* (Harrisburg, PA: Stackpole Books, 1967), 9.

43. Erna Risch, *Suppying Washington's Army* (Washington, DC: U.S. Army Center of Military Studies, 1981), 26. Also see Charles H. Lesser, ed., *The Sinews of Independence: Monthly Strength Reports of the Continental Army* (Chicago: n.p., 1976). Lesser was the first modern researcher to edit the available returns of the Continental Army.

44. Raphael, *A People's History*, 312.

45. James Thacher, *Military Journal of the American Revolution, 1775–1783* (Gansevoort, NY: Corner House Publishing, 1998), 161.

8

The Generals of the Armies

There were prejudices enough among the weak and fears enough among the timid, as well as other obstacles from the cunning: but the great necessity for officers of skill and experience, prevailed.

—John Adams

Officers are the very soul of an army: one might as well attempt to animate a dead body into action as to expect to employ an army to advantage, when the officers are not perfectly easy in their circumstance, and happy in the service.

—Thomas Jefferson

THE ORGANIZATION OF THE BRITISH ARMY

On the eve of the Revolution the British army, including all three arms of the service worldwide, numbered about 49,000 men. Its organization was based on approximately 70 regiments of foot, 28 regiments of cavalry and dragoons, some 50 companies of marines, and 48 companies of Royal Artillery arranged in four battalions. Many of the most junior regiments were left understrength in an effort at economy.[1] Large standing forces were economically impossible to justify to the British taxpayer. Americans found them redundant in the light of their own provincial forces and viewed them only as a threat to their liberty. No regular British troops were permanently stationed in America prior to the French and Indian War.[2] The Honourable East India Company maintained a private army in India, which somewhat freed the British to use their regulars more liberally in America.[3]

From the outbreak of the Revolution in 1775 to the peace of 1783, the infantry regiments of the British army increased in number from 70 to 102. No fewer than 12 of these were raised among the highland Scots, and all were created in response to the entry of France into the war. There were about 9000 regulars posted to America in 1775. By the end of the war in 1783, there were more than six times that number, representing more than 60 regiments. Additionally, almost 70 provincial regiments of loyalists were raised in America to serve against the rebels.[4]

Administration

Unlike the Americans, who needed to invent a national administration for both their army and navy from the outset of the Revolution, the British had an established administration in the Board of War for their army and the Board of Admiralty for their navy. The Board of Admiralty was the most powerful administrative office in the empire. The whole scheme emphasized the prevalence of the naval arm in British strategic thinking.

The Ordnance Department of the Admiralty controlled everything from arms and ammunition issued to soldiers to the detention of prisoners of war. The military testing facilities at Woolwich provided all the artillery and gunpowder for both the army and the navy. The chief engineer at Woolwich made all decisions affecting artillery, ammunition wagons, artillery limbers and carriages, firearms, edged weapons, and other accoutrements, including any innovations or changes. Both civilian and military gunsmiths "proofed" their weapons at Woolwich.

The Board of War was never as powerful as the Board of Admiralty. It was controlled by the secretary of war through the War Office. The position was held by Lord Barrington throughout the Revolution. The subsidiary offices of the army administration were the Paymaster's Office, the Judge Advocate's Office, the controller of army accounts, the apothecary-general, and the board of the Chelsea Hospital. The position of commander in chief of all the British armies in the empire became vacant in 1772 and was not filled until 1778, when it went to Sir Jeffrey Amherst.

This circumstance left the suppression of the revolution largely in the hands of the colonial secretary, George Lord Germain. The consequences of having the army under political control during the formative stages of the Revolution are incalculable, and any conclusions based on hypothetical scenarios would be highly suspect. It is certain, however, that Germain dealt with the generals serving in America in a biased and uneven manner, favoring some and discounting the advice of others because of their politics.[5]

Logistics and Supplies

The army relied directly on the Treasury to provide funds for its food and equipment, and the details of supply were left to the colonel of each regiment. This system resulted in a general lack of central authority, a wide variance in the quality of life among the regiments in peacetime, and a great deal of overlapping and frustrating waste of effort when preparing for active duty. The annual allotment of funds from the Treasury could be used to benefit the men or to line the pockets of the commander.

Regimental colonels purchased or inherited their commands. They could do almost anything they wished with their regiments, as long as the men were kept in fighting trim. The colonels usually provided for themselves by selling commissions to ambitious young men who wished to serve as officers. Commissions in the Guards, the Grenadiers, or the cavalry were highly regarded by truly ambitious men, and those posted to the oldest and lowest-numbered regiments cost more than those available in newly raised units.

The Crown accepted the system of selling commissions mainly because it helped to maintain the social and political status quo. Although the system rarely allowed truly incompetent men to rise to a position of overall command, it did prevent talented men with small means from attaining high rank and influence. There was a constant demand for commissions, and no ill-disposed officer was ever forced to serve in a particular campaign because he could always sell his commission to someone else.

THE BRITISH COMMANDERS IN AMERICA

On May 25, 1775, the British warship *Cerebus*, named for the mythological three-headed dog that guarded the gateway into the underworld, dropped anchor in Boston Harbor. The choice of a ship of that particular name was not lost on the Americans, for on board were three men who would figure prominently in the war. All three were members of Parliament, which guaranteed them a certain patronage in Britain. A London paper noted of their posting to America:

> Behold the Cerebus the Atlantic plough.
> Her precious cargo Burgoyne, Clinton, Howe.
> Bow, wow, wow![6]

Chart 8.1

**The Price of Commissions in the British Army: Approximate Cost in
Pounds Sterling in 1775**

LINE REGIMENTS

Rank	Price
Lieutenant Colonel	3,500
Major	2,600
Captain	1,500
1st Lieutenant	800
2nd Lieutenant	500
Ensign	400

ELITE REGIMENTS

Rank	Price
Lieutenant Colonel	5,500
Major	4,300
Captain	2,700
Lieutenant	1,500
Cornet	1,200

The Howe Brothers

Major General William Howe was a successful and popular officer
from a family steeped in military tradition. He had served in America
in the French wars, and had trained and commanded the light infantry
units that had scaled the cliff at Quebec in 1759. Howe was sent to replace Thomas Gage as British commander in chief in America with the
brevet rank of full general. William Howe was forty-six, the youngest of
three brothers—the late Lord Augustus Howe and the present Lord
Richard Howe.

Augustus Howe had been a model soldier, young and highly regarded
by the colonials. During the Seven Years' War, Augustus placed himself
in the hands of Robert Rogers and learned, first hand, his methods of
woodlands warfare and ranger tactics. Unfortunately, Augustus was
killed in a sharp fight at Ticonderoga in 1758. William had implemented
many of his innovations in 1772, when he was assigned to promote a
new light infantry drill for the flank companies of the regiments of foot.

William's elder brother, Richard, was an experienced naval officer. When the eldest Howe brother was killed, Richard was made Lord Howe, but he was popularly known as "Black Dick." In 1776 he was named commander of the North American Squadron, displacing Vice Admiral Thomas Graves. He resigned this position in 1778 when his brother William was recalled, and refused further commands until 1782. His long career thereafter was filled with success, and he ultimately became First Lord of the Admiralty.

William Howe was a moderate Whig whose political sympathies were generally on the side of the colonials. He initially refused a command in America. Howe not only condemned the conduct of the government, but he and Germain, the colonial secretary, had a long-standing dispute between them, which effectively precluded their cooperation. Howe numbered among his friends those who believed that conciliation was the only solution to the American problem. Only the direct intercession of the king caused Howe to accept the American assignment.

Howe was depressed and disgusted by Gage's bloody victory at Breed's Hill, but he remained in America to command the 1776 campaign for New York City and the 1777 campaign that captured Philadelphia. He was recalled to England in 1778 to answer charges that he had allowed Washington's army to escape destruction. Sir George Collier wrote, "Having to deal with a generous, merciful, forbearing enemy, who would take no unfair advantages, must have been highly satisfactory to General Washington, and he was certainly very deficient in not expressing his gratitude to General Howe for his kind behavior towards him." Nonetheless, Howe was a good soldier who followed orders and did all he thought best to surpress the rebellion.[7]

Henry Clinton

Major General Sir Henry Clinton was the longest-serving British commander during the Revolution. Clinton was born in 1738 in New York, where his father was the colonial governor. At 37 he was a seasoned soldier. Completely distraught by the unexpected death of his wife in 1772, he had recovered his mental health well enough by 1775 to accept an American assignment as second in command of the British army. In 1776 he was assigned to command the unsuccessful siege of Charleston, South Carolina. He was then sent to capture Newport, Rhode Island, after which success he was knighted in London. In 1777, he returned to New York, where he undertook the defense of the city. From here Clinton reached out into the "no-man's land" of Westchester County and challenged the American hold on the Hudson Highlands surrounding West Point.

Clinton made no attempt to dissuade Howe from his ill-timed operation against Philadelphia in 1777, which abandoned Burgoyne to his fate at Saratoga. In fact, in a vague exchange of dispatches with Howe, Clinton suggested that the forces in New York City were not immediately needed in the north. Nonetheless, Clinton did send a detachment under Brig. Gen. Vaughan up the Hudson, which should have "involve[d] General Gates in inexpressible embarrassment and difficulty, by placing him between two armies." However, Clinton gave no detailed instructions as to when or where the detachment should attempt to link up with Burgoyne. Vaughan's force was still more than forty miles from Albany when word reached him of Burgoyne's surrender.[8]

Clinton was chosen to replace Howe as commander in chief in 1778. During the next two years he continued an indecisive war of raids and counterraids, skirmishes, and minor encounters throughout lower New York, eastern New Jersey, and coastal Connecticut. He seems to have consistently underestimated the colonials as military opponents, yet he rarely strayed too far from the loyalist stronghold of New York. In 1780 he led a second attack on Charleston that proved successful, and then he quickly returned to New York, leaving Cornwallis in charge in the south.

John Burgoyne

The third officer to arrive on *Cerebus* was 53-year-old John Burgoyne. Known as "Gentleman Johnny" for his pretensions as a playwright, poet, and social commentator, Burgoyne was, nonetheless, a creditable field officer who had entered the service in 1740. He was present at the battle of Breed's Hill, which he described as "one of the greatest scenes of war that can be conceived. . . . Howe's corps ascending the hill in the face of entrenchments and a very disadvantageous ground warmly engaged to the left [by] the enemy . . . and in the arm of the sea, our ships and floating batteries cannonading them."[9]

Burgoyne retuned to England in 1776. Here he received a promotion to lieutenant general and the authority to implement a scheme to attack the Americans from Canada through the Lake Champlain-Lake George channel. This was not a new plan. Only a successful naval blocking action led by Benedict Arnold at Valcour Island in Lake Champlain had prevented Gen. Sir Guy Carleton from descending the lakes in 1776. Burgoyne's plan differed in that it would attempt to split the rebellious colonies in three pieces by simultaneously driving British armies west-to-east along the Mohawk River Valley from Lake Ontario, and south-to north from New York City by way of the Hudson River. Burgoyne would proceed north-to-south along the lakes in company with Hessian forces under Lt. Gen. August Baron von Riedesel, his second in command.

Burgoyne rapidly began his movement to the southern end of Lake Champlain and with little fuss took Fort Ticonderoga from the Americans, who abandoned it. However, his progress thereafter was impeded by his poor knowledge of the region and his reliance on local loyalists. Colonel Philip Skene, an ex-British officer serving as a loyalist aide to the general, had established a 25,000-acre estate near the head of Lake Champlain. He advised Burgoyne to march by way of his holdings, which incidentally would benefit by any roads built by the army as it advanced. Burgoyne therefore hacked a way through the wilderness instead of quickly advancing by way of Lake George and the army road from Fort Edward to Albany built in the previous war. Instead of floating down the 32-mile length of the lake in two days, his army moved a mere 23 miles through the forest in 24 days, obstructed by creative patriots who felled trees across every mile of his route and fired unremittingly on his working parties.

Bennington. Meanwhile, Burgoyne detached a group of Hessians, loyalists, and Indians to seek out horses in the nearby Connecticut River Valley that served as the boundary between New York and the New Hampshire Grants, now known as Vermont. It was from this region that Ethan Allen had raised the Green Mountain Boys, a loosely organized group of frontier militiamen and wilderness freebooters fighting for the patriots. Burgoyne's detachment was soundly whipped at Bennington by the militia under Gen. John Stark. This was the first of a number of military disasters that afflicted Burgoyne's campaign thereafter.

Fort Stanwix. The Mohawk Valley operation was entrusted to Lt. Col. Barry St. Leger, who believed the region to be filled with loyalist sympathizers who would turn out to support him. This hope failed to materialize, but St. Leger did attract a large contingent of Iroquois Indians from western New York. Instead of quickly imposing British dominance throughout the valley and moving on to cooperate with Burgoyne, St. Leger found himself conducting the siege of a stubborn force of Continentals (3rd New York Regiment) under Col. Peter Gansevoort, closed up in a strongly fortified position known as Fort Stanwix. Stanwix was strategically positioned, like a stopper in a bottle, at the western opening to the Mohawk Valley near present day Rome in central New York.[10]

The siege of Fort Stanwix was finally raised when the British commander fell victim to a stratagem conceived of by the ubiquitous Benedict Arnold. A young German boy, Yon Host, posing as an informer, caused St. Leger to believe that a large relieving force of Continental troops was advancing up the valley from the east. The British retired in utmost hast to Lake Oswego, leaving almost all of their baggage in their camp near the fort.

Oriskany. During the siege of Fort Stanwix, a sizable force composed of Mohawk Valley patriots under the command of militia general Nich-

The interior of Fort Stanwix in winter. The cannon sits on the parade ground of this fine National Park Service reproduction fort and park in Rome, New York. The church is a nineteenth-century structure.

olas Herkimer had in fact materialized from the countryside to threaten St. Leger's line of advance. Although he was too far away to cooperate with Gansevoort tactically, Herkimer fought a dogged battle with some of St. Leger's loyalists and a large number of allied Iroquois at Oriskany, about a dozen miles from Fort Stanwix, in late August 1777. Herkimer had 800 frontier militia and a few dozen Oneida Indians to oppose an almost equal force composed of Native Americans, John Butler's Tory Rangers, and John Johnson's Royal Greens, all led by Joseph Brant.

Herkimer's few Oneida scouts failed to detect an ambush set by the British in a remarkably small wooded ravine, and many patriots were killed in the opening fire. Struck in the knee by a musket ball that also felled his horse, Herkimer directed the battle while sitting against a tree on the field and quietly puffing on his pipe. He died at his home ten days after the battle of hemorrhaging during the amputation of his infected leg by an inexperienced doctor. The battle lasted all day, ending only when the participants grew too weary to continue. Both sides resorted to savage fighting with tomahawks, hatchets, and knives after a summer downpour wetted their powder.

Oriskany, while indecisive in itself, may have been the bloodiest encounter between irregular forces during the war. It is estimated that 200 patriots lost their lives and that half of Herkimer's force sustained wounds. Crown losses were also severe, but remain uncounted because they were sustained mainly by Brant's Indians. The most profound consequence of the battle was that it caused the badly mauled Indians to melt back into the interior to mourn their dead, leaving St. Leger bereft of much needed intelligence. The Indians were thereafter less resolute in their support of the Crown. St. Leger later admitted that this circumstance figured prominently in his abandonment of the siege of Fort Stanwix.

The Saratoga Campaign. Notwithstanding his detour through Skenesboro, Burgoyne found himself comfortably situated near Saratoga, New York, in early September 1777, with many days of good campaigning weather still before him. He believed that he would winter his army in Albany, which was little more than a dozen miles away, after joining with Howe's forces from the south. However, the third prong of Burgoyne's scheme never materialized. Howe had inexplicably taken his troops to attack Philadelphia instead. Burgoyne, at Schuylerville with fewer than 6000 effective troops, found himself faced by an ever increasing number of patriots arriving from all quarters.

Although denied support from both St. Leger and Howe, Burgoyne gamely fought two major battles in the Saratoga area against twice his number. The first was at Freeman's Farm on September 19, 1777. Although the Americans were officially under the command of Horatio Gates, it was Benedict Arnold who served as the American field commander during the battle. Burgoyne battled Arnold's men all day, and as night fell, Arnold retreated, leaving the battlefield to the British. The human toll of the day's fighting was remarkable—556 British casualties and 287 for the patriots. This was almost 10 percent of Burgoyne's force.

The second battle took place on October 9 at Bemis Heights. The American riflemen of Daniel Morgan were particularly effective during this encounter, decimating the British officer corps. Private Timothy Murphy of Morgan's rifles took careful aim at Brig. Gen. Simon Fraser, the commander of the British advanced corps, killing him from a great range, and thereby turned the tide of battle at an opportune moment.

Gates was in immediate command at Bemis Heights. He had inexplicably relieved Arnold of his duties in a moment of pique and confined him to his quarters, saying, "I have nothing for you to do; you have no business here." Nonetheless, Arnold left his tent as the sounds of battle reached a crescendo. He rode recklessly into the battle at the strategically placed Hessian redoubt, urging the Americans to redouble their efforts. When the position fell, it exposed Burgoyne's entire flank to attack. The next day Burgoyne attempted a retreat toward Ticonderoga but, despairing of a successful withdrawal before winter weather set in, he was forced to surrender.[11]

For the patriots, the Saratoga campaign represented a monumental change of fortune that breathed new life into the Revolution. They had decisively defeated a major force of regulars in the field for the first time. Although Gates allowed Burgoyne to sign a face-saving convention rather than a surrender, the Americans had clearly triumphed under circumstances that could not be dissembled by the ministry in London into anything other than a stunning defeat. They captured two lieutenant generals, two major generals, three brigadiers, all their staffs and sub-ordinate officers, and almost 5000 British and German privates, who were now interned as prisoners of the "Convention." Ticonderoga and Crown Point were evacuated by the Crown forces, and the garrisons recalled to Canada. All of northern New York up to its border with Canada was freed of the threat of invasion. At the end of 1777 the British "reluctantly admitted that the war was going to last longer than previously expected."[12]

Shortly after Saratoga, Burgoyne returned to England, where he had to face both hostility and ridicule. He never again served in a position of consequence. The same London newspaper that had announced the sailing of *Cerebus* now ran the rhyme:

> Burgoyne, alas, unknowing future fates,
> Could force his way through the woods,
> But not through Gates.[13]

A War Nearly Won

Charles Lord Cornwallis remains one of the most recognizable names in American history. A seasoned soldier, he was thirty-eight years old when he arrived in New York with the British invasion fleet of 1776. Cornwallis was immediately thrown into a series of battles with the Americans, each of them a resounding victory. At Fort Washington, 2800 patriots were taken prisoner and much of Washington's scarce supply of artillery, ammunition, and flour was taken. Major General Charles Lee wrote sarcastically of this disaster: "The ingenious maneuver of Fort Washington has unhinged the goodly fabric we have been building—there never was so damned a stroke." Cornwallis led the attack on Fort Lee, atop the clifflike palisades and chased Washington through the townships of New Jersey and into Pennsylvania.[14]

No one knew it at the time, but the British came closest to victory in that 1776 campaign. However, the tide of a "war nearly won" proved too easily turned by Washington's victory at Trenton. Nonetheless, in all of his operations Cornwallis lost only one encounter to Washington—at Princeton, New Jersey, in January 1777. He wintered in England and returned in the spring to play key roles at the battle of Brandywine and

Table 8.1

Principal Actions in the Southern Theater 1775–1781

Date	Location	Opponents		Victory
		Patriot	*Crown*	
1775	Great Bridge	Woodford	Dunmore	Patriot
1776	Moore's Creek	Moore	McLeod	Patriot
	Charleston	C. Lee/Moultrie	Clinton/Parker	Patriot
1777	Thomas Swamp	Baker	J. Prevost	Crown
1778	Savannah	R. Howe	Campbell	Crown
1779	Fort Morris	Lane	A. Prevost	Crown
	Port Royal	Moultrie	Gardiner	Patriot
	Kettle Creek	Pickens	Boyd/Hamilton	Patriot
	Savannah	d'Estaing	A. Prevost	Crown
1780	Charleston	Lincoln	H. Clinton	Crown
	Waxhaw	Buford	Tarleton	Crown
	Camden	Gates/DeKalb	Cornwallis	Crown
	King's Mountain	Shelby	Ferguson	Patriot
1781	Cowpens	Morgan	Tarleton	Patriot
	Haw River	H. Lee	Pyles	Patriot
	Guilford C. H.	Greene	Cornwallis	Crown
	Hobkirk's Hill	Greene	Rawdon	Crown
	Ninety-Six	Greene	Cruger	Crown
	Green Springs	Lafayette/Wayne	Cornwallis	Crown
	Eutaw Springs	Greene	Stewart	Crown
	Yorktown	Washington/ Rochambeau	Cornwallis	Patriot

the capture of Philadelphia. In 1778 he was made second in command of all British forces in North America, under Sir Henry Clinton.[15]

In 1780 Cornwallis and Clinton cooperated in the siege of Charleston and captured 5000 patriots under the command of Maj. Gen. Benjamin Lincoln. Cornwallis thereafter assumed sole command of the southern theater. Assured that the region was filled with loyal subjects, he began a series of operations designed to destroy the patriot resistance. Although he soundly defeated a second patriot army under Horatio Gates at Camden, the patriot forces refused to disappear.

Camden proved a Pyrrhic victory for Cornwallis. Because Gates behaved poorly after the battle, fleeing 120 miles alone and in terror on horseback, the patriot army came under the command of Nathanael Greene, a more able officer and a better strategist. Greene led Cornwallis to overextend his lines of supply while allowing him a series of strategically meaningless victories won at a great expense in terms of the lives of his men.

Guilford Courthouse. Nonetheless, the British bloodhound was unrelenting as he chased Greene through the south. At the battle of Guilford Courthouse in March 1781, Cornwallis, outnumbered and unfamiliar with the ground, ordered his artillery fired into a mass of advancing patriots mixed with his own men to prevent a defeat. An American officer wrote of this battle, "Cornwallis undoubtedly gained a dear bought victory." Thereafter Cornwallis's force was barely fit to continue in the field. Horace Walpole, Earl of Oxford, commented upon the report of the battle, "Lord Cornwallis' triumphs have increased our losses, without leaving any hopes."[16]

King's Mountain and Cowpens. Cornwallis, like Burgoyne, was plagued by a number of embarrassing defeats overseen by otherwise trustworthy and capable subordinates. Prominent among these were the destruction of a loyalist force under Maj. Patrick Ferguson at King's Mountain, South Carolina, by American riflemen, and the virtual annihilation of 1100 regulars and most of Banastre Tarleton's legion at Cowpens by Daniel Morgan's mixed force of Continental infantry, dragoons, and regional militia. Tarleton's defeat was particularly savored by the patriots, to whom he had previously shown little quarter and no compassion.

Eutaw Springs. The final meeting of Greene's forces and those of Cornwallis was at Eutaw Springs, South Carolina. Cornwallis, though his troops held the field at the end of the fighting, was too badly mauled to stay where he was. The ultimate result of his southern operations was to deplete his troops and exhaust his supplies. Greene had calmly supported the local patriot militias under leaders like Marion, Pickens, and Sumter. He had used the horsemen of Harry Lee and William Washington, and his own Continentals and riflemen, expertly. Without winning a single battle, Greene had closed an impenetrable arc around British-held Charleston.

Yorktown. In order to receive succor, Cornwallis was forced to abandon his baggage and retreat to Yorktown, Virginia. Here he fully expected to reestablish his communications and supply lines by means of the Royal Navy. This never took place, largely because of the timely arrival of the French navy. After a prolonged siege by American and French land forces under George Washington and Gen. Caron de Rochambeau, Cornwallis was forced to surrender in October 1781.

It seems clear that Cornwallis was not held at fault for the pall of defeat that overtook British arms in America after Yorktown. An American wit wrote of Cornwallis as he took ship for England in 1781:

Farewell, my Lord; may zephyrs waft thee o'er
In health and safety to thy native shore;
There seek Burgoyne, and tell him, though too late,
You blamed unwisely his unhappy fate;
Tell your deluded monarch that you see,
The Hand of Heaven upraised for liberty;
Tell your exhausted nation, tell them true.
They cannot conquer those who conquer'd you.[17]

THE ORGANIZATION OF THE PATRIOT ARMY

Army Departments

The structure of the patriot army was based largely on the Continental Association formed during the Stamp Act crisis. This was interwoven with the existing structure of provincial forces. Congress found that it had to build upon these foundation stones or risk losing the cooperation of the individual colonies. The inequities that followed serve to highlight the overall problem of prosecuting a regional war with troops assembled from a number of fiercely independent colonies. These problems transcended the bounds of command and rank to affect the distribution of supplies and provisions, the arrangements for shelter and uniforms, the appointment of field officers, and the planning of operations. Not only were the officers of the separate colonies fiercely independent, they were quite willing in many cases to have nothing to do with the Continental Congress, and would refuse to share their own supplies with their less fortunate comrades from other colonies.

Congress divided the colonies into four military districts known as departments, each with its own army and army commander. All of New England was to be known as the Main Department. It was to this army that Washington was posted in 1775 as commander in chief. The Middle Department encompassed the colonies of New York, Pennsylvania, New Jersey, Delaware, Maryland, and Virginia; the Southern Department embraced the two Carolinas and Georgia; and a Canadian Department was created in anticipation that the residents there might join the Revolution. It should be noted that this organization evolved and varied throughout the course of the war.

It would be unfair, incorrect, and naive to assume that the patriot army of 1775 suddenly sprang from the soil of America composed of farmers, shopkeepers, and mechanics, and commanded by a cadre of inexperienced lawyers, plantation owners, and merchants. Although almost all Americans were military amateurs, except for the youngest, most of the men had served in the French and Indian War in some capacity. The

Table 8.2

Principal Actions in the Northern Theater, 1775–1779

Date	Location	Opponents		Victory
		Patriot	*Crown*	
1775	Lexington	Parker	Smith/Pitcairn	Crown
	Concord	Prescott	Smith/Pitcairn	Patriot
	Ticonderoga	Arnold/Allen	De Laplace	Patriot
	Breed's Hill	Prescott	Howe/Gage	Crown
	Quebec	Arnold/ Montgomery	Carleton	Crown
1776	Long Island	Sullivan/Putnam	Howe/Clinton	Crown
	Harlem Heights	Washington	Howe	Crown
	White Plains	Washington	Howe	Crown
	Ft. Washington	Magaw	Percy/Knyphausen	Crown
	Trenton	Washington	Rall	Patriot
	Valcour Island	Arnold	Carleton	Crown
1777	Princeton	Washington/ Mercer	Mawhood/ Cornwallis	Patriot
	Ridgefield	Wooster/Arnold	Tryon	Crown
	Ticonderoga	St. Clair	Burgoyne	Crown
	Ft. Stanwix	Ganesvoort	St. Leger	Patriot
	Oriskany	Herkimer	Brant/Butler/Johnson	Indecisive
	Saratoga	Gates/Arnold	Burgoyne/Riedesel	Patriot
	Brandywine	Washington	Howe/Knyphausen	Crown
	Germantown	Washington	Howe/Cornwallis	Crown
1778	Monmouth	Washington/ C. Lee	Clinton	Indecisive
	Newport	Sullivan/ d'Estaing	Pigot	Patriot
1779	Greenwich	Putnam	Tryon	Crown
	Norwalk	Parsons/Betts	Tryon	Crown
	Stony Point	Wayne	H. Johnson	Patriot
	Paulus Hook	H. Lee	Sutherland	Patriot
	Lloyd's Neck	Tallmadge	Loyalists	Patriot

older ones had served side by side with the regulars on the frontiers as officers and NCOs in the provincial service.

The General Officers

Fewer than 200 general officers were created during the eight years of the American Revolution. From 1775 to 1783 30 men attained the rank of major general. All but a handful of these had initially served as brig-

Friedrich Wilhelm von Steuben came to America and told Congress that he had been a general in the Prussian Army. Actually, he had only been a major. Nonetheless, he did a magnificent job training the patriot army.

adier generals. Notable among the exceptions were Gen. George Washington—who was chosen commander in chief—and Charles Lee, Artemus Ward, Philip Schuyler, and Israel Putnam, all of whom were directly appointed major generals. Forty-eight brigadier generals served during the war. Among them were some who displayed notable ability, competence, and courage. Others were remarkably mediocre and commonplace.

The rank of major general was also conferred on several foreign gentlemen: the Marquis de Lafayette, Count Kasimir Pulaski, Baron Johann De Kalb, Philippe du Coudray, and Friedrich Wilhelm von Steuben. These were all capable men who proved important to the success of the American army. Pulaski was killed in action at Savannah in 1779, and De Kalb during the debacle at Camden in 1780. These two and Richard Montgomery, who was killed at Quebec in 1776, were the only major generals to die in action. Du Coudray, an expert in artillery, drowned within a month of his appointment. Lafayette served as an aide to Washington and as a field commander with great distinction. Von Steuben, although somewhat of a self-aggrandizing braggart, proved his worth by devising a simplified drill for the patriots. He is credited with training the patriot army to fight a European-style war rather than a frontier-style one. This was quite important, since only victory in these terms could bring European recognition of claims of American independence.

In 1777, under political pressure from Massachusetts, Benjamin Lincoln was promoted major general directly from the rank of regimental colonel. This appointment rankled the delagates to Congress from Connecticut, who were negotiating to have one of their own brigadiers chosen. Among these was Benedict Arnold, who was particularly galled at being snubbed. Lincoln seems to have been an able officer, but he suffered the single worst patriot defeat in the war in 1780, when he was forced to surrender his entire army at Charleston.

A Cadre of Leaders

With the selection of the four major generals of the army completed, Congress turned to the brigadiers. Because the commander in chief, one major general, and the adjutant general were all drawn from Virginia, the choice of brigadier generals was carefully prearranged to help avoid political difficulties with the individual colonies. Consequently, Massachusetts received three appointments, Connecticut two, and New York, New Hampshire, and Rhode Island one each. In order of their precedence these men were Seth Pomeroy of Massachusetts, Richard Montgomery of New York, David Wooster of Connecticut, William Heath of Massachusetts, Joseph Spencer of Connecticut, John Thomas of Massachusetts, John Sullivan of New Hampshire, and Nathanael Greene of Rhode Island.[18]

Ironically, the best field officer among the patriots seems to have been Benedict Arnold. Inasmuch as he ultimately proved a traitor to the patriot cause, Arnold has been justly placed on the trash heap of infamy, but there is little doubt that prior to his treason, he was America's best tactical commander. Rising from provincial colonel to brigadier, to major general, he appears at all the important junctures in the record of the war, and at critical moments in battle he offers the proper strategem to turn the trick on the British. After his treason was dicovered, Arnold returned to the war as a British major general and continued his successes on the battlefield in Virginia and Connecticut. Described by one biographer as being simultaneously "the luminescent hero and the serpentine villain," Arnold was nonetheless characterized by the troops who served under him as a "fighting general and a bloody fellow."[19]

The honor of best strategist seems to rest with the youngest of the patriot brigadiers, Nathanael Greene. A fallen-away Quaker, Greene began his carreer as a brigade commander serving with the Main Army. He was then chosen to reorganize the logistical morass of the army as quartermaster general, and as a major general he commanded the Southern Army from 1780 until the end of the war. It was he who successfully dissipated the strength of the British forces under Cornwallis, forcing him into Yorktown. Despite the fact that Greene never won a battle where he was the sole commander, he was considered by his contemporaries to be the finest military leader of the war save Washington.[20]

Wrangling over Rank

In addition to the selection of Washington as command in chief, Congress initially authorized a command structure of two major generals, five brigadier generals, and an adjutant general, who would rank as a brigadier. Intercolonial wrangling and politics caused this number to be increased by adding two major generals and three brigadiers more than was first envisioned. Giving in to the congressional delagates caused a good deal of unexpected trouble for the American army.

Artemus Ward, who was commanding the American forces besieging Boston, was made the senior major general of the Continental Army under Washington in the Main Department, while Charles Lee, a recent resident of Virginia (1773), was made the second major general in charge of the Southern Department. Philip Schuyler of New York was made the third major general, with responsibility for the Middle Department, and Israel Putnam of Connecticut was placed fourth, with no department under his immediate control. Of these five men—raised to the highest ranks of the patriot army by the Congress in 1775—only Washington remained in active service beyond 1780. All the others resigned, retired, or were dismissed from the service.

The selection of an adjutant general caused little difficulty at the time. Horatio Gates, a half-pay officer from the British army, was quickly appointed. Gates initially served with some distinction, but even in the early months of the war he seems to have entertained anti-Washington sentiments from among the general staff. Gates was particularly open in his written comments about Washington in some of his letters to Charles Lee, who was also a former British officer. He wrote of Washington as "a certain great man . . . most damnably deficient."[21]

John Adams was conscious of the unrest that plagued the officer corps, and he wrote about it to his wife, Abigail:

I am wearied to death with the wrangles between military officers, high and low. They quarrel like cats and dogs. They worry one another like mastiffs, scrambling for rank and pay like apes for food. I believe there is no principle which predominates in human nature so much . . . as this passion for superiority . . . but I never saw it to operate with such keenness, ferocity, and fury as among military officers. They will go to terrible lengths in their emulation, their envy, and revenge in consequence of it.[22]

The Conway Cabal

Gates allowed himself to become the nucleus of an anti-Washington plot known to historians as the Conway Cabal. Riding a wave of popularity after his success at Saratoga, Gates seems to have considered displacing Washington as commander in chief, by force if necessary. A mere sense of a plot was discovered through a tactlessly written letter to Gates from Brigadier Thomas Conway, an Irishman who had served in the French army. This document fell into Washington's hands at Valley Forge in 1778 and set off a series of recriminations and charges. However, there was no concrete evidence in the letter of anything other than indiscreet griping, and many historians seriously consider that no plot to unseat Washington ever existed.

Washington's Young Men

Washington surrounded himself with a number of young men of ability from outside the normal circles of political posturing and infighting. The general transmitted orders through them, and relied on them to carry out important and secret operations. These most trusted assistants included Alexander Hamilton, Henry "Light Horse Harry" Lee, Allen MacLean, Benjamin Tallmadge, and the Marquis de Lafayette, all of whom were in their early twenties.

Lee, MacLean, and Tallmadge were cavalry commanders from Virginia, Delaware, and Connecticut, respectively. All were conspicuously successful in raiding British supply lines and providing intelligence to the commander in chief. Tallmadge commanded a squadron of dragoons in Connecticut and led enterprising whaleboat raids on the loyalists across Long Island Sound. He served as Washintgton's chief of espionage, and may have controlled a dozen spies and informants working behind British lines in New York. MacLean was said to be Washington's favorite rider, and he was famed for defeating six British dragoons in a single encounter. He and Lee were particularly successful in foraging for supplies during the Valley Forge winter. Unfortunately, the two fell out after Lee was promoted as MacLean's commander. As a major in his own partisan corps, Lee led a successful attack on the British at Paulus Hook (Elizabeth, New Jersey), and Congress voted him a gold medal for his efforts—the only such award to an officer of lower rank than brigadier during the entire conflict. Lee went on to serve with great distinction in the southern theater of the war as an independent commander. His memoirs, edited by his youngest son, General Robert E. Lee, CSA, are a major source of information about the revolution in the Carolinas.[23]

Alexander Hamilton was Washington's secretary and most trusted aide. Raised to the rank of lieutenant colonel, Hamilton commanded a brigade under Lafayette at Yorktown. He served after the war in Washington's first cabinet as secretary of the Treasury. Hamilton proved to be the ultimate proponent of a strong federal government after the Revolution, and he was one of the authors of the collection of political works known as *The Federalist Papers*. Both Hamilton and Harry Lee were treated like sons by the childless Washington, and they returned his favor with loyalty in later years. It was Lee, then governor of Virginia, who eulogized Washington as "First in war; first in peace; and first in the hearts of his countrymen."[24]

Nineteen-year-old Marie Joseph du Motier, Marquis de Lafayette, was "smitten" with the notion of helping the Americans win independence from Britain. Congress granted Lafayette the rank of major general, but gave him no command. Washington took an instant liking to the young volunteer. Having been wounded at Brandywine, Lafayette was given command of a division of Virginia light infantry, which he directed with reasonable distinction at Monmouth. He later commanded two brigades in the attack on Newport. He returned to France in 1777 to garner support for the patriot cause, and served as a liaison between the French and American commanders in America. Lafayette commanded one of three major divisions of the allied army at Yorktown, and he returned to France immediately after the surrender. As an aristocrat, he was condemned by the radical faction of the French Revolution, but escaped. In 1824 he returned for a yearlong triumphal tour of the United States.[25]

THE PATRIOT COMMANDERS

Artemus Ward

After serving with distinction in the French and Indian War, Artemus Ward had become the commander of the Massachusetts militia upon the defection of William Brattle. Although he missed the battles at Lexington and Concord due to illness, he directed the actions at Breed's Hill (Bunker Hill), and he effectively contained the British army in Boston for several months. Notwithstanding his position as the senior major general in the chain of command, Ward was not officially designated second in command of the patriot army mainly because Charles Lee was thought by Congress to be better qualified for the post. Ward resigned his commission after the evacuation of the British from Boston in 1776, and he went on to serve in the Massachusetts government, in the Continental Congress, and in the U.S. House of Representatives.

Charles Lee

Charles Lee hardly looked the part of a military officer, being tall, angular, exceedingly thin, and hook-nosed. Surviving images of the man, which purport to be reasonable likenesses, seem to be caricatures or works of derision. Lee was a half-pay British officer who had risen to the rank of major general in the Polish army before moving to Virginia.

Lee was one of the earliest and most outspoken proponents of independence among those chosen to command the American forces. He also freely expressed an unabashed good opinion of his own qualities as a military commander, and he made a number of political blunders that painted him as immoderate and opinionated. He generally failed to hide his contempt for Washington, whom he considered a military amateur. One historian noted that Lee "failed to confine [himself] to purely military matters, and . . . freely commented on both internal and external political affairs, and urged his opinions upon various members of Congress."[26]

In December 1776, Lee was seized at an inn near Basking Ridge, New Jersey, by a party of British dragoons under circumstances that suggested to some that he had arranged his own capture. The infamous British commander Banastre Tarleton was leading the detachment of 17th Light Dragoons when they captured Lee. During the Seven Years' War, Lee had commanded this same regiment. An American aide to Lee, Capt. James Wilkinson, who admitted "being too inexperienced immediately to penetrate the motives of this enterprise," was suspicious of the circumstances of the capture and communicated them to Washington.[27]

Lee's capture was much celebrated by the British, who considered him a great asset to the American cause. Tarleton, then a mere subaltern, wrote that the capture was "a most miraculous event . . . appear[ing] like a dream."[28] Yet after spending a comfortable winter literally partying with the British staff in New York, Lee was exchanged for another officer in time to take command of the patriot army at the battle of Monmouth. Here he exhibited a conspicuous lack of confidence in his men and issued a string of questionable orders that caused a precipitous retreat before the advancing British regulars. Washington rode up to Lee on the battlefield in high dudgeon, had heated words with him, and relieved him of command on the spot. General Charles Scott of Virginia, who witnessed the confrontation, wrote, "[Washington] swore on that day till the leaves shook on the trees, charming, delightful! Never have I enjoyed such swearing before, or since. Sir, on that ever-memorable day he swore like an angel from Heaven." Lafayette, who was nearby, recalled that Washington took immediate command of the retreating troops and turned the tide of battle by his personal example. "Never had I beheld so superb a man."[29]

Washington relieved Charles Lee of command on the battlefield at Monmouth. He turned the tide of battle with his forceful presence. Lee was later dismissed from the service.

Although the battle of Monmouth ended in an indecisive draw, it was the last major encounter between the patriots and the regulars in the northern theater. The unrelenting efforts of Nathanael Greene and William Alexander (Lord Stirling), commanding the American flanks, suggested that the nature of the war had changed. Patriot troops, using a new drill devised by Von Steuben, fought a European-style engagement with the regulars for the first time. Although Von Steuben's drill was a much abbreviated and simplified form of the British exercise, it was obvious that the Americans had finally fielded a well-disciplined army under the command of knowledgeable officers.

After the battle Charles Lee was charged with disobedience, misbehavior, and disrespect to the commander in chief. Charges of treason and disaffection were considered, but they were not brought. As a result of a court-martial, Lee was suspended from command for one year, but his natural conceit caused him to write a public letter, which was deemed so insulting, contemptuous, and offensive to the honor of Congress that he was dismissed from the army.

Charles Lee died of natural causes in 1782. Defiant and egotistical to the end, in his will he wrote, "I desire most earnestly that I may not be buried in any church or church-yard . . . within one mile of any Presbyterian or Anabaptist meeting house, for since I have resided in this country, I have kept so much bad company while living, that I do not choose to continue it when dead."[30] Thomas Paine wrote of Lee, "He was above all monarchs, and below all scum."[31]

Philip Schuyler

A politically important landowner from Albany, New York, Philip Schuyler was made the third major general of the Continental Army and was given command of the Middle Department. Schuyler was the head of the powerful Whig faction in the New York legislature. But there was some concern in Congress about New York's reliability and enthusiasm for the American cause. Indeed, the province had not raised a single regiment of regular troops by the summer of 1775. The appointment of Schuyler was thought to ensure New York's cooperation in the revolution.

As Middle Department commander, Schuyler was responsible for the defense of all the provinces stretching from New York to Virginia, but the great distances involved and his own desire to maintain his headquarters near Albany made this task almost impossible. However, Albany controlled the strategically important southern end of the Lake Champlain-Lake George water route from Canada, deemed by some historians the most heavily fortified passage in all of British North America in the eighteenth century.[32] A generally gloomy man, Schuyler was far from confident that he could organize and discipline an army composed of militia. Their air of democracy and dedication to personal equality rankled his more aristocratic and haughty view of proper society. He doubted that an effective army could be formed from "amongst a people where so little distinction is kept up."[33]

Schuyler's downfall as a military commander came when his subordinate, Brig. Gen. Arthur St. Clair, abandoned the fort at Ticonderoga with unseemly dispatch at the first hint of Burgoyne's advance upon his position. Both St. Clair and Schuyler came to be held in great contempt by their military colleagues thereafter. American surgeon James Thacher wrote, "What could induce General St. Clair and the general officers with him to evacuate Ticonderoga, God only knows . . . It has been industriously reported that generals Schuyler and St. Clair acted the part of traitors to the country."[34] In this regard, John Adams wrote:

I think we shall never defend a post until we shoot a General. After that we shall defend posts, and this event, in my opinion, is not far off. No other fort will ever be evacuated without inquiry, nor any other officer come off without a court-martial. We must trifle no more.[35]

St. Clair, under suspicion because he had served as a regular British officer in the French wars, was acquitted of disaffection by a court-martial; and since Burgoyne was eventually forced to surrender his army at Saratoga, St. Clair had the satisfaction of knowing that "though he lost a post, he had eventually saved a state."[36] Schuyler, on the other hand, was "a complex figure with many attributes as well as some disabling traits." Horatio Gates, whom Schuyler disliked intensely, was appointed to replace him. The ultimate success of Gates at Saratoga led Schuyler to resign his commission. He went on the serve in the Congress.[37]

Israel Putnam

Known as "Old Put," Israel Putnam was selected as the fourth major general of the Continental Army. Then 57, Putnam was well known for a number of legendary incidents in his youth. He had been an officer in Rogers' Rangers, had narrowly escaped execution by French Indians, had commanded a provincial regiment against the French, and had been with Augustus Howe at his death. More recently he had fought the Indians during Pontiac's Rebellion. His many exploits made him a colorful and popular choice as an upper-echelon commander. More important, he was a resident of Connecticut, and his choice was designed to appease that colony and all of New England. A nineteenth-century poem noted of Putnam:

> In Gallic war a major made,
> Fort Edward's powder house he saved,
> When fire endangered all the post;
> And when before the Indian host
> He steered his craft o'er Hudson's falls,
> Saving his men from savage balls.[38]

Putnam was described by a contemporary as "corpulent and clumsy," but his legendary daring seemingly never left him. He was almost captured by a group of fast-moving British dragoons who attempted to take him as he ate lunch in a tavern in Cos Cob, Connecticut. Warned of their approach, "Old Put" crashed out of the tavern through a window, leaped upon his waiting horse, and outdistanced his pursuers by galloping down a set of stairs carved in a cliffside so steep that his pursuers did not follow.[39] Although he was popular and of "a bold and undaunted front," Putnam was no longer a capable field commander. After sharing command at Breed's Hill and Boston, he was relegated to training recruits and performing organizational duties in New England. He retired from field service in 1779 after suffering a minor stroke.

Disorganization. Even the most carefully made appointment of officers had the potential to cause problems for the Americans. Some of the

Israel Putnam was a legendary character, and his life was filled with
exciting escapes and adventures. Here he rides down a perilous slope
to elude his pursuers.

men, having held rank within their individual provinces, were superseded by their former subordinates. The most egregious case was that of
Israel Putnam, David Wooster, and Joseph Spencer. Putnam's appointment promoted him over both of his former superiors. When informed
of this circumstance, Wooster briefly returned his Continental commis-

sion to Congress and fell back upon his provincial rank; Spencer simply packed his belongings and left the army permanently.

Wearing two hats. David Wooster's dissatisfaction transcended his objections to serving under the aged Putnam. Wooster was himself sixty-four years old, but he was placed directly below several men of much less experience, distinction, and age. Moreover, Wooster had the rank and prestige of a major general in Connecticut while simultaneously holding the rank of brigadier in the Continental Army. It seems clear that Wooster "could with dexterity put on one [hat] or the other as the occasion demanded." He, more than any another general officer, used this circumstance to enhance his power or circumvent the orders of his superiors.[40]

In New York City, Wooster received orders from the New York Committee of Safety. He responded, "No provincial congress can with any propriety, interfere in the disposition of Continental troops, much less control the orders of any general officer. If the Continental Congress or the commander-in-chief, think proper . . . I shall expect their orders direct, and no man will with greater alacrity obey." Wooster also avoided legitimate orders with equal enthusiasm by claiming his privileges as a provincial major general.[41]

Chain of Command

Ambiguities in the chain of command plagued the army. In March 1776, Congress promoted John Thomas to command the Canadian Department. His appointment brought him into direct conflict with Schuyler in Albany, where both commanders chose to have their headquarters. Orders issued by Thomas were declared invalid by Schuyler because they originated within his department. Schuyler went so far as to charge some officers with insubordination. In these circumstances it became difficult to know whom to obey.

Washington viewed the situation with great foreboding. Department commanders had complete authority within their departments, yet they were directly responsible to Congress rather than to himself as commander in chief. To complicate matters, there were senior generals in the army, like Putnam, who had no department command. Should they be obeyed if they issued conflicting orders?

Matters of command were made worse by distance. Schuyler, whose responsibilties reached as far south as Virginia, stubbornly refused to quit Albany for a more centrally located headquarters in Pennsylvania or New Jersey. This precluded his effective control of situations so far removed in space and time. The same problem plagued the Southern Department, which was headquartered in Charleston, so removed from both Congress and General Washington that it was deemed a virtually independent command.[42]

NOTES

1. Stuart Reid, *King George's Army, 1740–93*. Vol. 1, *Infantry* (London: Osprey, 1995), 12; see also Charles Townshend, ed., *The Oxford Illustrated History of Modern War* (New York: Oxford University Press, 1997), 27.

2. See Brendan Morrissey, *Boston 1775: The Shot Heard Around the World* (London: Osprey, 1995), 25.

3. See Brian Gardner, *The East India Company: A History* (New York: Dorset Press, 1971), 188.

4. Morrissey, *Boston 1775*, 25.

5. Germain strongly favored Burgoyne and Cornwallis, and had many conflicts with Howe, Clinton, and Carleton.

6. William P. Cumming and Hugh Rankin, eds., *The Fate of a Nation: The American Revolution Through Contemporary Eyes* (London: Phaidon Press, 1975), 49.

7. Ibid., 110.

8. Surgeon James Thatcher, quoted in ibid., 161–162.

9. Quoted in Jeremy Black, *Warfare in the Eighteenth Century* (London: Cassell, 1999), 114.

10. An excellent re-creation of the fort as it appeared in the Revolution sits in the middle of downtown Rome, New York.

11. Cumming and Rankin, *Fate of a Nation*, 164–165.

12. Larry Bowman, *Captive Americans: Prisoners During the American Revolution* (Athens: Ohio University Press, 1976), 129–130.

13. Geoffrey Regan, *SNAFU: A Fascinating Compendium of Ill-Advised Attacks and Incomprehensible Campaigns* (New York: Avon Books, 1993), 43.

14. Cumming and Rankin, *Fate of a Nation*, 126.

15. Black, *Warfare in the Eighteenth Century*, 114.

16. Cumming and Rankin, *Fate of a Nation*, 305.

17. Ibid., 305.

18. Jonathan Gregory Rossie, *The Politics of Command in the American Revolution* (Syracuse, NY: Syracuse University Press, 1975), 12–16.

19. James Kirby Martin, *Benedict Arnold, Revolutionary Hero: An American Warrior Reconsidered* (New York: New York University Press, 1997), 10 and 2.

20. Henry Lee, *Memoirs of the War* (New York: Burt Franklin, 1970), 4.

21. Cumming and Rankin, *Fate of a Nation*, 128.

22. Ibid., 198.

23. See Noel B. Gerson, *Light Horse Harry: A Biography of Washington's Great Cavalryman* (Garden City, NY: Doubleday, 1966).

24. See ibid.

25. L. Edward Purcell and David F. Burg, eds., *The World Almanac of the American Revolution* (New York: Pharos Books, 1992), 352–353.

26. Rossie, *The Politics of Command*, 78.

27. Cumming and Rankin, *Fate of a Nation*, 130.

28. Ibid.

29. Ibid., 212–213.

30. James Thacher, *Military Journal of the American Revolution, 1775–1783* (Gansevoort, NY: Corner House Publishing, 1998), 465.

31. Ibid.

32. James M. Volo and Dorothy Denneen Volo, *Daily Life on the Old Colonial Frontier* (Westport, CT: Greenwood, 2002).

33. Jared Sparks, ed., *Correspondence of the American Revolution; Being Letters of Eminent Men to George Washington, from the Time of His Taking Command of the Army to the End of His Presidency*, 4 vols. (Boston: n.p., 1853), vol. 1, 4. Also see Rossie, *The Politics of Command*, 37–38.

34. Cumming and Rankin, *Fate of a Nation*, 148.

35. Ibid., 149.

36. Thacher, *Military Journal*, 153–154.

37. Purcell and Burg, *World Almanac*, 365–366.

38. Edward Johnson Runk, *Washington: A National Epic in Six Cantos* (New York: G. P. Putnam's Sons, 1897), 36.

39. Thacher, *Military Journal*, 147. These steps are still visible from US Route 1, the Post Road, in Greenwich, Connecticut.

40. Rossie, *Politics of Command*, 50–56.

41. Quoted in ibid., 49.

42. Ibid., 90.

9

Sinews of Wars

No copper, lead or tin is to be had between Albany and New York.
            —Captain Richard Varick to General Washington

Almost every species of camp transportation is now performed by men, who without murmur, patiently yoke themselves to little carriages of their own making, or load their firewood and provisions on their backs.

            —A Visitor to Valley Forge

WEAPONS

Long Arms

In the eighteenth century almost all military firearms were based upon a standard smoothbore flintlock technology. Most firearms, including pistols, fired a generally large lead ball between .63 and .75 caliber and weighing almost an ounce, but more than half a dozen different calibers were used during the war. The effective range of muskets remained under 100 yards, while the visually intimidating pistols were useful only at very close quarters. Rifle fire, by comparison, was particularly accurate even at ranges of 300 to 400 yards.

For a rifle to be fired accurately, the soldier needed a good deal more time to load it than if firing a musket. The rifleman precisely measured his powder for the range of his target, and he laboriously seated his ball in a leather or linen patch driven down the spiraled grooves inside the barrel that gave the ball a stabilizing spin like that of a well-thrown football. A well-aimed shot taken every two minutes was considered good marksmanship for riflemen, and virtually ensured a hit on a man-sized target with every shot at 100 yards.

Musket fire at three rounds per minute, using prepared paper cartridges containing the powder charge and ball, was the standard rate of fire among trained regulars. Four rounds per minute was an ideal to which most commanders aspired, and two per minute was what they actually achieved in the heat and confusion of battle. The musket ball was also rammed home, but it was looser fitting in the smooth barrel from which it came hurling with the same precision as a poorly hit golf-ball, slicing and hooking through the air. Since musket fire lacked precision, in a great volley of fire taken simultaneously, it was hoped that some portion of shot would fall among the ranks of the enemy. The training essential for the individual musketman was in quickly reloading and obeying his officers' commands on when, where, and at what angle to fire.

The difference between the rate of fire of the musket and the rifle left the rifleman exposed to sudden rushes by light troops or Indians as he engaged in the cumbersome process of reloading his weapon. For this reason riflemen often shifted their position after firing, or worked in pairs so that one might be loaded at all times. As the war progressed, it became common practice to team musketmen with riflemen so that the quicker loading muskets could protect the slower but more accurate rifles.

Sidearms

Most general officers carried light stabbing swords known as "court swords" or "hunting swords" that were symbols of their rank and not designed for serious hacking. Field officers usually supplied themselves with more practical weapons designed for cutting or slashing. A pistol or two might be clipped to the officer's belt or held in holsters fitted to the saddle of his horse. Most of the regular infantry were issued a bayonet in lieu of a sword, and the militia usually supplied themselves with a knife, and a hatchet or tomahawk. Some elite units carried swords as part of their regular equipment. Swords were carried by the cavalry along with a pair of pistols and a carbine. Grenadiers, light infantry, and some NCOs carried short cutting swords known as hangers. After the battle at Trenton, John Greenwood noted the need "to disarm the [Hessian] prisoners of their swords, with one of which every man was provided."[1]

By fixing a bayonet to the muzzle of his musket, a soldier changed it from a firearm to a long spear. Jeremy Black, a British historian of eighteenth-century warfare, has noted that "the introduction of the socket bayonet helped to change the face of the European battlefield." The combination of the two weapons (musket and bayonet) led to a degree of tactical flexibility and increased firepower unimagined in the previous century, when battlefields were dominated by a combination of musketeers, pikemen, and cavalry.[2]

The American colonial tradition with regard to its militia was rooted in the obsolete deployment of pikemen, and NCOs continued to carry a 7- to-8-foot-long spontoon as a symbol of their rank. Largely because bayonets were not available, Washington, who understood their usefulness, ordered folding pikes to be manufactured for the militia. However, few if any were issued. Americans were not initially encouraged to attack with the bayonets even when they had them. The colonial bayonet drills placed their emphasis on receiving the enemy rather than making charges. The patriots simply did not possess the discipline to maintain the linear formations employed in such attacks. Only at Stony Point, New York, did the patriots exhibit the discipline needed to bring off a successful bayonet attack. Despite the use of bayonets, pikes, swords, knives, hatchets, and tomahawks, hand-to-hand fighting on the battlefield was relatively uncommon, and it was remarked upon by contemporary observers when it occurred. Most casualties in the Revolution were caused by musket shot or artillery fire.

GUNPOWDER

No item was more important to the prosecution of the Revolution than gunpowder, but the Americans had very little capacity to supply their own. Nonetheless, the only battle of the Revolution which was lost due to lack of gunpowder was that on Breed's Hill. Even though Israel Putnam ordered the artillery cartridges broken open to provide powder for the muskets, the militia were overrun by the final charge of the British because they had expended all their ammunition. It is also certain that an unknowable number of operations may have been canceled or postponed due to a lack of the black, velvety material. As late as July 1780, the failure of a single shipment of gunpowder from France so distressed Washington that he wrote that it "ensured the continuance of the stalemate in the north."[3]

When Washington arrived at the patriot works surrounding Boston in 1775, he was told that there were 300 barrels of gunpowder on hand. However, upon ordering that a new supply of cartridges be distributed to the troops, he found that there was powder enough for only nine rounds per man, and none for the artillery. Washington was so struck by this revelation that he did not utter a word for half an hour. He wrote to Congress, "We are so exceedingly destitute [of gunpowder] that our artillery will be of little use." In order to conserve powder while investing the city, he limited the artillery to a single 9-pounder that belched fire periodically from the works on Prospect Hill.[4]

On Christmas Day, 1775, Washington reported to Congress, "Our want of powder is inconceivable. A daily waste and no supply administers a gloomy prospect." Three weeks later there was not a pound of gunpowder in the army's reserve. The entire rebellion hinged on the paper cartridges in the men's ammunition pouches and the fixed ammunition stored in the limber chests of the artillery. Standing orders were issued to the militia to "shoot no beast, bird, or mark, in order that they might husband their stock of powder and ball for the purpose of destroying British troops." Washington also ordered that no musket be loaded "until we are close to the enemy, and there is a moral certainty of engaging them." The problem of mounting guard with unloaded weapons was resolved by loading the muskets with undersized balls, called "running balls" in orders. This ball could easily be withdrawn at the end of a tour of guard duty.[5]

Patriots found that they could kick out the burning fuses of shells lobbed by the British into the patriot position as they rolled about the works before exploding. William Heath reported in his journal that "nearly five pounds of powder was taken from a single 13-inch British bomb." Moreover, bounties were issued to men who recovered spent cannonballs from the face of the earthworks, and many men amused themselves by digging in the soft soil for these newfound premiums.[6]

In the spring of 1776, Washington's immediate problem with respect to powder was solved by the timely capture of a British store ship loaded with ordnance supplies. Also, numerous privately consigned cargoes of munitions began to arrive from France and the Dutch islands in the West Indies. The Continental Congress consigned a 10-ton shipment of powder to the Main Army, and smaller quantities were brought in by agents of the individual colonies. With sufficient powder in New England to answer the immediate purpose, Congress stopped these transfers "borrowed" from other states, lest they fall into British hands. One of the great failures of the Royal Navy and British army at the beginning of the war was their inability to cut off these shipments of war material.[7]

On March 2, Washington opened fire on the city of Boston with 59 pieces of artillery from Fort Ticonderoga that had been dragged through the snow-filled forests of the Northeast by a detachment under the command of Col. Henry Knox. These included a wide variety of ordnance: a half-dozen 6- and 8-inch brass[8] mortars that weighed almost a ton each, two howitzers, 13 brass cannon, and 26 iron cannon. Knox had required 42 strong sleds and 80 yokes (pairs) of oxen to make the move. Washington bombarded Boston for 14 consecutive days and forced the

British to evacuate the city. However, the patriots had used all of the powder available to the provinces before the war, and all that had been imported since the beginning of hostilities, in gaining the city.[9]

Secret Shipments

Thereafter, the Second Continental Congress took steps to secure a supply of gunpowder adequate for pursuing its ends. Three New York merchants—Van Derbilt, Van Zandt, and Sands—secretly chartered a pair of swift ships, loaded them with good American wheat, and sent them out to return with gunpowder and other war material. The scheme recognized that the untested value of the new Continental dollar was not nearly as enduring as the value of good American wheat. Van Zandt also formed a partnership with Nicholas Law and Philip Livingston to bring in shipments of powder in exchange for permission from Congress to trade in items banned by the Continental Association. Law was the first to import a shipment under this agreement, but he withheld it, demanding a price of £30 sterling per hundredweight and a permit to export 12 tons of contraband trade goods. The powder bargain was made, but Congress realized that it needed to free itself of this type of mercantile extortion and develop a domestic supply of gunpowder. In the summer of 1776 the patriots began to receive powder, ordnance, musket, and flints through the services of Hortalez and Company, a front for the French government managed by the playwright Beaumarchais. French powder was produced through a chemical process, devised by the scientist Lavoisier, that utilized animal waste as a major ingredient. Hundreds of barrels of powder and other munitions were delivered to New York just prior to the British invasion.

The Composition of Gunpowder

The main ingredient in gunpowder was saltpeter, a nitrate salt of potassium. Carbon and sulfur were also needed. Carbon in the form of ground charcoal gave the powder its black color. Bulk quantities of sulfur (brimstone) could be imported from many islands in the West Indies blessed with volcanoes, or it could be extracted from the waters of the many sulfur springs that peppered the frontier regions. The towns of Schoharie, Mineral Springs, and Sharon Springs in central New York supported sulfur works for this purpose, and attracted the unwanted attention of loyalists and Indians throughout the war.

There were few places in the world, however, where saltpeter deposits could be mined directly. India was one of these, and Britain controlled an almost inexhaustible supply of saltpeter found there. France, having lost most of its possessions in the subcontinent in the Seven Years' War, developed a chemical process that used animal manure as a raw material for manufacturing saltpeter. Congress became dedicated to the idea that the united colonies could do the same as France, and "render themselves independent of foreigners for the supply of military stores."[10]

The delegates to Congress advanced schemes of every sort for the erection of artificial nitrate works, some of them without justification as to their practicality or economy. Agents were sent forth to test the theory of extracting nitrous salts from the earthen floors of stables, pigpens, cattle yards, and tobacco sheds. Plans were made for the collection of horse manure, pig droppings, and even human excrement. Little came of these collection projects, but several powder mills were built where the ingredients could be properly ground and mixed. The Board of War entered into a multiyear contract with two brothers from France, Nicholas and Mark Fouquet, who were to serve as instructors in the art of saltpeter production.

The Committee of Safety in Philadelphia issued a pamphlet detailing the home manufacture of saltpeter, titled "Several Methods of Making Salte Petre: Recommended to the Inhabitants of the United Colonies by Their Representatives in Congress." The New York committee issued another, "Essays upon the Making of Salt-Petre and Gunpowder." John Adams, who was particularly enthusiastic about the project, wrote, "Every stable, Dove House, Cellar, Vault, etc. is a mine of salt petre. Mould under stables, etc. may be boiled soon into salt petre."[11]

Public niter works were erected in Philadelphia and Virginia, and legislation provided bounties for private niter works and powder mills. Financial support was an important ingredient in erecting a powder mill because the grinding of the components of gunpowder was very dangerous. For this reason saltpeter was often ground alone and then combined with ground sulfur. The carbon was then added in small but increasing amounts until the proper mix was attained. Because the carbon would settle to the bottom of the barrel, it was not unusual to see artillerymen gently rolling barrels of powder about the parade grounds to remix the ingredients.[12]

The first successes in establishing local powderworks were in Massachusetts and Pennsylvania, but the hastily constructed and crude factories proved inadequate to supply the needs of a large army. In eighteen months of effort, about 50 tons of excellent propellent was produced from imported ingredients. Some 55 tons of gunpowder was made from domestic saltpeter by the time continuous supplies began to appear from the French. The Americans were hard-pressed for powder throughout the war, and were more dependent on foreign imports at the end of the war than at any time after its first year.[13]

Benjamin Franklin, who thought less of the domestic effort to produce powder than did John Adams, wrote in a half-joking manner that the colonials might adopt a bow-and-arrow technology to fight the war. Because arrows could be seen in flight, Franklin suggested that their fall would strike terror into the British troops, causing them to break ranks and run. Of course, bowyers and fletchers, who made bows and arrows, respectively, were even more scarce than the technicians and mechanics needed to produce gunpowder. The suggestion was made in jest, but it was not totally without practical merit. The effective range of the arrow and the musket ball were not that different, and arrows could be loosed at a much faster rate than musketballs could be fired. Moreover, they could be retrieved from the field of battle and reused.

Scarcity Felt by the British

Ironically, the British army also suffered several shortages of munitions during the course of the war. In 1778 a severe shortage was caused by powder being stored aboard ship in the damp hold for too long. The powder, which absorbed water vapor from the air, was ruined. It refused to ignite when sparks were applied, or it burned sporadically and slowly. Moisture caused the ingredients to separate as the saltpeter dissolved and recrystallized in its container. Part of the moisture problem may have been due to the lack of good American barrel staves, from which water tight containers for powder had previously been built. Some English-made barrels were so fragile that they could not be hauled overland by wagon.

British Adjutant General James Pattison reported in March 1779 that a large shipment of artillery and musket cartridges from England had been ruined due to wetting. The wooden bottoms on the munitions chests had rotted aboard ship, and the tin canisters of musket cartridges had rusted through due to the damp. The powder in the cartridges had become so hard as to be useless, leaving the British army in New York with a short-term shortage.[14]

ARTILLERY

Behold the ordnance on their carriages,
With fatal mouths gaping . . . and the nimble gunner
With linstock now the devilish cannon touches,
And down goes all before him.
                    —William Shakespeare, *Henry V, act III, prologue*

British Ordnance

Battalion guns were artillery pieces attached to a regiment of foot, usually set in pairs, and serviced by a combination of artillerymen, who

This modern replica is characteristic of the light 3-pound battalion gun with its implements and ammunition chest. The chest would be placed several yards behind the gun during firing.

worked the gun, and infantrymen, who helped to move it about the field for short distances. The two standard battalion guns of the British army in 1775 were the light 6-pounder and the light 3-pounder. Each pair of battalion guns was commanded by a subaltern, and a battery of two or more pairs by a captain. It required at least four men to fire a gun, but twice that number to do so efficiently. A single gun crew could contain 15 men, but six of these were dragropemen used to move the piece about the field. Two horses or oxen were detailed to pull each battalion gun and its limber on the march. Two more animals moved the spare ammunition wagon or cart. They required several drovers to oversee them while the gun was in action.

A combination limber and carriage for artillery was designed by William Congreve, who noted that it "enable[d] light 6 pounder and light 3 pounder guns to travel at a rate of six and even ten miles an hour, with four artillery men and 50 rounds of ammunition on the gun carriage." Congreve's thinking was innovative, and many of his ideas for the improvement of artillery were field-tested during the American Revolution. A letter written to the master general of artillery at Woolrich in late 1775 says in part, "The implements brought here by Captain Congreve . . . will be of great use in this country."[15]

The Congreve carriage should not be confused with the "galloper" carriage for very light pieces. The galloper initially served to carry the tiny "pound and a half" cannon and had, instead of a classic trail, a pair of "shafts so as to be drawn without a limber." Because it had ammunition boxes built into the carriage, it was "thought by some artillerists to be more convenient and preferable to other field carriages." With its lightweight carriage, it could be more readily moved about the field by just a few men. The galloper also carried 2-and 3-pounders, but it exhibited unsatisfactory recoil when mounted with larger guns.[16]

Battalion guns were normally positioned in the spaces between the companies to provide direct support to the infantry in battle. Their relatively flat trajectory and ability to fire canister allowed them to inflict terrible damage on an advancing enemy. However, artillery fire from flat-firing cannon could be masked by rolling or forested ground. Partly for this reason, howitzers and mortars capable of high arcing fire were developed. The battalion guns were sometimes massed on the flanks of the infantry line in "hastily thrown up earthworks," or in elevated positions with a wide view of the battle from which they could open a "vigorous cannonade" upon the enemy.[17]

As the war developed, it became common for British and Hessian infantry detachments marching into the interior to take one or two guns with them for close support. The apprehension of the British in these circumstances was that they might be overwhelmed, as they were on the road from Concord in 1775, by masses of patriot militia. It soon became obvious that the militia respected the awesome power of even small pieces of artillery. Extracts from hundreds of orders similar to that of Adjutant General James Pattison, issued in New York in 1778, illustrate this point:

Two 3 pounders and one cart, with 100 rounds of ammunition to each gun, are . . . to join the 71st Regiment. . . . For the Grenadiers, four 6 pounders, New Pattern; [for] the Light Infantry, four 3 pounders with shafts. One ammunition cart for each two guns; and each gun to be complete to 100 rounds.[18]

The artillery of the park, or train of artillery was composed of the pieces of ordnance that were not assigned as battalion guns. The park can be thought of as a reserve, or as a collection of specialized pieces better suited to siege warfare than the common battalion guns. The artillery park of General Burgoyne's army at Saratoga included 16 pieces with their own ammunition wagons, carts, and forges.[19] The Royal Regiment of Artillery was composed of "fireworkers" or "artillery artificers." These technologists were considered civilian experts who compounded shells and other explosive mixtures for the artillery. They came into existence in 1716 and remained a civilian branch of the service until long after the war.[20]

The British hired civilian teamsters to move their artillery pieces and ammunition rather than provide a detachment from their own forces for this purpose. These civilian contractors assumed all the risks to their livestock inherent in military operations. However, they "were loath to remain on the battlefield," and after depositing their cargo near the battle line, they withdrew. Thereafter, only by the force of their own muscles could the artillerymen shift the position of their piece. Partially for this reason very light pieces, firing rounds of two or three pounds, were in demand as supports for the army. Since insufficient ammunition was carried with the guns for a prolonged engagement, army commanders knew that "after a few salvoes the gunners had to rely on the ammunition wagons," and they remained apprehensive lest the teamsters not return to the field "on schedule." Field commanders were thereby limited in how they employed their artillery in battle.[21]

Patriot Artillery

Congress could not find a reliable source of cannon before the French alliance. During 1775 and 1776 the army relied on captured British artillery or older pieces owned by the provinces from the time of the French wars. The 59 pieces of artillery brought to Boston from Ticonderoga by Knox in the winter of 1775–1776 included some very heavy iron pieces that were not practical for use with line companies.

Heavy weapons were best suited for naval vessels, where their weight was not such a disadvantage. Experience showed that any shot smaller than 12 pounds did very little damage to the timbers of a warship, and 12-, 18-, 24-, and 32-pound projectiles were commonly used in naval engagements. The heaviest guns were almost always restricted to the lowest deck to improve the vessel's stability. The lightest guns (4-, 6-, and 9-pounders) were placed on the upper decks to work upon the rigging and decks. They were often supported by swivel guns, lethal man-killers that were too heavy to be held by hand.[22]

PROJECTILES

Artillery fired a wide variety of ammunition designed for specific purposes. The standard projectiles were solid iron cannonballs. The weight of these defined the size of the piece (as in 3-pounder or 6-pounder). Solid shot was used to destroy the timbers of ships and break down the walls of fortifications. Solid shot could be made to bounce along the field of battle, taking down men and horses or overturning and smashing enemy artillery like an errant bowling ball.

Hollow iron spheres filled with explosive powder were known as bombs or shells. They were commonly fired in a high arc by howitzers

Col. Herry Knox accomplished an amazing feat by moving 59 pieces of artillery through the snow from upstate New York to Boston.

and mortars that could elevate their barrels. Bombs or shells did their job by the force of their concussion, the lethal fragments of the shell flying in all directions. They were very effective when lobbed into fortifications and earthworks. The fuses were hollowed pieces of wood filled with powder. Because these were cut to a length corresponding to the estimated time before they exploded, bombs also had a remarkable pyschological effect, rolling about ready to burst with their fuses burning, scattering the frightened defenders.

A cluster of iron balls (like golf balls) fixed to a board within a canvas bag was known as grapeshot. This was most useful against the rigging of ships or when fired along the decks filled with gun crews or boarders.

This detail from a period painting of the battle of Princeton captures the power of the artillery, and shows the placement of the gun crew in action. Note the blowback that clears the fire tube from the vent.

It was essentially a naval round often confused with canister. The use of bar shot and chain shot also was generally limited to naval gunnery. These whirled through the air like a scythe, cutting the rigging or taking down the spars and masts of enemy vessels.

Canister was an effective killer at close range on the battlefield. It consisted of a tinned iron can the diameter of the bore of the piece and filled with from 60 to 100 lead musket balls of varying caliber. It was fired into advancing troops at ranges under 350 yards with the lethal effect of a giant shotgun. Cannon could be double-loaded with canister at very close range. Pieces loaded with canister could achieve remarkable rates of fire because they did not need to be carefully aimed to be effective.[23]

Ammunition for the artillery could be fixed, semi-fixed, or unfixed. Fixed ammunition implied that the projectile and the propellent were in a single piece, the ball attached by means of a wooden disk to a flannel bag holding the powder. Semi-fixed ammunition consisted of a projectile fitted to a wooden disk but with no powder bag attached. Unfixed ammunition was simply loose shot, ball, or canister introduced directly on top of the powder charge with only some cloth wadding between them. Fixed ammunition was the quickest to fire, and it was carried in the limber or ammunition chest.

The ignition of the charge through the touchhole at the rear of the cannon was accomplished by using quick matches and fire tubes. The quick match, cotton or worsted cord that looked like a piece of modern clothesline, was carried on a linstock. The ends of the quick match were ignited and smoldered somewhat like a lighted cigarette. It was used to light the fire tube, which was pushed into the touchhole. When the tube was ignited, the flame ran down into the piece and ignited the main charge. Tin tubes and quills, which were blown out of the touchhole upon firing, were almost always used in field service. A standard rate of fire among trained artillery crews using fixed ammunition was just under four rounds per minute, but this rate was difficult to sustain.[24]

STRATEGIC METALS

Iron

Iron was the basic metal for all long arms, pistols, swords, pikes, and bayonets; it was also needed to make fittings and implements for ordnance pieces, tires for wagon wheels, chains and fasteners for harness, hinges for the limber chests, shoes for horses and oxen, and other camp equipment such as nails, felling axes, froes for splitting shingles, and picks and shovels. It was estimated that, in addition, 1500 boxes of tin and 500 sheets of copper would be necessary to carry on the war effectively for one year.

Although the British had prohibited the establishment of mills for the slitting, rolling, plating, and forging of iron in 1750, Americans had developed a large number of iron mines, bloomeries, and ironworks for the production of unworked pig iron. America produced one-seventh of all the world's iron in 1775. A line of furnaces and ironworks stretched from South Carolina to New Hampshire. The difficulty in transporting the iron cannon produced at these locations, and the shot and shell that went with them, caused the ironworks within a particular region to be relied upon to supply each army department. Therefore, ironworks located in New England served the needs of the earliest stages of the war, while those in Maryland, New Jersey, and Pennsylvania became more strategically important during 1777 and 1778.

The process of casting large metal objects like artillery pieces was called founding. Some items could be used with some minor internal flaws, but artillery had to be perfect. For this reason the bore was drilled into the piece rather than left hollow in the casting. Although brass ordnance was considered preferable to that made of iron, the domestic production of brass or bronze guns by the patriots proved difficult because most failed to stand "proof." In proofing the piece, it was intentionally overloaded with powder and double shot to disclose any unseen flaw. Iron pieces were easier to cast correctly, and there were many iron founders in America who were experienced in casting pots, kettles, stove plates, and other household items.

The Brown brothers of Stirling, New York, cast 3000 small iron cannons, mortars, and swivel guns for the patriots during the war. The Salisbury furnance located in Connecticut dominated the production of large cannon, and it had a shot tower for making projectiles. Nonetheless, the total domestic production of artillery was small. Production was also hampered by the lack of trained artisans and foundry workers, who were called away to serve in the militia or state troops. Consequently, Congress asked the states to exempt experienced ironworkers from their enlistments.[25]

Lead

During the initial stages of the Revolution, the potential scarcity of lead for the production of musket balls created a great deal of apprehension. In 1775, Congress set up a series of bounties to increase the supply. Daniel Dunscomb and Samuel Pierce were appointed by Congress to serve as agents for the collection of "old lead." Window sash weights were torn from their casings, lead downspouts were ripped from buildings, lead roofing tiles were stripped away, and lead statues were pulled from their foundations. All were broken apart and melted down to make bullets. Small weights used on shopkeepers' scales and lead printers' type were excepted from requisition.

Militia Lt. Isaac Bangs of Massachusetts recorded the destruction of a gilded lead statue of George III in New York in July 1776. The statue had been erected at the end of the French and Indian War to honor the king, but it became the object of patriotic fervor when word of the Declaration of Independence reached the city. In it were "four thousand pounds of lead ... [which] is to be run up into musket balls for the use of the Yankees, when it is hoped that the emanations from the leaden George will make ... deep impressions in the bodies of some of his red-coated and Tory subjects."[26]

In 1776, a vessel from Marseille brought in 40 tons of lead, and another brought 7 tons just in time to help the patriots defend New York City. There were lead mines in Fincastle County, Virginia, that produced lead throughout the war. Lead was also available near York, Pennsylvania. The production of usable lead was simple. Heating the white lead oxide ore from the mines in a closed furnance produced a soft, silver-gray metal easily formed into musket balls in molds with eight to ten cavities.[27]

A more serious problem was sizing the projectiles to fit a wide variety of firearms. Rifles and pistols were generally made as individual pieces by gunsmiths, who provided bullet molds of the proper size for each piece. However, when ammunition was issued to the troops for their muskets, the balls had to be cast into suitable sizes and in proportion to the number needed by troops having different caliber arms. At one point in the war seven different calibers of ball were required by the American army, including some weighing almost an ounce. Heavy soft lead bullets did more than pierce the body. They broke and shattered bones, often requiring amputation when men were wounded in the arm or leg.

Washington noted that most of the army's weapons were either 0.75 or 0.69 caliber, representing common British and the French military rounds, respectively. The larger British ball could be cast at a rate of 16 balls per pound of lead (1 ounce), while the smaller French round gave 18 balls per pound. In 1777 Washington wrote to Commissary General Benjamin Flowers, requesting sorely needed ammunition: "If you have any 16ths & 18ths viz: cartridges which require so many to the pound now ready, you are to transmit them without a moments delay."[28]

At the battle of Briar Creek (Court Royal Island, South Carolina), the patriot militia were routed by the British after they suddenly found that oversized cartridges had been distributed to them for their weapons. In the court of inquiry that followed the battle, testimony was given by the officers in charge that the men were "so panic stricken" by the fact that the cartridges did not fit their guns that they could not be held in their lines. Over 1000 muskets were abandoned on the field by the fleeing troops, and hundreds of lives were lost. Only by closely examining the reports of his officers for "defects and abuses," and by calling the attention of the brigade commanders to these problems, was Washington able to bring about any improvement. He wrote, "[G]reat care must be taken to make the bores of the same size [in a company], that the balls may answer, otherwise great disadvantage may arise from a mixture of cartridges."[29]

FORTS AND FORTIFICATIONS

The techniques of fortification reached their apex in Europe during the late seventeenth century. The works built in Europe were huge, complex fortifications, manned by garrisons which were much smaller than the armies needed to attack them. The British raised several imposing stonework forts in North America during the French wars. Fort Carillon, known as Ticonderoga, was begun by the French as a wooden structure and finished by the British in stone. Fort Frederick, a star-shaped stone structure similar to Ticonderoga, was built in Maryland at great expense to the colonial government. Fort Crown Point, the largest stonework fortification built by the British in North America, was completed on the shores of Lake Champlain in the 1760s.

New permanent fortifications were expensive and often beyond the means of the colonials. Consequently, the patriots built few permanent fortifications, and their temporary ones seldom went beyond earthworks, wooden walls and blockhouses, and revetments composed of bundles and baskets made of saplings filled and backed by earth and sod. These could be laid out with simple surveying instruments and built with axes, shovels, picks, and baskets for moving the earth and sod. Charles Lee noted that the patriots were "skillful in the management of the instruments necessary for all military works, such as spades, pickaxes, and hatchets." The most extensive series of fortifications built by the patriots were around New York City in Manhattan, Brooklyn, the Bronx, Westchester and New Jersey.[30]

The patriots favored naming their entrenchments after the officers in their army (Fort Washington, Fort Greene, Fort Hamilton, and Fort Lee, for instance), or after their fallen heroes (Fort Montgomery, Fort Mercer). It was common for the troops who built the position to name it after their commanding officer (as in Fort Arnold, Fort Schuyler, or Fort Moultrie). Many of the fortifications along the Hudson River were named for prominent topographical features: Paulus Hook and Stony Point (initially British), or Verplanck's Point and West Point (American).[31]

Ironically, earthworks proved more effective than works of stone and morter in absorbing the lethal energy of cannonballs, and they all but eliminated wounds from ricochets and shards of stone ripped from the walls of masonry fortifications. They did nothing, however, to reduce wounds from splintered wood, which were most lethal because they easily became infected. One witness wrote in her journal, "Large quantities of fagots and screwed hay are collected for entrenching purposes, and what tells a plainer story than all the other preparations, two thousand bandages are in readiness for the wounds which it is expected will need them."[32]

MILITARY ENGINEERS

The patriots were blessed with several outstanding military engineers. One of these was Col. Rufus Putnam, brother of Israel Putnam. Rufus helped to plan and erect the fortifications in Boston, around New York City, and at West Point. Putnam was said to have freed a monumental boulder from the cliffside overlooking the narrows of the Hudson River at West Point, which came crashing down onto the banks of the river below the site of the fortifications. With bravado typical of his family, he mounted the boulder after it had come to rest, and jokingly christened it Fort Putnam. Putnam's Massachusetts regiment built the real Fort Putnam 600 feet above the Hudson River in 1778. Rufus Putnam served at Saratoga, and during 1778 and 1779 was a brigadier under Gen. "Mad Anthony" Wayne. He was the first surveyor general of the United States.

The other military engineer for whom the patriots were grateful was Colonel Tadeusz (Thaddeus) Kosciusko, one of the more effective European officers to enter the patriot service. Made a colonel of engineers by Congress in 1776, Kosciusko was initially assigned to the command of Horatio Gates. He helped to plan the entrenchments at Saratoga and was with Gates at the fiasco at Camden. He remained with the army in South Carolina and served under Nathanael Greene, as his transportation officer, during the race for the Dan River. Kosciusko was unsuccessful in driving the British from their fort at Ninety-Six in South Carolina. He thereafter served as a cavalry commander in the Southern Army. At the end of the war Kosciusko was made a brigadier general, but he returned to his homeland to lead an ill-fated attempt to secure Poland's independence from Russia.

At West Point, Putnam and Kosciusko helped to execute the plans of Cap. Louis de La Radiere, one of four French military engineers secured by Benjamin Franklin in Europe. Radiere laid out the plans for the fortifications following the precepts of the seventeenth-century French engineer Louis Vauban. He initially wanted to place the main American position at a different site along the Hudson River, which was rocky and more difficult to approach, but he was overruled by Washington, who felt that the deep soil of West Point would be easier to entrench. Moreover, the roads to West Point from the countrytside were better for moving supplies. West Point commanded a narrow bend in the river where the Royal Navy could not sprint by without tacking back and forth. Here a great chain and floating boom blocking the passage were placed from the western shore to Constitution Island. The position was overseen by Forts Webb, Wyllys, and Meigs,[33] which were designed to provide a field of crossfire against the enemy. Each fort was named for the colonel of the regiment that built and manned it. Fort Arnold was built here by the troops of Brig. James Clinton, to whose name it reverted after Arnold's treason. Captain Radiere died in action in 1780.

> The peaceful scene of beauty lay
> Prepared with bristling forts the fray
> Of revolution strife to bear
> On Constitution isle, and where
> Poplopen's Kill to Hudson's stream
> Descends, with chain and boom that seem
> To block the way at southern gate,
> But all in vain for war's stern fate . . .
> The works of war with Radiere
> The fortifying to prepare
> In plans, while Kosciuszko's rare
> Accomplishments the building crown
> Mount Independence with a frown

Of Rufus Putnam's fort the plain
O'erlooked, and lower rose the twain
Forts Webb and Wyllys named.[34]

NOTES

1. Jack Coggins, ed., *Boys in the Revolution: Young Americans Tell Their Part in the War for Independence* (Harrisburg, PA: Stackpole Books, 1967), 44.

2. Jeremy Black, *Warfare in the Eighteenth Century* (London: Cassell, 1999), 156–157.

3. Erna Risch, *Supplying Washington's Army* (Washington, DC: U.S. Army Center of Military Studies, 1981), 345. This work will provide most readers with an exhaustive study of the development of the Quartermaster's Department.

4. James M. Volo, "The Acquisition and Use of Warlike Stores During the American Revolution, Part II," *Living History Journal* no. 15 (Fall 1986), 10.

5. Risch, *Supplying Washington's Army*, 344–345.

6. Volo, "Acquisition and Use," 10.

7. Risch, *Supplying Washington's Army*, 345.

8. Brass is a combination of copper and zinc, while bronze is made by mixing copper with tin. Most ordnance pieces were some combination of the two alloys. The term "bell metal" was also used.

9. Risch, *Supplying Washington's Army*, 358.

10. Volo, "Acquisition and Use," 11.

11. Ibid.

12. See John Muller, *A Treatise of Artillery, 1780* (Bloomfield, ON: Museum Restoration Services, 1977).

13. See Dorothy Denneen Volo and James M. Volo, *Daily Life in the Age of Sail* (Westport, CT: Greenwood, 2002), 233–234; Risch, *Supplying Washington's Army*, 344–345.

14. Volo, "Acquisition and Use," 4.

15. Adrian Caruana, *The Light 6-pdr. Battalion Gun of 1776* (Bloomfield, ON., Canada: Museum Restoration Services, 1977), 6.

16. Muller, *Treatise of Artillery*, 114, 115.

17. George W. Platt, *An Account of the British Expedition Above the Highlands of the Hudson River and of the Events Connected with the Burning of Kingston in 1777* (Kingston, NY: Ulster County Historical Society, 1860), 135.

18. Adrian Caruana, *British Artillery Ammunition, 1780* (Bloomfield, ON: Museum Restoration Services, 1979), 13–14.

19. Caruana, *The Light 6-pdr.*, 8.

20. Carson I. A. Ritchie, "A New York Diary," in *Narratives of the Revolution in New York* (New York: New York Historical Society, 1975), 208–209.

21. L. Edward Purcell and David F. Burg, eds., *The World Almanac of the American Revolution* (New York: Pharos Books, 1992), 77.

22. Volo and Volo, *Daily Life in the Age of Sail*, 205–207.

23. Cannon could also be loaded with *langrage*, an assortment of nails, pieces of chain, broken glass, pebbles, and other debris. The use of *langrage* was considered improper in civilized warfare, and it was reserved to pirates and smugglers.

24. Caruana, *British Artillery*, 3–4.

25. Risch, *Supplying Washington's Army*, 359–362.

26. William P. Cumming and Hugh Rankin, eds., *The Fate of a Nation: The American Revolution Through Contemporary Eyes* (London: Phaidon Press, 1975), 100. A piece of this statue was rescued from the Norwalk River in Wilton, Connecticut, in the 1970s by an associate of the authors. It has since disappeared into the custody of the state.

27. Risch, *Supplying Washington's Army*, 336.

28. Letter of George Washington, August 28, 1777, to Benjamin Flowers, in Washington's papers (Washington, DC: Manuscript Division, Library of Congress).

29. James M. Volo, "The Acquisition and Use of Warlike Stores During the American Revolution," *Living History Journal* (Spring 1986), 30.

30. Robson, *American Revolution*, 153–154.

31. Charles Townshend, ed., *The Oxford Illustrated History of Modern War* (New York: Oxford University Press, 1997), 26–27.

32. Dorothy Dudley, *Theatrum Majorum: The Diary of Dorothy Dudley* (New York: Arno Press, 1971), 57.

33. The men were Cols. Samuel B. Webb of Massachusetts, and Samuel Wyllys and Return Johnathan Meigs of Connecticut.

34. Edward Johnson Runk, *Washington: A National Epic in Six Cantos* (New York: G. P. Putam's Sons, 1897), 77.

10

Food and Forage

The Colonel, putting his hand in his pocket, took out a piece of an ear of Indian corn burnt as black as coal. "Here, eat this," he said, "and learn to be a soldier."

—Private Joseph Plumb Martin

LAND TRANSPORTATION

During the French and Indian War the British command almost despaired of having adequate wheeled transport.[1] The British were better prepared to deal with the problems of land transportation during the Revolution. They hired everything from four-horse carriages to sledges pulled by teams of oxen from loyalists, and they hired all their drivers and teamsters as well. The ammunition carts, hospital wagons, and traveling forges that were not readily available in America were shipped over from Britain. The vast number of vehicles needed by an eighteenth-century army operating overseas can be summed in "a single statistic." The British continually employed a monthly average of 739 wagons, 1958 horses, and 760 teamsters during the war.[2]

In 1776, Washington's quartermaster general, Thomas Mifflin, found a sufficient number of carts and ox teams to move the patriot army to New York without resorting to impressment. Massachusetts alone provided 300 wagons. However, within a few months, Mifflin needed an additional 200 wagons because so many had been lost in the retreat across New Jersey. He was authorized to spend $300,000 to provide this transport. This included more than $72,000 for the monthly payroll of the wagoners, teamsters, and packhorse men.[3]

Baggage

The ancient Roman legions called the baggage train of their army *impedimenta*, and it certainly was an encumbrance, or impediment, to rapid movement. Washington deemed the baggage carried by some officers for their comfort an "absurdity," and he enjoined them to pack up and send away all trunks, chests, and furniture that were not strictly necessary to their functions as field commanders. "Officers should retain their blankets, great coats, and three or four shifts of under clothes, and . . . the men should, besides what they have on, keep only a blanket, and a shirt apiece, and such as have it, a great coat." Moreover, some of the soldiers were in the habit of secreting items in the battalion baggage wagons. This was often done with the connivance of the NCOs. It was the duty of the wagonmasters to prevent such actions.[4]

Horses

It was quickly found impractical for the British to transport horses from Europe by ship. The difficulties of providing sufficient water, forage, and room for horses aboard ships caused a terrible loss of animals when a voyage took longer than expected. Moreover, those which did survive needed many months to recover their full health. The British were forced to purchase, lease, or requisition horses in the rural areas of America that generally supported the revolution. Theft, straying, lameness, and death left the army constantly in need of new mounts.

Washington had less trouble finding appropriate horseflesh mainly because the patriots controlled some of the most productive areas in colonial America in terms of breeding. Virginia, Connecticut, and parts of Pennsylvania had developed a domestic market for horses, but officers and mounted dragoons were usually required to provide their own mounts. Draft animals were purchased or leased by agents of Congress.[5]

The number of riding and wagon horses with the American main army in the fall of 1778 was estimated to be 10,000. Steps were taken to disperse the excess horse herds during the winter encampments so that forage could more easily be found. No officer was to keep more horses than permitted to his rank, nor any additional mounts within 40 miles of the encampments. The lowest-grade company officers were permitted two mounts each, while general officers had no restrictions. The continuing need to haul wood, straw, and other materials for sheltering the troops was assigned to country teams hired locally. The owners of these teams were made responsible for their animals as part of their service contracts.

The need to supply ample forage and pasturage for horses and other draft animals proved a constant difficulty for the British and American armies throughout the war. The open fields of the southern and middle colonies provided grass in summer and early autumn, but in winter neither impressment nor purchase of hay seemed to relieve the shortages in feed. The poor quality of the roads connecting the southern colonies to the winter encampments in New Jersey prevented forage from being transported effectively. Hundreds of horses perished each winter for want of forage as the pastures failed in autumn. With each annual campaign in the spring, the horses that had successfully wintered with the army had to be fed and cared for to restore them to usefulness. A separate Commissary of Horses was established by the Congress in 1776–1777, which authorized the purchase of 15,000 bushels of oats and 1800 tons of hay annually for this purpose.[6]

Congress directed that the Light Dragoons be dispersed to various states, thereby relieving some of the demand for forage in a single region. Durham, Connecticut; Lancaster, Pennsylvania; and Winchester, Virginia became favored wintering sites for this purpose. This option left the army dangerously exposed to a surprise attack even though some mounted troops were retained. Fortunately, the British attempted few winter operations, choosing instead to winter in comfort in the cities.[7]

A troop of the Virginia Light Horse, described as "beautiful" and "splendid," was retained at Valley Forge in the winter of 1777–1778.[8] These Virginians, under the command of "Light Horse Harry" Lee, were active in preventing British raids on patriot provisions, and they raided British supply columns with notable success. The *New Jersey Gazette* of January 14, 1778, noted:

A troop of Dragoons in Bland's Regiment, seldom having more than 25 men and horses fit for duty has since the first of August last, taken 124 British and Hessian privates, besides 4 commissioned officers, with the loss of only one horse. This gallant corps is under the command of Captain Lee, Lieutenant Lindsay and Cornet Peyton, whose merits and services it is hoped will not be passed unnoticed or unrewarded.[9]

Size and Breeding. Washington ordered that any horse more than 16 hands in height (4 inches per hand at the withers) be reserved for the use of the general staff. Ostensibly this was to ensure that the general officers could see and be seen while directing the movements of their troops. While horses of this stature are fairly common today, in the eighteenth century horses were a good deal smaller. A detailed account of the

the size of 299 horses for a regiment of British light horse shows that 46 percent were of 15 hands and 28 percent were under 15 hands in height.[10]

Hands	Horses
16	4
15 ½	74
15	138
14 ½	83

Americans relied almost entirely on breeds common to Europe for their horseflesh. The tall and graceful breed of horse known as the Thoroughbred had just begun to gain attention in the South. The saddle and draft horses available to colonials were generally bred from the hardy cobs, large ponies, and common horses easily recognized by the frontier immigrants from Europe. Thus, men were mounted on generally smaller animals than the larger warhorses of nineteenth century cavalry. Contemporary drawings and sketches by Baron Ludwig von Closen, an aide-de-camp to General Rochambeau, bear this out. Although crudely drawn, they are the only images of cavalry done from life during the war. The smaller stature of these animals facilitated the mounting and dismounting expected of the dragoon, who often served afoot.[11]

Americans seemed particularly attached to their mounts even under the most trying of circumstances. Many patriots, who should have provided officers for infantry companies, chose to serve in the mounted arm, even if that meant serving as privates. At one point, South Carolina alone had more than 2000 mounted militia, a number that all of New England could not match. At the battle of Cowpens, the majority of the militia who turned out to support Daniel Morgan's riflemen and William Washington's dragoons were mounted. Only by the most persuasive arguments did these men abandon their horses at the rear of the patriot line. They fired a few rounds as infantry, discreetly retreated in good order, and returned as mounted pursuers of a routed enemy.

Draft Animals

The first heavy draft horses used to pull wagons and plows, such as the immensely powerful Shire and Belgian breeds, were not introduced into America until 1800. In the absence of a particular breed, large individual animals were used in this service. More often, oxen were hitched to heavy loads in colonial America. The great number of iron oxshoes found at Revolutionary era sites attests to their popularity as draft animals. Oxen utilized their front feet to gain traction, and like four-wheel drive vehicles, they could move more weight through mud and snow than horses, which applied their strength almost entirely from their rear legs only. Oxen were also less likely to run away and to be peevish; but they were prone to foot disease and had to be trained from a very early age to work in pairs. An oxen fancier noted, "The ox is a most noble animal, patient, thrifty, durable, gentle, and easily driven."[12]

Hay and Grain

Nathanael Greene, when serving as quartermaster general in 1778, ordered that stores of grain and hay for the livestock of the army be established at intermediate posts along the American lines of communication. At Trenton, New Jersey, and at Head of Elk, Maryland, 200,000 bushels of grain and a proportionate stock of hay were stored; on the lines from Reading, Pennsylvania, on the Schuylkill River, to Lancaster, on the Susquehanna River, 100,000 bushels; among the several posts from the Delaware River to the Hudson River, another 100,000; and at Allentown, Pennsylvania, a store of 400,000 bushels of grain and hay was to be laid up for use by the army in southern New Jersey. All the hay was tied up in bundles, and crews of local farmers were hired to transport it.[13]

Wagons

As part of his duties, Greene estimated the number of wagons and teams needed to move a single brigade composed of four regiments. There was one wagon in each brigade dedicated to the entrenching tools and another for spare ammunition, four wagons for the commissary stores, and four more for forage for the wagon teams. Each of the four regiments had four wagons for its own provisions and baggage, and the brigadier general was allowed one for his own use and that of his headquarters staff. This made a total of 27 wagons per brigade. Added to this number were the wagons and carts of the mounted dragoons, the headquarters staff, the engineers, the quartermasters, and the artillery train. At the time of Greene's estimate, Washington was planning the movement of 19 brigades of the Continental Army, which would require 551 wagons and teams in proportion.

Each of the 68 artillery fieldpieces assigned to the Main Army was capable of independent movement on its own wheeled carriage and limber, but each piece required not only a team of its own but one for an ammunition wagon as well. Also included in the artillery train were 50 spare ammunition wagons, 8 baggage wagons, 6 commissary wagons, 20 traveling forges (mounted on two-wheeled carts), and 4 wagons for the artillery artificers and their supplies. The ammunition and ordnance stores included barrels of powder, musket balls, musket cartridges, flints, fuses, and artillery implements. The unopened barrels of gunpowder were transported in covered wagons, and the fixed cartridges were moved in two wheeled carts, called tumbrels, that had a slightly peaked wooden roof covered with oilcloth to keep out the rain.

The dragoons required 28 wagons for their provisions, tents, extra horse equipment, and forage for their horses. The engineers and sappers needed 25 wagons for tools; the Quartermaster Corps, 40 for its stores; the commissary, 50 for provisions; and the hospital, 20 for its meager list of equipment. Washington's staff and the army headquarters were assigned 47 wagons. In addition, 60 wagons were assigned to the army as a whole to supply forage for the teams. To supplement this, the dragoons carried large linen bags in which to collect hay when on the march. Greene's total for the entire army in 1778 came to a remarkable 977 wagons or carts, and 1071 teamsters to drive them.[14]

FOOD FOR THE REDCOATS

Because the patriots controlled the rural areas of the colonies, almost all the food eaten by the redcoats had to be shipped across the Atlantic. Although many of the documents detailing this process are missing, it is certain that supplying the British army in America was a remarkable feat. Over 2 million pounds of dried biscuit crossed the ocean from January 1775 to January 1778 alone. An account of the British commissary in New York from 1774 until 1781 showed the expenditure of more than £22,000 on foodstuffs. The list of items is staggering, and it includes bread, spirits, beef, pork, flour, raisins, pease, oatmeal, rice, oil, butter, cheese, vinegar, and sauerkraut. Also included were nonedible items associated with storing provisions, such as jars, casks, bags, and barrel hoops. There was, nonetheless, a constant shortage of foodstuffs for the British soldier, and the redcoats rarely had enough to eat.[15]

The Daily Ration

The daily ration for a British soldier on duty was determined by the Treasury to be: 1 pound of bread or biscuit; 1 pound of beef or 9 1/7 ounces of pork; 3/7 pint of pease; 6/7 ounce of butter or 1/7 ounce of cheese; 2/7 ounce of flour or 1/7 ounce of rice or oatmeal. One gill (equal to 2 ounces) of vinegar was provided. Each man had a daily rum ration of 1 gill, which was mixed by the NCOs into the water in his canteen to prevent him from saving it up for a good drunk. Other drinks were sometimes made available by the commanding officer, including wine, small beer, and spruce beer. The relatively boring diet could be relieved by the men's personal expenditure for food items, or by unauthorized foraging and stealing.[16]

The food issued from the store was often spoiled, moldy, or musty.

Some of it may have sat aboard transports for more than six months as the ships from England crossed the Atlantic in adverse weather. For a period of some months in both 1778 and 1779, the British army in New York City suffered greatly from a lack of adequate provisions because the victualing ships from Cork, Ireland, took twice as long as usual to cross the Atlantic.

The biscuit or bread was notorious for being virtually indestructible, and it resembled neither biscuit nor bread. A probably apocryphal story circulated among the regulars that their biscuit had been captured from the French in the last war and kept in storage for the present one. Made with flour, a little salt, and just enough water to make a stiff dough, the biscuit was baked into 4-inch, rock-solid cakes about half an inch thick. The men had to soak it to make it edible, or nibble it about the edges. It could be broken up with the butt of a musket or a cannonball, and mixed with some salt, water, and fat to make a sort of hot pudding.

When the biscuit was poor, it was either too hard, or moldy and wet. It was noted for being filled with weevils, but these creatures did not detract from its nutrional value. They could be evicted by toasting the cracker or breaking it up into a mug of hot liquid and skimming off the pests. The biscuit provided a good-quality ration when combined with other foods, and a man could exist on as few as three crackers a day. Fresh bread was available when soldiers were in garrisons, and the British used the many bakeries of New York and Philadelphia to provide both hard and fresh bread for the men stationed there.

MILITARY PAY

The pay for British military personnel, set by Parliament, is well documented. Common soldiers in the British army and seamen in the Royal Navy were paid at a rate of 6s a week. Those who rose in rank or displayed extraordinary skills, such as an army NCO or a naval petty officer, might rate an additional shilling and some pence weekly. The military wage included provision of a minimum of food and shelter for the individual, but nothing for the family of a married man. Moreover, the wage was subject to levies for equipment, uniforms, and fines.[17]

The British citizen serving his country was particularly underpaid and underappreciated. The difference between civilian and military wages continued for centuries. At the beginning of the eighteenth century, a merchant seamen could expect an average wage of about 12s weekly, whereas the naval wage for a man of equal ability remained fixed at little more than 6s. In 1697 Daniel Defoe described this dichotomy. "[O]ur seamen lurk and hide and hang back in time of war . . . for who would serve king and country and fight and be knocked on the head at 24s. a month, that can have 50s. without that hazard?" A private in the regular infantry could expect to find a similar discrepancy between his weekly wages and those of a day laborer.[18]

Although the practice of paying substantial enlistment bounties to both army and navy enlistees was established in Britain during the reign of Charles II, in the next hundred years, to the accession of George III in 1760, the military pay schedule remained unaltered. American military personnel were given wages similar to those of the redcoats, but the British were always paid in stable sterling silver coin rather than in debased colonial coin or paper, which varied widely in value.

PROVISIONING THE CONTINENTAL ARMY

The patriot army that surrounded the British at Boston was composed of militia and provincial troops from many colonies. Each colony had its own rules for providing rations to its troops. When Congress authorized the creation of the Continental Army, it put aside the colonial regulations and set a uniform daily food allowance for the entire force. This allowance "compared favorably with that allowed the British soldier," and remained in effect with little change for the duration of the war.[19]

Congress fixed the components of the daily ration as follows:

1 pound of beef, or ¾ pound pork, or 1 pound salt fish, per day. 1 pound of bread or flour per day. 3 pints of pease or beans per week, or vegetables equivalent, at one dollar per bushel for pease or beans. 1 pint of milk per man per day, or at the rate of 1/72 of a dollar. 1 half pint of rice, or one pint of Indian meal per man per week. 1 quart of spruce beer or cider per man per day, or nine gallons of molasses per company of 100 men per week. 3 pounds candles to 100 men per week for guards. 24 pounds of soft or 8 lbs. of hard soap, for 100 men per week.[20]

The combination of daily and weekly allowances with monetary values in the regulations leaves the actual day-to-day diet of the American soldier somewhat obscured. In the summer of 1776, the daily ration was valued at a little over 8d New York currency, but in a single year, inflation had brought its value to 3s 4d (40d)—a 400 percent increase! The rising cost of food simply did not permit the purchase of many of the items listed in the ration. Moreover, the substitution of plentiful foodstuffs for scarce ones required the specific authority of Congress, and this power was not granted until 1778.

Until 1777 the Subsistence Department was directed by Commissary General Joseph Trumbull, who provided a more generous allowance of salt pork, fresh beef, and beer than that prescribed. As the Middle Department became almost depleted of provisions by the constant operations of the army in eastern Pennsylvania and New Jersey during 1777,

Table 10.1

**Paymaster's Scale for the Continental Army in 1777:
Approximate Monthly Wage in Shillings and Continental
Dollars***

Rank	Wage	
(or function)	*Shillings*	*Dollars*
Colonel	450	60
Lt. Colonel	400	54
Major	350	46⅔
Chaplain	300	40
Adjutant	200	26⅔
Surgeon	200	26⅔
Surgeon's Mate	160	21⅓
Quartermaster	160	21⅓
Captain	300	40
Lieutenant	200	26⅔
Ensign	160	21⅓
Sergeant	90	12
Corporal	60	8
Private	50	6⅔**

*Wage based on 7s 6d per Spanish dollar paid in Continental paper currency.
**As established by Congress for Continental infantry. Privates serving as dragoons and artillerymen, and militia serving outside their state, received 8⅓.

the provisioning of even the minimum uniform allowances became infrequent. The discrepancies among those rations the men received, those to which they were entitled, and those to which they had become accustomed became a constant source of grumbling.

Beef and flour were generally plentiful "in such an extensive and abundant country" unless their transportation failed, but men could not maintain their health on an unremitting diet of bread, meat, and water.[21] Fresh vegetables, cider, and vinegar were necessary to prevent scurvy and maintain good health. Washington wrote, "Our soldiers, the greatest part of the last campaign [1777], and the whole of this [winter], have scarcely tasted any kind of vegetable, had but little salt, and vinegar, which would have been tolerable substitute for vegetables.... Neither have they been provided with proper drink. Beer and cider seldom comes [*sic*] within the verge of the camp, and rum in much too small quantities."[22]

There was a great deal of waste among the soldiers. The men were ordered to combine their meat and vegetables into stews and soups in company kettles provided for the purpose, but most ignored the orders, choosing to roast the meat over open fires, thereby losing a good deal of caloric value in the wasted drippings. Heavy iron kettles, abandoned on the march, often dotted the landscape. Excess fresh beef, taken from the cattle herds that followed the army, and salt pork in opened barrels was often thrown away or left uneaten until they putrefied. Barrels of flour, once opened and allowed to be wetted, became moldy, or unscrupulous bakers took the surplus and sold it to the local population.

The soldiers could supplement their diet by purchasing food from local farmers or from sutlers who stocked such items. With little money to buy provisions, the soldiers sold their metal buttons or carried their flour allowance into the country to trade for other foodstuffs. Dorothy Dudley noted, "Many have had opportunity to work at their trades of shoemaking, tailoring, and the like, or add to their income by selling such things as nuts, apples, and cider, which make a little variety in their daily diet."[23] However, the officers considered this commerce a pretext for malingering and an opportunity for the soldiers to defraud the local inhabitants. Washington understood the scope of these problems and took steps to offset them, but it is clear "that his orders brought no permanent improvement in conditions."[24]

The period during which food was most scarce occurred immediately after the army evacuated New York City in November 1776. Left behind in the retreat from New York were thousands of barrels of foodstuffs. At Fort Lee alone, 1000 barrels of flour had been abandoned because there were not enough wagons to transport them. This left the army facing the winter with as little as five days' rations. This was the most severe shortage of food during the war, but there was plenty of wheat to purchase in Pennsylvania. With Washington's army consuming 200 barrels of flour daily, Commissary General Trumbull estimated that 20,000 barrels of flour could be had from Philadelphia—enough to supply the army for more than half a year.

However, the lack of the barrels proved to be of greatest concern to the Quartermaster's Department. The demand for foodstuffs placed a great strain on the ability of the countryside to produce enough barrels to safely transport such huge quantities of wheat flour, pease, meal, cider, vinegar, beer, salt beef, and salt pork. Moreover, the barrels had to be watertight, and those used for beef or pork could not be reused for flour. The New York Committee of Safety took steps to increase the supply of these containers by exempting from their enlistments all the coopers in the counties south of Albany.[25]

Bread

The patriots utilized "hard bread," or biscuit, quite as often as the British when on campaign. The Commissary Department put many of the bakers' ovens in Connecticut into the full-time production of hard bread for the patriot army. The cakes, or crackers, could be carried in the haversacks of the men, and several days' rations would neither spoil nor crumble. Private Martin recalled that, even newly baked, the biscuits were "nearly hard enough for musket flints." Nonetheless, when he had the opportunity to freely pilfer a cask of biscuits, he took "as many as I could . . . a dozen or more in all, and . . . I stowed them away in my knapsack."[26]

In 1777 Congress appointed Christopher Ludwick, "a skillful, patriotic German baker," as the director of baking for the Continental Army, with the idea of furnishing freshly baked bread for the troops. Ludwick promptly took over the ovens near Morristown, New Jersey, and began the erection of "public ovens" in Pennsylvania and New Jersey. By the end of 1779, Ludwick was producing 1500 loaves of fresh bread daily, but he felt that the process was wasteful of flour. He recommended that only hard bread be issued as a ration. Washington supported Ludwick, and ordered him to establish hard bread production at West Point. Here Ludwick produced a daily supply of 6000 to 8000 pounds of hard bread until 1781.[27]

Congress then intended to stop the issue of loose flour to each man in the ration. However, Washington was quick to point out that the flour could be mixed with a little water and baked on a flat stone by the individual soldier into a "firecake" with little trouble. Nonetheless, unless the soldier was an accomplished fireside cook, the cake came out either soggy or burned around the edges. In any case it definitely lacked flavor, being described as tasting like wallpaper paste or an old cedar shingle.

As an alternative to a constant diet of hard bread, Washington recommended that each brigade make fresh bread in camp by erecting temporary ovens made of local stone and mortar, and he ordered that portable ovens made of sheet iron be procured from the iron foundry at Ringwood, New Jersey. Although designed to travel with the army, these ovens were of considerable size; only two could be carried in a wagon. By the end of 1778 one metal bread oven had been assigned to each brigade, and bakers had been found from among the men to operate them. However, Christopher Ludwick had been correct, and fresh bread simply could not be made in camp efficiently. The army thereafter reverted to a hard bread ration in the field.[28]

Meat

Meat, either salted or fresh, made up the bulk of the army ration. Initially there was little concern over the ability of the provinces to supply enough livestock to meet the needs of the army. New England was, at the time, a region noted for its production of hogs and cattle. The export of salted pork and beef was a thriving industry there before the war. The most productive areas of hog and cattle breeding were solidly in the control of the patriots and out of the reach of the British. However, it was found that even these resources could be strained. The demands of two armies—the Main Army, with Washington in Pennsylvania, and the Northern Army in New York, poised to receive an attack from Canada—drew a constant supply of meat from the same region, placing the supply of livestock under tremendous pressure. Livestock was driven to within a few miles of where it was needed and slaughtered there with greater efficiency and less cost than salting and packaging the meat and moving it by wagon. Ultimately, live cattle and hogs were secured from western New Jersey, Delaware, Maryland, and Pennsylvania until the supply was exhausted.

Salt

Because the Commissary Department initially had planned to preserve its meat near where it was raised, most of the salt imported into the country was directed to New England, and a slaughterhouse and curing facility were erected at Medford, Massachusetts. However, as the seat of war shifted to New Jersey, and then to the South, the difficulty of transporting hundreds of casks of salted meat many hundreds of miles became apparent. Thereafter, Congress ordered that the meat be preserved in the southern states, particularly North Carolina, to which large shipments of salt from the West Indies were directed for that purpose.

Pork was favored over beef for salting because it was easier to preserve, and it tasted better than preserved beef. Salt beef sometimes tasted so bad that the soldiers referred to it as "salt horse." Veteran soldiers sometimes declined a piece of fresh beef for a good piece of salt pork, but recruits had to learn to ignore the overwhelming salty favor and appreciate its nutritional qualities. The amount of salt used in the preserving of pork was staggering, often equaling the weight of the meat itself. Salt pork needed to be soaked to remove some of the salt before it could be used, but it could last unspoiled for a long time in a properly sealed barrel. However, once the barrel was opened, it needed to be cooked quickly or it would spoil.

Pork was also made into bacon, and large amounts of bacon were shipped north from the southern states. Bacon was a common colonial

Washington visiting the troops at Valley Forge.

foodstuff with a taste that was highly acceptable to most soldiers. It was made from the sides or flanks of the hog, kept in a slab, soaked in brine, and finally cured in a smokehouse. This operation flavored the meat and also retarded the growth of bacteria, so that bacon could be kept for long periods of time even under adverse conditions. Thick slices could be cut from the slabs over several days with little noticeable deterioration of the remainder. Several cooked slices of thick bacon could be placed in a haversack, wrapped in an oilcloth, and carried on the march without spoiling for several days. With this bacon and eight or ten hard bread crackers, the soldiers of the army could freely maneuver away from their supply lines for several days.

Starvation at Valley Forge

The quantity of provisions on hand as the patriot army went into winter quarters at Valley Forge in December 1777 seemed satisfactory. Various quantities of hard bread, flour, salt fish, salt pork, and rum were deposited in stores in Carlisle, York, and Lancaster in Pennsylvania and at Trenton and Newton in New Jersey. Moreover, foodstuffs in quantity had been placed in various magazines thought to be outside the reach of the British in New England, in the Southern Department, and in the North around Albany. Estimates were made that a large number of cattle could be driven to Valley Forge from Connecticut, and that sufficient quantities of beef and pork would be salted and barreled before the winter. The army had wintered at Morristown in 1776–1777, where provisions were plentiful and easily obtainable, a situation that caused the estimates for the winter of 1777–1778 at Valley Forge to be overly optimistic.

The heavy consumption of meat in the Middle Department had made local livestock scarce, and by the fall of 1777 the British had cut off several avenues by which a fresh supply of meat could be acquired by the patriot army. Although more than 3000 head of cattle were available in Bucks County, Pennsylvania, Washington's army was consuming beef at the rate of 800 head per week. In a mere four weeks this supply was exhausted. The British control of the Delaware River was particularly effective in cutting off the supply of salted pork and bacon available from storehouses in Virginia and the Carolinas. The British had also destroyed a considerable store of provisions at Peekskill, New York, and at Danbury, Connecticut. These losses had not been made up by the time the patriots went into winter quarters.

As the enemy advanced on Philadelphia in August 1777, many of the regional stores of flour and salted provisions had been removed to Lebanon and Carlisle, Pennsylvania, as a precautionary measure, but insufficient stores had been retained for the army. Congress had removed much of the army's provisions to Ulster County, New York, with the understanding that Washington would winter nearby, but this proved strategically impossible because the army's continued presence near Philadelphia was deemed essential. At the same time all wagons, boats, and horses in the path of the British army had been moved south, making the transportation of supplies more difficult than it usually was during the winter months. The lack of meat at Valley Forge increased the army's use of bread from 200 barrels per week to 400 barrels per week. The transportation of vast amounts of hard bread, with one wagon needed to move a mere six or seven barrels, became almost impossible, especially as the local teamsters increasingly feared that their wagons and teams would be impressed once they entered the patriot camp.

Moreover, the British army, which occupied Philadelphia, was purchasing provisions in the same general region as the patriots' encampment. The farmers of the region had a stock of grain, but they refused to sell it to Washington for fear that they would not be paid. British money, unlike the Continental dollar, suffered far less devaluation during the war. When grain was to be had, the local millers working for the patriots produced fewer than ten barrels of flour per day even under the watchful eyes of armed guards. Unscrupulous agents, previously serving as suppliers of fresh beef to the patriots, turned about to sell hundreds of cattle to the British, and many of the inhabitants of Chester County, Pennsylvania, were later prosecuted by local patriots for supplying the British with provisions.

However, the main cause of the starvation experienced at Valley Forge must be laid at the door of Congress, which began a major reorganization of the Commissary Department in the midst of the 1777 campaign and failed to complete it in time to provide for the wintering of the army. Commissary General Joseph Trumbull and many in his staff resigned their posts as Congress took steps to end a number of abuses that had crept into the Subsistence Department since 1775. Trumbull was briefly replaced by his deputy, Ephraim Blaine, who lacked sufficient authority to run the department efficiently.

Blaine was superseded after several months by William Buchanan, who reported directly to the Board of War. Buchanan did not act aggressively in getting his department reorganized. This was partially because he did not recognize the deterioration that had taken place under Blaine and partially because he lacked the authority to act in the smallest regard without the direct consent of Congress. The delegates were simply overmanaging the department. During the Valley Forge winter of 1777–1778, the Subsistence Department was unable to react to the needs of the army as they became clear. Historian Erna Risch has noted, "[T]he complete breakdown of transportation and the failure of Congress to appoint an active Quartermaster General were fundamental factors in promoting the distressing conditions at Valley Forge."[29] Confined to poorly designed shelters and denied proper nutrition, the soldiers suffered a mortality of almost 25 percent between December 1777 and June 1778.[30]

Misery at Morristown

Although the winter at Valley Forge is quite properly considered a triumph of the patriots over the twins evils of starvation and exposure, much more hostile conditions were encountered at Morristown in the winter of 1779–1780. That winter, the second spent at Morristown by the army, was "the most bitter and prolonged not only of the Revolution but also of the entire eighteenth century."[31] A violent snowstorm hit the region in early January, and both cattle and supply wagons found the snow-filled roads impassable.

Private Benjamin Gilbert wrote of the storm's effect on the Morristown encampment: "At 11 o'clock forenoon [January 2] it began to snow very hard . . . I lay under 4 inches of snow all night. In the morning [January 3] the snow was midleg deep in the hut. It snowed all day."[32] Repeated storms and frozen harbors made the delivery of supplies irregular, with prolonged periods between deliveries. Soldiers went without any meat for six to eight days at a time, and they often lacked bread for more than a week. "The pattern of supply throughout these months was one of acute shortage temporarily relieved by the arrival of small quantities of provisions" that barely kept the troops alive.[33]

Joseph Plumb Martin's story of the winter at Morristown is one of severe privation and danger. "The poor soldiers had hardships enough to endure without having to starve," he wrote. He was disillusioned at having to march "naked, fatigued, and starved" in winter weather from his quarters in New England to New Jersey simply in order to build "habitations to starve and suffer in."[34] Many men were exposed to snows that were 4 to 6 feet in depth with no shirts, no shoes, and no blankets. For those who were not immediately stricken, illness was never far from their minds. The death rate from starvation and disease at Morristown that winter exceeded that of the prisoners of war held by the British in the damp and cold prison hulks in Wallabout Bay.[35]

Water

Washington understood the need to provide clean, fresh water for the army. In one of the first orders (July 4, 1775) that he issued as commander in chief at Boston, he wrote: "No person is to be allowed to go to [the] fresh-water pond [for] fishing or on any other occasion as there may be a danger of introducing the small pox into the army."[36] Private Elijah Fisher noted that "the water we had to drink and to mix our flour with was out of a brook that ran along by the camp, and so many a dippin and washin [in] it . . . made it very dirty and muddy."[37]

Soldiers carried a canteen or water bottle with them as part of their kit. These items were usually made of tinned iron, but wooden canteens and leather-covered glass bottles were widely used, especially by the colonials. They usually held a quart. Orders to the contrary, little notice was taken of where the soldiers filled their canteens, but the many fast-running streams, brooks, and private wells that dotted the American countryside usually provided sufficient potable water. Dr. James Thacher noted the many "brooks, winding in every direction, among rude clefts and precipices." Although the eighteenth-century soldier had no concept of germs, the addition of rum to the water in the canteen served to kill many of the bacteria it contained. Maintaining the health of the men in this manner was mistakenly attributed to a unique ability of the rum to fortify the soldiers against disease.[38]

FORAGING

Whether British or patriot, soldiers were death to a farmstead. Acres of potatoes, cribs full of corn, fruit orchards, chicken coops, hog pens, gardens green with vegetables, and stocks of hay all went in short order once foragers arrived. Some part of the army was detailed to forage almost every day, usually protected by a detail of mounted dragoons and light infantry. Well-disposed patriot or loyalist families understood the terrible necessity of providing food for the troops who championed their cause, but they often found their larders plundered by both sides and their own families facing privation or worse. A once prosperous region could also be laid waste by runaway slaves, deserters, and other civilians searching for provision for themselves.

Joseph Plumb Martin described an incident that arose from a search for Tory refugees at Westchester, a village some miles east of the King's Bridge in Bronx County.

We found no enemy in this place, but . . . here was a plenty of good bread, milk and butter. We were hungry as Indians, and immediately "fell to, and spared not," while the man of the house held the candle and looked at us as we were devouring his eatables. I could not see his heart . . . but I could see his face and that indicated pretty distinctly what passed in his mind. He said nothing, but I believe he had as like his bread and butter had been arsenic as what it was. We cared little for his thoughts or maledictions; they did not do us half so much hurt as his victuals did us good.[39]

NOTES

1. A journal entry in Andrew J. Wahll, ed., *The Braddock Road Chronicles, 1755* (Bowie, MD: Heritage Books, 1999), 151, 154.

2. Robin May, *The British Army in North America, 1775–1783* (London: Osprey, 1997), 13–14. This was a monthly average, with fewer wagons being used in winter operations than during the rest of the year.

3. Erna Risch, *Supplying Washington's Army* (Washington, DC: U.S. Army Center of Military Studies, 1981), 66–75.

4. Ibid., 73–74.

5. Report of Quartermaster General Nicholas Biddle, November 25, 1778, quoted in ibid., 112.

6. Ibid., 41.

7. Ibid., 112.

8. James Thacher, *Military Journal of the American Revolution, 1775–1783* (Gansevoort, NY: Corner House Publishing, 1998), 162.

9. *New Jersey Gazette*, January 14, 1778.

10. Bryan Fosten, *Wellington's Light Cavalry* (London: Osprey, 1983), 25. The statistics given were for the 10th Hussars in England. Similar data for the Scots Greys, considered heavy cavalry, still evidences more than 50 percent at 15 hands or less.

11. See Brendan Morrissey, *Yorktown 1781: The World Turned Upside Down* (London: Osprey, 1997), 59.

12. James M. Volo and Dorothy Denneen Volo, *Encyclopedia of the Antebellum South* (Westport, CT: Greenwood, 2000), 172–173.

13. Risch, *Supplying Washington's Army*, 107.

14. Ibid., 64–96, 78–79n.

15. May, *The British Army*, 24.

16. Ibid., 13–14.

17. M. Dorothy George, *London Life in the Eighteenth Century* (Chicago: Academy Chicago Publishers, 1999), 165–167.

18. John Laffin, *Jack Tar* (London, Cassell, 1969), 66.

19. Risch, *Supplying Washington's Army*, 189n.

20. Ibid.

21. John C. Fitzpatrick, ed., *The Writings of George Washington*, 30 vols. (Washington, DC: n.p., 1931–1939), vol. 8, 441.

22. Risch, *Supplying Washington's Army*, 206.

23. Dorothy Dudley, *Theatrum Majorum: The Diary of Dorothy Dudley* (New York: Arno Press, 1971), 57–58.

24. Risch, *Supplying Washington's Army*, 193.

25. Ibid., 198.

26. George E. Scheer, ed., *Private Yankee Doodle* (New York: Eastern Acorn Press, 1962), 23.

27. Risch, *Supplying Washington's Army*, 196.

28. Ibid., 195.

29. Ibid., 207.

30. James Kirby Martin and Mark Edward Lender, *A Respectable Army: The Military Origins of the Republic, 1763–1789* (Arlington Heights, IL: Harlan Davidson, 1982), 101.

31. Scheer, *Private Yankee Doodle*, 169n.

32. Rebecca D. Symmes, ed., *A Citizen-Soldier in the American Revolution: The Diary of Benjamin Gilbert in Massachusetts and New York* (Cooperstown, NY: New York Historical Association, 1980), 62.

33. Risch, *Supplying Washington's Army*, 228.

34. Scheer, *Private Yankee Doodle*, 166.

35. Ibid., 288.

36. John Rhodehamel, ed., *Washington: Writings* (New York: Penguin Books, 1997), 176.

37. Risch, *Supplying Washington's Army*, 194.

38. Thacher, *Military Journal*, 163.

39. Scheer, *Private Yankee Doodle*, 140.

11

Clothing and Shelter

Soldiers, without nails, and almost without tools, except the ax and
saw, provided for their officers and themselves comfortable and convenient quarters, with little or no expense to the public.
—American Surgeon James Thacher

CLOTHING

In the eighteenth century, militiamen were expected to supply most of
their own arms, accoutrements, and clothing. This resulted in a wide
array of individualized equipment, which was practical but lacked any
hint of uniformity. Some of the militia officers may have had military
uniforms, but the common soldiers did not. George Washington silently
campaigned for the appointment as commander in chief by wearing his
provincial uniform from the French and Indian War to Congress each
day. Many officers arrived in Boston in 1775 in provincial uniforms.
Colonel William Prescott wore a dark blue uniform lapelled and faced
in a military manner. While supervising the construction of entrenchments in the heat of the day, he discarded his uniform coat and put on
a banian, a light linen coat much like a long robe. "His hat and wig were
laid aside; his bald head glistened with sweat, as he went about . . . en-
couraging his men or driving them to their labor with sharp commands."[1]

Evidence suggests that initially there was a little uniformity of dress
among the rank and file, each man wearing what he thought best for his

These are some of the very few illustrations of patriot soldiers done from life during the war. From left to right: a black soldier of the Rhode Island light infantry, an infantryman from a "hat" company, a rifle man, an artilleryman with his linstock, and a mounted light dragoon.

own comfort and circumstance. The backcountry militia companies commonly wore the same garments in which they pursued their daily life on the frontier. This would include a linen shirt and a waistcoat of wool or linen, covered with an outer garment of heavier linen known as a hunting frock, which was usually held closed with the same belt that held a knife or hatchet. The choice of wool or linen outerwear was made according to the season, but most men dispensed with woolen coats in favor of a warm woolen blanket. In an army destitute of traditional woolen uniforms, lying "on the cold and often wet ground without a blanket and with nothing but thin summer clothing was tedious."[2]

A leather ammunition pouch, a powder horn, a haversack, and a canteen were worn on straps that crossed the chest. The straps were ordinarily of white or black leather, and the soldiers carried white pipe clay or a black ball of wax to maintain their appearance. Black wax was also used on shoes, boots, and cartridge boxes as waterproofing. Ammunition was made up into cylindrical paper cartridges for ease of distribution and loading, and a powder horn, if used at all, was only for priming powder. The haversack was usually of heavy white linen. In it the soldier carried his meager lot of personal items, such as a Bible, a razor, and a bowl or cup, as well as several days' cooked or dry rations.

Headgear

A wide variety of caps, hats, and kerchiefs were used to cover the head. Most men wore broad-brimmed felt hats, either flat or turned up in a variety of ways: the civilian tricorn, the military bicorn, or a hat with the left side pinned up to stay out of the way of the musket when

Chart 11.1

Typical Equipment and Clothing for an Infantryman, Continental Army: 1777–1783

CLOTHING

Summer	Winter	Field Uniform*
Military Cocked Hat	Woolen Hat/Cap	Fatigue Cap or Round Hat
Leather Neck Stock	Woolen Scarf	Neck Cloth
Linen Shirt (2)	Woolen Sweater	Hunting Shirt
Knee Breeches or Overalls (2)	Knee Breeches or Overalls (2)	Leather or Linen Trousers
Thread Stockings (2 pr.)	Wool Stockings (1 pr.)	
Garters (1 pr.)	Garters (1 pr.)	Cloth ties (1 pr.)
Shoes (1 pr.)	Shoes (1 pr.)	Moccasins (1 pr.) Boots (officers)
Linen Waistcoat	Woolen Waistcoat	
Regimental Coat	Regimental Coat	Hunting Frock or Coatee
Canvas Gaiters, Half or Full	Woolen Gaiters	Indian Leggings or Wraps
Cloak (officers or night guards)	Cloak/Greatcoat	Capote (blanket coat)

ARMS

Firelock (musket), bayonet and bayonet carriage, cartridge box and sling, cartridges (24 to 60), hammerstall, flash guard, hatchet or tomahawk (optional), sword and sword carriage (NCOs, officers, and elite units), spontoon (NCOs)

EQUIPMENT*

Linen haversack, canteen or water bottle (1 qt.), wool blanket, knapsack, oiled ground cloth, musket tool, vent pick and brush, cleaning patches (or tow), extra flints (4), muzzle tampion, lock cover, belt or pocket knife, spoon, cup and plate, housewife (sewing kit), candles, tinderbox, mittens or gloves, ice creepers, Bible or prayer book (optional)

*Additional uniform or equipment as authorized by the regimental commanding officer.

at shoulder arms. Small-brimmed hats, known as round hats, were also popular. Knitted stocking caps of wool often sported a saying such as "Liberty" or "Liberty or Death." Americans generally eschewed the wearing of wigs, preferring to tie back their natural hair in a queue or to shave their heads. Nonetheless, some officers wore wigs, and some units were issued flour and lard with which to powder their hair for formal affairs, a common practice in the British service.

Most patriot soldiers wore some type of decoration on their hats to denote their membership in a particular unit. During the French and Indian War, the local militia unit from Norwalk, Connecticut, marching off under Captain Thomas Fitch to join the colonial forces massing in Albany, was dressed in such a variety of common workmen's clothing and civilian dress that it seemed unlike a proper military unit. The commander's sister, to provide some level of uniformity, gave each man a chicken feather for his hat. When the men arrived at the encampment, a surgeon among the British regulars took the opportunity to write a poem derisive of the colonials. This was later set to a common tavern tune, and became the song "Yankee Doodle." Ironically, during the Revolution the Americans adopted the song as an anthem illustrative of their independent spirit.[3]

The devices found on hats in the Revolution included pine branches and other forms of vegetation, colored feathers and plumes, and fabric or leather cockades. Riflemen seem to have favored some form of natural greenery. Initially most infantry units adopted a simple ribbon cockade of white, but this was deemed too much like those used in the Scottish Revolt of 1745–1746. Thereafter, black cockades made of grosgrain ribbon or dyed leather were adopted for private soldiers. Since loyalist militia often wore red cockades, the black ones came to signify the patriot forces. After the French alliance of 1778, a black cockade with a white center representing the alliance was adopted by many Continental units. The cockade was usually attached to the upturned left side of the hat with a single button in its center. Some of the elite units among the cavalry and light infantry used plumes as well as cockades to enhance the bearskin or horsehair roaches on the crests of their leather helmets.[4]

Breeches

Most eighteenth-century civilian men wore knee-length breeches, but recent research suggests that many more men wore full-length trousers, or overalls than was originally thought. In this regard "breeches" seems to have been a generic word like the word "pants" today. Most breeches were of wool or heavy linen, but leather ones were common among special troops such as cavalry, sappers, and riflemen. The breeches were exceedingly full in the seat, fitted to the leg or ankle with buttoned flaps, and could be taken in or let out with a network of laces at the back of the waistband. The front was provided with a trapdoor "fall" or a French-style button fly. Overalls were fitted to the lower leg and covered the shoe, while the knee breeches left the lower leg covered only by a knitted stocking of cotton or wool.

Footwear

Most American soldiers wore leather shoes, or moccasins of deerskin or elkskin, rather than boots. Boots, which posed difficulty in marching, seem to have been favored only by officers, cavalrymen, and other mounted personnel. Soldiers of both armies commonly covered their lower legs with linen or woolen gaiters, which wrapped about the leg and were buttoned on the outside of the calf. A strap went under the shoe to help keep them in place as they were tugged at in the mud and tall grass. Linen canvas gaiters, sometimes called spatterdashers if they were very tall, were often tarred to provide waterproofing. Woolen gaiters were used in winter to provide the lower leg with protection from the cold and snow. Backcountry volunteers often covered their lower legs with Indian leggings of wool or with "leather stockings."[5]

An eyewitness at the battle at Breed's Hill wrote of the colonial militia, "To a man, they wore small-clothes [shirt, waistcoat, and breeches], coming down and fastening just below the knee, and long stockings with cowhide shoes ornamented by large buckles, while not a pair of boots graced the company. The coats and waistcoats were loose and of huge dimensions, with colors as various as the barks of oak, sumach [*sic*] and other trees of our hills and swamps, could make them and their shirts were all made of flax, and like every other part of their dress, were homespun."[6]

Riflemen from the backcountry displayed a more unusual appearance than rural farmers and townsmen. Dorothy Dudley noted, "A company of riflemen . . . has just joined our army,—a most singular body of men, dressed in Indian costume, with brown linen hunting-jackets confined by wampum belts, leggings and moccasins elaborately trimmed with beads, and a simple round hat. Each carries a tomahawk or knife stuck in his belt, and his own unerring rifle which he brought from his home in the backwoods."[7]

Regimental Uniforms

Attempts were made to differentiate among the troops of different states in the Continental army by assigning them specific colors for their regimental uniforms. However, it proved impossible to provide formal coats of one color with military facings (lapels, collars, and cuffs) because no sufficient quantity of wool in one color could be had. Ultimately Washington divised a system that assigned different facing colors to troops from the three regions of the colonies without regard to the background color of the coat. New England states were assigned white lapels, collars, and cuffs; the middle states, red; and the southern states, light blue. Field officers wore the uniforms of their regiments. General officers and their staff were to be uniformed in dark blue woolen coats of military cut with buff facings. These distinctions were thought to facilitate a better control of the troops on the field of battle, and they attempted to duplicate the look of a European-style army with its parti-colored regimental uniforms—a propaganda need of which Washington was keenly aware.

In October 1778 a large shipment of surplus clothing and equipment arrived from France. The small clothes were all white; the military coats were blue or brown with red facings. They were assigned to the different states by lot.[8] The resulting distribution of these coats somewhat obscured the overall geographic color scheme of Continental uniforms, but the warm French uniforms relieved the dire need of the army for woolen winter clothing. The regiments were also issued heavy watchcoats of gray wool, one for every four men, to be used on picket duty. Lacking these, sentries served wrapped in blankets.

The Hunting Frock

The patriot rifle companies were drawn mainly from the backcountry of Pennsylvania, Maryland, and Virginia. They were "remarkably stout and hardy men; many of them exceeding six feet in height." Their clothing was that of the backwoodsman, failing entirely to approach anything military in style. Yet it was well suited to the vicissitudes of the weather and the physical exertion that would be expected of soldiers. Each man wore a characteristic hunting frock, or shirt, of heavy unbleached linen that had a shoulder cape and lines of fringe of the same material: "a kind of loose frock, reaching halfway down the thigh, with large sleeves, open before and so wide as to lap over a foot or more when belted." Each unit, in the absence of formal military attire, was ordered to dye its linen hunting frocks a uniform dark color, but no particular hue was designated. The order was widely ignored, leaving many frocks white, but others were dyed brown, blue, green, gray, or even purple, with both matching and contrasting fringes.[9] The Marquis de Lafayette noted that the patriot army was "ill-armed and still worse clothed. . . . [but] the best clad wore hunting-shirts [or] large grey linen coats."[10]

Washington came to appreciate the linen hunting shirt both as a practical garment and as a means of strategic deception and tactical subterfuge. The British came to associate the fringed frocks with the riflemen whom they both detested and feared, and more than once they over-estimated the lethal abilities of a force of patriots in hunting frocks by mistaking them for riflemen at a distance.

Insignia

The need to distinguish between officers and the rank and file was the subject of one of Washington's earliest general orders. Although the patriots elected their own officers, Washington was no democrat. The Continental army was not to be a mass of republican-minded citizen-soldiers commanded by "plain, russet-coated captains."[11] He wanted a modern, European-style force in which "everyone is made to know his place and keep in it."[12] Rather than simply detailing a system for denoting rank, Washington's plan was directly focused on creating a "great distinction" between the officers and the men.[13]

The commander in chief would wear a light blue sash across his breast, between his coat and waistcoat, and in like manner other general officers would wear differing colors. Major generals would wear purple; brigadiers, pink; aides-de-camp, green. Field-grade officers were to place brightly colored cockades upon their hats and sashes of silk or other fine cloth about their waists, and were to provide themselves with swords as part of the insignia of their rank. Epaulets made of metal thread were to be worn on both shoulders by senior officers, on the right shoulder only by captains, and on the left only by lieutenants. The adoption of the epaulet was not universally popular with American officers, especially those from New England, because it was regarded as a French ornament.

Many officers also sported gorgets, a kidney-shaped metal plate of silver or brass worn about the neck on a ribbon or cord as a symbol of leadership. The gorget, a European affectation based on an armored neck protector worn by knights since medieval times, was now only symbolic rather than functional. Many militia officers provided themselves with gorgets, and it was not unusual to see an officer attired in a linen hunting frock and overalls, adorned with a ruffled shirt, gorget, sword, and sash of raw silk. Native American officers, on both sides, were often given gorgets as a symbol of their authority.[14]

As in any army, noncommissioned officers, sergeants and corporals, were the backbone of the army. NCOs were relied upon to act as a positive influence on the men in camp and on the march. They were placed on the ends of each rank to maintain its alignment, and steady the men in battle. They wore the same uniform as the rank and file of their regiment. Orders regarding the details of their display of rank were issued annually, with many variations causing untold confusion among students of the period. NCOs were required to fasten strips of colored cloth on their shoulders, sometimes singly and sometimes in pairs. Red

George Washington as he appeared in his Virginia militia uniform. Note the sash and gorget.

cloth generally denoted a sergeant; blue or green, a corporal. In addition, sergeants wore woolen sashes about their waists. They often carried lightweight muskets, or fusils, with barrels slightly shorter than the average, or they sported short pole arms known as spontoons.

SHELTER

When Washington arrived at Boston in 1775, he found the patriot army housed in a wide variety of makeshift wooden and canvas shelters, which he described in a letter to Congress:

Some are made of boards, and some of sail-cloth. Some partly of one and partly of the other. Again others are made of stone and turf, brick or brush. Some are thrown up in a hurry; others curiously wrought with doors and windows, done with wreaths and withes, in the manner of a basket. Some are your proper tents and marquees, looking like the regular camp of the enemy. In these are the Rhode Islanders, who are furnished with tent-equipage, and everything in the most English style.[15]

Washington almost immediately devised a plan to erect 120 barracks near Boston, each to house 100 men. The barracks were to be 90 by 16 feet in size, and their cost was estimated at £100 each. Meanwhile, steps were taken to house the troops in private residences and public buildings. When the British evacuated Boston, the patriot militia melted back into the countryside or transferred to the city of New York. Nonetheless, barracks at Cambridge and Dorchester Heights were completed in 1776, but the owners of the land on which they were built began to dismantle the vacant buildings as early as 1779, in order to convert the lumber to their own use.

As the scene of the war shifted, Washington again became concerned with providing proper shelters in which his troops might pass the winter months of 1776–1777. Boards and shingles, bricks, stone, lime, and other materials were procured by the Quartermaster's Department, and three companies of carpenters, each consisting of 30 men, a captain, and other officers, were raised from among the soldiers of the army. Barracks were constructed for about 2000 troops near the Hudson River at Peekskill and Fishkill. Each building was 36 feet long, 19 feet wide, and had side walls 7 feet in height. However, the corps of carpenters proved too few to erect all the housing that had been planned, and more than 100 militiamen were assigned to help on the project.

Throughout the war, additional permanent barracks (as opposed to temporary wooden huts) were raised by the patriots at Trenton, Albany, West Point, and other places. Major General Schuyler wrote, "They [the soldiers] are crowded in vile barracks, which, with the natural inattention of the soldiery to cleanliness, has been productive of disease, and numbers are daily rendered unfit for duty."[16] Private Joseph Plumb Martin noted that his barracks had "rats enough, had they been men, to garrison twenty West Points."[17]

Shelter was almost nonexistent when soldiers were in the field on active campaign. Private Martin wrote:

The soldiers' whole time is spent in marches, especially night marches, watching, starving, and in cold weather, freezing and sickness. If they get any chance to rest, it must be in the woods or fields, under the side of a fence, in an orchard or in any other place but . . . a comfortable one, lying on the cold and often wet ground.[18]

Martin's journal provides detailed descriptions of how the soldiers built their own winter quarters. His regiment constructed satisfactory wooden huts in Connecticut in 1778 with little supervision from its officers. The quartermaster simply issued axes, handsaws, froes (for splitting shingles), augers (for drilling holes), mallets, and other hand tools, and set them to work. These huts had no foundations or wooden floors, and they were built directly on the ground with whole logs interlocked at the corners, in the manner of a frontier cabin.

In 1779, with the army in winter camp in Morristown for the second time, every facet of the construction process seems to have been more carefully supervised. The organization of the camp was so controlled that "no one was allowed to transgress . . . on any account whatever."[19] The huts were constructed of tree trunks notched at the corners. The spaces between the logs were filled with a mixture of clay, mud, and straw known as chinking. The roof was covered with large wooden slabs made by riving, splitting lengthwise modest lengths of green logs. Riven roofing was considered quicker and easier to make than common shingles, and it required only a skeleton of rafters for support. A timber chimney plastered in clay, or one of stone if it was available, was centered on one of the short walls, and a door or window was made by sawing through the logs. The soldiers built their own huts and those of their officers.

Sergeant Major (later Ensign) Benjamin Gilbert of Brookfield, Massachusetts, detailed the difficulty of providing a sound chimney for his hut: "We built a chimney and it smoked like the Devil." On the following day, he noted, "We altered our chimney and it carried smoke very well." A few weeks later, he wrote again, "We pulled down our chimney and began to build anew. . . . We got our chimney up so high as to build a fire [the same day]." The increased height of a chimney improved its ability to draw away the smoke that generally filled the hut from the ceiling to within a few feet of the floor. A poorly designed chimney was

The author inspects the construction of a typical soldiers' hut at Fort Lee, New Jersey. The building was destroyed by arsonists in 1999. There are plans to rebuild it on the same site.

inefficient in producing heat and left the choking men with red and watering eyes.[20]

The huts built by the troops at Morristown were 12 feet wide, 16 feet long, and had 7-foot sidewalls. They were supposed to house 12 to 18 men each. Surgeon James Thacher noted that the "soldiers, without nails, and almost without tools, except the ax and saw, provided for their officers and themselves comfortable and convenient quarters, with little or no expense to the public." The design of these huts remained the standard for winter quarters for the remainder of the war. Barracks and huts were used as winter quarters only.[21]

Tents

The active campaigning season usually began in the late spring and ran into the early winter. The soldiers were, therefore, under some sort of canvas shelter for most of the year, under a wide variety of weather conditions ranging from dry heat to wet, snowy cold. When on the move, the soldiers used a canvas wedge tent, which was carried in the baggage wagons. Sometimes called the common tent, the wedge tent was formed of sheet canvas stretched over a horizontal bar some 6 or 7 feet long, supported at both ends by an upright pole of about the same length.

An eighteenth-century illustration of the layout of a British camp. Note the neat rows of soldiers' tents and the wide spacing of those of the officers in the background. The circles in the foreground are the regimental drums.

One end of the wedge was split up the center into two flaps, which could be opened and fixed back to provide ventilation, or tied closed in foul weather. The whole tent was sewn in one piece.

The rectangular floor space of a common tent was about 6 feet square. The wedge shape, which varied somewhat between armies, usually allowed a man of medium height to stand erect only in the very center under the crossbar, but six men could easily find room to store their meager equipment and sleep on the floor.

Other fabric structures set up about the encampment might include the diminutive bell tents for protecting the stack of muskets; horsemen's tents, which were much like the wedge but had an additional area at the rear for saddles and tack; wall tents, which were used for stores, headquarters, or temporary hospitals; and marquees, which were oval in outline and usually reserved for general officers. Tents provided protection from moderate rainfall, and they broke the wind somewhat. However, they did little to shelter the men in downpours, and could be ripped from their moorings by high winds.

Mounted men carried 4-foot-squares of painted canvas to protect their horse furniture, and each foot soldier was expected to have a piece of oilcloth the size of his blanket to use as a ground cloth or makeshift sleeping bag. Their main purpose was to prevent the morning dew from

wetting everthing and to help retain the men's body heat. Special tents
of painted canvas were used for storing powder.

One of the responsibilities of the quarter guard of the army was to
ensure that the tents stayed in place in high winds. They were also expected to be the first to fight fires that might break out among the canvas
structures in the camp. For this reason cooking fires were always placed
away from the sleeping area.

There were also dangers from which cloth tents could not shelter the
troops. An NCO noted the danger of lightning in his diary for July 1,
1779:

In the afternoon we had a very hard shower of rain and extreme hard thunder
one clap of which struck in our regiment [in camp on Constitution Island] and
not one company in our regiment but that had some men hurt. . . . One man . . .
was struck dead on the spot and seven more rendered unfit for duty. There was
five and thirty that was struck. . . . After the lightning left our regiment it ran
down the road and crossed the river on the [West Point] chain up to Fort Clinton.
Struck two men there.[22]

Like many other strategically important materials in the colonies, fabric for the construction and repair of tents was in short supply. Canvas
duck was the principal textile used in the manufacture of tents, and
almost 22 yards of the material was needed to make one common tent.
As early as 1775, Congress took steps to develop a secure source of canvas. In 1776 "country linen fit for tents" was selling at the absurd price
of 3s 6d per yard. A secret committee of Congress was assigned the task
of importing canvas and stout linen sailcloth from France or Holland,
and bounties were authorized for the development of domestic sources
of hemp, flax, and cotton. Nonetheless, the stocks of textiles in the colonies were quickly used up. There was such a shortage of canvas that
some members of the Marine Committee half-jokingly feared that the
ships of the navy might be "stripped of sails so that the soldiers might
have tents."[23]

Many of the army's tents were lost during the evacuation of New York
in 1776 because of a lack of transportation. The shortage was made worse
when the reserve store of tents at Danbury, Connecticut, was burned by
the British in 1777. Washington shortly thereafter authorized the use of
wedge tents only. This allowed "one soldier's tent for the field officers
of each regiment, one for every four commissioned officers, one for eight
sergeants, drummers, and fife players, and one for every eight privates."[24]

Thereafter, the number of men assigned to each tent fluctuated between six and eight, and while this seems a crowded condition, the space
allotted by this system was not unreasonable. It must be remembered

that at least one-third of the army was constantly on guard duty, and the ranks of the men became thinner as the campaign season continued, due to sickness and battle casualties. Although six to eight men may have drawn a single tent at the beginning of the campaign, as few as four privates may have actually had to share it at any time. An NCO noted in June 1779, "I drawed a tent [all] to myself [because] Sergeant Wing went to hospital." In 1781, a conservative estimate showed that 3000 tents were available for the American army of 12,000, and Washington's army of 5000 at Yorktown had a total of 2000 common tents to share among them.[25]

CAMP LIFE

The science of setting up an encampment was called castramentation, derived from castra, the Latin word for a camp. An officer from each regiment was designated as the castramentation officer. He had the task of finding suitable ground, from within the area that the army commander chose, for the encampment of his regiment. A standard plan of encampment by brigade was followed, but some regiments with less able officers were always allotted poor, wet, or rocky ground. The regimental camp was broken down into long lanes or streets of tents. In the textbook scheme the NCOs were given positions at the ends of the company streets, and the lowest-ranking officers were billeted some small distance from the troops in order to maintain social distinction and inhibit fraternization. By this method a hierarchy of housing passed through the entire camp, with the highest-ranking officers placed farther and farther from the troops, but always within easy access to them. The artillery, cavalry, and riflemen had camps of their own, separate from the line troops.

Private Joseph Plumb Martin provided evidence that the grand scheme of company streets set out in a grid was not always followed.

At a place in New Jersey called Basking Ridge . . . it was cold and snowy; we had to march all day through the snow and at night take up our lodgings in some wood[s], where, after shoveling away the snow, we used to pitch three or four tents facing each other, and then join in making a fire in the center. Sometimes we could procure an armful of buckwheat straw to lie upon, which was deemed a luxury.[26]

Soldiers also took the step of raising their tents off the ground and filling the space between the canvas and the ground with flagstones or pieces of sod. Sergeant Major Gilbert noted that although orders were issued against the practice, "We raised our tent two foot from the ground and made walls with flaggs."[27] Gilbert was a sergeant at the time (1778), and his diary repeatedly noted the raising of tents with "flaggs" and "boards." Moreover, he noted, in April 1778: "We built a chimney to our tent."[28] Certainly the individualization of the common tents must have distracted from the orderly lines of tents suggested by the regulations.

Diversions

The regimen of daily life in the camps allowed little in the way of free time. Drill, fatigue duty, cutting trees and brush, collecting firewood and water, foraging, and service at the outposts consumed most of the soldiers' day. Just keeping warm and supplied with dry clothes required a great deal of effort. Nonetheless, individuals and groups did find some time for entertaining activities. Writing letters and journals, reading, whittling, and drawing were common entertainments. Simple musical instruments were played in camp. Games such as checkers (draughts), chess, and dice were popular with small groups, as were card games. Board games, common in civilian life, were often drawn on a simple piece of canvas, and stones, bones, and corncobs served as game pieces. Gambling was strictly forbidden by the Articles of War, but the prohibition was almost impossible to enforce. Dorothy Dudley, who lived in camp with the patriot army, noted in her diary, "There has been a good deal of card playing and gambling of various kinds. The enforced quiet of the soldiers has been irksome, and they enliven the monotony in any way they can devise."[29]

Cleanliness

The patriot army was often described, even by its own officers, as filthy and nearly naked. This should not be taken too literally by students of the period. An eighteenth-century man was considered naked if he appeared in public dressed only in his smallclothes. Certainly the patriots were ragged in their appearance, but they probably had more of their bodies covered than most persons who are considered fully clothed today. No free white male of the eighteenth century would appear in public in his shirtsleeves without a waistcoat. Those doing heavy work wore a smock or apron. Only slaves and indentured servants appeared in their shirts, and it was improper for even male slaves to go without shirts.

Personal cleanliness was a serious and ongoing problem in the army. Eighteenth-century persons tolerated a good deal more dirt, grime, and odor than people today. Outer clothing was brushed or sponged clean rather than washed. The bedding used by the soldiers was made of straw-filled ticking fabric that seemingly bred vermin and lice. Young John Greenwood noted in his journal:

Barracks life as it is portrayed at Fort Stanwix in Rome, New York. The folks in the foreground are playing draughts (checkers).

I had the itch so bad that my breeches stuck to my thighs, all the skin being off. There were hundreds of vermin on me owing to a whole month's march and having been obliged for the sake of keeping warm to lie down at night among the soldiers who were huddled close together like hogs ... When I arrived at my father's house in Boston, the first thing done was to bake my clothes [in the oven to destroy the vermin] and then to annoint [*sic*] me all over with brimstome [powdered sulfur].[30]

Soap was issued to each regiment as part of the weekly ration. The men were expected to use the soap not only to clean their bodies but also to launder their smallclothes. For every 100 men, 24 pounds of soft soap or 8 pounds of hard soap was issued weekly, an allowance that fell well below what which was needed to maintain cleanliness. The soldiers also sold their allowance of soap in the countryside to obtain additional foodstuffs. Washington issued numerous orders on sanitation, health, and the policing of the camps and barracks. "His soldiers, however, persisted in being woefully oblivious of the need to maintain sanitary surroundings."[31]

Health

The sciences of medicine and health care were in a woefully backward state in the eighteenth century. Many of the most closely held precepts of medicine, such as bleeding victims to produce a cure, were rooted in erroneous or fanciful premises concerning how the human body worked. Moreover, the concept of germs as the cause of infection was unknown, and infection was thought to be associated with bad odors and mists that crept along the ground. With sober sincerity, doctors pronounced miasmic fogs the cause of epidemic diseases. Visual cleanliness and an inoffensive smell were considered adequate in terms of sanitation, and pleasing fragrances were thought to balance out the evil effects of offensive odors.

Disease was the great killer of soldiers in eighteenth-century armies. Fever and dysentery were more dangerous than firearms and bayonets, and generals feared that sickness would overcome their armies in the field. For this reason the patriot army—at least the Continentals—was inoculated against smallpox by 1777. This procedure should not be confused with the modern form of inoculation. All those soldiers who had not previously been exposed to the disease where given a mild case by having the scabs of a man infected with cowpox rubbed into scatches made on their skin. This commonly caused a few pockmarks, a mild fever, and a temporary disability. The inoculation itself was dreaded by the men, who did not properly understand the process, but it was seldom fatal among men in good health. The precaution taken by the patriots was a major innovation in military science and an advancement in health care.

The most feared epidemic disease for an army, however, was "putrid fever" or "camp fever," which was typically a form of typhoid or typhus passed through the water supply. There was no inoculation for this, and doctors had no clue to the source. Other diseases, such as scurvy, pleurisy, pneumonia, and the "bloody flux" seem to have decimated the army periodically. Surgeon James Thacher noted, "Their diseases . . . are so malignant, that it is feared they will baffle all the skill of the physician." Sulfur was sometimes burned to fumigate the huts, and items were washed in vinegar in an effort to stem the spread of these diseases.[32]

Scurvy, most common among seamen, also attacked the army. It was thought to originate from a prolonged diet of highly salted provisions and bad water. In fact, the main cause of scurvy was a deficiency of vitamin C, which could be made up by adding fresh vegetables and fruits to the diet. It was a terribly disabling affliction, and without treatment could cause death. William Hutchinson experienced the ravages of the disease and lived to write about it. His descriptions of its symptoms are some of the most graphic recorded in the eighteenth century.

I found myself taken with a pain under my left breast . . . [M]y armpits and hams grew black but did not swell, and I pined away to a weak, helpless condition, with my teeth all loose, and my upper and lower gums swelled and clotted together like a jelly, and they bled to that degree, that I was obliged to lie with my mouth hanging over the side of my bunk, to let the blood run out. . . . [W]ith fresh provisions and fomentations of herbs I got well . . . in eighteen days.[33]

Hospitals and Care of the Sick

Wounded men, without the benefits of any painkillers save rum, faced a miserable end if infection or gangrene set in. Heavy, slow-moving bullets shattered the bones of arms and legs, injuries requiring amputation. Brave fellows whose skulls proved "too thick for a ball to penetrate" might linger in extreme agony with "no parent, wife or sister, to wipe the tear of anguish from their eyes, or to soothe the pillow of [inevitable] death."[34] Soldiers prayed to be killed cleanly in battle rather than return with a major wound. The child's saying "Cross my heart and hope to die," was originally a soldier's prayer for a quick death on the battlefield by a bullet aimed at the straps of his equipment crossing his chest. One man, having received an apparently nonfatal bayonet wound to the thigh, died in agony three years later of the infection that set in. Nonetheless, Dr. Thacher noted that if the "patient is athletic and has not sustained a very copious loss of blood . . . he [might] eventually recover, which is to be ascribed principally to the free use of the lancet [bleeding] and such abstemious living [fasting] as to reduce him to the greatest extremity."[35]

Thacher described a military field hospital at the battle of Saratoga, staffed by 30 surgeons and their assistants:

This hospital is now crowded with officers and soldiers from the field of battle; those belonging to the British and Hessians, are accommodated in the same hospital with our own men, and receive equal care and attention. The foreigners are under the care and management of their own surgeons. . . . The English surgeons perform with skill and dexterity, but the Germans, with few exceptions, do no credit to their profession. . . . [being] uncouth and clumsey . . . [and] destitute of all sympathy and tenderness towards the suffering patient. Amputating limbs, trepanning fractured skulls, and dressing the most formidable wounds . . . a military hospital is particularly calculated to afford examples for profitable contemplation, and to interest our sympathy and commiseration. . . . Mutilated bodies, mangled limbs and bleeding, incurable wounds [are] no less revolting . . . [than the] miserable object languishing under afflicting diseases of every description . . . the awful harbingers of approaching dissolution [death].[36]

Nursing

There was no formal corps of nurses (male or female) to staff the hospitals. Surgeons' mates did all they could in this regard. Following an

outbreak of smallpox among the troops, Washington ordered commanding officers of regiments to "assist Regimental Surgeons in procuring as
many women of the army as can be prevailed on to serve as nurses."
He also noted that they would be "paid the usual price," suggesting that
there was at least an informal arrangement for nursing staff.[37]

General Washington also specified the duties to be performed by these
women:

The nurses, in the absence of the [surgeons'] mates, administer the medicine and
diet prescribed for the sick according to order; they obey all orders they receive
from the matron; not only to be attentive to the cleanliness of the wards and
patients, but to keep themselves clean; they are never to be disguised with liquor;
they are to see that the close-stools or pots are . . . emptied as soon as possible
after they are used. . . . [T]hey are to see that every patient, upon his admission
into the hospital is immediately washed with warm water; and that his face and
hands are washed and head combed every morning . . . that their wards are
swept over every morning or oftener if necessary and sprinkled with vinegar
three or four times a day; nor are they ever to be absent without leave from the
physicians, surgeons, or matron.[38]

NOTES

1. Christopher Ward, *The War of the Revolution* (New York: Macmillan, 1952),
81.

2. Jack Coggins, ed., *Boys in the Revolution: Young Americans Tell Their Part in
the War for Independence* (Harrisburg, PA: Stackpole Books, 1967), 73.

3. Norwalk, Connecticut, claims the distinction of being the home of Yankee
Doodle. A local bridge, part of Interstate 95, is known as the Yankee Doodle
Bridge.

4. North Callahan, *Royal Raiders: The Tories of the American Revolution* (New
York: Bobbs-Merrill, 1963), 95.

5. David Hackett Fischer, *Albion's Seed: Four British Folkways in America* (New
York: Oxford University Press, 1989), 732–733.

6. Ward, *War of the Revolution*, 78.

7. Dorothy Dudley, *Theatrum Majorum: The Diary of Dorothy Dudley* (New
York: Arno Press, 1971), 28.

8. The blue initially went to troops from North Carolina, New Jersey, New
York, and Maryland, and both colors were distributed to those from Delaware,
Pennsylvania, Massachusetts, Virginia, and New Hampshire. The Canadian reg-
iment of Colonel Moses Hazen drew brown.

9. Fischer, *Albion's Seed*, 732–733.

10. Ward, *War of the Revolution*, 559.

11. Simon Schama, *A History of Britain: The Wars of the British: 1603–1776* (New
York: Hyperion, 2001), 197.

12. Ward, *War of the Revolution*, 104.

13. Ibid., 104.

14. Ibid., 559.

15. Erna Risch, *Supplying Washington's Army* (Washington, DC: U.S. Army Center of Military Studies, 1981), 140.

16. Ibid., 145.

17. Ibid., 146.

18. Coggins, *Boys in the Revolution*, 76.

19. George E. Scheer, ed., *Private Yankee Doodle* (New York: Eastern Acorn Press, 1962), 168.

20. Rebecca D. Symmes, ed., *A Citizen-Soldier in the American Revolution: The Diary of Benjamin Gilbert in Massachusetts and New York* (Cooperstown, NY: New York Historical Association, 1980), 60–61.

21. Risch, *Supplying Washington's Army*, 150.

22. Symmes, *A Citizen-Soldier*, 54.

23. Risch, *Supplying Washington's Army*, 147.

24. Ibid., 148.

25. Symmes, *A Citizen-Soldier*, 53.

26. Scheer, *Private Yankee Doodle*, 166.

27. Symmes, *A Citizen-Soldier*, 53.

28. Ibid., 29.

29. Dudley, *Theatrum Majorum*, 57.

30. Coggins, *Boys in the Revolution*, 45–46.

31. Risch, *Supplying Washington's Army*, 193.

32. James Thacher, *Military Journal of the American Revolution, 1775–1783* (Gansevoort, NY: Corner House Publishing, 1998), 145.

33. William Hutchinson, *A Treatise on Naval Architecture* (Liverpool: T. Billinge, 1794), 286–289.

34. Thacher, *Military Journal*, 113.

35. Ibid., 255.

36. Ibid., 112–113.

37. John C. Fitzpatrick, ed., *Writings of Washington*, vol. 9 (Washington, DC: U.S. Government Printing Office, 1933), 497.

38. Ray Raphael, *A People's History of the American Revolution* (New York: New Press, 1991), 110–111.

12

Tory, Refugee, Traitor, Spy

Had I been a magistrate, I would, at every hazzard, have interposed my authority in suppression of the outrage. But this was not the only instance which convinced me that I wanted the nerves for a revolutionist.

—Alexander Graydon, a Loyalist

WHIGS AND TORIES

For the great majority of Anglo-Americans, loyalty to the king, Parliament, and the traditions of British government was the "normal condition" of political life. Some historians believe that the Whig, or Patriot, Party in America aspired to make changes in the social order and attempted to convert the ordinary citizen into a revolutionary. However, Whig political principles were not novel. They were deeply rooted in the old traditions of Magna Carta, the Grand Remonstrance, the Declaration of the Rights of Englishmen, and the political philosophies of Thomas Hobbes, John Milton, and John Locke. All the British ministries of the Revolutionary period were ostensibly those of the Whig Party. However, the American Whigs had so far outstripped the Whig Party in Britain, in terms of the evolution of their political thought, that those in England found it difficult to understand the actions of those in America.[1]

The Tory Party was founded in large measure on "the aristocracy of culture, of dignified professions, of official rank and hereditary wealth."

Supporting the Tories were many of the most substantial businessmen, the richest landowners, the clergy of the established church, and the legally appointed officers of the empire. The Tories had only briefly controlled Parliament in 1762–1763, but they had the ear of the king. American Tories exhibited the "natural conservatism of all prosperous men," to maintain the stability and dominance of the system that had proved the foundation of their own power or wealth—in this case the government of King George III.

Possibly due to the natural reticence that sometimes accompanies a secure place in the establishment of an unquestioned social prominence, the Tories in America did not come forward to be heard until after the Revolution touched them personally, depriving them of their property or dislocating them from their homes.[2] The editor of *Rivington's Gazetteer*, James Rivington, wrote that the Tory Party had been unfairly "censured for remissness in not having exerted themselves sufficiently" during the earliest days of the troubles between the colonies and Parliament. "The truth of the case was that they saw and shuddered at the gathering storm, but durst not attempt to dispel it lest it should burst on their own heads."[3]

The Tories "rested content in a state of indolence and languid inactivity," failing to enlist in volunteer companies of like-minded persons and take up arms, as had those who had aligned themselves with the rebellion. They simply relied, as they had in the past, on the bureaucracy of government to maintain the status quo, and on the British regulars to fight their fight. When they finally took up arms, many of their military operations were misdirected, ineffective, and uncoordinated because they failed to develop an effective leadership and a strong organization of their own.[4] British army officials deemed the initial response to rebellion "unwisely left too much in Tory hands."[5]

Loyalists

Many Americans were loyal because they feared to join the revolution; others, because they disagreed with its aims. Many feared "how helpless the Colonies would be against the invasion of a foreign power if there were no protection by the mother country."[6] Some persons were loyal because their family or friends chose the side of the king; others, because their personal or political enemies had chosen to be rebels. Family loyalty and kinships bonds were very important in determining which side, if any, an individual chose; and political feuds and personal antagonisms often carried more weight than the more insubstantial issues of taxation, representation, and the rights of Englishmen.

Some historians believe that the loyalists in America numbered up to one third of the population. This estimate is largely based upon a comment made by John Adams, who calculated that one third of Americans were Tories, another third Whigs, and the rest undecided. There may have been as many as 100,000 loyalists in New York state alone, and little Delaware was home to more than 20,000. But these were the bastions of loyalism in America in terms of numbers. Half of New Jersey may have been loyal, but the pockets of loyalism were scattered, geographically isolating most Tory sympathizers. In New England, loyalism was all but exterminated by 1776, and the absolute number of loyalists in the less populous southern colonies, though considerable, was never as great as the Crown's best estimates.[7]

While it is certain that many loyalists helped the British during the war in the matters of supply, manpower, and information, there is no evidence that active loyalism was as widely practiced as John Adams seemed to suggest. It seems certain, in fact, that the radicals among both patriots and loyalists were a minority of positive and determined men who represented the extremes of either position. Between them lay the "wavering neutral masses ready to move unresistingly in the direction given by the success of either Whig or Tory."[8]

In 1775 a desperate attempt was made in New York to arouse loyalist sentiment against the patriot Congress. The city had served as the headquarters for the British army since the French wars, and its commercial interests were closely allied to those of a stable and legitimate government. This gave the loyalist movement in New York the support of an established garrison and the strength of the city's financial interests. The many refugee families flocking to the city for protection may have given the British a false impression of the overall number of loyal colonials, which would help to explain their constant hope that overwhelming numbers would turn out to support their military operations.

Test Oaths

Many undecided colonials were required by the rebels to take a test oath, and all who equivocated were bound over to the patriot controlled courts for trial. Most of these proceedings were carried out "under the form of the law,"[9] but political, legal, and civil disabilities were the "invariable results" of a refusal to take the oath. Imprisonment, special taxation, and confiscation of property and arms were among the common penalties imposed in various states.[10] By the summer of 1776, the Tory was "no longer regarded as a political opponent to be coerced, but as a traitor deserving retributive justice."[11] Major William Pierce, a southern patriot, wrote, "The two opposite principles of Whiggism and Toryism have set the people of this country to cutting each other's throats, and scarce a day passes but some poor deluded Tory is put to death at his door."[12] A patriot soldier who found loyalists "obnoxious," when asked if he would "murder" loyalist refugees if he found them, answered, "It is impossible to commit murder [on] refugees."[13]

A humorist among the Tory masses penned a parody of Hamlet's soliloquy that served to demonstrate the pitiable position into which some loyalists were placed when faced with the test oaths:

> To sign or not to sign, that is the question
> Whether 'twere better for an honest man
> To sign, and be so safe; or to resolve,
> Betide what will, against associations.
> And by retreating shun them. To fly—I reck
> Not where; and by that flight, t'escape
> Feather and tar and thousand other ills
> That loyalty is heir to; 'Tis a consumation
> Devoutly to be wished.[14]

Hector St. John de Crevecoeur, a Frenchman married to an Anglo-American girl, anguished over the dilemma presented to him by the choice of loyalty to the traditional forms of monarchical rule or to the "innovations" of democracy offered by the revolutionaries.

How easily do men pass from loving, to hating and cursing one another! I am a lover of peace. . . . If I attach myself to the Mother Country, which is 3,000 miles from me, I become what is called an enemy to my own region; if I follow the rest of my countrymen, I become opposed to our ancient masters: both extremes appear equally dangerous. . . . What can an insignificant man do in the midst of these jarring contradictory parties, equally hostile to persons situated as I am?[15]

The Tory Menace

When the British evacuated Boston, they took with them to Halifax "102 officials of the Crown, 18 clergymen, 105 rural residents, 213 mechanics and similar tradesmen, as well as some 382 farmers."[16] However, many of those deemed Tories by the radical patriots remained behind or fled to New York. Samuel Adams wrote to another patriot, Dr. James Warren, describing his feelings about those with Tory sympathies remaining in America.

In my opinion, much more is to be apprehended from the secret machinations of these rascally people than from the open violence of British and Hessian soldiers, whose success has been in a great measure owing to the aid they have received from them. . . . Indeed, my friend, if measures are not soon taken, and the most vigorous ones, to root out these pernicious weeds, it will be in vain for America to presevere in this generous struggle for the public liberty.[17]

A late nineteenth-century historian summarized the reaction of the loyalist refugees to being hounded from their homes and businesses. "[W]ith nothing to do, [they] needed no tempter to find reckless things for their idle tongues to say. One hoped that the rebels would swing for it; another wanted to see the blood streaming from the hearts of the leaders, but would be content to see them become turnspits in the kitchen of some English noble." Madame Higginson, a Tory noted for her lack of self-restraint, declared that it would be "a joy to ride through American blood to the hubs of her chariot wheels." Loyalist rhetoric demanded that the patriot leaders be put to the sword, and those in rebellion have their houses destroyed and their possessions plundered. "It is just that they should be the first victims to the mischief they have brought upon us."[18]

Many fighting men were recruited by the British from among this displaced, ill-disposed, and merciless population, and it is not surprising that loyalist regiments were associated with many of the atrocities that came to characterize the war.[19] As many as 8,000 men volunteered to serve in Loyal American units or on loyalist privateers. Most were hard fighting, dependable, and generally effective as soldiers. "The refugees possessed a zeal which, with their intimate knowledge of the country, rendered them very useful" to the Crown.[20]

More New Yorkers fought for George III than for George Washington. The refugees in New York supplied as least 15,000 recruits to the regular British regiments and the warships of the Royal Navy. New York supplied more troops to the British cause than any other city in America or Europe, about 25,000 in total. "All of the remaining colonies furnished about as many more, so that we may safely state that 50,000 soldiers, either regulars or militia, were drawn into the service of Great Britain." These represented fully half of the Crown forces in America, making the Revolution more of a civil war between Americans than a war of independence from Britain.[21]

THE PLIGHT OF THE REFUGEES

The terrors of civil war always create refugees on both sides, and the Revolution was no different from other civil wars in this respect. Thousands of loyalists sat out the war in the British-held urban centers of America because they had nowhere else to go. If they could, loyalists flocked to the British strongholds in the cities, especially New York, where their number "constantly grew in size and in hopeless dependence."[22] As winter approached in 1777, hundreds of women and children arrived at the refugee camps, being "friends of the government" fleeing the persecution of the rebels. "They were sent off by order of the committees, councils of safety &c. with little more than their wearing apparel,

A contemporary illustration of the great New York fire of 1776.

being robbed of their furniture, cattle, &c. and their farms given to strangers."[23]

The New York Fire

A great shortage of housing in the city of New York was made worse by an immense fire, said to have been set by patriot arsonists, that completely destroyed one thousand buildings in the city in late 1776. According to Ambrose Serle, General Howe's secretary, "Some rebels . . . were caught with matches and fire-balls about them. One man, detected in the act, was knocked down by a Grenadier [and] thrown into the flames for his reward." A strong wind increased the rapidity of the flames' spread, which "extended in a line for almost the length of a mile . . . in a vast conflagration." The whole British military garrison and the sailors from the fleet were called out to aid the municipal fire department, but they could not suppress the fire until a third of the city was in ashes. Many more buildings were severely damaged. St. Paul's Church was spared, but Trinity Church was destroyed.[24]

Many women and children were said to have perished in the fire, and many residents lost all their possessions. The extent of the fire created a serious shortage of bedding, clothing, furniture, and household implements, and it destroyed many of the warehouses, shops, and workplaces that might have furnished replacements. Lumber and building materials were thereafter held at a premium, and patriot control of the hinterland made their importation difficult.

There were 21,000 residents in the city of New York in 1775. By February 1777 this figure had grown by 11,000, not including the army. These could not be crowded into less than 2000 remaining structures. Moreover, because of the extraordinary number of inhabitants imposed on the British administration, loyalist refugees were allocated little in the way of firewood, food, candles, or clothing. A rebuilding project was undertaken, but it was delayed by the effects of unremitting graft and corruption. The general feeling among the loyalists was that more money should have been spent on the relief of their more immediate sufferings. Dependent refugee families were often left destitute because their men were away on duty with a Tory regiment. Although the families of volunteers received half rations from the army while they served, no system for forwarding a husband's military pay to his wife was in place. Many loyal husbands and sons were incarcerated in rebel jails with no provision made for their loved ones' survival. Charitable subscriptions for the refugees were taken up among the residents of the city, but as the war dragged on, it seemed the wiser course for most New Yorkers to maintain the meager remnants of their wealth as a contingency against British defeat.

The Camps

Many of the permanent residents of Manhattan wanted the refugees out of the way. Left with little hope of finding decent lodgings in the city, the refugees resorted to living in shacks, huts, or other improvised shelters in the "camps" in the Bronx. The camps were described as "wretched" and "deplorable," but they did have a dependable supply of firewood and fresh water. The former estate of the patriot merchant Robert Morris, known as Morrisania, held one of the largest concentrations of loyalist refugees in all the colonies save Halifax, Nova Scotia.[25]

British General Samuel Graham placed the camps "where a stream runs [the East River], separating New York from the mainland." He further wrote, "A considerable space of ground outside the lines was occupied by . . . the loyal refugees [who] had taken up their abode in the deserted farmhouses, from whence they continually sent out foraging parties."[26] Lieutenant John von Krafft, a Hessian officer, wrote, "All the wood for fuel, building and fortifying was procured in Morrisania, a piece of land back of number 8 redoubt which once belonged to a Rebel Colonel. In his fine house not far from our camp the Generals were in the habit of lodging. . . . Among the [refugees] that arrived there were some unfortunate persons of high social rank."[27]

Another concentration of refugee families was in Queens County. "All

The camps were filled with refugee families who were forced to spend great amounts of time outdoors, cooking, washing, and caring for themselves. These reenactors are dressed for late November weather.

the women and children belonging to the regiments [the Loyal Americans] . . . had quarters given them on Long Island at Flesching-Fleg [Flushing]." Because the camps were located just within the fringe of British control, they were, on occasion, openly attacked by patriot forces. They were not without defenses, however. Flushing had its Loyal American Regiment and Morrisania served as a base for De Lancey's Refugee Corps. In many cases the patriots used the presence of these units as an excuse for attacking the camps. Nonetheless, husbands and sons, who enlisted as soldiers in an effort to regain their property from the rebels by helping in its reconquest, were often swept away from their families by an army administration whose view of the war effort often encompassed a broader geographical conflict than the volunteers had imagined. Von Krafft reported that the women and children refugees at Morrisania and Flushing were simply left behind when "the regiments . . . sailed for South Carolina" with the rest of the British army.[28]

If a refugee woman lost her husband to the fates of war, she was under some constraint to find herself a new spouse or risk being taken off the rations list by a callous army administration. Certain soldiers took advantage of the dire predicament of these desparate women. Von Krafft, who himself secretly married Miss Cornelia de la Metre, the daughter of a refugee widow living at Kingsbridge, reported, "A certain sergeant of

[an] English regiment, a handsome fellow, had been married sixteen times to women of the town by different English and German chaplains, through shrewd contrivances, without the consent of his officers and told me that he hoped to do so again, before making up his mind to take the last one in earnest."[29]

Prostitution

A city the size of New York normally supported a small population of harlots. However, crowding a financially desitute population of helpless women together with a restless mass of soldiers without wives almost ensured that prostitution would become epidemic. Many women refugees, and even teenage girls, were reported by contemporary observers to have taken up prostitution, selling themselves to the soldiers in order to survive. The dire circumstances of these desperate women can not be understated, nor should a quick moral judgment be made of their behavior by persons unafflicted by similar levels of destitution and need. The permanent residents of the city, however, often incorrectly regarded such amorous economics as simply opportunism.[30]

Ironically, an area of the city near the remnants of Trinity Church, misnamed the Holy Ground, became a prime location for prostitution, and the residents of the district were described as "impudent, immodest, and brutal." Many orders were issued admonishing the men to keep out of the way of temptation and "to avoid lewd women."[31] Lieutenant Von Krafft was generally disappointed in the behavior of both the men and the women in these circumstances. "I chiefly despised them for their imprudence, when I saw what promiscuous exchanges were made."[32] A typical punishment for a couple caught trading in promiscuity was that the woman would be "well watered under a pump, and every officer and soldier . . . tried and punished by court-martial."[33]

Municipal Corruption

When Sir Guy Carleton took command of the New York garrison in April 1782, he opened a vigorous offensive against all kinds of corruption in the city. The refugee population considered a great number of minor British officals to be dishonest in their dealings with them. These included persons responsible for rebuilding the city, and for providing food and temporary shelter for the refugees. A small army of bureaucrats had flourished under the military government, including barracks masters, land commissioners, building inspectors, livestock feeders, hay collectors, hay weighers, timber commissioners, lumber inspectors, firewood and charcoal inspectors, provisions providers, and ration deliverers. The loyalist population of the city praised Carleton for "clean[ing] out the entire group of leeches."[34]

By the end of the war most loyalists had suffered the confiscation of their property, disenfranchisement, dislocation, or social isolation at the hands of the rebels. Intoxicated by their victory over Britain, the patriots drove the most determined elements among the remaining loyalists from the country. At least 7000 left the city of New York when the last remnants of the British army took ship for Halifax in 1783. In October 1783, Parliament made a small provision for the loyal Americans who served with the British army or in the refugee regiments. Each officer was entitled to receive 1500 acres of land in Canada, and each private, 50 acres. "Those that had lost any part of their property and could give sufficient proof thereof, were to receive apart from [the land], royal compensation, but not to exceed £2000." In this way all but the most wealthy loyalists were indemnified for their financial losses, but not for the personal pain brought about by dislocation, upheaval, or the loss of loved ones.[35]

THE NEUTRAL GROUND

The patriots held all of New England and the region from the Hudson Highlands of New York to the Canadian border after 1778. The British commanded Manhattan, much of the Bronx, and all of Staten Island and Long Island. Much of present-day Westchester County thereby became "neutral ground." Both armies attempted to patrol the disputed region in order to use its resources as an open larder for provisions. Once the southern colonies became the main focus of the war about 1779, the neutral ground evolved into a region constantly upset by the small war, the *petite guerre*, which provided continual conflict until the British evacuation in 1783.

Small combined detachments of mounted and dismounted troops, composed of regulars, militia, or loyalists from both armies, swept the area, confiscating livestock and forage, and offering battle to any willing enemy force with which they came in contact. James Thacher noted, "This vicinity is constantly harassed by small parties of volunteers on our side, and parties of Royalists and Tories on the other, who are making every effort to effect mutual destruction; seeking every opportunity to beat up each other's quarters, and to kill or capture all who are found in arms. This is to be considered a very hazardous situation; it requires the utmost vigilance to guard against surprise."[36]

The neutral ground was also the haunt of loyalist "cowboys" and patriot "skinners"—so named because of their affinity for stealing livestock and robbing persons of their goods along the highways, respectively. These persons, usually in small groups of less than a half dozen, fought a partisan war of their own. The Whig propaganda charged that the royal authorities in the city, "heartily fatigued with having so many importunate hungry Tories hanged upon them, have come to a kind of compromise with these wretches. They are now to prowl for their own living and maintain their families by plunder and robbery."[37]

However, evidence suggests that most of the cowboys and skinners were mere miscreants, "banditti and villains," who lacked any true form of fidelity to either cause. They stole horses and cattle "under some pretense," and drove them across either the British or the American lines, where they accepted pay in "coveted specie" from either the British or the patriots. Preserved meats, root vegatables, and other provisions were quickly confiscated by either group for its own use, leaving the residents of the neutral ground destitute of food for the winter. So common were theft and countertheft that loyalist residents in patriot-controlled areas "were obliged to make good all robberies committed within their county, and they were specially taxed for the purpose."[38]

Such actions were often overlooked by American authorities as resulting from "excessive zeal" when patriot soldiers were treating with "Tories and other suspected persons."[39] Moreover, local Committees of Safety officially "appropriated loyalist property for Continental purposes" by cutting timber, herding livestock, or gathering in hay, grain, or fruit found on Tory lands under the terms of impressment legislation, which promised future payment. However, as the war progressed, the tendency of the patriots to simply confiscate loyalist property became "less restrained," and many Tory estates were simply declared "forfeited altogether."[40] Some efforts were made by the committees to prevent individuals from plundering the loyalists for their own benefit, but the legal disposition of loyalist property was such that "if the revolution succeeded, the proceeds would fall to the coffers of the state."[41]

AN ARMY OF PHANTOMS

The British had no idea that a regional conflict begun in Boston in 1775 would spread so quickly through all the colonies. One of the important strategic failures of the British was that they waited too long to actively support the loyalist population in the other colonies, particularly those in the South. In the first months of the war almost 1,000 loyalists were raised in North Carolina among the Scots who had settled there. Dressed in their kilts and marching to the skirl of bagpipes, they swore a special oath of loyalty to the king before the royal governor. Most of these loyal Scots resided in just eight counties of North Carolina, the only ones in the colony to send no representatives to the Continental Congress. An additional smaller number of loyalists responded with less ceremony to Lord Dunmore's call for support in Virginia.

However, these loyalists rallied too soon and in numbers too small to resist the frenzy of the rebels without the support of British regulars. At the battle of Great Bridge in Virginia in December 1775, almost half of the 400 British troops involved were Scottish loyalists. They were soundly defeated by the patriot militia. Thereafter, Lord Dunmore evacuated as many loyal persons as possible to the ships of the Royal Navy in Norfolk. These loyalists left with him when he abandoned the colony. Over 1000 North Carolina patriots under Col. James Moore blocked the march of 1500 loyal Scots at a bridge over Moore's Creek near the Cape Fear River in February 1776. The Scots were bravely led by Col. Donald McLeod, and they attacked the entrenchments of the patriots with a variety of firearms, broadswords, and dirks, bagpipes resounding over the gunfire. The battle "lasted three minutes," with 50 Scots killed, including McLeod, hundreds of loyalists captured, and the remainder scattered to the frontier regions. This patriot victory shattered any strength that the Tories could muster in the South for some time.[42]

For several years small groups of loyalists managed only sporadic victories like that at Thomas Swamp, Florida, but with the war in the Northeast in stalemate, the British once again turned their efforts south, taking Savannah in December 1778. There might still be enough loyal Americans in the South to overwhelm the rebels. If the British regulars showed strong support for the loyalists, royal authority in the South might be completely reestablished. The patriots sent a force of 2000 men into South Carolina after the fall of Savannah to regain the initiative. They were met by an equally determined force of 700 loyalists, many of whom were refugees or persons who had "joined [the British] after their first successes." Caught by the Americans, commanded by Colonel Andrew Pickens, at Kettle Creek in Georgia, the loyalists were mercilessly butchered. In less than an hour 40 loyalists were killed and 75 captured. The rest of the loyalist force scattered. Of those captured, 70 were tried for treason to the United States and found guilty. Five of the prisoners sentenced to die were immediately executed by hanging.[43]

The capture of Charleston, South Carolina, in May 1780, and the victory at Camden in August, temporarily revitalized loyalist support, and when Lord Cornwalis invaded North Carolina, a large number of Tories turned out in the frontier regions of the state to support him. As the British army scored its victories in the South, small bands of Tories formed in response. Many inhabitants of the region, who had previously been lukewarm to the Crown, came foward to swear alligence to the king in victory, if only to attempt to save their property. Others, more determined, "kept up a continual struggle" with the local patriot leaders like Thomas Sumter, Andrew Pickens, and Francis Marion, and they carried the war into the frontier regions.[44]

More than 1000 loyalists assembled near the Blue Ridge Mountains in what is now Tennessee, under the able leadership of British Major Patrick Ferguson. This loyalist force was well-armed, and its leader was a serious professional officer. The backcountry patriots, mostly mounted riflemen of Scotch-Irish descent, pursued these loyalists remorselessly. Ferguson chose to turn and make a stand at a steep peak known as King's Mountain on October 7, 1780. The patriots surrounded him, and from behind trees, they laid down a deadly rifle fire on Ferguson's men. The loyalists made three determined bayonet charges in an attempt to break out, but each was turned back. Finally, Ferguson was killed, and with his death the battle ground to a halt. Every loyalist in the fight was killed, wounded, or captured. The loyalist dead numbered 157, while the patriot losses were 28 dead and 52 wounded. This patriot victory "drain[ed] much blood from southern loyalist support" and dissuaded many Tories from coming forward thereafter.[45]

SUPPRESSING LOYALISM

When detected by the Committees of Safety, loyalists were sometimes arrested on charges of disaffection to the cause and confined in jails. The worst of these prisons was undoubtedly the Simsbury Mines in Connecticut, where scores of men were confined underground in the dark and damp galleries left behind by the copper miners. Even in August the temperature in the mines rarely rose above 45°F, and water constantly dripped down the rock face, making the environment cold and damp. The prisoners were not made to work in the mines. There was no place where the floor was not tilted and irregular, so few men of average height could stand upright. Although the patriots "intended to provide decent jails," there was just not enough space in the local prison buildings and warehouses to confine so many loyalists.[46]

The patriot courts seemed prone to sentence men to death rather than to confinement. A Tory newspaper editor wrote of the patriot courts, "They [want] rebel foragers exchanged as prisoners of war, but Refugees for the same work [are] treated and executed as traitors."[47] At least 105 loyalists were sentenced to hang in New Jersey alone. This rather ruthless attitude on the part of the patriots of New Jersey may have been in response to the fact that there were so many totally disaffected communities in the state.[48]

Many loyalists, and patriots for that matter, found themselves victims of lynching without the formality of a trial. Such incidents often reflected local hatreds and petty personal vendettas that predated the hostilities.[49] At least four persons were hanged in a series of associated incidents in New Jersey involving two opposing groups, one ardently loyal and the other equally dedicated to the rebellion. Serving as ad hoc "irregulars," each used the pretext of the war to execute members of the opposition with no justification other than revenge.[50]

Delaware, only recently torn from Pennsylvania's governance, was composed of three counties: New Castle, Kent, and Sussex. The people had united in resisting the measures of the English Parliament with respect to taxation, but they were greatly divided in their attitude toward open warfare. The Tory population of the colony outweighed that of the Whigs, and a third party of Quaker pacifists made up a significant portion of the residents. In Kent County, the Tories held a nominal majority, but in Sussex they may have made up 90 percent of the residents. Only in New Castle County did the Whigs hold a slim majority, 52 percent. The Whigs had worked hard to create support for the Continental Congress, and by their tireless efforts they had made Delaware a part of the Revolution. The patriots held the state only by actively suppressing the rest of the population.[51]

In 1775 Lord Dunmore personally helped organize 1500 Tories in Delaware, and in 1776 the Royal Navy landed agents in the state to help direct loyalist resistance. Congress instructed the Committee of Safety to disarm all the loyalists in the state whom they deemed hostile. When word of this proposal reached the loyalist leaders, a petition to the Congress was circulated to which 5000 Tories attached their signatures. Squire John Clark was sent to Philadelphia to plead the Tory case for the maintenance of their civil rights; but he was arrested and the petition was destroyed.[52] A loyalist plot to burn the city of Dover was discovered on June 10, 1776, in time to prevent its completion, and Congress immediately detached a force of 3000 men under Col. Samuel Miles to Lewes, Delaware, to overawe the 1500 Tories who had gathered there.

One month after the adoption of the Declaration of Independence, 600 loyalists again assembled at Lewes during an election and allowed only those friendly to the king to vote. Caesar Rodney and Thomas McKean were thereby removed as congressional delagates and replaced by the more conservative John Evans and John Dickinson. A "lukewarm patriot" named John McKinley was elected president of Delaware, and many patriot-leaning judges were replaced by Tories. "There was not a Whig [left] in the General Assembly from Kent or Sussex Counties."[53]

These results were reversed in 1777 with considerable effort by the Whig Party. Rodney was elected president of the state, and he immediately took steps to stem the growing loyalist power. A Test Bill was passed that required every citizen to take an oath of allegiance to the state and to Congress. Another act provided for the confiscation of all the property of those found to be doing business with the British. A person failing to comply with these acts was expressly prohibited from serving in any political capacity. These steps deprived the loyalists of the ability to act within the government or through the courts. They therefore turned to open resistance.

In April 1778, an armed group of 150 insurrectionists led by Cheney

Clow marched on Dover, burned a small fortification, stole some goods, and destroyed a quantity of military stores. Clow's men were then defeated in a brief battle with an equal force of patriot militia under Lt. Col. Charles Pope. Clow was apprehended in 1782 and executed after the war.[54] Another serious loyalist effort, known as the Black Camp Rebellion, was made in 1780. About 400 Tories terrorized the Whig population of Sussex County by seizing their weapons, kidnapping their militia officers, and generally placing the coutryside in an uproar. Patriot forces pursued these Tories into the swamps, and 37 men were arrested and tried for treason. Found guilty, they were sentenced by the court to the most hideous punishment of being hanged, drawn, and quartered. However, all the prisoners were later paroled by the General Assembly.[55]

WILLIAM TRYON

One historian has called William Tryon "the evil genius of the royal cause in America" because of his many successes in prosecuting the loyalist cause through raids on patriot strongholds. Once the governor of North Carolina, Tryon was assigned the task of governing New York just in time to face the beginnings of the insurrection. When the Revolution began in Boston, Tryon asked for, and received, a commission as a major general of loyalist forces in America. He proved invaluable as the military leader of the loyalist resistance.[56]

Tryon operated with a force of more than 2000 loyalists encamped on Long Island. He organized a stronghold on the north shore near Glen Cove, and from there launched amphibious raids across Long Island Sound into Connecticut. In 1777 he led his troops to burn the colonial stores at Danbury and Ridgefield. In this raid, Maj. Gen. Daniel Wooster was killed; Benedict Arnold assumed command of the local troops and drove Tryon back into the sea. Tryon's most damaging raids were made in 1779 against Fairfield, Westport, and Norwalk, Connecticut.[57]

The Burning of Norwalk

The town of Norwalk was almost completely destroyed in 1779. Tryon's landing at Calf Pasture Beach in Norwalk harbor was the largest amphibious operation undertaken by loyalists during the war. He attacked with 2000 troops carried in 26 ships, and was joined by the King's American Regiment from Huntington, who "crossed over in flat-boats to Old Well [South Norwalk]."[58]

Tryon was opposed by fewer than 400 patriot troops, of whom 150 were Continentals under Brig. Gen. Samuel H. Parsons. In five separate encounters, the outnumbered patriots harassed and skirmished with Tryon's men. The fights at Flax Hill, Pudding Lane, and France Street lasted two hours. Old Well quickly went up in flames, but it took five hours for Tryon to dislodge the dogged patriots from the business district of the town. The most serious encounter, resulting in a stalemate, took place in an area known as "The Rocks." Here, with six small cannon placed in advantageous positions on a rocky outcrop by Captain Stephen Betts, General Parsons held off repeated attacks by Tryon's men, who simply could not dislodge the small group of patriots.[59]

Tryon's own report of the Norwalk operation noted 20 British killed, 96 wounded, and 32 missing. As far as is known, the patriot defenders lost four killed and one wounded. However, 400 patriots could not keep six times their number at bay simultaneously. While Tryon fought at The Rocks, his detachments sacked the town and burned all but 30 buildings in the area. These were spared the torch when the female residents claimed "the loyalty of their husbands to King George." The official communication of the disaster to Congress noted the total destruction of 80 homes, 87 barns, 17 shops, and 4 mills. Two churches were destoyed— the Congregational, which was purposely fired, and the Episcopal, which was accidentally set afire by burning cinders from a nearby building. Moreover, "The [British] destroyed all the saltpans of the people along the shore, and towed to their fleet every whaleboat in the harbor, with the magazine and stores gathered in the town for the [patriot] army. All the whaling and other vessels at the dock or in the river were burned." Of the 5 vessels burned, 2 were newly built privateers, and more than 60 whaleboats were seized.[60]

The destruction severely taxed the citizens of the area, who were left "in extreme poverty and in unpleasant relations towards those [loyalists] among their neighbors who had been the instruments of despoiling them." In consideration of damages amounting to almost $120,000, Congress granted Connecticut a large tract of land in northern Ohio. At the end of the war much of this grant, known as the Firelands, was settled by displaced residents from Norwalk who moved west to the frontier.[61]

SPYS AND TRAITORS

John Andre

It was through the neutral ground in New York that Maj. John Andre, adjutant to the British commander in the city, passed in order to meet with Benedict Arnold in September 1780. Overwhelming evidence suggests that Arnold was plotting treason with Andre with regard to turning over the patriot stronghold at West Point to the British. Andre was captured on his return from meeting with Arnold, during which he was given the plans of the fortifications and the disposition of the 3000 patriot troops defending the post. Although a great iron chain had been set across the river to prevent the Royal Navy from ascending the Hudson, the fall of the fortifications on one bank or the other would have made the position untenable by the patriots.

Andre, dressed in civilian clothes, was initially stopped by a trio of "skinners" who were probably intent on robbery. However, when they found the damning documents in the major's boot, they became suspicious that they had come across a more profitable piece of good fortune. Andre was given over to a local outpost commander, Lt. Col. John Jameson, who unfortunately sent word of the capture of a suspected spy to West Point. Arnold immediately took flight, escaping by boat to the Royal Navy cutter *Vulture*, which was patrolling the Hudson River below the chain.

Washington was willing to trade Andre for Arnold, and he put this offer in writing to General Clinton, the British commander in chief. When Clinton failed to turn over Arnold, Andre was brought before a military court. He was found guilty of espionage, having been discovered behind American lines out of uniform. He was sentenced to death. It is universally accepted that Andre was well liked by all the patriot officers who came into contact with him during this trying period. He acted the part of a gentleman throughout, barely flinching when he found he was to be hanged and not shot. Andre's body was returned to the British after the war, and it was interred in Westminster Abbey in England.

Benedict Arnold

The list of Benedict Arnold's honors in battle is remarkable: the capture of Forts Ticonderoga and Crown Point; the capture of the British garrison and a naval vessel at St. John's that gave the Americans control of Lake Champlain; his overland march to Quebec and the siege of that city, in which he was wounded; his naval action at Valcour Island that stemmed the British advance from Canada in 1776; his leadership in attacking the British column that had burned Danbury and Ridgefield, Connecticut, in April 1777, which made him a major general; his relief of Fort Stanwix in 1778; and his leadership at the battle of Saratoga, during which he received a second crippling wound.

Although his battle record won him popular distinctions as "America's Hannibal" or "America's Xenophon," or simply as "Washington's fighting general," his lack of influence in Congress—even among the delegates of his home state of Connecticut—kept him from being rewarded with important commands. Having been sent to the backwaters of military precedence as military governor of Philadelphia, only Washington's personal patronage won him the important post at West Point.[62]

Arnold was often overly aggressive and combative in his dealings with his military peers, and he was particularly tactless in matters of politics.

He had notable confrontations with several important patriots, including Col. Ethan Allen, Col. Moses Hazen, and Maj. Gen. Horatio Gates. He considered Congress to be capricious in its judgments and narrow-minded in allowing political influence, rather than military merit, to dictate the advancement of officers. "Had Arnold been less passionate about protecting and defending his honor and good name, he might well have avoided falling into the abyss of embittered resentment that plagued him." He came to be considered a pariah among his fellow officers and a disgruntled, troublesome, and base-born person by Congress.[63]

Arnold's young wife, Peggy Shippen, is often accused of engendering his treason because of the loyalist sympathies of her Philadelphia family. This may or may not have been true. Peggy Shippen was a lovely teenager when Arnold married her. Little is known of the strength of her loyalist sentiments, but it is certain that she felt Arnold was misused and underappreciated by the patriots. Arnold certainly felt jusified in his attempt to hand over West Point to the British. "He even fancied himself a pied piper of reconciliation whose willingness to act decisively . . . would encourage other worthy patriots, most particularly disgruntled soldiers in the Continental army, to come to their senses, renounce the Revolution, and revert to their natural British allegiance. In his imagination he envisioned thousands of disillusioned Americans following his own bold example."[64]

After escaping to the British lines in New York, Arnold accepted a commission as a major general in the British army. He led several raids on patriot positions in coastal Connecticut, and he burned the town of New London. During a raid on Groton, the patriot commander of Fort Griswold, Col. William Ledyard, was killed while surrendering his sword, an act for which Arnold was blamed although Col. Edmund Eyre was in direct command of the British detachment. Arnold thereafter turned to the South. With a force of 1600 men, including the Queen's Rangers of loyalist Lt. Col. John Simcoe, he attempted to seize or destroy patriot property throughout coastal Virginia in 1781. Under Arnold's orders Simcoe destroyed iron foundries, powder mills, machine shops, and stores of valuable tobacco. Arnold burned and ransacked parts of Richmond and Petersburg. Clandestine efforts were made to kill or capture Arnold while he was in America, but he eluded capture during the war. He died in poor economic circumstances in Britain.

Benjamin Church

The discovery that Dr. Benjamin Church was a British spy shocked the patriot community. Church had been one of the inner circle of patriot leaders in Boston, and he had been made surgeon general of the Army of Observation. In 1775, his duplicity was discovered when a coded letter entrusted to a prostitute for delivery was intercepted by Nathanael Greene. Deciphered by two cryptologists, the letter was clearly an intelligence report to the British. Church was tried by a court-martial and found guilty in October, but the Articles of War then in effect called only for him to be cashiered and imprisoned. He was eventually allowed to sail for the West Indies, but his ship disappeared en route.

James Rivington

As the editor of the *New York Gazetteer*, sometimes called *Rivington's Gazetteer*, James Rivington "at various times seemed to be the friend of both Whig and Tory—or neither." He was a friend and correspondent of Henry Knox before the war, but as the war progressed, his natural conservative leanings brought him and his newspaper firmly into the loyalist camp. His printing office was twice destroyed by the New York mob led by Isaac Sears, who disliked Rivington intensely. However, there is documentary evidence that Rivington may have been a paid double agent working for George Washington while "at the same time acting his role as Tory." Although he never openly admitted his activities as a spy, he enjoyed a good deal of prominence in New York after the war.[65]

Nathan Hale

The best-known person to serve as a spy for the patriots was 21-year-old Nathan Hale. This graduate of Yale had taught school in East Haddam and New London in Connecticut, but he had accepted a commission as a lieutenant in the 7th Connecticut Militia in 1775, and he fought during the siege of Boston and the battle of Long Island. Hale had recently accepted a captaincy in the rangers of Thomas Knowlton when Washington asked for a volunteer to gather intelligence behind the British lines. Disguised as a traveling teacher, Hale left the patriot lines on Harlem Heights in Manhattan and crossed over to British-held Long Island by boat.

Hale was captured trying to return to his own lines on September 21, 1776, with incriminating papers on his person. Since he was out of uniform and in disguise, General Howe ordered him hanged immediately. Hale reportedly went to the gallows remarkably composed. His final words were reported by a British officer in attendance at his death: "I only regret that I have but one life to lose for my country." The manner of Hale's death fired patriot propaganda, nineteenth-century anecodatal hagiography, and twentieth-century schoolbooks. He was, however, clearly a spy, and the conditions of his execution were well within the protocols reserved for such persons.[66]

NOTES

1. Claude Halstead van Tyne, *Loyalists in the American Revolution* (Ganesvoort, NY: Corner House Historical Publications, 1999), 2.

2. Ibid., 5.

3. Ibid., 6.

4. Ibid., 169.

5. Ibid., 187.

6. Charles E. Green, *The Story of Delaware in the Revolution* (Wilmington, DE: Press of William N. Cann, 1975), 185.

7. John C. Miller, *Origins of the American Revolution* (Boston: Little, Brown, 1943), 379.

8. Van Tyne, *Loyalists*, 158.

9. Otto Hufeland, *Westchester County During the American Revolution, 1775–1783* (Harrison, NY: Harbor Hill Books, 1982), 94.

10. Van Tyne, *Loyalists*, 136.

11. Ibid., 100.

12. Ray Raphael, *A People's History of the American Revolution* (New York: New Press, 1991), 82.

13. George E. Scheer, ed., *Private Yankee Doodle* (New York: Eastern Acorn Press, 1962), 141.

14. North Callahan, *Royal Raiders: The Tories of the American Revolution* (New York: Bobbs-Merrill, 1963), 68.

15. Richard B. Morris and James Woodress, eds., *Voices from America's Past: The Times That Tried Men's Souls, 1770–1783* (New York: McGraw-Hill, 1961), 30.

16. Callahan, *Royal Raiders*, 76.

17. Morris and Woodress, *Voices*, 31–32. The letter was written in 1777.

18. Van Tyne, *Loyalists*, 43–44.

19. The loyalist New Jersey Volunteers were accused of a massacre of prisoners at Fort Griswold, Connecticut, in 1781.

20. Van Tyne, *Loyalists*, 178.

21. Ibid., 183.

22. Ibid., 146.

23. Holly A. Mayer, *Belongs to the Army* (Columbia: University of South Carolina Press, 1996), 11.

24. William Pierce Randel, *The American Revolution: Mirror of the People* (Maplewood, NJ: Hamond, 1973), 95–95.

25. John Charles Philip von Krafft, *Journal of John Charles Philip von Krafft* (New York: Arno Press, 1968), 123.

26. Carson I. A. Ritchie, "A New York Diary," in *Narratives of the Revolution in New York* (New York: New York Historical Society, 1975), 230.

27. Von Krafft, *Journal*, 123–124.

28. Ibid., 126.

29. Ibid., 140.

30. J. T. Flexner, *States Dyckman: American Loyalist* (Boston: Little, Brown, 1980), 23–24. See also Christopher Hibbert, *Redcoats and Rebels: The American Revolution Through British Eyes* (New York: Avon, 1991), 79.

31. Callahan, *Royal Raiders*, 75.

32. Von Krafft, *Journal*, 140–141.

33. Mayer, *Belongs to the Army*, 111.

34. Thomas Jefferson Wertenbaker, *Father Knickerbocker Rebels* (New York: Charles Scribner's Sons, 1948), 163.

35. Von Krafft, *Journal*, 194.

36. James Thacher, *Military Journal of the American Revolution, 1775–1783* (Gansevoort, NY: Corner House Publishing, 1998), 255.

37. Van Tyne, *Loyalists*, 182.

38. Hufeland, *Westchester County*, 274.

39. John T. Hayes, *Connecticut's Revolutionary Cavalry: Sheldon's Horse* (Chester, CT: Pequot Press, 1975), 20.

40. Van Tyne, *Loyalists*, 274.

41. Ibid., 275.

42. Bart McDowell, ed., *The Revolutionary War* (Washington, DC: National Geographic Society, 1967), 80; L. Edward Purcell and David F. Burg, eds., *The World Almanac of the American Revolution* (New York: Pharos Books, 1992), 74.

43. McDowell, *Revolutionary War*, 142.

44. Van Tyne, *Loyalists*, 185.

45. McDowell, *Revolutionary War*, 159; James Kirby Martin and Mark Edward Lender, *A Respectable Army, The Military Origins of the Republic, 1762–1789* (Arlington Heights, IL: Harlan Davidson, 1982), 166.

46. Van Tyne, *Loyalists*, 237. This jail and mine complex is now a national landmark. The authors have visited these mines, which are near their home.

47. Van Tyne, *Loyalists*, 176.

48. Martin and Lender, *A Respectable Army*, 93.

49. Van Tyne, *Loyalists*, 187.

50. James M. Volo, "The Status of Prisoners of War in the American Revolution," *Living History Journal* 32 (October/November 1987), 6–7.

51. Green, *Story of Delaware*, 181.

52. Ibid., 182.

53. Ibid., 183.

54. Ibid., 214–215.

55. Ibid., 185.

56. Callahan, *Royal Raiders*, 77.

57. D. Hamilton Hurd, ed., *History of Fairfield County Connecticut* (Philadelphia: J. W. Lewis, 1881), 513.

58. Ibid., 503.

59. Ibid., 498–499. Scores of cannonballs have been retrieved from the area of the battle of The Rocks, attesting to the severity of the encounter on both sides.

60. Ibid., 497.

61. Ibid., 498.

62. James Kirby Martin, *Benedict Arnold, Revolutionary Hero: An American Warrior Reconsidered* (New York: New York University Press, 1997), 414.

63. Ibid., 414.

64. Ibid., 4.

65. Callahan, *Royal Raiders*, 64.

66. Katherine Bakeless and John Bakeless, *Spies of the Revolution* (New York: Scholastic Books, 1959), 106–107.

13

Women at War

We may destroy all the men in America, and we shall still have all
we can do to defeat the women.

—Charles Lord Cornwallis

POLITICAL AWARENESS

The brave deeds and tremendous hardships of the soldiers during the
Revolution have long been recognized and saluted. Equal accolades have
often eluded the sacrifices and efforts of American women during this
same period. In the wake of the Townshend Acts and the Tea Act, boycott organizers turned to the housewives of America for support. There
was little necessity to convince the women of the contributions they
could make. The ladies quickly realized that their economic decisions
had important political implications. They rallied to the cause, making
what contributions they could in light of their social class, personal resources, and physical abilities.

As disputes between the colonies and the British empire moved from
impassioned rhetoric to armed conflict, women were called upon to
make even greater sacrifices. When men marched away to defend their
homes, their wives and daughters took up the men's labors and shoul-
dered them along with the already burdensome obligations of
eighteenth-century homemaking. Quietly, women stepped in to fill the
void. They worked on the farm or in the shop, fed and clothed the chil-

dren, kept the home intact, and supplied the armies with the necessities of life. The spirit of the patriot woman was an invaluable factor in the struggle for independence.

The social climate of pre-Revolutionary America severely limited women's roles and generally excluded them from the political process. Yet in the decade between the Stamp Act and the Declaration of Independence, women became more politically aware. Some men among the patriot radicals believed that it was essential for women to become actively involved in political expression if the economic boycotts set in place by the Continental Association were to be successful. Nevertheless, whatever was asked of women in the political crisis needed to remain within the broader bounds of acceptable gender roles.

Christopher Gadsden, a delegate to the First Continental Congress from South Carolina, wrote an open letter to his colleagues explaining this strategy:

[W]hat many say and think is the *greatest difficulty* of all we have to encounter . . . is to persuade our wives to give us their assistance, without which 'tis impossible to succeed. . . . [O]ur political salvation at this crisis, depends altogether upon their strictest economy, that the women could, with propriety, have the principal management thereof; for 'tis well known, that none in the world are better economists, make better wives or more tender mothers, than ours. . . . Only let their husbands point out the necessity of such conduct . . . their affections will soon be awakened [and] they will then be anxious and persevering in this matter.[1]

In an article in the *South Carolina Gazette*, William Tennent III, an itinerant minister among the Scotch-Irish in the Carolina backcountry, took a more direct approach. Urging women to eschew the use of tea, he encouraged them to take action in the strongest language: "Yes, Ladies. You have it in your power more than all your committees and Congresses, to strike the stroke, and make the hills and plains of America clap their hands."[2]

Mercy Otis Warren was one of the few women to give public voice to her political sentiments. Mercy was the sister of James Otis, a leader of the Revolution. She wrote several satirical plays and corresponded with many prominent figures in colonial society, including Samuel Adams, George Washington, Thomas Jefferson, Elbridge Gerry, and Alexander Hamilton. She maintained especially close contact with John and Abigail Adams.

She structured her political comments within plays, none of which were performed on stage because Mercy had specifically written them for publication in the newspapers. Such writing was commonly used to express ideas to the public. Through her plays Mercy revealed her contempt for the Tory administration in Boston and her passion for Whig ideology. "The Adulateur," which first appeared in *The Massachusetts Spy*, criticized Thomas Hutchinson's activities as lieutenant governor of Massachusetts and glorified such radicals as Sam Adams and her brother, James. "The Defeat" continued to mock Hutchinson. "The Group," her most popular play, focused on Hutchinson's family and showed her disdain for Americans who maintained their loyalty to the Crown.

In 1776 General Burgoyne, in his self-appointed role as playwright, penned *The Blockade of Boston*, a satire that mocked the colonials and glorified the British. Performances of this play infuriated the patriots. Mercy Warren quickly penned a play in answer, "The Blockheads; or the Affrightened Officers: A Farce," a scorching personal attack on the British regulars and the Crown forces as a whole. There has been some controversy as to whether Mercy was the author of this work, since it contained some very candid language, but it is often linked to her. In another work, "The Motley Assembly: A Farce," she maintained a more democratic perspective that focused on a different target, women of the upper social classes who remained absorbed in a world of fashion and luxury. Mercy believed that a woman's primary focus should be her family, but asserted that it was important for women to be aware of politics in order to better serve their families.

Embracing the Cause

It did not take much convincing for some women to join the patriot effort, and it became somewhat fashionable in certain circles to do so. On January 31, 1770, almost four years before the Boston Tea Party, a group of 426 women of Boston signed an agreement not to drink any tea until the tax upon it was repealed. Even nine-year-old Susan Boudinot embraced the pledge. While a guest in the home of New Jersey's loyalist governor, William Franklin, the young girl was offered a cup of tea. Susan accepted the refreshment, curtsied, raised the cup, and threw the liquid out the window.[3]

Editors of patriot newspapers, always searching for propaganda pieces, began capitalizing on the "spinning bee." Women had long participated in spinning bees, usually held at the minister's home, in order to spin fiber that would later be made into cloth for his personal wardrobe. Following the imposition of the Townshend duties in 1767, this traditional activity, now redirected to the purposes of the boycott by producing cloth, was given prominence in certain papers and exalted as having the most patriotic of motivations. The *Boston Evening Post* reported, "[T]he industry and frugality of American ladies must exhaust their character in the eyes of the world and serve to show how greatly they are contributing to bring about the political salvation of a whole continent."[4]

Many members of the clergy promoted such domestic activities. Congregational ministers in New England were particularly active in emphasizing the frugality, economy, and industry characteristic of traditional Puritanism. Peter Oliver, a loyalist, charged that rebel ministers preached "manufactures instead of Gospel. They preached about it and preached about it, until the women and children, both within doors and without, set their spinning wheels a whirling in defiance of Great Britain. The female spinners kept on spinning for 6 days of the week; and on the seventh, the parsons took their turns and spun out their prayers and sermons to a long thread of politics."[5] Jack Smith, a college student at the time of the Revolution, noted, "There was no hesitation about preaching political sermons in those days. Ministers would have deemed themselves to have entirely failed their duty, had they not expressed their views in regard to what was right and wrong on public questions."[6]

In urban areas across the colonies, young women began to assemble with their spinning wheels in daylong demonstrations of patriotic fervor. New York teenager, Charity Clarke, wrote to an English cousin that "[h]eroines may not distinguish themselves at the head of an Army," but "armed with spinning wheels," women could contribute to the preservation of colonial liberties.[7] For women in rural areas and those of limited means, spinning was less a trendy expression of patriotic ideals than a more genuine domestic necessity, yet the symbolism of the act could be considerable. A Connecticut farm girl, Betsy Foote, noted in her diary in 1775 that she had carded wool all day and spun ten knots of wool in the evening. This was a likely day's work for a young woman at any time, but Betsy added to her entry, "and felt Nationly into the bargain."[8]

What began as symbolic support for an economic and political ideal quietly crept into a way of life. Dorothy Dudley summed up the situation in a letter in 1776: "This year had been one of severe trial for us all. Of course there has been reason for great economy both in household and dress. Tea is a comfort put from us with resolution, though its absence from our tables is cuttingly felt by many. As far as possible we patronize only home manufactures, and ourselves use the spindle to diminish the necessity for foreign material."[9]

As the war raged on, women engaged in a variety of activities to support the troops in the field. Many of their methods capitalized on domestic skills and were almost an extension of their household work. The family papers of Helen Evertson Smith reveal that "[s]pinning yarn and knitting stockings, preparing bandages and scraping lint, filled every patriotic woman's every moment that could be spared from the daily cares of her family."[10] Some of these endeavors took on the form of community action. The Literary Club of Sharon, Connecticut, for instance, passed a resolution that at debating meetings, "all of the women and such of the men as were not engaged in speaking or reading are expected to knit stockings or do some other work to help [the] brave and suffering soldiers in their desperate struggle to gain Liberty."[11]

On a spring evening in 1777, Mrs. Smith invited her neighbors to come to her home with "every pewter dish they could spare." By the evening's end "many gallons of good bullets had been made from the cherished pewter articles, which had been melted and merrily run through bullet molds." For many evenings following this event, there were "trencher bees"[12] at which young men "cut and shaped maple and poplar wood into dishes, which the women made smooth by scraping with broken glass, and polished with the clean white sand of powdered limestone."[13] Undoubtedly these ladies possessed some imported china dishes that they could have used instead of these wooden replacements. However, they may have been hesitant to use such fragile items, knowing that under the restraints of war they would be impossible to replace if broken, and impossible to use without seeming less than fully dedicated to the patriotic cause.

Shirts of Country Linen

Women of prominence used their position to rouse support for the troops. In June 1780, Ester Reed of Philadelphia published a broadside, "The Sentiments of an American Woman," which declared that American women were resolved to do more than dispatch "barren wishes" for the army's success. She desired women to be "really useful," like the "heroines of antiquity."[14] Drawing upon role models of strong women from the Old Testament, Roman and Greek legends, and a history of female monarchs on the English throne to argue her case, Reed outlined a plan for women to donate the money now saved by shunning imports to the American troops. The broadside proved to be highly inspirational. Three days after it appeared, 36 prominent women of Philadelphia met to develop a strategy to actualize the scheme. The ladies began a fervent campaign to solicit funds, which were to be known as "The Offering of the Ladies."[15] No donation was too small, and no one was excluded from their appeal, including servants. By the completion of the campaign in July, more than $300,000 in Continental dollars had been collected from 1600 individual supporters.

The endeavor garnered considerable notoriety in the press that helped in spreading the plan. Reed and the other organizers wrote to prominent women in neighboring regions, imploring them to implement a similar effort. Women's associations in New Jersey, Maryland, and Virginia took up the challenge, and many variations of the idea were initiated. Geography and limited financial resources prevented all the campaigns from having the same degree of success as that in Philadelphia, but they did raise additional funds.

Reed's original plan called for the donations to be presented to Martha Washington, who would see that they reached the soldiers and would not be spent on items that Congress should be supplying to the army during the normal course of its operation. By the time the collection was completed, however, Mrs. Washington had returned to Virginia, and Reed had to deal with General Washington himself. The general was concerned that giving funds to the soldiers directly might cause "irregularities," "disorders," and "discontent" among the troops, and he countered with a plan of his own to use the money to supply the soldiers with much-needed shirts. He suggested that the ladies make the shirts themselves, in order to eliminate the cost of seamstresses. Recognizing that Washington would not yield in his opinion, the ladies altered their plan.

Reed died before the process was completed. However, under the guidance of Sarah Franklin Bache, country linen was purchased, and the women commenced to put their needles to work. The Marquis de Chastellux, a general officer with the French army in America, described a visit to Bache's house: "She conducted us into a room filled with work lately finished by the ladies of Philadelphia. This work consisted neither of embroidered tambour waistcoats, nor of network edging, nor of gold and silver brocade. It was a quantity of shirts for the soldiers of Pennsylvania. The ladies bought linen from their private purses, and took pleasure in cutting them out and sewing them. On each shirt was the name of the married or unmarried lady who made it, and they amounted to twenty-two hundred."[16] Bache once told Washington, "We wish them to be worn with as much pleasure as they were made."[17]

My Country! Oh! My Country!

There are countless instances of women bringing food and supplies to the troops and providing aid to the wounded when the army was encamped nearby. The diary of Elizabeth Drinker, a Quaker, contains a number of entries similar to this one: "[W]ent this afternoon in the rain ... with a jug of wine-whey and a tea-kettle of coffee for the wounded men." Many such endeavors were casually recorded with equal brevity in diaries, journals, and letters written during the natural flow of women's daily activities. Such deeds were not portrayed as acts of radical patriotism nor feats of heroism. They were recorded simply as the fulfillment of a woman's natural duty to her community.[18]

Yet it was not always easy to reach the needy troops. A contemporary observer recounted how the resourceful women of Charleston managed to deliver supplies to patriot troops outside the British-held city. "The women would often procure passes [from the British] to go to their farms or plantations in the country. They seized this occasion for carrying forth supplies of cloth, linen, and even gunpowder and shot to their countrymen. . . . These commodities were concealed beneath their garments; and, in preparation for their departure, the dimensions of the good women were observed sensibly to increase. At length it was noticed by the officers on guard, that the lady, who when she left the city was of enormous bulk, would return reduced to a shadow . . . [and] a jury of spinsters was provided and the fat ladies were taken into custody."[19]

Many towns served as storage facilities for supplies for the troops. Here, too, it was the women who took charge. "Almost all of the able bodied male inhabitants more than seventeen years of age were enrolled in the armies, and the work pertaining to the stores was carried on by the women and children under the direction of a few old men."[20] The British raid on Ridgefield, Connecticut, must have dealt a huge emotional and economic blow to those charged with overseeing the stores. "[A] large quantity of the public stores had been deposited in the Episcopal church, and the first work of the soldiers was to remove them into the street and burn them. . . . In a few hours eighteen hundred barrels of pork and beef, seven hundred barrels of flour, two-thousand bushels of wheat, rye, oats, and Indian corn, clothing for a regiment of troops, and seventeen hundred and ninety tents were burned. The smoke arising from the destruction of this property was strangulating and filled the whole air, while the streets ran with the melted pork and beef."[21]

Having a husband away at war increased the physical burden of an already demanding lifestyle even when families were safe from marauding troops. A man, who was a child during the war, remembered: "My mother had the sole charge of us four little ones. . . . When my father was permitted to come home [on leave], his stay was short. . . . Sometimes we wondered that [Mother] did not mention the cold weather, or our short meals, or her hard work, that we little ones might be clothed, and fed, and taught. But she would not weaken his hands, or sadden his heart, for she said a soldier's life was harder than all."[22]

Temperance Smith recalled what life was like after her husband, a parson, left to minister to the troops.

I had no leisure for murmuring. I rose with the sun and all through the long day I had no time for aught but my work. So much did it press upon me that I could scarcely divert my thoughts from its demands, even during the family prayers. . . . I should have been sending all my thoughts to heaven for the safety of my beloved husband and the salvation of our hapless country. Instead of which I was often wondering whether Polly had remembered to set the sponge for the bread or to put water on the leach tub, or to turn the cloth in the dying vat, or whether the wool had been carded for Betsy to start her spinning wheel in the morning, or Billy had chopped light wood enough for the kindling, or dry hard wood enough to heat the big oven, or whether some other thing had not been forgotten of the thousand that must be done.[23]

The letters between Capt. Nathan Peters and his wife, Lois, provide an insight into the adversity faced by the wives of the men who went to serve in the army. When Nathan, a saddler and leather worker, set out in 1775 to respond to the fighting around Boston, he left his pregnant wife to care for a small child of less than a year, to manage their home, and to run their business. From the beginning, Lois found that continuing what she referred to as "the Trade" was not going to be easy. She complained, "I can't collect one penny."[24] She soon asked Nathan to "send home a power of attorney" so she could pursue clients who were avoiding their debts to him.[25] Lack of cash confounded her operation of the saddler's shop, and Lois sought Nathan's approval for an arrangement with a journeyman, who agreed to work in the shop and take his pay in board and stock for his labor on completed saddles. "It is so difficult to carry on the Trade that I see no way possible at present, for we can't get our plush nor trimming without money."[26] Two months later she wrote, "[I] have done the best I could to carry on the Trade but can't any longer for want of stock of all kinds."[27]

While trying to run the business, Lois constantly made shirts to send to her husband despite the difficulty in getting the necessary fabric. "I shall send by [H]errick 1 cake of chocolate and some of my good old cheese."[28] Lois also continued to manage the homestead. "I have been very much put to it to get help to cut our hay. I am like to have it all cut today. The drought has been very severe and the grass is very poor."[29] In another letter she wrote, "I have got my corn harvested and have about eighty bushel[s]."[30]

As both Christmas and the birth of their child drew near, Lois's situation grew worse. "I shall hope that you will by that time be home and see about your business yourself for I am almost tired of the fatigue of it. I have nobody to do one chore for me only what I hire. [I] should think it would be well to send Joseph[31] home if he is willing to come and you can have him dismissed for it grows cold and I am not so well able to undergo hardships at some times and I want wood cut at the door and fires made and many things done that I am obliged to hire some done and some go undone."[32] Although Lois gave birth soon thereafter, her worries about her family continued. "[O]ur dear son is sick. [I] am in hopes it [is] only a great cold and worms. Our daughter is well. Mother is sick with camp distemper but is better."[33]

Perhaps the most telling remarks of hardship and suffering are those dealing with Nathan's absence. Two days after Christmas, Lois wrote, "I have looked for you 'til I am almost out of hope of your coming home at all. It would be a great comfort to me to have you come home and stay this winter. . . . I live a very sorrowful and lonesome life. Our dear son is well and says he wants Daddy."[34] Later she wrote, "[I]f you lived as lonesome and felt as melancholy as I do you would be be glad of a line from me. . . . If I could only have the enjoyment of my dear husband to live with me, I should think myself as happy as this world could make me."[35] After more than a year's separation, Lois's agony deepened: "My only comfort is at present in the dear little pledges of our love. When I see them, I see my dear. Must I deny myself the pleasure of him? I was going to say, 'No!' I must refuse myself that pleasure when so glorious a cause calls him away from my arms. My country! Oh! My country! Excuse, my love, the anguish of a soul that has you always painted before her."[36]

Prolonged separation of husband and wife brought anxiety, longing, and pain. Mercy Warren wrote to her husband, "Oh! these painful absences. Ten thousand anxieties invade my bosom on your account and some times hold my lids waking many hours of the cold and lonely night."[37] Mary Bartlett penned the following to her spouse: "Apples scarce, plumbs in the garden plenty. Pray do come home before cold weather, as you know my circumstances will be difficult in the winter, if I am alive."[38] Abigail Adams became so desperate for news of her husband that her nine-year-old son, John Quincy, became post rider for her, traveling the 11 miles between Braintree and Boston with the latest reports of the war.[39]

While the men went off to meet the war, too often the war came to meet the women who were left behind. Abigail Adams detailed the events of one night: "I went to bed about twelve, and rose again a little after one. I could no more sleep than if I had been in the engagement; the rattling of the windows, the jar of the house, the continual roar of the twenty-four pounders; and the bursting shells give us such ideas, and we realize a scene to us of which we could form scarcely any conception."[40]

The stress brought on by the bombardment of the Boston suburb of Charlestown by the Royal Navy took its toll on all family members. John Quincy Adams recalled:

For the space of twelve months my mother with her infant children dwelt, liable every hour of the day and the night to be butchered in cold blood, or taken and carried into Boston as hostages. My mother lived in unintermitted danger of being consumed with them all in a conflagration kindled by a torch in the same hands which on the 17th of June [1775] lighted the fires of Charlestown. I saw with my own eyes those fires, and heard Britannia's thunders in the Battle of Bunker Hill, and witnessed the tears of my mother and mingled them with my own.[41]

Such fears were not unfounded. Eliza Wilkinson wrote to a friend of facing British foragers bent on robbing her home outside of Charleston, South Carolina.

I heard the horses of the inhumane Britons[42] coming—the raiders bellowing out the most horrid oaths and imprecations. I had no time for thought—they were up to the house—entered with drawn swords and pistols in their hands crying, "Where are those women rebels?" The moment they spied us, off went our caps, to get a paltry stone and wax pin, which kept them on our heads; at the same time uttering abusive language, and making as if they would hew us to pieces with their swords.... They began to plunder the house of everything they thought worth taking; our trunks were split to pieces, and each mean wretch crammed his bosom with the contents. I represented to him the times were such we could not replace what they had taken from us, and we begged him to spare me only a suit or two; but so far was his callous heart from relenting, that casting his eyes toward my shoes, "I want them buckles," said he.... They took my sister's earrings from her ears, her and Mrs. Samuell's buckles, demanding her ring from her finger, and after bundling up all of their booty, mounted their horses; each wretche's bosom stuffed so full, they appeared to be afflicted with some dropoisal disorder.[43]

Some years later Wilkinson described the accumulated emotional toll of incidents like this one on her family and herself.

The whole world appeared to me as a theatre, where nothing was acted but cruelty, bloodshed and oppression; where neither age nor sex escaped the horrors of injustice and violence; where lives and property of the innocent and inoffensive were in continual danger.... We could neither eat, drink nor sleep in peace; for as we lay in our clothes every night, we could not enjoy the little sleep we got. The least noise alarmed us; up we would jump, expecting every moment to hear them demand admittance. In short, our nights were wearisome and painful; our days spent in anxiety and melancholy.[44]

INDIAN ATTACK

Residents of frontier areas were often subjected to attack by Native Americans allied with the British. One of the more horrific attacks occurred in the Wyoming Valley of Pennsylvania. Women, children, and old men were hurried by their captors into the wilderness with no opportunity to prepare themselves for the arduous journey. Shortly after they set out, "the Indians got out of control," and some prisoners were subjected to ghastly tortures and even death. The terrified survivors panicked, and many escaped through a swamp known as "the Shades of Death." From the woods over the following days came an intermittent succession of "mothers carrying dead babies, women learning of their widowhood on the trail, children being born, and old folks dying."[45]

Elizabeth Farmar, whose home was spared, declared, "Most of the houses near us have been either burnt or pulled down as would have been the case with us if we had not stayed in it even at the hazard of our lives."[46]

The Van Alstines of Canajoharie in central New York were beset by raiders, their horses taken, and their house plundered. All their clothing was taken. Beds were ripped open and the feathers shaken out so that the cloth ticking could be carried away. The intruders broke the window glass throughout the house. Mrs. Nancy Van Alstine's shawl was ripped from her neck. Buckles were ripped from the shoes of her aged grandmother, and the shoes flung in the woman's face. Fortunately, the family was spared any personal harm, a fact that Mrs. Van Alstine attributed to her acquaintance with Joseph Brant and Sir John Johnson.

With everything lost, the family subsisted on corn, which they made into corn cakes, but they suffered greatly from the elements, having no warm clothing and no windows. Frustrated by the suffering of her loved ones, Mrs. Van Alstine proved herself an extraordinary woman. Armed with courage and accompanied by her teenage son, she set out through deep winter snow to right this injustice to her family. The pair arrived at a nearby Indian village when the men were out hunting and it was populated only by women and small children. Mrs. Van Alstine approached the principal dwelling near which their family horses were tied. Here she was confronted by a native woman. Van Alstine requested food, saying that she had never turned away a hungry Indian.

As soon as the native woman went to prepare something to eat, Van Alstine began to search the premises. She soon found her copper teapot and several other personal items, which she gave to her son to put in their sleigh. The Indian woman returned and became distressed at the visitors' actions. Knowing that the Indian woman probably could not read, the resourceful housewife took a paper from her pocket and showed it to her, informing her that it was a pass signed by "Yankee Peter," a man of great influence among the Indians. Thus, she and her son were permitted to leave. As they left the village, Mrs. Van Alstine instructed her son to cut the halters of their horses, knowing that once free, they would return home.

The family passed a tense night, anticipating some form of retaliation. Shortly after daylight, Indian warriors appeared with the intent of ransacking her barn. Instructing her family to remain inside, Mrs. Van Alstine ran to the barn and attempted to bar the door. She was thrown down by the leader of the party, but arose and reassumed her defensive position. The Indian raised his musket, threatening to shoot her, but the determined woman simply bared her neck in defiance. After a tense moment he lowered his weapon, and the band retreated. Recalling the event to a British officer, the Indian who led the party praised Van Alstine's courage, saying that if there were fifty such women among the patriots, the Indians would never have troubled the inhabitants of the valleys.[47]

Many patriot families were taken captive in these raids. In the attack on Wyoming, Mrs. Campbell was dragged off into western New York with her children and mother. During the journey her mother was killed by a single tomahawk blow to the head because she was unable to keep the pace, her older children were distributed among various Indian groups, and her infant was taken from her arms when she reached the Seneca country. Campbell was placed with an Indian family for the winter, and she used her needlework skills to make and repair garments in return for corn and venison. In 1779 she was sent to the British stronghold at Fort Niagara, and shortly thereafter was exchanged for the wife and sons of a loyalist raider, Colonel John Butler.[48]

SEXUAL ABUSE

The possibility of rape by enemy soldiers was a fear with which women had to live. The *Pennsylvania Evening Post* reported of Lord Cornwallis's troops in New Jersey: "Besides the sixteen women who had fled to the woods to avoid their brutality and were there seized and carried off, one man had the cruel mortification to have his wife and only daughter (a child of ten years of age) ravished. . . . [A] girl of thirteen years of age was taken from her fathers house, carried to a barn about a mile, there ravished, and afterwards made use of by five more of these brutes."[49]

Thirteen-year-old Abigail Palmer gave a deposition to the Continental Congress describing the horrors she experienced at the hands of some British regulars. The soldiers entered her home, dragged her to a back room, and "three of the said soldiers ravished her." For three successive days thereafter, "diverse soldiers would come to the house and treat her in the same manner." The soldiers also raped her aunt and a young friend who had come to console Abigail on the third day of her travail. "The said soldiers ravished them both and then took them away to their camp, where they [were] both treated by some others of the soldiers in the same cruel manner."[50]

Such conduct was a violation of military law, and the officers would never have allowed such treatment of women of their own social class to go unpunished. However, when it came to country women, Lord Rawdon, leader of the infamous Irish Volunteers, often bragged of the sexual conquests of his "healthy and spirited" troops. "A girl cannot step into the bushes to pluck a rose without running the most imminent risk of being ravished, and they are so little accustomed to these vigorous methods that they don't bear them with the proper resignation, and of consequence we have most entertaining courts-martial every day."[51]

CAMP FOLLOWERS

As the war dragged on, many women joined their husbands in the patriot camps rather than face humiliation and starvation. Such a drastic move would be taken only in the most dire circumstances. The large body of civilians, collectively referred to as camp followers, traveled with the army, providing supplies, services, and emotional support. Camp followers usually included servants, slaves, sutlers,[52] contractors, bureaucrats, and military employees, but as the war progressed, it was increasingly composed of the displaced families of soldiers. A British intelligence report regarding the patriot army at White Plains in 1778 found that "Women and Waggoners [make] up near half of their army."[53]

Many women camp followers took on additional duties in order to alleviate the added stress their arrival placed on their husband's meager pay. The army had a need for laundresses, cleaning women, seamstresses, and nurses. Colonel Ebenezer Huntington wrote to his brother in 1780, "[M]y washing bill is beyond the limits of my wages. I am now endeavoring to hire some woman . . . to do the washing for myself and some of the officers."[54] By providing services that were still within the gender-specific roles expected of them in the eigthteenth century, women helped to legitimize their presence with the army. A body of enterprising women could fill some of the voids left by the inadequately run Quartermaster's and Commissary departments. When a women joined her husband in the field, she generally exposed herself to many of the same dangers he faced. General Washington asked Sarah Osborn if she was not afraid of the cannonballs, to which she replied, "It would not do for men to fight and to starve, too."[55]

It is important to note that the rough jokes and snide remarks of a sexual nature often associated with women camp followers are more characteristic of the armies of the American Civil War than those of the Revolution. The role of women with the army, outside of any personal relations with their husbands, was to remain of a nonsexual nature. Married women were to be provided with certificates to that effect, which detailed the name of their husband and his regiment. Unmarried women were ordered to be "sent off," but no distinction was made for older girls, perhaps the daughters or siblings of the soldiers. Officially prostitution was banned in the camps, and those found practicing the trade were made to feel unwelcome. Confirmed prostitutes would have found the hard coin of the British paymaster far more attractive than the paper currency of the patriots in any case. However, it proved impossible to police all the hundreds of legitimate sexual relationships among husbands, wives, and lovers in the camps in order to cull out the illicit ones.[56]

An army camp might seem a strange place to see so many women and children, but the displaced families of patriot soldiers had no choice but to follow the army.

Life with the Army

Patriot women rarely sought refuge in the cities, as loyalist women did, because the urban centers were largely controlled by the British. In the absence of a sanctuary with family or friends, they were forced to follow the patriot army in order to come under its protection. The lot of these women was one of hardship and sacrifice. The army was described in a letter written by a lady outside of Boston in 1777 as having "great numbers of women, who seemed to be the beasts of burden, having bushel baskets on their backs, by which they were bent double. The contents seemed to be pots and kettles, various sorts of furniture, children peeping through gridirons and other utensils—some very young infants, who were born on the road—the women barefoot, clothed in dirty rags."[57] An officer described these women as "the ugliest in the world. . . . [T]he furies who inhabit the infernal region can never be painted half so hideous as these women." Most were reported to have one or more children with them, "few with none."[58]

The presence of wives and children with the army, although it could not be avoided without creating distress among the supporters of the

American cause, was generally thought to be a great burden. In August 1777, Washington wrote, "In the present state of the army, every incumberence [*sic*] proves greatly prejudicial to the service; the multitude of the women in particular, especially those who are pregnant, or have children, are a clog upon every movement. The Commander-in-Chief therefore earnestly recommends it to the officers commanding brigades and corps, to use every reasonable method in their power to get rid of all such as are not absolutely necessary."[59] Washington hoped to limit "the proportion of women which ought to be allowed to any number of men, and to whom rations shall be allowed." From time to time, quotas were discussed, but they were never really put into practice.[60]

In this regard, the total of women's rations was established at a fifteenth of the issues for noncommissoned officers and privates. The wives could earn their rations by taking up work, and rates of pay were established for washing and other duties. However, in a cash-starved army, "the soldier, nay the officer, for whom they wash has naught to pay them."[61] The general understood, however, that ultimately he "was obliged to give provisions to the extra women in [the] regiments, or lose by desertion, perhaps to the enemy, some of the oldest and best soldiers in the service."[62]

It was generally expected that the camp followers would refrain from marching among the ranks of men. When the army marched into Philadelphia in 1777, Washington gave detailed orders as to the appearance and decorum of the column. "If any soldier shall dare to quit his ranks, he shall receive thirty-nine lashes at the first halting place afterwards. . . . Not a Woman belonging to the army is to be seen with the troops on their march thro' the City."[63] An eyewitness recounted, however, that the women were determined to be with their men, although they were "spirited off into the quaint, dirty little alleyways and side streets." Nonetheless, the army had barely passed through the main streets of the town before the women "poured after their soldiers again, their hair flying, their brows beady from the heat, their belongings slung over one shoulder, chattering and yelling in sluttish shrills as they went, and spitting in the gutters."[64]

Approximately 25 general orders were issued by Washington concerning women among the forces. The majority of them dealt with women riding in the wagons of the army: "Any woman found in a wagon contrary to this regulation is to be immediately turned out."[65] The repeated requests for women to refrain from riding on the wagons suggests that they largely failed to comply with the general's expectations. Nonetheless, women who could ride on horseback were considered an asset if they would serve as drovers and thereby "diminish the number of drivers taken from the army."[66]

This nineteenth-century illustration is of "Molly Pitcher," whose real name was Mary Hays. All the women who brought water to the men on the battlefield were known as "Molly Pitchers."

On the Battlefield

There are several stories of heroic actions by women camp followers who took up their husbands' posts when they fell in battle. Over time it is likely that many of the details of their service have become mythologized or otherwise exaggerated. Mary Ludwig Hays, who has come to be known as "Molly Pitcher," may well be the best-known woman to have served in battle. Mary, like many other women known as "Molly Pitchers," carried water to relieve the thirst of soldiers in battle. The legend claims that at the battle of Monmouth, Mary Hays saw her husband, an artilleryman, hit by a British shell. She dragged him out of the way of further harm, and then returned to the battle, taking his place at the cannon. While Mary is believed to have been present at the battle, there is evidence that her story may be an amalgamation of the deeds of many women.

Private Joseph Plumb Martin recalled a scene he witnessed at the battle of Monmouth that day.

A woman whose husband belonged to the artillery and who was then attached to a piece in the engagement, attended with her husband at the piece the whole time. While in the act of reaching a cartridge and having one of her feet as far before the other as she could step, a cannon shot from the enemy passed directly between her legs without doing any other damage than carrying away all the lower part of her petticoat. Looking at it with apparent unconcern, she observed that it was lucky it did not pass a little higher, for in that case it might have carried away something else, and continued her occupation.[67]

Margaret Cochran Corbin served at her husband's side when he fell at his artillery piece at Fort Washington. It is said that she immediately took his place and continued there until she, herself, was wounded. Margaret was the first woman to receive a lifetime pension from the United States for her service-related disability received in action.

Officers' Wives

The wives of officers in the American army were not as likely to accompany their husbands on campaign as were those of the lower classes. Nor were they considered camp followers. Being from that part of colonial society which was generally better off financially allowed the wives and families of officers to find sanctuary among a wider range of friends and relatives capable of supporting them in the interim. The massive redistribution of populations during the war severely strained these resources, however, and individual households thought to be out of the way of the enemy swelled to accommodate fleeing friends and relatives. Jean Blair voiced her frustration when twenty "guests" sought refuge in her home in 1781. "I hardly ever knew the trouble of house keeping before, a large family and continual confusion and not any thing to eat but salt meat and hoecake and no conveniences to dress them."[68]

Traveling with an army was both arduous and dangerous even for the wives of officers. The baggage train of the army, complete with women, children, and wounded, might be attacked by the enemy, and detachments were made from the army to deter such operations. Any man with the means to provide for his family away from the army would never willingly subject them to such experiences. Nonetheless, some officers' wives did meet their husbands in winter quarters when the army was not on the move. The practice was begun when Martha Washington and some other ladies joined their husbands outside Boston for the winter of 1775–1776.[69] In 1778, Lafayette wrote to his wife in France from the encampment at Valley Forge, "Several staff officers are having their wives join them in camp. I am very envious—not of their wives, but of the happiness that this opportunity brings them. General Washington has also resolved to send for his wife."[70]

The official attitude toward these women was greatly different from that toward soldiers' wives. Officers' wives were considered ladies, and as such were accorded respect appropriate to their social station or the rank of their husbands. These women also made contributions to the war effort in their own way, by mending uniforms, sewing shirts, and knitting stockings for the soldiers. From time to time they visited the camps, dispensing food to the hungry and offering encouragement to the sick or emotionally distressed.

The gathering of the officers and their ladies during the winter created a kind of social season complete with dinners and dances, albeit considerably subdued from those of the prewar period. Dorothy Dudley wrote on January 30, 1777: "Madame Washington has enlivened the monotony of her winter among us by a reception, on the seventeenth anniversary of her wedding day. The fine old Vassall mansion was in gala dress, and the coming and going of guests brightened the sober aspect of the General's head-quarters."[71] Several months later Dudley further elaborated on the event in a letter to a friend, "No display, no extravagance; but simple taste suited to this time of universal economy, characterized all the arrangements."[72]

Major General Nathanael Greene wrote of the social regime he experienced during the winter of 1778–1779: "I spent a month the most agreeable and disagreeable I ever did a month in my life. We had the most splendid entertainment imaginable; large assemblies, evening balls, etc. It was hard service to go through the duties of the day. I was obliged to rise early and to go to bed late to complete them. In the morning a round of visiting came on. Then you had to prepare for dinner, after which the evening balls would engage your time until one or two in the morning."[73]

FOLLOWING THE REGULARS

British and German troops also had their share of camp followers. When eight regiments of British regulars arrived in the colonies in January 1776, each consisted of almost 700 officers and men. Allotted to each regimental organization were 60 women and 12 servants. These regiments were followed by a detachment from Jamaica of 374 officers and men, and 40 women. A month later almost 1200 officers and men were accompanied by 80 women, and soon thereafter another 2300 soldiers arrived with 160 more women. These data seem to reflect a rough proportion of 12 men to 1 woman.[74] Feeding the women was another concern. "The quartermasters of corps [are] to subsist their women and children on board ship, with flour and rice only, till further orders, and that it be issued to them with economy. A small quantity of fish may be given to them with it."[75]

Nonetheless, as the regulars traveled, it was not unusual for them to accumulate additional camp followers from among the women they encountered along the way. Attempts were made to limit the number of these hangers-on. "The commanding officers will be answerable the

This young woman has taken a Hessian soldier as her husband. If he dies in battle, she will be forced to find another, or be driven from the camp. She carries all her belongings, including a small cooking pot.

number of women with their respective corps does not exceed 4 per company . . . [and] those be the best behaved and bring and keep no children with them." Although accurate numbers do not exist for these additional women, the British Commissary's figures of 1777 suggest the ratio of men to women to be about 8 to 1 among the British and 30 to 1 among the Germans. In 1781, figures show that the ratio of men to women was then 4.5 to 1 among the British and 15 to 1 among the Germans. The growing number of women with the army may have reflected an increased number of loyalist refugees attaching themselves to Crown forces as the war turned against the British.[76]

The encumbrance of women caused problems for the king's troops similar to those experienced by Washington's forces. General William Howe issued 26 orders concerning women. Conspicuous among these were those dealing with rations and the order of march. "The women of the army are constantly to march upon the flanks of the baggage of their respective corps, and the Provost Martial has received positive orders to drum out any woman who shall dare disobey this order."[77] Any woman abandoned by the army lost the privilege of drawing rations. Finally, the conduct of the women was a major issue, and those who marched with the army came under a strict form of military justice. One soldier's wife who was determined to have received stolen goods was sentenced to "one hundred lashes on her bare back, with a cat-o'-nine tails, at the cart's tail, in different portions of the most conspicuous parts of the town, and to be imprisoned three months."[78]

British and German army officers also took their wives on military expeditions. The Baroness Fredericke von Riedesel may be the best-known of all those who crossed the Atlantic to be with their spouses. She published a detailed memoir of her journey from Germany with her small children and of how she tried to support her husband as she traveled with him on campaign. "I remained about an hour's march behind the army, and visited my husband every morning in the camp. Very often I took my noon meal with him, but most of the time he came over to my quarters and ate with me."[79]

INFORMANTS AND SUPPORTERS

Some women took a very active role in the campaigns of their respective armies. Nancy Morgan Hart, Dicey Langston, and Lydia Barrington Darragh each found herself in possession of information that could be valuable for the patriots. Waiving concern for their personal safety, each found a way to deliver the information to the troops. Sisters-in-law Grace and Rachel Martin, whose husbands were away fighting the British, learned of a British courier who was carrying important dispatches. The two women, dressed in their husbands' clothing and brandishing rifles, hid in the woods through which the courier and his escort had to pass. They surprised the group and demanded the papers. The women then melted back into the forest and delivered the documents to the American camp.

Elizabeth Zane was among those in the settlement at Fort Henry, Virginia, when 350 British and Indians attacked. The supply of gunpowder soon ran low. A cabin only 60 yards outside the walls was known to contain a substantial cache. Although many of the men among the defenders volunteered to retrieve it, Elizabeth was able to convince them that she was the obvious choice. The young woman may have aroused the curiosity of the attackers, but she arrived at the cabin unmolested. Her return trip was not so simple. With the powder tied in a cloth on her shoulder, the fearless young woman sprinted back to the fort as sharpshooters attempted to distract the enemy. The gunpowder that Elizabeth brought was enough for the settlers to hold off the attackers, who eventually gave up.

Sybil Ludington

The job of the alarm riders did not end with the first battles of the Revolution. Individual couriers served throughout the war. One of the most interesting persons to serve in this capacity was sixteen-year-old Sybil Ludington. Sybil was at home in Fredericksburg, New York, on the evening of April 26, 1777, when word reached her that British maj. gen. William Tryon was poised to burn the town of Danbury, Connecticut, twenty-five miles away. Sybil saddled her horse, Star, and rode a circuit of almost forty miles through Carmel, Mahopac, and Kents Falls, New York, warning the militia. Although the roads were dark and unfamiliar to her, Sybil succeeded in rousing enough men to help drive the British south along the Norwalk River, where they retreated to ships waiting in Long Island Sound.

WOMEN IN UNIFORM

Deborah Sampson[80] took a bold step when giving her support to the cause of liberty. One night the young woman left home and journeyed thirty miles north to another community, where, dressed as a man, she enlisted in the Fourth Massachusetts Regiment as a youth, "Robert Shurtleff." Deborah was slightly wounded in battle several times. Fearing detection, she insisted each time upon treating her own wounds. Her fraud was uncovered when she contracted a fever and was hospitalized. "Private Shurtleff" was then honorably discharged from service in October 1783. Deborah's experience was not unique. Military records show that in August 1777, "Samuel Gay" of Massachusetts was "discharged, being a woman, dressed in men's cloths."[81] Another woman, Sally St. Clair, is said to have kept her gender concealed until she was killed during the battle of Savannah. These are only a few women known to have served. There may have been others of whom no record exists, or those whose secret was never discovered. In every case where a woman was discovered passing as a man, she was discharged from the service.

It may seem strange that a woman living in such close quarters with men could conceal her gender for so long, but several eigthteenth-century social presumptions made such a deception much easier than it would be today. Clothing did much in this period to establish the trade, wealth, and gender of the wearer. If you dressed as a merchant, it was assumed that you were a merchant. People did not generally dress out of their station, and women did not dress in male attire. Biases about the physical, emotional and intellectual abilities of women, as well as limitations regarding acceptable female roles, forestalled the concept of a female soldier and minimized the likelihood of the men raising suspicions about another soldier's gender. It is likely that a young, thin woman in disguise would be seen as a male youth of frail physique who had not yet begun to shave. The disguise would be even more complete if the woman was physically strong and able to sustain the rough language and behavior of her fellow soldiers.[82]

TRAGIC LOYALTY

Much of the frontier warfare was carried on by "Tory bands in league with the Indians."[83] In June 1777, many of the families on the New York frontier were apprehensive due to Burgoyne's advance with a large army composed of British regulars, loyalists, and allied Indians. Jane McCrea, the daugther of a Scottish Presbyterian minister from New Jersey, was one of these. When Jane's widowed father died, she went to live with her brother, John, in Fort Edward, New York, near the southern end of Lake George. Here she was befriended by the loyalist McNeil family, and in 1775 she became engaged to a young local man named David Jones, who was a loyalist lieutenant with Burgoyne's army.

Early on the morning of June 27, 1777, Jane and Mrs. McNeil were captured by Indians. There was no question that the Indians were British allies, yet the two women were taken away separately toward the British army. According to McNeil, her party of Indians stumbled into a group of patriots, who fired upon them several times with little effect, and she arrived at the British camp without further incident. Here she reported Jane McCrea's capture. That evening a Wyandot Indian returned to the British camp displaying the long blonde tresses of McCrea as a trophy. The offending Indian told of an American attack on their party during which Jane was killed by patriot musket fire. He had taken the scalp as a simple matter of course. The Indian and many of his companions had disappeared from the British camp by the next morning.

Burgoyne was mortified by the incident. An officer in the camp reported, "The cruelties committed by [the Indians] were too shocking to relate, particularly the melancholy catastrophe of the unfortunate Miss McCrea, which affected the general and the whole army with the sincerest regret and concern for her untimely fate." Evidence taken from the body suggested that McCrea had indeed been shot through the body three times, but her skull was intact. This suggested that the tale told by the Indians may have been true, since it was common for captives who were killed to be bludgeoned upon the head before scalping.[84]

The Americans jumped upon the story as a primer for their lagging propaganda campaign against Burgoyne: "Miss McCrea was . . . carried into the woods, and there scalped and mangled in a most shocking manner . . . [by] a murderer employed by you. Upwards of one hundred men, women, and children have perished by the hands of the ruffians to whom it is asserted you have paid the price of blood."[85] The immediate effect of the story was to bring hundreds of uncommitted frontier settlers to the side of the patriots at the Saratoga battlefield.

NOTES

1. Richard Walsh, ed., *The Writings of Christopher Gadsen* (Columbia: University of South Carolina Press, 1966), 83.

2. Mary Beth Norton, *Liberty's Daughters: The Revolutionary Experience of American Women, 1750–1800* (Boston: Little, Brown, 1980), 159.

3. Carol Berkin, *First Generations: Women in Colonial America* (New York: Hill and Wang, 1996), 175.

4. Linda K. Kerber, *Women of the Republic: Intellect and Ideology in Revolutionary America* (Chapel Hill: University of North Carolina Press, 1980), 42.

5. Ray Raphael, *A People's History of the American Revolution* (New York: New Press, 1991), 108.

6. Helen Evertson Smith, *Colonial Days and Ways* (New York: Century, 1901), 301–302.

7. Norton, *Liberty's Daughters*, 169.

8. Ibid.

9. Dorothy Dudley, *Theatrum Majorum: The Diary of Dorothy Dudley* (New York: Arno Press, 1971), 67.

10. Smith, *Colonial Days*, 263.

11. Ibid., 275.

12. Trenchers were wooden bowls and plates common in the eighteenth century.

13. Smith, *Colonial Days*, 245.

14. Norton, *Liberty's Daughters*, 178.

15. Ibid., 179.

16. Elizabeth F. Lumis Ellet, *Domestic History of the American Revolution* (New York: Charles Scribner, 1859), 254. Author is usually listed as Mrs. Ellet.

17. Norton, *Liberty's Daughters*, 187.

18. Elaine Forman Crane, ed., *The Diary of Elizabeth Drinker: The Life Cycle of an Eighteenth Century Woman* (Boston: Northeastern University Press, 1994), 65.

19. Ellet, *Domestic History*, 224–225.

20. Smith, *Colonial Days*, 311.

21. D. Hamilton Hurd, *History of Fairfield County, Connecticut* (Philadelphia: J. W. Lewis, 1881), 642.

22. Selma R. Williams, *Demeter's Daughters: The Women Who Founded America 1587–1787* (New York: Atheneum, 1976), 255–257.

23. Smith, *Colonial Days*, 226–227.

24. William Guthman, *The Correspondence of Captain Nathan and Lois Peters* (Hartford: Connecticut Historical Society, 1980), 10.

25. Ibid., 15.

26. Ibid., 21.

27. Ibid., 24.

28. Ibid., 20.

29. Ibid., 19.

30. Ibid., 25.

31. Joseph Crary was Lois's brother, who also had enlisted in the local company.

32. Guthman, *Correspondence . . . Peters*, 27.

33. Ibid., 45.

34. Ibid., 28.

35. Ibid., 34.

36. Ibid., 48.

37. Carl Holliday, *Women's Life in Colonial Days* (Williamstown, MA: Corner House Publishing, 1968), 101.

38. Milton Meltzer, ed., *The American Revolution: A History in Their Own Words 1750–1800* (New York: Thomas Y. Crowell, 1987), 78.

39. Holliday, *Women's Life*, 304.

40. Ibid., 308.

41. Ibid., 304.

42. There were reports of patriots looting loyalist homes as well.

43. Caroline Gilman, ed., *Letters of Eliza Wilkinson During the Invasion and Possession of Charleston, S.C. by the British in the Revolutionary War* (New York: Arno Press, 1969), 28–30.

44. Ibid., 31, 43.

45. Howard Swiggett, *War Out of Niagara: Walter Butler and the Tory Rangers* (New York: Columbia University Press, 1933), 360–361.

46. Norton, *Liberty's Daughters*, 199–200.

47. Smith, *Colonial Days*, 244–248.

48. See James M. Volo and Dorothy Denneen Volo, *Daily Life on the Old Colonial Frontier* (Westport, CT: Greenwood, 2002), for information on the reasons Indians took captives and how they were treated.

49. Linda Grant DePauw and Conover Hunt, *Remember the Ladies: Women in America, 1750–1815* (New York: Viking, 1976), 86.

50. Raphael, *A People's History*, 134.

51. Henry Steele Commager and Richard B. Morris, *The Spirit of Seventy-six: The Story of the American Revolution as Told by Participants* (New York: Harper & Row, 1975), 424.

52. Sutlers were merchants who sold liquor and other staples to soldiers. These purveyors transported their goods to camp and set up business. Some followed the troops as they moved. Licensed sutlers had to agree to follow army regulations and to obey orders. Occasionally, nonlicensed vendors made their way in to camp either by stealth or by oversight.

53. Holly A. Mayer, *Belongs to the Army* (Columbia: University of South Carolina Press, 1996), 1.

54. Walter Hart Blumenthal, *Women Camp Followers of the Revolution* (Salem, NH: Ayer, 1992), 63.

55. Meltzer, *The American Revolution*, 145.

56. Kerber, *Women of the Republic*, 56.

57. Ellet, *Domestic History*, 93.

58. Mayer, *Belongs to the Army*, 126.

59. John C. Fitzpatrick, ed., *Writings of Washington*, vol. 9 (Washington, DC: U.S. Government Printing Office, 1933), 17.

60. Ibid., 203.

61. Ibid., 78–80. For rates of pay, see Kerber, *Women of the Republic*, 56.

62. Fitzpatrick, *Writings of Washington*, 78–80.

63. Ibid., 126.

64. John Hyde Preston, *Revolution 1776* (New York: Harcourt, Brace, 1933), 179.

65. Fitzpatrick, *Writings of Washington*, 347.

66. Kerber, *Women of the Republic*, 56.

67. Joseph Plumb Martin, *Private Yankee Doodle: Being a Narrative of Some of the Adventures, Dangers and Sufferings of a Revolutionary Soldier* (Boston: Little, Brown, 1962), 132–133.

68. Norton, *Liberty's Daughters*, 200.

69. Mayer, *Belongs to the Army*, 15.

70. Blumenthal, *Women Camp Followers*, 86.

71. Dudley, *Theatrum Majorum*, 55.

72. Ibid., 69.

73. John Tebbel, *George Washington's America* (New York: E. P. Dutton, 1954), 308.

74. Blumenthal, *Women Camp Followers*, 15–16.

75. Ibid., 41.

76. Ibid., 18–19.

77. Ibid., 43.

78. Ibid., 42.

79. Baroness Fredericke Riedesel, *Letters and Journals* (New York: Arno Press, 1968), 116.

80. Deborah Sampson is often identified by her married name, Gannett, the name under which she petitioned the government for a pension. At the time of her service she was not married.

81. Raphael, *A People's History*, 125.

82. See Dorothy Denneen Volo and James M. Volo, *Daily Life in the Age of Sail* (Westport, CT: Greenwood, 2002), 170–173.

83. Claude Halstead van Tyne, *Loyalists in the American Revolution* (Gansevoort, NY: Corner House Historical Publications, 1999), 184.

84. John Koster, "Jane McCrea, Remembered as a Victim of American Indian Brutality, May Have Died Under Different Circumstances," *Military History* (June 2000), 16.

85. Ibid.

14

Sacrifice, Shortage, and Substitution

The exactions of the Mother Country had rendered it impossible for any but the wealthiest to import anything to eat or wear, and all had to be raised and manufactured at home, from bread stuffs, sugar and rum to linen and woolen for our clothes and bedding.

—Mrs. Smith of Sharon, Connecticut

FOOD

It was not until 1796, when Amelia Simmons published *American Cookery*, that the first cookbook written by an American author appeared. Prior to that, American cooks referred to English works for culinary guidance. Cookbooks had been published in the colonies since 1742 but, like *The Compleat Housewife* by Eliza Smith, first printed in London in 1727, these were wholesale reprints of older English works. The only acknowledgment of its American audience in the 1772 Boston edition of Susannah Carter's *The Frugal Housewife* was the inclusion of two plates engraved by Paul Revere. Hanna Glasse's *The Art of Cookery Made Plain and Easy* was one of the best-selling cookbooks in 1776, and it was an essential reference for several prominent Americans. George Washington and Thomas Jefferson each owned a copy. Benjamin Franklin, an avid proponent of "American cookery," had recipes from the Glasse book translated into French in preparation for his trip to Paris in 1776.

No mention was made in these books of squash, cranberries, pumpkins, or other items introduced to the colonists by Native Americans.

Although certain American ingredients such as turkey, tomatoes, chocolate, and vanilla had made their way into English works by the mid-eighteenth century, their appearance in cookbooks was in no way in deference to American tastes. It merely showed the evolution of English taste. In some cases these ingredients were identified with other European countries. Ironically, the beans commonly referred to in English works as "French beans" were in fact, American. Glasse's instructions on how "To dress Haddocks after the Spanish-way" required the inclusion of American "love apples [tomatoes], when in season."[1]

Receipt Books

Recipes, or receipts, as they were known, were copied by hand and kept in booklet form for future reference. These receipt books included far more than foods, and contained formulas for household cleaning agents, cosmetic aids, and medicine. New receipts were shared within a community or could be copied from almanacs, publications that reached a much wider proportion of the population than cookbooks, which were generally owned only by the wealthy.

Diarists and letter writers commonly documented special meals served at holidays and feasts, but little was ever written about the mundane, day-to-day fare upon which most people survived. Although they appeared on eighteenth century menus, the average colonial never tasted ice cream or enjoyed lemon tarts. Citrus fruits, like lemons and oranges, and pineapples were available only in seaport towns, and even then their high cost was prohibitive to the average pocketbook. Pineapples brought home by seamen were left on the front steps of the home as a symbol of hospitality and welcome. Their distinctive shape was sometimes incorporated into ornaments and door knockers.[2]

Some insight into dining patterns can be gained from soldiers who interacted with the local residents. A patriot colonel, a prisoner taken at Fort Washington, was paroled and billeted with a family in Flatbush, New York. While the accommodations were very clean, he initially found it difficult to adjust to the meager fare of the poor family. He recalled, "A sorry wash was made of a sprinkling of bohea,[3] and the darkest sugar on the verge of fluidity, with half-baked bread,[4] and a little stale butter, constituted our breakfast. At our first coming, a small piece of pickled beef was occasionally boiled for dinner, but to the beef, which was soon consumed, there succeeded clippers or clams; and our unvaried supper was supon or mush, sometimes with skimmed milk, but more generally with buttermilk blended with molasses, which kept for weeks in a churn, as swill is saved for hogs. I found it, however, after a little use, very eatable; and supper soon became my best meal."[5]

Thomas Anderson escaped from the prison ship *Jersey* and traversed Long Island, making his way to safety. He recorded the kindness of a woman in Suffolk County. "I had nothing more to say than to apprise her that I was penniless. In a few moments she placed on the table a bowl of bread and milk, a dried blue fish roasted, and a mug of cider."[6]

Diet

Menus reflected the season's bounty and maintained a strongly regional character. Economics was also a key factor. Affluent residents in cities and on plantations dined on far more sophisticated fare than the average rural farmer. A British traveler visiting Virginia plantations in 1775 reported that the breakfast table was replete with "roasted fowls, ham, venison, game, and other dainties. Even at Williamsburg it is the custom to have a plate of cold ham on the table; and there is scarcely a Virginia lady who breakfasts without it."[7] This could scarcely be considered a typical breakfast for those scraping out a living on a frontier farmstead, or providing for a retinue of apprentices and journeymen in a household dedicated to trade. Moreover, it was not unusual for breakfast to include leftovers from the previous evening's meal. This was not simply a thrifty practice; it was extremely practical in the days before modern refrigeration.

Rural farmsteads produced almost all the foodstuffs required for daily use. Meat that was raised for consumption was supplemented by game. What was not to be consumed immediately was preserved by drying, smoking, pickling, or salting. Autumn's harvest brought with it several weeks of intensive labor during which nature's bounty was preserved. To survive the winter a family needed barrels of salted pork, crocks of corned beef, and racks of smoked or sugar-cured ham, bacon, and sausage. Root vegetables such as beets, cabbage, carrots, onions, parsnips, potatoes, radishes, turnips, and winter squash were stored in root cellars, or packed in straw and stored in barrels.[8] The straw acted as a barrier to prevent the spread of spoilage to the entire barrel. Carrots were often buried in boxes of sawdust. Other vegetables, such as corn, beans, and peas, were dried.

Green corn was preserved by turning back the husk, leaving only the last, very thin layer, and then hanging it in the sun or a warm room to dry. When it was needed for cooking, it was parboiled and cut from the cob. Sweet corn was parboiled, cut from the cob, dried in the sun, and stored in a bag that was kept in a cool, dry place. It could also be dried in the husk and then buried in salt. Whole string beans, and slices and strips of squash and pumpkin, were strung on a thread and hung to dry. Vegetables could also be preserved by making them into catsups and relishes. "Catsup" was the general name given to sauces that were made from vegetables and fruits. Cabbage was made into sauerkraut by pickling.[9]

While city dwellers had access to more exotic foods and imports than country residents, they were far removed from the land's natural bounty of game, fruits, and berries. They were dependent upon rural producers to supply them with fresh foodstuffs. It was not uncommon for city residents to maintain small garden patches or fruit trees to supplement their market purchases.

Cooking

When the colonists first settled in America, they cooked much in the manner of the Native Americans who taught them. As time went on, they adapted their traditional ways of cooking to the foods that were available. European and native cooking techniques thereby evolved with time and the availablity of cookware. It would be an error to think that cooking was done over the flames of the fire. Fireplace cooking was best accomplished by using the heat of hot coals produced at the back of the fireplace. Coals were produced by burning hardwoods, like oak and hickory, rather than resinous woods, like pine and spruce, that flamed brightly but quickly lost their heat. A family farmstead carved from a stand of pine trees, therefore, might be hard pressed to provide the proper wood for heating and cooking.

Boiling was the most common method of cooking. A boiling pot required little attention, thus allowing the busy housewife to attend to her myriad other duties. It also required only one pot that could be hung in the fireplace from a lugpole or crane. Cooking temperatures were adjusted by raising or lowering the pot through the use of pothooks, chains, or a mechanical trammel. Stews, thick soups, and porridges were commonly made by this method, and a pot of dried beans or peas might be found soaking in warm water on the hearth at almost any time of day.

Roasting was also popular. The problem with this method was that the food needed constant attention in order to assure even cooking. The task of turning the roast often fell to a small child. A roast or bird could be hung vertically from a pair of cords fastened inside the chimney. When twisted, the cords wound and unwound around each other for quite some time and with an amazing regularity that more evenly cooked the meat. Very wealthy families sometimes had a weighted clockwork device for the purpose of rotating meats. Reflector ovens, which reflected the fire's heat to the back of the roast as it turned, were less expensive than more intricate devices. They contained a hinged door at the back that could be opened to permit basting, and a place for a tray to collect the drippings. Meat might also be broiled on a gridiron placed over coals on the hearth apron.

Roasting often lost the fats and drippings of the meat to the flames. Today we shun fatty meats, but maintaining the caloric count of fatty foods was important in a time when food resources were limited. Frying retained the juices of the meat and was done in long handled, three-legged skillets called spiders. Frying pans were also used to cook food other than meats in oil, fat, lard, or butter. Flat disks of cornmeal, wheat flour, bread dough, and the meats of acorns or chestnuts were sometimes prepared in this manner into hoecakes or journey cakes. Batters of many types and spoon breads were dropped into boiling oils to cook them. Oil and lard were more easily preserved than butter, which, if unsalted, turns rancid very quickly in the absence of cool temperatures.

Baking was done in an oven built into the fireplace. Sometimes bake ovens were separate structures built outside the home and covered with a little wooden roof that extended a few feet in front of the oven. In either case, a fire was built in the oven and kept burning until the bricks were hot. Every baker had her own method of knowing when the proper temperature had been reached. The coals and ashes would then be swept out, the flue closed, and the food placed within. Mrs. Smith of Sharon, Connecticut, recalled to her children, "[B]y five o'clock [in the morning] the bread was ready to be molded, the hickory coals were lying in great glowing mass on the oven bottom, casting a brilliant light over its vaulted top and sending such a heat into my face when I passed by the oven mouth that it caused me to think then, as it always does, of Nebuchadnezzar's firery furnace, seven times heated."[10]

The majority of the baking was done once a week in order to best utilize the labor represented in the vast amount of firewood required to heat the oven. Breads would be baked in the hottest oven, followed by meat pies, fruit pies, and more delicate pastries. Baking could also be done in lidded cast-iron pots. These pots, sometimes called Dutch ovens by students of the period, had short legs that permitted them to sit on coals in front of the fire. The heavy lids of these pots had a raised rim that permitted the placing of coals on top of the pot. In this way the food received heat from both above and below. All types of pies could be conveniently baked in such an oven.

BEVERAGES

Since the quality of water was always questionable, most meals were served with beer or cider. Rural housewives brewed what was known as "small" beer every week or so, and it was consumed shortly after brewing. "Strong" beer was brewed annually in the fall, and in most cases it was made by those with expertise in the craft. Cider was an excellent way to preserve the apple harvest. The liquid from the pressed fruit was allowed to ferment naturally in jugs or barrels in the cool of the cellar until it was mildly alcoholic. Cider that was served in taverns usually had a slightly higher alcoholic content than that made at home because sugar was added during the fermentation process. New Englander Josiah Bartlett evidenced a regional preference among ciders when he wrote to his wife from Philadelphia, "I am sorry to hear there is like to be a scarcity of cider, as I sensibly feel the want of it here, where there is always a scarcity or rather where they never use much of it, and what is made is very inferior to the New England cider. If you will purchase a few barrels . . . I should be glad of a little (after so long fasting from it) when I return home."[11]

Boycott

The boycott of tea was one of the most popular endeavors of patriots during the years leading to the Revolutionary War. Eschewing tea became a badge of honor among many colonial households, although it was not always easy to abstain from this popular beverage. Throughout the colonies hundreds of women pledged to forgo the use of the unjustly taxed leaves. Newspapers waged campaigns against tea. To dissuade people from using the brew some boycott leaders and patriot newspapers circulated stories that tea was a poisonous brew, responsible for stomach ailments and nervous disorders. They asserted that tea bred lice and fleas. It was even suggested that the tea was prepared for export by being pressed into its container by the bare, dirty feet of Chinese workers.[12]

Prior to the boycott of the Continental Association, tea was commonly served in the morning as part of breakfast or in the late afternoon as a social event. Colonials preferred their tea strong and brewed it dark. Bohea was so popular that the name came to be used as a slang term for tea itself. Lighter teas, such as Souchong and Hyson, comprised only about 10 percent of the colonial imports.[13] The tax on tea was mainly felt by the more affluent colonists, to whom tea drinking had become a social ritual.

To properly serve tea, a hostess needed a profusion of ancillary items in addition to the tea kettle, teapot, and teacups. Serving tea required the right tea table, canisters, bowls, saucers, spoons, strainers, a milk or cream pitcher, sugar container, sugar tongs, and a slop bowl.[14] Few common people could afford the tea, let alone the paraphernalia needed to serve it in proper form. Custom even dictated the arrangement of the serving pieces. On a round table the cups and saucers would be arranged in a circle. On a rectangular table, the drinking vessels would be lined up in rows. In either case, the teapot was the centerpiece of the arrangement, flanked by the sugar and creamer on one side and the slop bowl on the other.

Liberty Tea

The colonial housewife experimented with a variety of native plants in an effort to find a palatable substitute for tea. Made from the four-leaf loosestrife plant, liberty tea was extremely popular. The stalks were stripped of the leaves and boiled. The leaves were placed in an iron kettle and basted with the liquor from the stalks. Finally, the leaves were oven dried. Over time the term "liberty tea" has been applied to any of the homegrown tea substitutes devised by creative colonists.

Ribwort, strawberry, elderberry, blackberry, and currant leaves were used as substitutes, as were sassafras, dittany, sage, and thoroughwort (boneset). Some teas also included flowers, such as the blossoms of linden, elder, red clover, chamomile, violets, and roses. Other teas came from the bark of sassafras or willow trees, or from twigs of the sweet gum, seeds of fennel and dill, and the fruit of the rosebush, commonly known as rosehips. In the Carolinas a plant that thrived in the sandy soil yielded Yeepann tea. Oswego tea, which bore the name given to it by the Native Americans who originally introduced it to the colonists, was popular in the Midatlantic region. It was brewed from bee balm leaves and flowers, lemon balm, and mint. Hyperion tea was made from raspberry leaves. An advertisement of the day boasted, "The use of Hyperion or Labrador tea is everyday coming into vogue among people of all ranks."[15]

Forsaking their beloved tea was difficult for many. Lois Peters beseeched her husband, "I should be glad of a little tea among the rest of my wants."[16] Baroness Frederika von Riedesel, wife of a Hessian general, sensed the depth of the colonial passion for tea during her stay in a Virginia tavern. As she prepared tea for herself and her husband, she noted that the woman of the house "watched greedily, for the Americans loved tea very much, but had decided not to drink any more, because the tea tax was the cause of the war."[17]

A Boston newspaper contained the following verse in support of the tea boycott:

> Throw aside your Bohea and your green Hyson tea,
> And all things with a new fashioned duty;
> Procure a good store of the choice Labradore
> For there'll soon be enough here to suit ye;
> These do without fear, and to all you'll appear
> Fair, charming, true, lovely and clever;
> Though the times remain darkish,
> Young men may be sparkish,
> And love you much stronger than ever.[18]

In the absence of tea, many colonists turned to coffee. Between 1770 and 1790 coffee consumption in the American colonies increased more than sevenfold.[19] In 1774, John Adams reported in a letter to his wife the following conversation upon his arrival at the home of the Hudsons after a long journey. He said to Mrs. Hudson, "Madam! Is it lawful for a weary traveler to refresh himself with a dish of tea, provided it has been honestly smuggled, or paid no duties?" She replied, "No, sir! We have renounced all tea in this place, but I'll make you coffee." Adams noted that he had drunk coffee every afternoon thereafter and "borne it very well." He concluded, "Tea must be universally renounced, and I must be weaned."[20]

Coffee, like tea, was imported, but it never became the symbol of protest that tea was. Once trade became interrupted by the war, coffee, too, became difficult to acquire. A variety of nuts and grains were parched and boiled in an attempt to find a suitable substitute. Rye grain and chestnuts were the most common choices. Mrs. Smith recalled drinking "wheat coffee (which was all we could get in those days, and a poor substitute it was for good Mocha)."[21] The *New York Gazette and Weekly Mercury* hoped to inspire women to forgo tea, reporting that a group of New Hampshire women "made their breakfast upon rye coffee."[22]

Chocolate was another popular warm beverage among affluent colonists. It was imported in blocks. To make a pot of chocolate, a quantity was shaved from the block and boiled in water. Milk and sugar were added according to taste. The supply of chocolate, too, soon fell victim to the war.

SHORTAGES AND SCARCITY

As Britain cut off the regular channels of trade to the American colonies, certain commodities became increasingly difficult to obtain. Sugar, salt, and molasses quickly fell into short supply. West India molasses nearly doubled in price. Medicine and pins were almost impossible to obtain. The shortages were exacerbated by merchants who sought to profit from the situation. In July 1777, such opportunism turned a group of Massachusetts women into a raging mob. Abigail Adams wrote, "You must know that there is a great scarcity of sugar and coffee, articles which the female part of the state is very loath to give up, especially whilst they consider the scarcity occasioned by the merchants having secreted a large quantity."[23]

A similar situation occurred when a merchant's wife sought to avoid conflict by offering sugar for $4.00 a pound. An outraged group of 22 women, escorted by two soldiers, seized the sugar and distributed it at a considerably reduced price. Small dramas like these took place until the merchants' stockpiles were exhausted. "Some stores have been opened . . . and the coffee and sugar carried into the market and dealt out by pounds."[24]

Colonists tapped their personal resourcefulness and natural resources in order to discover replacements for scarce and highly taxed foodstuffs. Sugar was used mainly by families of wealth. It came in very hard cones, called loaves, that weighed 8 to 10 pounds each. The sugar, having a consistency of hard candy, would be removed from the loaf into usable quantities by the use of a sugar nipper. Less affluent colonials made greater use of molasses, which also was imported but less expensive. In some areas, sugar and molasses were replaced by maple syrup or maple sugar produced domestically and sold for about a quarter of the price of a white loaf sugar. Honey was another alternative sweetener, but it was seasonal and not widely available. Adaptive cooks discovered that juice squeezed from cornstalks could be used as a sweetener. When dried and boiled, pumpkin pulp was found to be a substitute for molasses. Bakers wishing to sweeten a cake batter often used chopped apples, dried blueberries, pumpkin, or squash. Such ingredients added flavor as well as a bit of sweetening.

The difficulty of importing molasses caused a secondary shortage in the availability of rum. The average American drank almost 4 gallons of rum annually, a practice that colonials hoped to maintain during the war years, not in pursuit of inebriation but because rum was thought to fortify the drinker and help prevent disease. With the shortage of molasses, the price of rum soared. Some innkeepers were so outraged by the enormous increase in the price of rum that they agreed to buy no more until the price was reduced.[25]

Salt

The lack of salt was a particularly serious problem. Salt was one of the main means of preserving meat. Congress intervened in the salt shortage advising provincial authorities "to regulate the price." The local authorities also offered bounties for its production. Many seaside communities erected salt pans, long, covered troughs through which seawater slowly flowed. Throughout the process of passing from pan to pan, the heat of the sun evaporated the water, leaving a thick paste of sea salt that was appropriate for preserving provisions.[26]

When a New Jersey woman received a bushel of salt as a gift from her sisters, she noted, "Being so rich, we thought it our duty to hand out a little to the poor around us, who were mourning for want of salt; so we divided the bushel, and gave a pint to every poor person who came for it—having an abundance for our own use."[27] Alternatives to salt as a preservative were sought, and a lye extracted from walnut ashes was discovered to be an effective preservative, although it did little to improve the flavor of the food.

Foraging and raiding troops were responsible for shortages in rural areas. Loyalist raiders targeted the salt pans of the patriots for destruction. They pillaged rebel homes, taking valuables, clothing, and food. On a farm in North Carolina, "They immediately entered and plundered the house of everything, carrying away also the corn and wheat."[28] In Philadelphia, the Hessians "plunder[ed] at a great rate, such things as wood, potatoes, turnips &c."[29] The nineteenth-century historian Mrs. Elizabeth F. Lumis Ellet recorded, "During the summer, families through the country, near the scene of warfare, lived chiefly on roasted corn, without bread, meat or salt."[30] Murderous gangs of loyalists so devasted the Carolinas that it prompted a verse:

> Carolina, South and North,
> Was filled with pain and woe:
> The Tories took their neighbors' worth,
> And away a Whig must go.[31]

The residents of Redding at first welcomed the proximity of "the dusty battalions" of friendly troops in their winter encampment, but they came to look at their presence with mixed emotions.

A few months' acquaintance opened their eyes to some of the ways of the soldiers, and caused them to speed the army in the spring as heartily as they welcomed them in the autumn. The soldiers . . . plundered the neighboring farmers, whether Whig or Tory, with the utmost impartiality. To them a well-stocked poultry-yard or a pen of fat porkers offered irresistible inducements . . . [U]nder cover of night droves of fat cattle . . . were killed and eaten with as little formality as they were taken.[32]

Shortages were often only regional. In need of flour, Lois Peters wrote to her husband, Nathan, that "there is flour to be bought very cheap at [New] York and it is very scarce here. If you could send me a barrel by Mr. Safford, I should be very glad."[33] After providing medical aid to some gondola men and their wives, Mrs. Morris of Burlington, New Jersey, set about engaging one of the grateful recipients of her charity to deliver into British-held Philadelphia "a quarter of beef, some veal, fowl and flour" for her aged father and sisters in the city. Two nights later, the man returned "with a letter, a bushel of salt, a jug of molasses, a bag of rice, some tea, coffee and sugar and some cloth for coats for [her] poor boys," all of which were available in the city.[34]

A poem by "Anonymous Molly Gutridge" summed up the concerns brought on by these shortages.

> For salt is all the farmer's cry,
> If we've no salt we sure must die.
> We cannot get bread nor yet meat.
> We see the world is nought but cheat. . . .
> These times will learn us to be wise.
> We now do eat what we despis'd.
> I now have something more to say.
> We must go up and down the Bay.
> To get a fish a-days to fry.
> We can't get fat were we to die.[35]

Flour

Abigail Adams painted a desperate picture of privation and need in Massachusetts when she wrote to her husband in 1777:

I wish the men of war [were] better employed than in taking flour vessels since it creates a temporary famine. Here, if I would give a guinea for a pound of flour I don't think I could purchase it. There is such a cry for bread in the town of Boston as I suppose was never before heard, and the bakers deal out but a loaf a day to the largest families. There is such a demand for Indian corn and rye, that a scarcity will soon take place in the country. . . . The meat that is carried to market is miserably poor.[36]

Leonard Gansevoort, Jr., of Albany wrote to Leonard Bronk of Cox-sackie in 1778, seeking his assistance in the face of dwindling supplies: "[R]especting the Flour which I spoke to you about. I would be glad if you would let me know whether you have it to spare. I am greatly in Want of it as I have not any."[37] Gansevoort continued to rely on Bronk to help him, and in 1782 he wrote, "Hard times. I have no butter and am now obliged to send my Negro down to you for some. He has money to pay for whatever he can get . . . Polly says she wants vinegar. If you can help her to some you will do her kindness. We want a great many things for the Winter . . . which are most necessary."[38] Four months later he wrote again, "Polly begins to grow uneasy whenever she looks at her little store of butter. If you can help her . . . you will greatly oblige."[39]

Lois Peters took a more proactive approach, writing to her husband, "[B]utter and cheese [were] never so high here since my remembrance as now. Cheese [is] six pence and butter nine and ten pence per pound. So if you could send some money by my brother, I could . . . buy me a cow and I think it would be very profitable."[40] New Englander Juliana Smith, writing about her Thanksgiving celebration in 1779, details other shortages and how resourceful cooks coped with them. "All the baking of pies & cakes was done at our house and we had the big oven heated and filled twice each day for three days before it was all done. . . . Neither love nor (paper) money could buy raisins, but our good red cherries dried without the pits, did almost as well and happily Uncle Simeon still had some spices in store."[41]

"Of course we have no roast beef. None of us have tasted beef this three years back as it must all go to the army, and too little they get, poor fellows," she wrote. For the feast Juliana's family was able to get "a fine red deer, so that we had a good haunch of venison on each table. These were balanced by huge chines of roast pork at the other ends of the tables. Then there was on one a big roast turkey and on the other a goose, and two big pigeon pasties . . . [and] an abundance of good vegetables of all sorts."[42]

Juliana also noted, "Our mince pies were good although we had to use dried cherries. . . . The pumpkin pies, apple tarts and big Indian pudding lacked for nothing save appetite. . . . Of course we had no wine. Uncle Simeon has still a cask or two but it must be saved for the sick, and indeed, for those well, good cider is a sufficient substitute. There was no plum pudding but a boiled suet pudding stirred thick with dried plums and cherries was called by the old name and answered the purpose."[43] She was further delighted with new vegetable that her Uncle Simeon had grown from seeds imported from England just before the war, and her uncle hoped to have enough the following year for everyone. "It is called Sellery [sic] and you eat it without cooking."[44]

The Cost of Food

Food prices rose and shortages continued throughout the war. When a city was occupied or after the countryside had been ravaged by the armies, what little was left, commanded enormous rates. In 1780, Abigail Adams reported the rampant inflation in Boston: "Beef, eight dollars per pound; mutton, nine; lamb, six, seven and eight. Butter twelve dollars per pound; cheese, ten. Sheep's wool, thirty dollars per pound; flax twenty."[45] In Philadelphia, with its surrounding countryside stripped almost bare by two competing armies of foragers, "[P]rovisions are so scarce with us now, that Jenny gave 2s 6d per lb. for mutton this morning—The people round the country do not come near us with anything, what little butter is bought is 7s 6d."[46] Mary Bartlett of Kingston, New Hampshire, noted the extravagant prices: "molasses found at six pence per gallon . . . New England rum five shillings per gallon, West India seven and six pence per gallon, cotton wool four shillings per pound, Bohea tea ten shillings per pound, and other things in proportion."[47]

NOTES

1. Hannah Glasse, *The Art of Cookery Made Plain and Easy* (Alexandria, VA: Cottom and Stewart, 1805), 239.

2. In her record of Thanksgiving Day, 1779, Juliana Smith noted that her brother, who was returning from college, brought two oranges for the grand-mothers. Unfortunately, the extravagant treats suffered greatly during his three-day journey, and froze in his saddlebags. Too valuable to waste, the frozen del-icacies were soaked in water and eaten nonetheless.

3. Bohea, a popular black tea, was named for the hills of China where it was grown.

4. Fuel would have been very scarce at the time. Undercooking may have been one way of conserving fuel.

5. Elizabeth F. Lumis Ellet, *Domestic History of the American Revolution* (New York: Charles Scribner, 1859) 112. The author is usually listed as Mrs. Ellet.

6. Ibid., 121–122.

7. William Peirce Randel, *The American Revolution: Mirror of a People* (New York: Routledge, 1973), 65.

8. Root cellars were stone and earth structures that provided insulation main-taining a temperature generally between 50 and 60°F.

9. See Dorothy Denneen Volo and James M. Volo, *Daily Life in Civil War America* (Westport, CT: Greenwood, 1998).

10. Helen Evertson Smith, *Colonial Days and Ways* (New York: Century, 1901), 229.

11. Milton Meltzer, ed., *The American Revolution: A History in Their Own Words, 1750–1800* (New York: Thomas Y. Crowell, 1987), 79.

12. Benjamin W. Larabee, *The Boston Tea Party* (New York: Oxford University Press, 1964), 8, 28, 144.

13. Ray Raphael, *A People's History of the American Revolution: How Common People Shaped the Fight for Independence* (New York: New Press, 1991), 17.

14. Prior to refilling a cup of tea, the dregs of the last cup were spilled into the slop bowl.

15. Alice Morse Earle, *Customs and Fashions in Old New England* (Williamstown, MA: Corner House Publishers, 1969), 181.

16. William Guthman, ed., *The Correspondence of Captain Nathan and Lois Peters* Hartford: Connecticut Historical Society, 1980), 35.

17. Selma R. Williams, *Demeter's Daughters: The Women Who Founded America 1587–1787* (New York: Atheneum, 1976), 228.

18. Larabee, *The Boston Tea Party*, 27–28.

19. Raphael, *A People's History*, 17.

20. Williams, *Demeter's Daughters*, 228.

21. Smith, *Colonial Days*, 229.

22. Mary Beth Norton, *Liberty's Daughters: The Revolutionary Experience of Amer-ican Women, 1750–1800* (Boston: Little, Brown, 1980), 159.

23. Williams, *Demeter's Daughters*, 264.

24. Ibid.

25. Arthur Meier Schlesinger, *The Colonial Merchants and the American Revolu-tion 1763–1776* (New York: Frederick Ungar, 1957), 590.

26. Carol Berkin, *First Generations: Women in Colonial America* (New York: Hill and Wang, 1996), 180–181.

27. Ellet, *Domestic History*, 69.

28. Ibid., 185.

29. Elaine Forman Crane, ed., *The Diary of Elizabeth Drinker: The Life Cycle of an Eighteenth Century Woman* (Boston: Northeastern University Press, 1994), 66.

30. Ellet, *Domestic History*, 215.

31. Ibid., 217.

32. D. Hamilton Hurd, *History of Fairfield County, Connecticut* (Philadelphia: J. W. Lewis, 1881), 595.

33. Guthman, *Correspondence. . . . Peters*, 35.

34. Ellet, *Domestic History*, 68–69.

35. Williams, *Demeter's Daughters*, 264–265.

36. Letter of Abigail Adams to John Adams, March 8, 1777, in *The American Revolution: Writings from the War of Independence* (New York: Library of America, 2001), 302.

37. Raymond Beecher, ed., *Letters from a Revolution 1775–1783* (Albany: Greene County Historical Society and New York State American Revolution Bicentennial Commission, 1973), 23.

38. Ibid., 45.

39. Ibid., 46.

40. Guthman, *Correspondence . . . Peters*, 43.

41. Smith, *Colonial Days*, 292–295.

42. Ibid.

43. Ibid.

44. Ibid.

45. Williams, *Demeter's Daughters*, 264.

46. Crane, *Diary . . . Drinker*, 65.

47. Meltzer, *American Revolution*, 78.

15

Diversions

Employ thy time well—if thou mean to enjoy leisure.
—Benjamin Franklin, *Poor Richard's Almanac*

COMMUNITY EVENTS

Gatherings in rural communities were grounded in agricultural activities such as barn raisings, logging bees, and harvest activities. It was common for the women of the community to gather in order to supply a community need, such as cloth for the local minister's family. One woman who attended a spinning bee "did the morning work of a large family, made her cheese, etc. and then rode more than two miles, and carried her own wheel, and sat down to spin at nine in the morning, and by seven in the evening spun 53 knots, and went home to milking."[1]

The custom of spinning bees was seized upon by promoters of the boycott who sought to commandeer the practice and to convert it to a political statement. Spinning bees took on a new meaning as women gathered together to spin not solely for charity but to also to demonstrate their commitment to shun imported fabrics and their passion for home manufactory. However, "the planting and the harvests of the absent soldiers must take precedence of those who remained at home."[2] The papers of the Smith family describe a series of "husking bees" that took place in 1777. The corn of a local "patriot who was absent in the service of his country" was brought to the largest barn in the town. There "[m]en and women, bond and free, boys and girls, 'quality' and 'commonality,' natives and refugees, all toiled together," the work "made as pleasurable as possible by songs and storytelling."[3]

These assemblages provided sufficient manpower for arduous or tedious labor, but they also created an excuse for a social gathering, such as this one during an otherwise bleak and serious period:

> After the evening's task was done and all had adjourned to the house, the different social grades sorted themselves apart. . . . In the broad and high basement were the slave quarters, where in front of blazing logs in wide fireplaces, they roasted potatoes in the ashes, and partook of apples, nuts and cider. . . . In the great kitchen, in whose fireplace an ox might have been roasted whole, another set enjoyed themselves in a similar manner; and in the generous dining-room . . . [a] more sumptuous repast was served. After the supper, reels and contra-dances, where the feet beat merrily to the entrancing strains of . . . "Caius Tite's" fiddle, gave a sportive finish to an evening which after all was done, had not been a long one, for all must be up and toiling again by daybreak or before.[4]

SEWING AND KNITTING

Sewing was always a very important activity. The household needed bed linens and towels, clothing required mending, and growing children always needed something larger. Although sewing was a regular part of her routine chores, spinning and needlework could be a welcome opportunity for a woman to sit down and relax while still being productive. Sewing could be brought along while visiting and done while socializing. The simplicity of the task allowed it to be done by the limited light of the fire at night. Elementary sewing, such as mending and hemming, required little attention and permitted a woman to converse or to listen to someone reading.

Mastery of the needle was essential for all women, young girls were taught needle skills at an early age and were expected to master them. Many samplers, handed down as family treasures, demonstrate tremendous skill even though they were wrought by prepubescent girls. Young Sally Wister proudly made a note in her journal of a conversation she had with a light dragoon officer who was quartered on her family's property. "Observ'd my sampler, which was in full view. Wish'd I would teach the Virginians some of my needle wisdom; [he said] they were the laziest girls in the world."[5] Surely the officer was flattering Sally. Even women who could afford to have servants do their sewing, needed some skill so that they could instruct the servants and direct the work. Women of means also had the free time and the financial means to engage in what is referred to as fancywork. They made decorative items such as bed hangings, Bible covers, chair seats, and pot holders with involved designs done in embroidery, crewel, and tambour work.

Once hostilities opened, women turned away from producing such luxuries and toward more basic needle skills, such as sewing shirts or knitting stockings for the troops. Awareness of the need to be productive was strong. Dorothy Dudley wrote in 1775: "[M]y life for a time runs in a different current from its wont. Our hands are soldiers' property now; jellies are to be made, lint to be scraped, bandages to be prepared for waiting wounds. Embroidery is laid aside and spinning takes its place. Oh, there is such urgent need for economy!"[6] A young woman given refuge in the home of Maj. Gen. Israel Putnam noted, "My amusements were few; the good Mrs. Putnam employed me and her daughters constantly to spin flax for shirts for the American soldiery; indolence in America being totally discouraged."[7] John Smith, detained with his father on their journey to New Haven by a snowstorm, noted, "As no one could be allowed to remain idle in such times of pressing need, my father and I helped to mold bullets for the soldiers' muskets, while gentle Mrs. Reeve sat busily knitting on yarn stockings for their feet."[8]

An event at the Morristown camp illustrates the sweeping commitment of patriot women to productivity.

I was never so ashamed in all my life. You see, (we three wives) thought we would visit Lady Washington, and as she was said to be so grand a lady, we thought we must put on our best bibbs and bands. So we dressed ourselves in our most elegant ruffles and silks, and were introduced to her ladyship. And don't you think we found her knitting and with a (check) apron on! She received us very graciously, and easily, but after the compliments were over, she resumed her knitting. There we were without a stitch of work, and sitting in State, but General Washington's lady with her own hands was knitting stockings for herself and her husband![9]

As the afternoon progressed, Mrs. Washington took the opportunity to remind her visitors that it was very important "that American ladies should be patterns of industry for their country." She appealed to them, saying, "We must become independent by our determination to do without what we cannot make ourselves. Whilst our husbands and brothers are examples of patriotism, we must be patterns of industry."[10] Nonetheless, some domestic handiwork was mandated by law because the troops were in desperate need of clothing. Several states set production quotas for towns. The residents of Hartford, Connecticut, for example, were required to produce 1000 coats and waistcoats and 1600 shirts.[11]

READING

For those of sufficient wealth to enjoy a bit of leisure time, reading was a popular pastime. Affluent diarists often briefly noted that they spent time reading. Reading was also enjoyed as a group activity, and it was common for one person to read while others listened and worked on sewing or knitting.

With the exception of newspapers, almanacs, sermons, and political pamphlets, most reading material in the colonies, at the beginning of the Revolution, was imported from London. One rare exception was John Dickinson's *Letters from a Farmer in Pennsylvania*. Sales of this 1768 work were so strong that it may well be considered a best-seller. Thomas Paine's *Common Sense* and John Trumbull's *M'Fingal* were the only two other publications to attain such popularity. Other popular works were generally of British origin. These included Oliver Goldsmith's *The Vicar of Wakefield*, Laurence Sterne's *Tristram Shandy*, Daniel Defoe's *Robinson Crusoe*, Lord Chesterfield's *Letters to His Son*, and Dr. John Gregory's *A Father's Legacy to His Daughters*.[12]

Lucinda Lee Orr spent two months visiting family in Virginia in 1782, during which time her social life was a whirlwind of visits to different plantations, dinners, teas, and parties. Nonetheless, Lucinda spent a fair amount of time reading. She had a great passion for novels, which were somewhat more popular in the South than in North. Writing to her friend Polly, Lucinda noted that she had read *Lady Julia Mandeville*. "I was much affected. Indeed, I think I never cried more in my life reading a novel; the style is beautiful, but the tale is horrid." In certain quarters, novels were thought to be too stirring for female minds. Lucinda may have agreed. "I have for the first time in my life just read Pope's *Eloiza*. . . . [C]uriousity [*sic*] led me to read it. . . . [T]he Poetry I think beautiful, but do not like some of the sentiments. Some of *Eloiza* is too amorous for a female I think." Lucinda also reported, "Mrs. A. Washington has lent me a new novel called *Victoria*. I can't say I admire the tale, though I think it prettily told." She read *Malvern Dale*, which she fancied was "something like *Evelina*,"[13] and passed an evening reading *Belle Stratta-gem* to her guests.

Fifteen-year-old Sally Wister, a Quaker, made several notations of having "read and work's in turns,"[14] one person reading aloud while others worked. She reported that one evening a dragoon officer billeted in her home outside Philadelphia "took up a volume of Homer's Illiad [*sic*], and read to us." To her delight, "He [read] very well, and with judgment."[15] She was overjoyed to have been brought "a charming collection of books" that included *Joseph Andrews, Juliet Grenville, Caroline Melmoth* and some of *Lady's Magazine*.[16]

Generally, even young women's taste in reading material favored religious, philosophical, or practical topics rather than fiction or humor. Mercy Otis Warren, herself a writer of poetry and plays, counseled her niece, Rebecca Otis, "Throw away no part of your time, in the perusal of . . . the puerile study of romance. . . . [L]eave your leisure to improve your taste, to cultivate your mind, and enlarge your understanding by reading."[17] Even young Lucindia Lee Orr cautioned a friend, "[R]ead something improving. Books of instruction will be a thousand times more pleasing (after a little while) than all the novels in the world. I own myself I am too fond of novel-reading; but by accustoming myself to reading other books I have become less so. I have entertained myself all day reading *Telamachus*. It is really delightful and very improving."[18] Anna Rawle Clifford of Philadelphia wrote in her journal, "Reading French this morning. We have got into *Telamachus*, which is much more interesting than the little fables we were reading before."[19] Ann Rawle Clifford had a particular treat when she spent the day "in looking over the magazines from New York which Benjamin Shoemaker had brought down in the morning."[20] She also reported, "I amuse myself in the evening with Rochefoucault's moral maxims."[21]

The most popular practical works of the period were Jonathan Edwards's *Sermons*, John Witherspoon's works on the Gospels, George Whitfield's *Domestic Medicine or the Family Physician*, Bishop Burnet's *History*, Alexander Pope's *Essay on Man*, Joseph Priestley's *Experimental Philosophy*, and Claredon's *History of the English Rebellion*. Wealthy patrons also sought to anchor their libraries with reference works such as Duhamel's *Husbandry*, Bailey's or Johnson's *Standard Dictionary*, or the *Dictionary of Arts and Sciences*. The *Frugal Housewife and Complete Woman Cook* was popular among women.[22]

Private Collections

Only those of comfortable means could afford to own books. Booksellers in larger cities, like Henry Knox of Boston, had to diversify their offerings if they were to enjoy financial success. They often advertised that they carried ledgers, account books, and stationery; books on divinity, history, law, physics, and surgery; schoolbooks on mathematics, grammar, the classics, and geography; and Bibles. A nineteenth-century study of printing calculated that there were, however, more than fifty booksellers in the colonies. Philadelphia led the way with twenty-one. Boston had seventeen. New York had four. New Haven and Charleston each had three. Newburyport, Salem, Newport, Providence, Hartford, Lancaster, Germantown, Wilmington, Annapolis, and Savannah each had one.[23] Many southern aristocrats had developed an appetite for the accumulation of literary works, and some private plantation libraries were impressive in their size and breadth of subject matter. Thomas Jefferson drew up a list of titles for "the common reader" of his own class "who has not leisure for any intricate or tedious study" that comprised 379 volumes worth more than £100 "in plain bindings."[24]

Libraries

In rural areas, the clergy frequently had the largest collection of books in an area. Many of these men made their volumes available to those who were interested. In this manner the books within a community were often carefully passed from friend to friend in an informal kind of circulating library. Most large cities had subscription libraries. Benjamin Franklin had helped found the first such library in Philadelphia. Users had to pay a fee in order to use the facility. These libraries were found in corners of public buildings or even in private homes. One exception was the Redwood Library in Newport, which was designed by Peter Harrison, who was considered to be one of the most prominent architects of the period. The residents of Charleston were proud of their library. A bequest to the Charleston Library in 1771 of more than 800 volumes made it the best in the South. It even paid the librarian a living wage, a unique practice in a day when colleges assigned professors to the library as part of their duties or paid a nominal fee to an untrained caretaker.

Literary Clubs

One area of Connecticut seems to have been particularly ripe with avid readers and inquiring minds. Prominent residents of Sharon founded the Sharon Literary Club in January 1779. The purpose of the organization was "to promote a taste for the study of *Belles Lettres* and of logic, and to gain some skill in the useful Freeman's *Art of Debate*." Literary clubs of this type were very popular during the nineteenth century, but this must have been quite unusual in its time.[25]

Meetings were held on every Monday evening throughout the year, except from May to the end of September. They would commence with selected readings from books that the members were supposed to be pursuing, such as Caesar's *Commentaries on the Gallic Wars*, Plutarch's *Life of Hannibal*, and Fenelon's *Telemachus*. The readings were then subject to the criticisms of the club's members. After the meeting ended, refreshments were served. This was sometimes followed by an hour of dancing. Seventeen dwellings were mentioned as hosting meetings. At alternate meetings the club was mainly a debating society for the men.

In October 1779 the club established a publication so that the talents of the members might be cultivated in writing as well as reading and speech, and each was expected to make a periodic contribution. The *Clio* was a "Literary Miscellany" issued bimonthly. It contained odes, essays, proverbs, puzzles, sketches, and jokes. "The large, coarse-textured sheets of foolscap [were] ruled down the center of each page to form two columns, and the several sheets are tied together by cords of braided, homespun, unbleached linen thread." The pages were "legibly written in the script of different hands." The contents compared favorably with those of printed literary periodicals of the day. Absent from the paper was any commentary on political issues. This is very odd, considering that the community strongly supported the patriot cause.[26]

Newspapers

Newspapers enjoyed a broader readership than books. The newspapers of the time differed greatly from the daily papers of today. Most were published weekly. Subscriptions were costly. Exclusive of postage or carrier fees, weekly papers averaged 8s a year. Readers of one publication often exchanged their paper with subscribers of another. Colonial papers carried local "news" but also copied articles that appeared in other publications in other cities which may have been weeks old. The news was anything but "late breaking." A report of an important battle or a measure passed in Parliament was more likely to have arrived by a courier or traveler. To fill space, newspapers relied on prose and poetry heavy with sentimentalism, reflection, and affectation of virtue, often copied from London magazines in order to give the publication an air of sophistication.

Newpapers commonly accepted the contributions of patrons who fancied themselves writers. As political tensions heightened, flowery verses were replaced by Whig rhetoric or Tory recriminations. Local political and religious leaders took up the pen in order to rouse public opinion to one cause or the other. Using classical pseudonyms such as "Lucius" and "Brutus," young men, often collegians, were welcomed contributors who passionately spread patriotic fervor. Publications such as *Rivington's Gazetteer* became vehicles for loyalist propaganda, while others, such as Boston's *New England Chronicle*, promptly changed its name to the *Independent Chronicle* and added to its bannerhead "An Appeal to Heaven" with the "figure of a Continental soldier on one side . . . and a scroll 'Independence' on the other."[27]

Newspaper editors controlled the tenor of their publications, and those who supported positions unpopular in the region they served, suffered harsh consequences that ranged from lost revenue to broken presses. Some Tory papers folded. In Boston the Tory editor of *The Chronicle* closed his doors and fled to England. After seventy-two years of publication, the colonies' oldest paper, the *News-Letter*, printed its last issue in 1776. Some newspapers with a divided readership sought to maintain their income by trying to be objective and neutral, but impartiality was often viewed as a lack of patriotic spirit. Many truly objective publications suffered as much as those blatantly pro-British. The *Boston*

Evening Post prided itself on presenting both sides of controversial issues, but following the events at Lexington and Concord, it suspended publication.

Some newspaper editors changed their politics completely. The *Massachusetts Spy*, printed by Isaiah Thomas, initially took a bipartisan position, but shifted support to the patriot party after the fighting at Lexington. When the British occupied New York, John Gaine moved the *New York Mercury* to Newark, New Jersey, to avoid persecution by the regulars. When he returned to the city, he renamed the publication the *Gazette and Weekly Mercury* and gave it a decidedly Tory slant.

James Rivington's *Gazetteer* started out maintaining a neutral position, but was stormed twice by Liberty Boys for printing pro-Tory articles. After Lexington, Rivington felt obliged to place the following public notice:

As many publications have appeared from my press which have given great Offense to the Colonies, and particularly to many of my fellow Citizens; I am therefore led, by a most sincere regard for their favorable Opinion, to declare to the Public, that Nothing which I have ever done, has proceeded from any Sentiments in the least unfriendly to the Liberties of this Continent, but altogether from the Ideas I entertained of the Liberty of the Press, and of my duty as a Printer. I am led to make this free and public Declaration to my Fellow Citizens, which I hope they will consider as a sufficient Pledge of my Resolution, for the future, to conduct my Press upon such Principles as shall not give Offense to the Inhabitants of the Colonies in general, and of this City in particular, to which I am connected by the tenderest of all human Ties, and in the Welfare of which I shall consider my own as inseparably involved.[28]

The *Gazetteer* eventually had to cease publication for a time, but resumed throughout the British occupation of New York as the *Royal Gazette*. Ironically, Rivington experienced a good deal of personal popularity in the city in the postwar years.

In Philadelphia the *Evening Post* began by supporting the patriot party. When the British took the city, it joined two other city newspapers in promoting the Tory position. Once the British pulled out, the paper resumed its pro-patriot stance. This was too much for most readers, who resented any publication that could undergo such frequent and dramatic ideological changes, and the publication's readership declined dramatically.

It was not unusual for women to be newspaper publishers. Margaret Draper continued the publication of the *Boston Newsletter* after the death of her husband in 1774. An advocate of Tory politics, the paper continued in print until the evacuation of the British from the city. Mary Katherine Goddard assumed control of *The Maryland Journal and Baltimore*

Advisor from her brother, and published the newssheet from 1775 to 1784.

As the war raged on, printers were faced with a severe shortage of paper, which prior to the nineteenth century was produced from rags. Rag paper is acid free, sturdy, long-lived, and does not yellow. Many eighteenth-century documents, written on this paper, are in better condition than those more than a century younger printed on wood pulp paper. While rag paper mills existed in both Massachusetts and Pennsylvania, the scarcity of cloth fiber seriously curtailed paper production. In some cases collectors went door-to-door in order to obtain fabric remnants. This naturally caused the price of newspapers to rise considerably and, in some cases, the quality of the paper to diminish.

Almanacs

A number of almanacs enjoyed widespread popularity from colonial times through the Revolution and into the nineteenth century. Franklin's *Poor Richard's Almanac*, which was published from 1732 to 1757, is without a doubt the most famous one of the colonial period, but it was not the only one. Almanacs were printed as pamphlets. They contained a mixture of practical suggestions for managing the home or farm, vague weather forecasts, sagacious maxims for living, and appealing stories for entertainment. In addition to a chronicle of dates, and calculations of the phases of the moon, eclipses, and tides, a typical issue might contain "a prescription for using asses' milk to cure consumption, a poem on the universe, together with receipts for making quince wine, and for the cure of worms in sheep, or of the swollen head for young turkeys."[29] The *Boston Almanac* also printed stage distances between chief towns, the civil list of the Massachusetts province, and the dates of court sessions. This combination of utilitarian and recreational reading made the almanac very popular to the sensible American.

Like other native publications during the war, almanacs showed their Whig or Tory support. Portraits of John Hancock, George Washington, and other patriot leaders appeared in issues, accompanied by suitable lyrics or acrostics. One almanac printed the *Speech of Galagacus to the North Britons*, in which he incited his army to fight for their liberties. A bookseller advertising in the *Independent Chronicle* argued, "This speech alone breathes such a spirit of heroism and liberty that it ought to be read by every friend of his country, and is alone worth treble the price of the almanac."[30] Almanacs that continued in print during the Revolution included Gleason's *Bickerstaff's Boston Almanac*, Rivington's *New Almanack & Ephemeris* by "Copernicus", and Rittenhouse's *Maryland, Virginia and Pennsylvania Almanac*.

Pamphlets

The most influential and widely read medium of communication of the day was the pamphlet. Thomas Paine's *Common Sense* (1776) is the best illustration of the effectiveness of this printed form. No other work of patriotic fervor was so well received or so widely quoted by the American public. Pamphlets were more affordable than books, and their ability to respond to the immediacy of an issue made them highly desirable. Theological discourses and sermons, printed in pamphlet form, were particularly popular. Well-advertised pamphlets of this genre included *Heaven upon Earth, A Penitential Crisis, The Whole Duty of Women, The Religious Education of Daughters*, and *Serial Sermons for the Days of the Week*.

GAMES AND WAGERING

Not all recreational time was spent in lofty pursuits. In higher social circles an evening might well be spent playing chess, checkers, or backgammon. Cards were widely denounced from the pulpit, but both men and women of leisure passed a great deal of time playing card games. Tokens in the shape of fish or other animals, fashioned in bone or ivory, were often used in place of coins as table stakes. Whist and cribbage were particularly popular.

There was a genre of board games involving dice and token pieces moving about a predetermined path, similar to the modern children's game Chutes and Ladders. Very popular as tavern games, these included Snake and The Game of Goose. Wagers were made and forefeits were added to the pot according to the play of the game. Other games, such as Shut the Box and Shove Ha'penny, utilized real boards and mechanical devices. Many of these involved wagers on every round or turn. A good deal of money might be in the pot at the end of the game.

Despite the unfavorable attitute toward wagering, men of the Revolutionary era were passionate gamblers. They would bet on virtually anything: dice, cards, cockfights, elections, horse races, shooting matches, or the fall of a leaf. The Marquis de Chastellux had the opportunity to observe another popular diversion and gambling opportunity. He came upon the Willis Ordinary, which he described as "a solitary place." He was surprised to find there a "numerous assembly, and was informed it was a cockfight. [A] diversion ... much in vogue in Virginia."[31]

Horse Racing

Horse racing was much favored by those in the upper classes, and regular race courses were maintained. A traveler in Virginia, Thomas Anbury, noted: "At Williamsburg there is a very excellent course of two,

three, or four mile heats."[32] Races were held throughout the colonies
before the Revolution, and match races between two contestants were
advertised and well attended by all classes of people with money to bet.
Well before the identification of the modern quarter horse breed, Anbury
was quite amazed at the colonial fascination for racing horses over a
course just a quarter-mile long. He wrote:

Near most of the ordinaries there is a piece of ground cleared in the woods . . .
where there are two paths about six or eight yards asunder which the horses
run in. I think I can say without the slightest exaggeration . . . that even the famous Eclipse could not excel them in speed. . . . These [quarter horses] are trained
to set out in this manner at the moment of starting. It is the most ridiculous
amusement imaginable, for if you happen to be looking another way, the race is
terminated before you can turn your head. . . . [V]ery considerable sums are billeted on these races. Only in the interior parts of this province are these races
held, for they are very much laughed at and ridiculed by the people in the lower
parts, about Richmond and other great towns. At Williamsburg there is a very
excellent course of two, three, or four mile heats.[33]

The love of horse racing led to an interest in breeding racing stock,
particularly of horses tracing their lineage to one of three Arabian stal-
lions of the previous century: the Byerly Turk, the Darby Arabian, and
the Godolphin Arabian. These horses were the foundation sires of Thoroughbred racing in Britain. The famous Eclipse, mentioned by Anbury,
traced his lineage to the Darby Arabian, and was the sole ancestral sire
of all American racing Thoroughbreds. Horses were also developed for
the more personal diversions offered by hunting and saddle riding. Outstanding horseflesh was extensively bred in Virginia, Pennsylvania, Maryland, and Connecticut. The Morgan breed, whose sire was an
outstanding stallion born during the Revolution, was not identified until
after the war.[34]

Lotteries

Churches and colleges, as well as towns, seized on the gambling mania
as a vehicle for raising capital. Public lotteries were held in order to fund
construction and to pay off public debt. New York held a lottery in 1780
in order to fund fire buckets for the city. The following year another was
held to raise funds to relieve the plight of needy loyalist refugees. Lotteries were even held to help fund the patriot military. One such was
organized by Benjamin Franklin in order to pay for cannon for the army.
The success of public lotteries inspired private parties to hold their own
lotteries, which offered books, furniture, jewelry, real estate, and the like
rather than cash prizes. Deceitful practices led to legislation that severely
limited lotteries, and even reputable organizations had to file documents

in advance that detailed the method of the drawing, the names of the managers, the number of tickets and the number of prizes, and the amount to be deducted from each award, which generally ranged from 12.5 to 15 percent of the pot.

PUBLIC HOUSES

The differences between inns, taverns, and ordinaries are lost on students of the period today, but they seem to have been clear enough at the time. In an era before the demonization of alcohol as the cause of social ills, taverns were a popular gathering place for men of all classes. Some served food, and all served liquor. The bar, which was often secured by a slatted gate after closing, was generally the center of attention. Johann David Schoepl wrote, "I stopped at the Tavern Formicola which was naturally much crowded. . . . Every evening there came generals, colonels, captains, senators, delegates, judges, doctors, clerks and gentlemen of every weight and caliber to sit around the fire, drink, smoke, sing, and swap anecdotes or political theories. Very entertaining, but Formicola's not being a spacious house, I found the crowd embarrassing."[35]

The taverns of Philadelphia had a particularly unsavory reputation as tippling and disorderly houses, filled with drunks and prostitutes, respectively. The Indian King was the oldest and most reputable of the city's public houses, and it was here that Ben Franklin and his associates met. Other prominent taverns included the Crooked Billet and the City Tavern. The Tun Tavern was the main source of volunteers for the newly formed corps of American marines. In New York City, Bolton's Tavern was renowned for its food. It was here that Washington gathered with his chief officers for a farewell glass of wine at the conclusion of the war. Fraunces Tavern was another establishment of high repute in the city. Boston's Green Dragon was used by the Order of Masons as a meeting place, and the patriot agitators Joseph Warren, Samuel Adams, James Otis, and Paul Revere often met there to solidify their arguments against British rule. In Virginia, Gadsby's Tavern was popular with the residents of Alexandria, and Christina Campbell's, Chauning's, and the Raleigh Tavern were popular with the members of the House of Burgesses in Williamsburg.

Inns and ordinaries furnished lodging and food to travelers. Accommodations were designed for male travelers only. While traveling, the Marquis de Chastellux complained, "They make nothing in America at an inn of crowding several people into the same room."[36] Few places offered private quarters, and the weary traveler often had to share a room as well as a bed with another guest. Ladies who traveled at this time prearranged their journey, making provisions to stay with relatives, friends, or friends of friends. When this was not possible, a lady would write to a clergyman, who would arrange for lodging with a suitable family. Larger inns often had one spacious public room that could be rented for a concert, lecture, or ball, or for use by sleigh ride parties stopping for supper and dancing. The prominence of these places and their convenience to travelers made them obvious choices for public auctions, meetings, and political rallies.

Prior to the war, many public houses bore names such as The King's Arms or The Royal George in honor of the Crown. As tensions heightened, many changed their names to less politically charged ones, such as The Punch Bowl or The Bull's Head, in order not to alienate any patrons. Following the siege of Boston even the British Coffee House was rechristened the American Coffee House. In Tory strongholds the retention of a British name generally advertised the politics of the patrons who frequented the establishment.

DANCING

An extremely popular diversion, which was enjoyed equally by men and women, rich or poor, was dancing. Rural dances often took the form of an informal frolic composed of square dances and reels held after a community gathering. In cities, more formal balls were held. The Marquis de Chastellux described a ball that took place in Philadelphia in 1780.

At Philadelphia, there are places appropriated for the young people to dance in. . . . A manager or Master of Ceremonies presides at the methodical amusements; he presents to the gentlemen and lady dancers, billets folded up containing each a number; thus fate decides the male or female partner for the whole evening. All the dances are previously arranged and the dances are called in their turns. These dances, like the toasts we drink at table, have some relation to politics; one is called *The Successful Campaign*, another *Bourgoyne's Defeat*, a third *Clinton's Retreat*. The managers are generally chosen from among the most distinguished officers of the army.[37]

Some managers may have been carried away by their military habits. A story was told of "a young lady who was figuring in a country dance, having forgot her turn through conversing with a friend, [the manager] came up to her and called out loud, 'Give over, Miss, take care what you are about. Do you think you come here for your pleasure?' "[38] Balls were so much a part of the social life of the "gentile class" that they were even held by the officers during military encampments. Nathanael Greene recalled a particular visit by Washington. "We had a little dance at my quarters. . . . His Excellency and Mrs. Greene danced upwards of three hours without once sitting down. . . . Upon the whole, we had a pretty little frisk."[39] Following the alliance with France, Henry Knox wrote, "We had . . . a most genteel entertainment given by self and officers. . . . We had above seventy ladies . . . and between three and four hundred gentlemen. We danced all night—an elegant room, the illuminating fireworks, &c. were more than pretty."[40]

THEATER

Stage acting was a late arrival to the colonies. Religious prejudices against theatrical entertainment greatly limited its appeal. It was not until September 5, 1752, in Williamsburg, Virginia, that the first dramatic performance ever given by a regular company of actors in an auditorium was presented. Audiences in Maryland and Virginia were more open to theater than those in the North with their Puritanical heritage, but gradually attitudes toward stage performances changed. By 1761 a regular theater was opened in New York City under the patronage of Governor De Lancy despite vigorous opposition by the Assembly and the city's religious leaders. By 1772 performances were commonly given once or twice a week in both New York and Philadelphia. The strong religious prejudices of Puritan New England supported laws that strictly forbade theatrical performances, especially the comedies and farces of playwrights like Sheridan and Molière. More serious works, like the plays of Shakespeare or Thomas Mallory attracted less bitter criticism, but still fell under the proscription. Many Britons disagreed with colonial bans, and asserted that an act of Parliament allowing public exhibitions had the effect of overriding such provincial prohibitions. Theatricals thus became identified with the Tory cause, and attracted passionate acrimony from among the most conservative Whigs. Once war broke out, many plays and other frivolous amusements were prohibited by local laws throughout the colonies. While the British were in possession of Boston, New York, and Philadelphia, performances were given for officers and Tory sympathizers. One such performance was *The Blockade of Boston*, a play written by General Burgoyne to mock the Continental troops.

LECTURES

In some communities elocution plays were executed as a series of readings that eventually merged into the complete recitation of a play or of a whole opera. Presented as a public speaking exercise, these performances, or lectures, were a means of circumventing local theatrical bans. Nonetheless, the lecture was an established and legitimate form of amusement that was sometimes advertised as a philosophical experiment "for the entertainment of the curious."[41] Lectures were generally presented as a vehicle to expand the mind. One lecture in Philadelphia was touted as a discourse on "pleasant and useful geography,"[42] in which the figure and motion of the earth, and the moon's effect on the tide and wind were revealed. Some lecturers conducted experiments with electricity that perpetuated, expanded, and popularized Franklin's work of midcentury. Others produced suction with a vacuum pump, presented botanical or zoological information, or pretended to show how iron could be heated by cold water.

MUSIC

Audiences also gathered for musical performances. Like balls, concerts, recitals, and chamber performances were commonly done by subscription, and they attracted a "very polite company." In larger cities a series of performances might take place weekly over a period of six or eight weeks, in what was referred to as a concert hall. These concerts could be vocal solos, duets, or occasionally a chorus. Instrumental performances on the violin, French horn, hautboy (oboe), or harpsichord were popular. On a special occasion of public note, a regimental band might perform. Occasionally concerts were given as benefits for a local music teacher or church organist who arranged and conducted the performance himself. Most musical performances were private affairs at social gatherings in homes where young ladies and gentlemen demonstrated their talents to the guests.

PHYSICAL ACTIVITIES

Outdoor pastimes included a form of bowling, quoits, shooting, horseback riding, fishing, hunting, ice skating, and swimming. Benjamin Franklin was renowned for his swimming ability, and as a young man even considered a professional pursuit of swimming in England. Social class dictated the degree of organization and flamboyance of any physical activity. Horseback and carriage riding was done individually or in parties. In warm weather carriage parties might be the prelude to a picnic where, in addition to the food, participants enjoyed fishing, kite flying, and games of blindman's buff or of forfeit. Winter brought sleighing and skating parties that sometimes culminated in an evening of dinner and dancing at a local inn.

Naturally, once fighting broke out in an area, all frivolous activities ceased. The war, however, tended to move from one region of the colonies to another over eight years. After the active fighting moved on, many resumed the amusements they had enjoyed prior to the war. A high social life flourished in areas under British control, which ignored local bans and social correctness. Rebecca Franks of Philadelphia wrote of her stay in New York in 1778, "You have no idea of the life of continued amusement I live in; I scarce have a moment to myself. . . . I have a ball this evening at Smith's where we have one every Thursday. . . . [Y]ou [can] chose [*sic*] at either Plays, Balls, Concerts or Assemblys."[43]

NOTES

1. Laura Thatcher Ulrich, "Daughters of Liberty: Religious Women in Revolutionary New England," in Ronald Hoffman and Peter J. Albert, eds., *Women in the Age of the American Revolution* (Charlottesville: University of Virginia Press, 1989), 226–227.

2. Helen Evertson Smith, *Colonial Days and Ways* (New York: Century, 1901), 263–264.

3. Ibid.

4. Ibid, 264–265.

5. Sally Wister, *Sally Wister's Journal: A True Narrative* (Bedford, MA: Applewood Books, 1995), 46.

6. Dorothy Dudley, *Theatrum Majorum: The Diary of Dorothy Dudley* (New York: Arno Press, 1971), 35.

7. Elizabeth F. Lumis Ellet, *Domestic History of the American Revolution* (New York: Charles Scribner, 1859), 51.

8. Smith, *Colonial Days*, 306.

9. Jeanne Munn Braken, ed., *Women in the American Revolution* (Carlisle, MA: Discovery Enterprises, 1997), 48–49.

10. Ibid.

11. Joan R. Gunderson, *To Be Useful in the World: Women in Revolutionary America, 1740–1750* (New York: Twayne, 1996), 67.

12. William Peirce Randel, *The American Revolution: Mirror of a People* (New York: Routledge, 1973), 181.

13. Alice Morse Earle, *Colonial Dames and Good Wives* (New York: Frederick Ungar, 1962), 192–193.

14. Wister, *Journal*, 39, 40.

15. Ibid., 50.

16. Ibid., 38–39.

17. Linda K. Kerber, *Women of the Republic: Intellect and Ideology in Revolutionary America* (Chapel Hill: University of North Carolina Press, 1980), 240, 253.

18. Earle, *Colonial Dames*, 193.

19. Elizabeth Evans, *Weathering the Storm: Women of the American Revolution* (New York: Charles Scribner's Sons, 1975), 291.

20. Ibid.

21. Ibid., 290.

22. James Schouler, *Americans of 1776: Daily Life During the Revolutionary Period* (New York: Dodd, Mead, 1906), 122–123.

23. Randel, *The American People*, 181.

24. Arthur Pierce Middleton, *A Virginia Gentleman's Library* (Williamsburg, VA: Colonial Williamsburg Foundation, 1952), 3.

25. Smith, *Colonial Days*, 270–271.

26. Ibid., 277–278.

27. Schouler, *Americans of 1776*, 153.

28. Randel, *The American Revolution*, 211.

29. Schouler, *Americans of 1776*, 140.

30. Ibid., 141.

31. Alfred, J. Morrisi, ed., *Travels in Virginia in Revolutionary Times* (Lynchburg, VA: J. P. Bell, 1922), 43.

32. Ibid., 28.

33. Ibid.

34. James M. Volo and Dorothy Denneen Volo, *Encyclopedia of the Antebellum South* (Westport, CT: Greenwood, 2000), 132–133.

35. Morrisi, *Travels in Virginia*, 55.

36. Schouler, *Americans of 1776*, 80.

37. Earle, *Colonial Dames*, 213–214.

38. Ibid., 214.

39. John Tebbel, *George Washington's America* (New York: E. P. Dutton, 1954), 140.

40. Ibid.

41. Schouler, *Americans of 1776*, 110.

42. Ibid.

43. Alice Morse Earle, *Costume of Colonial Times* (New York: Charles Scribner's Sons, 1894), 30–31.

16

Fashion

Though this body is not clad with silken garments, these limbs are
armed with strength, the Soul is fortified by Virtue, and Love of
Liberty is cherished within the bosom.
> —Charity Clarke, writing to an English cousin

'TIS THE FASHION

The way people dressed in the eighteenth century identified their social
class and often their profession as well. Fashion defined the person, and
people did not aspire to dress outside their class. A somber suit of sturdy
woolen broadcloth was the standard daily wear for most professional
men, such as lawyers, doctors, clerks, and public officials. Black was the
choice for almost all clergymen. Warm weather brought out suits of
lighter colored linen. Ostentatious colors and impractical fabrics, characteristic of gaudy young aristocrats known as Italian Macaronis, were
generally used by the upper classes only at the most fashionable social
gatherings. The term *Macaroni* was applied to an outlandish style of male
dress made popular in Europe in midcentury. It appears in a derisive
context in "Yankee Doodle," which was written by a British officer in
1757 and set to a tavern tune by the Americans, who adopted it, along
with the tune "Chester" as an unofficial national anthem.

> Yankee Doodle went to town,
> A'riding on a pony.

Stuck a feather in his hat,
And called it Macaroni.

People living in the rural areas of the colonies were much less affected by the extremes of fashion. Since they generally had to rely on homespun linen and wool, they were more concerned about practicality than style. Nonetheless, on the eve of the Revolution, prosperity had propagated a small social class in the colonies that was infatuated with fashion and finery. Styles mimicked those found in London or Paris, and affluent city dwellers anxiously awaited the arrival of "fashion babies" to learn what was in vogue across the ocean. These dolls were meticulously dressed, male and female, in the latest fashions and were the precursors of the printed fashion plates of the next century. Colonists of means became accustomed to importing the finest wools, linens, silks, satins, brocades, and other products of British mills. Listings of fabrics for sale made up perhaps the single greatest category of newspaper advertisements.

HAIR

Wigs

The wig (periwig or peruke) was a symbol of rank and position among merchants, planters, clerics, and professionals. Wigs were common among the fashionably attired, particularly in urban areas, and the hair could be arranged to suit a wide spectrum of tastes. Popular styles included the "bag wig," in which long hair was tied into a "tail" at the back and secured in a small silk bag. Dandies favored the "cadogan," which secured the long hair in two places. The "square wig" had hair that fell in a loose, shoulder-length, page style that was greatly favored by judges and clergy. Most men preferred the more conservative "major bob," which kept the hair close to the head and was accentuated by two or three rows of tight curls at the temples. Apprentices or other men of lower station generally chose the "minor bob," a bushy style with a center part and secured tail.

The cost of a wig varied with the quality of its construction and the materials used. Complexity and quality were a symbol of a person's social status. Therefore, there was no effort made to conceal the fact that one wore a wig. A contemporary wigmaker's advertising claimed:

To ecclesiastical perukes he gives a certain demure, sanctified air; he confers on the tye-wigs of the law an appearance of great sagacity and deep penetration; on those of the faculty . . . he casts a solemnity and gravity that seems equal to the profoundest knowledge. His military smarts . . . [endow] the wearer [with] a most warlike fierceness.[1]

A wig of high-quality human hair might cost as much as £3. Less expensive wigs made of the hair of cow, goat, or horse could be purchased for as little as 10s. Colors favored in the eighteenth century included white, black, grizzle (a mix of white and black), brown, and flaxen. Reds, like auburn and chestnut, were less fashionable. Maintaining the wig could be costly, and the more complex styles had to be professionally reworked every couple of weeks. Simpler styles could be brushed and cleaned much like one's own hair, and curling irons and ceramic rollers that looked like scissors and pieces of chalk, respectively, could be heated and used to set curls.

To ensure a good fit and to increase comfort, many wig wearers shaved their heads. They often wore a simple turned-up cap when relaxing indoors, working in their shop, or taking an informal walk. These caps could be of simple linen or fancy brocade, and they were often embroidered by a loved one as a gift. Some members of the upper classes affected an oriental style by wearing turbans while lounging at home or talking with neighbors across the backyard fence. It was not uncommon for a man to greet guests in his home dressed in a banian (a formal robe) and an embroidered cap.

Many men of high social rank did not follow the fashion of wearing wigs during the Revolutionary period, and those of the patriot party generally eschewed wigs entirely. These men would dress their own hair in the prevailing style. Most men of the yeomanry queued or clubbed their hair, wearing the tail tied with a ribbon or in a black silk bag. For more formal occasions they might turn a pair of curls at the temples, and would grease their hair and dust the coiffure with white powder.

Hair Half-a-Yard High

Women in the colonies generally did not wear wigs, although they did add in hairpieces to provide extra volume to their own hair or to enhance an arrangement with curls. This was in sharp contrast to the fashion in Europe, where some ladies sported hairstyles of such outlandish width and height that the hair had to be supported by wire frames and wads of wool or tow padding. The back hair was strained up in a maze of loops or short curls. All was kept in place with globs of pomade, dusted with white powder, and surmounted with lace, ribbon, pom-poms, gauze, beads, jewels, flowers, or feathers. By the last quarter of the eighteenth century these towers, or "talematongue," had risen until some structures measured half a yard in height. The style, like that of the male Macaroni, was farcical and the subject of many caricatures.

Colonial women, however, endeavored to create certain elements of that look. The fashionably high forehead that was accentuated by the absurd hairdos of European gentry, was achieved by severely brushing the hair back in order to reveal a full face. Additional height was achieved with padding. A Salem, Massachusetts, hairdresser advertised in 1773: "Ladies shall be attended to in the polite constructions of rolls such as may tend to raise their heads to any pitch they desire."[2] A Philadelphia newspaper of the same period carried an advertisement by a wigmaker that he had created a hair roll which weighed only 3 ounces, compared to the former 8 ounces.[3] The remainder of the long tresses were secured back in some way or worn tightly curled. Prepubescent girls usually wore their hair loose. A Hessian officer made note of women's hairstyles during the war. "They friz their hair every day and gather it up on the back of the head into a chignon at the same time pulling it up in the front . . . sometimes, but not often, they wear some light fabric on their hair."[4]

Overdone hairstyles, like men's wigs, quickly dropped out of favor when the war began, as can be seen in a poem by a patriot urging moderation with respect to hairstyles.

> Ladies you had better leave off your high rolls
> Lest by extravagance you lose your poor souls
> Then hand out the wool, and likewise the tow
> 'Twill clothe our whole army we very well know.[5]

COUNTRY LINEN AND HOMESPUN

The political fracture with England also spawned a fashion break. Colonists who once anxiously awaited news of the latest styles from the homeland shunned English fashion. Eliza Wilkinson noted in a letter, "[N]ever were greater politicians than the several knots of ladies, who met together. All trifling discourse of fashions, and such low little chat was thrown by, and we commenced perfect statesman."[6] Although the importation of cloth from France or Holland would not violate the boycott, whimsy and ostentation in dress were abandoned. As anti-British sentiment grew, many of even the wealthiest colonists became resolved either to make or to buy coarser American cloth as a statement of their devotion to the cause. It became a matter of genuine pride for a woman to use the spinning wheel on behalf of her country. Just as Daughters of Liberty agreed to drink no tea, they also swore to wear no garments of foreign make.

Spinning bees became so popular that it was not uncommon to see groups of women carrying their spinning wheels through the streets as a political statement. At Rowley, Massachusetts, "Thirty-three respectable ladies of the town met at sunrise with their wheels to spend the day at the house of the Rev'd Jedekiah Jewell, in the laudable design of a spinning match. At an hour before sunset, the ladies there appearing neatly dressed, principally in homespun, a polite and generous repast of American production was set for their entertainment.[7] Even Martha Washington served as an active supporter of the movement. She told a friend that she kept sixteen spinning wheels in constant operation at Mount Vernon. Although these were probably powered by her slaves, Martha was not beyond spinning for herself.[8]

The *Massachusetts Gazette* of November 9, 1767, contained a poem which suggested that women might renounce marriage to any man who did not join the ladies in their boycott of British manufactures.

> First then, throw aside your topknots of pride,
>   Wear none but your own country linen,
> Of Economy boast, let your pride be the most,
>   To show clothes of your own make and spinning.
>
> What if home-spun they say, is not quite so gay,
>   As brocades, yet be not in a passion.
> For when once it is known, this is much worn in town,
>   One and all will cry out—'Tis the fashion.
>
> And as one and all agree that you'll not married be
>   To such as will wear London factory,
> But at first sight refuse, 'till e'en such you do choose
>   As encourage our own manufactory.[9]

The continued desire for finer fabrics called for resourcefulness. Some families attempted to grow their own mulberry trees and cultivate silkworms. However, the silkmaking process required too much labor to support any large-scale commercial production of fabric. Fringe-and-lace maker James Butland advertised in the August 1774 issue of the *Pennsylvania Packet* that "any person having silk of their own may have it manufactured into . . . silk stockings, sewing silk, ribbons &c."[10] Tory Louisa Susannah Wells wrote an account of her discomfort in America. She complained, "I used to darn my stockings with the ravellings of another, and we flossed out our old silk gowns to spin together with cotton to knot our gloves."[11] Martha Washington showed two of her own dresses of cotton striped with silk with great pride, explaining that the silk stripes in the fabrics were made from the unravellings of brown silk stockings and old crimson damask chair covers.

Simplicity of dress and the use of fabrics of home manufacture became synonymous with patriotic fervor. Dorothy Dudley attended a reception given by General Washington and his wife in January 1776 and recorded the event in her diary. She noted, "Of course simplicity of dress was noticeable—no jewels or costly ornaments—though tasteful gowns, daintily trimmed by their owner's own fingers, were numerous."[12] In less formal situations Martha Washington chose to dress with great frugality. When she arrived at her husband's winter quarters in a private home at Morristown, she was initially mistaken by the homeowner for a domestic "in a plain russet gown with a white handkerchief neatly folded over her neck."[13]

As the conflict dragged on, the use of homespun became somewhat less voluntary. Temperance Smith of Connecticut noted, "[T]he extractions of the Mother Country had rendered it impossible for any but the wealthiest to import anything to eat or to wear, all had to be raised and manufactured at home from bread stuffs, sugar and rum to the linen and woolen for our clothes and bedding."[14] Lois Peters wrote to her husband, "You talked of sending back . . . some old shirts . . . I stand in great need of them to clothe my children. New [clothing] is not to be had and what I shall do I can't tell."[15] Lois bemoaned the fact that she could not meet her husband's request to send him new shirts. "[T]here is not a yard of hollon [Holland linen] to be had here."[16]

Those who lived behind British lines had no difficulty in obtaining imports, particularly if they were willing to supply desperately needed fresh produce in exchange. Rebecca Franks of Philadelphia was visiting New York in 1778 when she wrote of New York society, "The Dress is more ridiculous and pretty than anything I ever saw—great quantity of different colored feathers on the head at a time. The Hair dress'd very high . . . I have an afternoon cap with one wing, tho' I assure you I go less in the fashion than most of the Ladies—[There is] no being dress'd without a hoop."[17]

Once independence was declared and the separation of colony and mother country became established, some people felt less compelled to display their patriotic fervor by abstaining from imported articles. A Hessian officer observed that when the women in New York "go out, even though they be living in a hut, they throw a silk wrap about themselves and put on gloves. They also put on some well made and stylish little sunbonnet . . . [they] have fallen in love with red silk or woolen wraps." He speculated that "the wives and daughters spend much more than their incomes allow. The man must fish up the last penny he has in his pocket. . . . Nearly all articles necessary for the adornment of the female sex are very scarce and dear. For this reason they are wearing their Sunday finery. Should this begin to show signs of wear I am afraid that the husbands and fathers will be compelled to make peace with the Crown if they would keep their women folk supplied with gewgaws."[18]

Some enterprising people realized that this returning taste for articles of dress and luxury presented an opportunity for great profit. In January 1779, Benjamin Franklin's daughter noted, "There never was so much dressing and pleasure going on in the capital."[19] General Wayne received a letter echoing this sentiment. "[E]very lady and gentleman endeavors to outdo each other in splendor and show." General Greene remarked that the luxury of Boston was "an infant babe" to that of Philadelphia.[20] With avarice a stronger motive than patriotism, a new business, referred to as the Illicit Trade, persisted on Long Island during the entire war. Smugglers bought goods in the city of New York under the guise of offering them for sale to the King's loyal subjects on Long Island. The goods were, however, secretly loaded onto small vessels that were then "run" across Long Island Sound, to be delivered to certain dealers who were willing to pay the high prices in anticipation of a large profit for themselves. Lois Peters's husband was serving with the patriot army in New York when she wrote, "It is almost impossible to buy cloth here for one shirt. Hope you will be able to buy all you can that is a good penn'worth."[21]

The cunning of profit seekers spawned many frauds and schemes related to scarce goods. Sometimes the owner of a well-filled store on Long Island would conspire with whaleboat men to carry off his goods at night and convey them to Connecticut for their mutual financial advantage. The next day the claim of a rebel raid was asserted, and suitable rewards were offered by the appropriately indignant merchant.

While government policy prohibited any intercourse with the enemy, some officials, knowing there was little likelihood they could eliminate the activity, simply shared in the profits. At other times, provincial committees sought out illicit traders. In need of clothing for the troops, the state of New York was forced to employ secret agents to enter into a clandestine arrangement in order to procure British cloth. Connecticut dabbled in unlawful traffic until the popular outcry became unbearable. Even the British took part when it seemed in their best interest. In 1778, Governor Tryon used an intermediary to offer rum, sugar, and tea in exchange for American beef.

The British commandant in New York employed every possible means to restrict the illicit trade. Those wishing to transport goods out of the city were examined to ascertain their loyalty to the King and were required to have a permit that specifically detailed every article purchased. Stories circulated of victimized shoppers who, having made a purchase on impulse that was not listed in their permit, had their items seized by watchful guards, motivated by their ability to confiscate contraband and turn it to their own use.

Even when prohibited goods were not expropriated, the guards were given a share of their value as a reward for vigilance. Even this was not without its conspiracies. The owner of a boat loaded with another man's imports would set out from Long Island and conspire with the crew of an American privateer to have it captured. The goods would then be taken to a New England port, where the Admiralty court would condemn and sell them, sometimes at outlandish prices. Later, the conspirators would divide the profits. By this means British merchandise became available without violating any prohibitions. In Norwich, Connecticut auction sales "of a variety of European and other goods by piece or pattern" were held twice weekly.[22]

NOTES

1. Thomas K. Bullock and Maurice B. Tonkin, *The Wigmaker in Eighteenth Century Williamsburg* (Williamsburg, VA: Colonial Williamsburg Foundation, 1959), 16.

2. Alice Morse Earle, *Customs and Fashions of Old New England* (Williamstown, MA: Corner House, 1969), 295.

3. James Schouler, *Americans of 1776* (New York: Dodd, Mead, 1906), 90.

4. Alice Morse Earle, *Costume of Colonial Times* (New York: Charles Scribner's Sons, 1894), 31.

5. Earle, *Customs and Fashions*, 292.

6. Caroline Gilman, ed., *Letters of Eliza Wilkinson During the Invasion and Possession of Charleston, S.C. by the British in the Revolutionary War* (New York: Arno Press, 1969), 17.

7. Carl Holliday, *Women's Life in Colonial Days* (Williamstown, MA: Corner House, 1968), 111.

8. Ibid., 112.

9. Ibid., 160. Also see Selma R. Williams, *Demeter's Daughters: The Women Who Founded America 1587–1787* (New York: Atheneum, 1976), 229–230.

10. Susan Burrows Swan, *Plain & Fancy: American Women and Their Needlework, 1650–1850* (Austin, TX: Curious Works Press, 1997), 18–19.

11. Williams, *Demeter's Daughters*, 258–259.

12. Dorothy Dudley, *Theatrum Majorum: The Diary of Dorothy Dudley* (New York: Arno Press, 1971), 56.

13. Elizabeth F. Lumis Ellet, *Domestic History of the American Revolution* (New York: Charles Scribner, 1859), 73. The author is usually listed as Mrs. Ellet.

14. Helen Evertson Smith, *Colonial Days and Ways* (New York: Century, 1901), 226–227.

15. William Guthman, *The Correspondence of Captain Nathan and Lois Peters* (Hartford: Connecticut Historical Society, 1980), 32–33.

16. Ibid., 16.

17. Earle, *Costume of Colonial Times*, 31.

18. Ibid., 32.

19. Ellet, *Domestic History*, 164.

20. Earle, *Costume of Colonial Times*, 34.

21. Guthman, *Correspondence*, 29. "Penn'worth," a contraction of "penny's worth," was used to indicate good value.

22. Ellet, *Domestic History*, 128.

17

Burning Frontiers

Thayendaneagea, of the martial brow,
Gayentwahga, Honeyawas, where are they?
Sagoyewatha, he is silent now;
No more will listening throngs his voice obey....
Gone are my tribesmen, and another race,
Born of the foam, disclose with plough and spade
Secrets of battlefield and burial place,
And hunting grounds, once dark with pleasant shade,
Bask in the golden light.

—Read at the centennial celebration of
Sullivan's campaign against the Iroquois[1]

THE CONTEST FOR FRONTIER ALLIES

The American Revolution was characterized by brutal and violent warfare on the frontiers. Almost from the onset of hostilities, the British military determined to wage war by inciting the Indians to attack the outlying settlements. "The proximity and interconnectedness of Indian and colonial communities throughout large areas of North America gave the backcountry warfare of the Revolution a face-to-face nature that heightened its bitterness."[2]

Initially both loyalists and patriots put themselves forward as the legitimate heirs to the Native American alliances forged by the British during the French wars. The patriots faced a more difficult task in trying to bring the Indians to their side. Their agents came to the tribes too late and with too few presents to cement many friendships. British agents, already established among the Indian nations, were more successful than congressional ones in bringing the frontier tribes to their cause.

Many tribes openly aligned themselves to the Crown at the beginning of the conflict because they thought the British would quickly win the war or because they had formed a hatred of the patriot settlers in the previous decade. The Scotch-Irish settlers in particular had a long history of illegally occupying Indian land, "hewing their way through the woods, killing Indians when it suited them, and developing a righteous indignation against the restraining orders which came from the government."[3] The frontier people "were Indian haters first, last, and always. For them, all Indians lived by murder and deserved death on sight." Some patriots used the Revolution as an excuse to continue their murderous ways under the guise of a crusade for political rights.[4]

The British agents reportedly did all in their power to "induce all the nations of Indians to massacre the frontier inhabitants of Pennsylvania and Virginia and paid very high prices in goods for the scalps the Indians brought in." From their base near Detroit, British agents Charles Langlade and Colonel Henry "Hair Buyer" Hamilton played a diplomatic tug-of-war over the Great Lakes tribes with the main American agent at Fort Pitt, Colonel George Morgan. At Fort Niagara, Sir Guy Johnson oversaw the effort to convince the Indians of western New York to take up arms against the patriots. With the added influence of his cousin, Sir John Johnson, and of the Mohawk war leader Joseph Brant, Sir Guy was able to bring four of the six nations of the Iroquois Confederacy to the British side.

Sir John Johnson, son of the late Sir William Johnson, actively joined the Tories of his Royal Greens and Brant's Indians in the field. He was one of the most active loyalist leaders on the frontier. The father-and-son team of John and Walter Butler were also particularly active in harassing the settlements with their Tory Rangers. Dressed in short, dark green coatees, Indian leggings and moccasins, and carrying tomahawks and muskets, Butler's Rangers accompanied the Indians in raids throughout New York and Pennsylvania.[5]

The Crown's agents among the Indians were effectively opposed only by Rev. Samuel Kirkland, a Congregational missionary to the Iroquois. An ardent patriot, Kirkland was able to win the help of the Oneida and Tuscarora for the patriots by appealing to them on religious grounds, suggesting that the Crown would force the Anglican religion upon them if the patriots lost.[6] With the exception of Kirkland's successful appeals, only by threatening the tribes with massive retribution could the agents of Congress hope to maintain Indian neutrality. Colonel Morgan told the tribes at Fort Pitt, "If the foolish people who have struck us so often, will grow wise immediately they may yet avoid destruction." Otherwise, the patriot army would "trample them into dust." However, Morgan found that some of the tribes "were determined not to listen." They viewed his attempts to negotiate a neutrality "with increasing contempt." However, time would demonstrate that the Indians had failed to correctly gauge the resolve of the patriots.[7]

The Indians were assured by the British agents that they need not fear to "take up the hatchet against the Americans." Convinced that the redcoats would defeat the patriots as they had the French, the Indians undertook a series of frontier raids that demoralized the residents of the settlements. The attack on Wyoming Valley, Pennsylvania, in July 1778, by Iroquois warriors and loyalist rangers under the command of Maj. John Butler, was one of the worst of these raids. It was closely followed by the burning of Cherry Valley, New York, by a mixed force of Indians and loyalists under Capt. Walter Butler. These attacks in particular seem to have been pivotal in moving Congress to action. Immediately thererafter the Board of War concluded that a major operation against the Indians could not be avoided.[8]

PATRIOT TRIBES

Certain tribes were friendly to the patriots, including a small number of Delawares, all the Stockbridge and Mohegan Indians, and many of the Abenakis of New Hampshire and Maine. While the loyalty of the Delawares was always suspect, that of the Stockbridge and Mohegan warriors of New England was not. Almost two dozen Stockbridge Indians were killed in a single encounter while fighting for the patriots in the Bronx on a bluff overlooking the Van Cortlandt mansion.

The most crucial circumstance with regard to Indian allies proved to be the wresting away of the Oneida and Tuscarora warriors from the Iroquois Confederacy. Although the Six Nations reportedly could field 2000 warriors, it was the Iroquois failure to maintain their traditional tribal unity that proved most important. A firm stand by the Confederacy in favor of the Crown would have posed an almost impossible strategic problem for the patriots because many neutral tribes were poised to follow their lead. It was particularly comforting to the patriots, therefore, that the Iroquois failed to provide a unified front in the Revolution.

The New England Frontier

The powerful Abenaki nation had no great love for either "Britons or Bostonians."[9] Sir Guy Carleton, the British commander in Canada, seems to have underestimated the independent spirit of the Abenaki. He or-

dered them about in an arrogant and condescending manner, and refused them presents of arms and ammunition unless they proclaimed
undivided support for the Crown. Nonetheless, Washington was sur-
prisingly pleased when he was greeted by a delegation of Abenaki leaders at the camp at Cambridge, pledging their services in the cause of
liberty even before the British had evacuated Boston. Abenaki warriors
served as scouts for Benedict Arnold's expedition up the Kennebec
River of Maine and were standing with the patriots before the walled
city of Quebec in 1776. Congress responded to the Abenaki in the most
positive terms possible, and was helped immensely in cementing good
relations with the tribe in 1777 by the defeat of Burgoyne's army at Saratoga.

Joseph Louis Gill, the son of two whites adopted into the Abenaki
nation during the French wars, proved an effective representative of the
patriots among his people. Known as the "White Chief of the Saint Francis Abenaki," he seems to have formed around himself a hard core of
native support for the patriots. Estimates of the number of Abenaki warriors available to prosecute a war vary widely, from as few as 200 to as
many as 2000.[10] A company of Indian Rangers was formed under Gill,
who was granted an officer's commission by Congress. These rangers
patrolled the forests along the border with Canada, freeing the patriots
of the task. However, as the war dragged on and the outcome grew less
certain, Gill increasingly flirted with the British in Canada. This somewhat split Abenaki loyalty. Thereafter, groups of Abenaki scouts, ostensibly on opposite sides in the war, carefully avoided each other in the
wilderness areas, hoping that at the end of the war the whole tribe might
with some assurance gain an advantage from the ultimate winner of the
conflict.[11]

The Southern Frontier

The Catawbas of South Carolina, surrounded by patriot settlers, "did
the sensible thing from the first and supported the Americans."[12] The
Cherokees, on the other hand, attempted neutrality and found themselves in the deplorable situation of being caught between loyalists and
patriots, who both assumed they were hostile.[13] As a consequence of their
indecision, a number of minor expeditions were undertaken in 1776
against Cherokee villages.[14] These raids drove many of the Cherokees to
seek help from the redcoats, but the Crown largely failed to support
them. They were attacked again and again. In 1779 a major expedition
of patriot militia and volunteers was launched under Maj. Evan Shelby
and Maj. Andrew Williamson. The raid was timed with the harvests,
leaving the women and children among the Cherokees little to eat for
the winter. In 1781 Col. Andrew Pickens of South Carolina pushed his

men through the same Cherokee towns one more time. In 1782 a survivor of these outrages described the patriot raiders as "madmen."[15]

THE BRITISH ALLIES

Prominent among the allies of the British were Iroquois who sought arms and ammunition from them at Fort Niagara. Senecas, Cayugas, and Mohawks joined the British almost immediately in a series of daring raids directed at the patriot settlements. The less decisive Onondaga did not join them until 1779. The pro-British Iroquois warriors also attacked the villages of their kinsman, the Oneidas and Tuscaroras; and the Oneidas burned several Mohawk dwellings in retaliation. For the Iroquois, the Revolution was truly a war in which "brother killed brother."[16]

The Senecas, who had joined Pontiac in 1764, placed many of their former hatreds aside and rejoined the redcoats. They clearly saw the American Revolution as a war to defend their homelands against white encroachment.[17] The great war leaders of the Senecas were Gayentwahga, known as Cornplanter, and Sayenqueraghta, a distinguished old warrior of seventy known as Old Smoke. These men initially clung to a stubborn neutrality, but individuals and groups of Seneca warriors persisted in making "commitments [to the British] that undermined the consensus politics that traditionally guarded against rash decisions."[18] One Indian diplomat confided to an American agent that he could "no longer control [his] fighting men," who were turning "to the north" to join the British in Canada.[19]

THE NEUTRAL NATIONS

Many Indian nations tried to maintain neutrality in the white man's civil war, but the patriot militia on the frontier exhibited a peculiar inability to determine who among the native population were enemies and who were simply trying to remain neutral. Throughout the war many Indians "clung to a neutrality that cost them dearly."[20] In 1777, a few patriots foolishly murdered an important diplomat named Cornstalk and thereby drove the neutral Shawnees to the side of the British. The Onondaga struggled to maintain a neutrality until patriots burned their crops in 1779. In 1780 a group of patriots attacked a Moravian town filled with neutral Delawares without provocation, killing 96 men, women, and children. Two years later, a similar attack took place on a Delaware village near Pittsburgh.

Some of the tribes of the trans-Mississippi west, including Sioux, Chippewas, Fox, and Sauk, initially rallied to the agents of the Crown because the patriots had no representatives in their villages. However, an ill-advised British attack on the Spanish town of St. Louis in 1780 ended in utter failure and the Crown suffered a serious blow to its prestige among the Indians. This single failure seriously diminished the appetite of the western tribes for war against the patriots or their European allies.

JOSEPH BRANT

The Seneca leaders Cornplanter and Old Smoke "did not always enjoy a warm, working relationship" with the powerful Mohawk war leader Joseph Brant (Thayendanegea) even though they all belonged to the Iroquois Confederacy. Brant, at age 32, was initially thought of as an upstart "with great pretensions, but little experience" in warfare, but he quickly came to be viewed as the foremost war leader among all the Iroquois. Brant left the Mohawk Valley in 1775 and traveled with Guy Johnson to Montreal, where plans were made for the Iroquois to raise the King's standard across the frontier. Because he could speak the dialects of all the Iroquois nations, and was noted for his devotion to the Johnsons, Brant was made Captain of the Six Nations Indian Department.[21]

Near Fort Niagara, Brant established a group of volunteers that included both Indians and whites, whom the patriots considered renegades. He attracted most of his warriors from among the Mohawks, who had always been the most loyal of the Iroquois to the English. Brant generally failed, however, to influence the Oneida and Tuscarora warriors. Moreover, although he was recognized as a senior war leader, he became easily embroiled in disputes with the leaders of the other Indian nations allied to the Crown. Nonetheless, Brant was "a man of exceptional ability, high character, and strong convictions."[22]

Brant distinguished himself throughout the Revolution by leading numerous raids on patriot settlements. He was so active in pursuing the war in the New York and Pennsylvania border region that he was identified by eyewitnesses as simultaneously leading raids that were hundreds of miles apart—a physical impossiblity. It has been determined, however, that his efforts were remarkably wide-ranging. Brant led several major raids in New York: on Cobleskill and Sharon (1778), on Springfield and Andrustown (1778), on German Flats (1778 and again in 1782), on Vrooman's Land (1780), on Harpersfield (1780), on Schoharie and Stone Arabia (1780), and on Ballston and Saratoga (1780). He also led the attack on the Minisink settlements in the Delaware Valley of Pennsylvania in 1779, and he helped, along with Cornplanter, to burn the Canajoharie district of New York in 1780.

THE WYOMING MASSACRE

The British victory at Wyoming in June 1778 was overwhelming, but the atrocities committed against the military and civilian captives by the

Table 17.1

Principal Operations on the Frontiers 1775–1781

Date	Location	Opponents		Victory
		Patriot	*Crown*	
1775	Reedy River, SC	Richardson	Cunningham	Patriot
1776	———	———	———	———
1777	Fort McIntosh, VA	Winn	Tory militia	Crown
	Fort Henry, VA	Patriot militia	Native Americans	Indecisive
1778	Cobleskill, NY	Patrick	Brant	Crown
	Alligator Bridge, FL	R. Howe	E. Clark	Crown
	Wyoming, PA	Z. Butler	J. Butler	Crown
	Kaskasia, OH	G. R. Clark	Unopposed	Patriot
	Andrustown, NY	Residents	Brant	Crown
	Boonesboro, KY	Boone	Tories/Indians	Patriot
	Unadilla, NY	Wm. Butler	Native Americans	Patriot
	Cherry Valley, NY	Alden	W. Butler/Brant	Crown
1779	Vincennes, OH	G. R. Clark	Hamilton	Patriot
	Clinch River, TN	Shelby	Native Americans	Patriot
	Onondaga, NY	Van Schaick	Native Americans	Patriot
	Minisink, PA	Hathorn/Tuster	Brant	Crown
	Newtown, NY	Sullivan	W. Butler/Brant	Patriot
	Licking River, KY	D. Rogers	S. Girty	Crown
1780	Mohawk Valley, NY	Residents	J. Johnson/Brant	Crown
	Lake George, NY	Residents	J. Johnson/Brant	Crown
	Middleburg, NY	Woolsey	J. Johnson/Brant	Indecisive
1781	Currytown, NY	Local militia	Tories/Indians	Crown
	Sandusky, OH	Crawford	W. Butler	Crown

Indians galvanized the frontier patriots. Those settlers who were not caught unaware by Maj. John Butler's force of Indians and loyalist rangers, fled to the sanctuary of Forty Fort, one of the more substantial of several fortifications and blockhouses in the Wyoming Valley. The 24th Regiment of Connecticut militia[23] assembled at the fort under Col. Zebulon Butler and marched out to intercept the attackers with little comprehension of their actual number. The engagement that followed, sometimes known as the battle of the Butlers, was decisive, and no quarter was given by the British to the patriots. More than 300 of the residents were slain, and the valley was laid waste.[24] The inhabitants were made "totally dependent on the public, and . . . absolute objects of charity."[25] It was reported that the raiders "left about 230 women widows."[26]

Largely because of this attack, Washington determined to mount an offensive against the Indians and resolved "to carry the war into the heart of the country of the six nations; to cut off their settlements, destroy their next year's crops, and do them every other mischief of which time and circumstance will permit."[27] Congress agreed, thinking it more efficient to march a thousand men, well led by a few determined officers, into Indian country and destroy it, rather than to "garrison the frontier settlements with three times their number."[28]

As a direct result of these decisions, Maj. Gen. John Sullivan and Brig. Gen. James Clinton were directed to burn and plunder most of Iroquoia in 1779. While the Continentals acted in the eastern villages, the militia and frontier volunteers of Col. Daniel Brodhead mounted a separate operation from the west. The patriots attacked the towns of the Iroquois on the Mohawk River and those of the Delaware and the Muncee on the Allegheny.[29]

THE INDIAN CAMPAIGNS

The patriot strategy in the frontier war was aimed directly at the Indians rather than at the British. Their plan was to destroy the villiages and burn the crops "late in the season when there was insufficient time for raising another crop before winter."[30] It was expected that the Indians would flee before the onslaught of the patriot forces, and with "nothing to subsist upon but the remains of last years corn," they would be forced to beg provisions from the British at Niagara.[31]

There was only one major military engagement during the Sullivan-Clinton campaign of 1779. This was at Newtown (Tioga), New York. The loyalist commander, Maj. John Butler, attempted to persuade his Indian allies to fall back before the weight of the patriot advance, but the Indians, led by Joseph Brant, stubbornly refused to budge. Butler then set his 800 men to work creating a fortification: "Having possession of the heights we would have greatly the advantage should the enemy direct their march that way." Sullivan's 3200 troops, seeing the strength of Butler's position, attacked from both flanks and the center with infantry and light artillery. Meanwhile, the troops of generals Enoch Poor and James Clinton, overcoming serious topographical impediments, managed almost to encircle the less numerous British force, who, apprehending the danger, fled to the rear with their wounded and dying. "The battle of Newtown was so decisive that the panic-stricken enemy did not [thereafter] fire a single gun at the army on its march." Sullivan's expedition found nothing but empty villages along a 300-mile circuit through the Iroquois heartland, it being "impossible [for the British] to keep the Indians together."[32]

One of the more remarkable, but passing, achievements of the Sullivan-Clinton campaign was an engineering feat accomplished by James Clinton's troops. Having arrived at Lake Otsego, near the head of the Susquahanna River, with 200 boatloads of provisions for Sullivan's army, Clinton found the river so shallow as to be impassable. He ordered a dam built across the mouth of the lake to get a sufficient head of water to float the boats. After five weeks the dam was broken, and the boats were launched on the ensuing flood. "Forty miles was made in just two days by this method."[33]

With the loss of only 60 men from all causes, including sickness and snakebite, Sullivan crossed central New York and part of Pennsylvania in just 35 days, leaving behind a number of new roads and bridges, which helped to facilitate white settlement in the region after the war. In his official report to Congress, Sullivan noted that he had burned 40 Indian towns. "We have not left a single settlement or field of corn in the country of the [Iroquois], nor is there even the appearance of an Indian on this side of Niagara." The quantity of corn destroyed amounted to 160,000 bushels. The patriots also destroyed the plum, peach, and apple orchards of the Indians by cutting down trees or girdling their trunks. It would take decades to renew the agricultural produce of these trees.[34]

Colonel Daniel Brodhead, generally lacking restraint with regard to Indian fighting, set "a high standard for murder" during his phase of the operation.[35] Broadhead wrote to General Sullivan after several weeks of campaigning, "I think [the Indians] are willing by this time to make peace, but I hope it will not be granted them until they are sufficiently drubbed for their past inequities."[36] Brodhead's raids on the neutral Delaware villages at Coshocton and Lichtenau, Ohio, were particularly violent. In his official report, he noted, "The troops remained on the ground three whole days destroying the towns and cornfields. I never saw finer corn, although it was planted much thicker than is common with our farmers."[37]

The murder of a Delaware leader, Red Eagle, and the execution of all the male captives over the age of 12 during Brodhead's operations, drove many of the Indian nations that had remained neutral into the arms of the British. The frontier militia became fearful of retaliation by the Indians and, recognizing their own excesses and believing that it was essential for the safety of their own families to return to their homes, began to desert Brodhead's command almost immediately.[38]

The Burning of the Valleys

In 1778 Joseph Brant established his headquarters at Onondaga, the ancestral center of the Iroquois Confederacy. From here he led more than 300 loyalists and Indians against the patriot settlements along the rivers and creeks that fed into the Mohawk River. Loyalists and Indians ranged throughout the New York frontier, falling particularly on the old

German and Dutch settlements in the Schoharie, Cobleskill, and Mohawk valleys.

Brant burned the town of Cobleskill and plundered nearby Sharon in 1778. Ten houses and the patriot sulfur works at Sharon Springs were completely destroyed. Only by retreating to one of the three forts in the valley were the residents saved from destruction. A detachment of militia caught Brant in the open and engaged him; 25 patriots were killed and several were taken prisoner. Abraham Wemple, who later helped to bury the patriot dead, reported that one of the settlers was "butchered in the most inhumane manner . . . his body cut open and his intestines fastened around a tree several feet distant."[39]

The raid on nearby Cherry Valley a few months later was particularly violent. Many women and children were taken prisoner by the Indians and many settlers were killed. Because some of these killings took place after the settlers had surrendered, the Cherry Valley raids were judged a massacre. Such reports completely terrorized the residents of the frontier region. More than 200 dwellings were burned during similar raids on German Flats, Vrooman's Land, Harpersfield, Schoharie, Stone Arabia, Ballston, and Saratoga in 1780. These tactical operations, coordinated by British headquarters in Canada, came to be known as "The Burning of the Valleys."[40]

In 1780 the patriot governor of New York, George Clinton, wrote with great foreboding of the results of these campaigns: "Schenectady may now be said to become the limits of our western frontier." Nonetheless, rather than increasing the support for the British among the residents of western New York, many loyalists took advantage of the opportunity afforded by these raids to abandon their homes and retreat with the Crown forces to Canada or Niagara. This left central New York, with its potential to provide foodstuffs, forage, and raw materials for the Continental Army, almost completely in patriot hands.[41]

The War in the Ohio Country

In 1775 George Rogers Clark went to Kentucky from Virginia as a surveyor and land speculator. When the Indians sided with the British in 1776, he became the natural leader of the patriot forces who opposed them in the region. He was made a lieutenant colonel of provincial forces by the colony of Virginia and was authorized to raise troops to carry out his operations. In 1777 Clark repelled an Indian attack on Harrodsburg, sent patrols to the Illinois country, and formulated plans for the conquest of the Ohio country. He also took measures to suppress the Indian attacks on the westernmost settlements. Clark believed that no punishment was too great for the Indians allied to the Crown. He wrote, "To excel them in barbarity was and is the only way to make war upon Indians and make a name among them." In one encounter Clark personally bludgeoned to death with a tomahawk several Indian captives, in order to fill the Native Americans of the region with fear.[42]

Having trained a body of men by summer 1778, Clark marched cross-country for six days and surprised the British garrision at Kaskaskia on July 4. The French inhabitants of the region were happy to recognize the legitimacy of the patriot government, and the entire Illinois country was captured without the loss of a single man. Clark then began a program of pacification among the Indians of the region, but he was countered by British Governor Henry "Hair Buyer" Hamilton. In 1779 Clark marched about 170 men through the swamps and tributaries of the Wabash River basin and appeared before the frontier headquarters of the astonished Hamilton at Vincennes in midwinter, demanding his surrender. By claiming that he had many more men that he really did, Clark overcame the willingness of the formidable British garrison to resist.

Only the small size of his actual force kept Clark from attacking Detroit directly. In 1780, he established Fort Jefferson near the mouth of the Ohio River and reached out from this post to defend his outpost at Cahokia, Illinois, and the Spanish settlement at St. Louis. He then returned to Kentucky and gathered 1000 men to invade and destroy the Shawnee villages in that region. In 1782 he led another force against the Indian villages on the Great Miami River. This was his last important service during the Revolution. The hardships and exposure to cold and wet conditions endured by Clark during the war led to an infirmity in his middle years that crippled him before his time. His younger brother William was one of the leaders of the Lewis and Clark expedition that surveyed the Louisiana territory in 1805.

NOTES

1. Frederick Cook, *Journals of the Military Expedition of Major General John Sullivan Against the Six Nations of Indians in 1779 with Records of the Centennial Celebrations* (Auburn, NY: Knapp, Peck & Thompson, 1887), 529. The Mohawk Thayendanegea (Joseph Brant), and the Senecas Gayentwahga (Cornplanter), Honeyawas (Farmer's Brother), and Segoyewatha (Red Jacket) were all considered important Indian leaders against the patriots by those celebrating Sullivan's victories a century after the event. All the Senecas named were present during the Wyoming massacre.

2. Colin G. Calloway, *The American Revolution in Indian Country: Crisis and Diversity in Native American Communities* (Cambridge: Cambridge University Press, 1999), 4.

3. Louis B. Wright, *The Atlantic Frontier: Colonial American Civilization, 1607–1763* (New York: Alfred A. Knopf, 1951), 224.

4. R. Douglas Hurt, *The Ohio Frontier: Crucible of the Old Northwest, 1720–1830* (Indianapolis: Indiana University Press, 1996), 67.

5. See Howard Swiggett, *War Out of Niagara: Walter Butler and the Tory Rangers* (New York: Columbia University Press, 1933).

6. Hurt, *Ohio Frontier*, 76.

7. Ibid., 76–77.

8. Ibid., 65.

9. Calloway, *American Revolution*, 68.

10. Samuel Adams Drake, *The Border Wars of New England, Commonly Called King Williams's and Queen Anne's Wars* (Williamstown, MA: Corner House, 1973), 150n.

11. For a more detailed account of Joseph Gill, see John C. Huden, "The White Chief of the St. Francis Abenaki," *Vermont History* 24 (1956), 207, 337–338.

12. Calloway, *American Revolution*, 43.

13. Ibid., 58.

14. Ibid., 49.

15. Ibid., 50.

16. Ibid., 34.

17. Hurt, *Ohio Frontier*, 85. See also 78.

18. Gavin K. Watt, *The Burning of the Valleys: Daring Raids from Canada Against the New York Frontier in the Fall of 1780* (Toronto: Dundurn Press, 1997), 27.

19. Hurt, *Ohio Frontier*, 66.

20. Calloway, *American Revolution*, 39.

21. Watt, *Burning of the Valleys*, 26.

22. Barbara Graymont, *The Iroquois in the American Revolution* (Syracuse, NY: Syracuse University Press, 1972), 53.

23. Wyoming was then claimed by the state of Connecticut based on its original charter.

24. Thomas E. Byrne and Lawrence E. Byrne, eds., *The Sullivan-Clinton Expedition of 1779 in Pennsylvania and New York* (Elmira, NY: Chemung County Historical Society, 1999), 4.

25. Cook, *Journals*, 147.

26. Ibid., 107–108.

27. Calloway, *American Revolution*, 51.

28. The men referred to are General Armstrong (no first name) and Col. Daniel Broadhead. Calloway, *American Revolution*, 47–48.

29. Cook, *Journals*, 4.

30. Calloway, *American Revolution*, 47.

31. Ibid., 56.

32. Cook, *Journals*, 302.

33. Byrne and Byrne, *Sullivan-Clinton Expedition*, 10–11.

34. Ibid., 29. Sullivan resigned his commission upon his return from the expedition in order to serve as a delegate to Congress.

35. Hurt, *Ohio Frontier*, 85–86.

36. Letter of Daniel Broadhead to Maj. Gen. John Sullivan, August 6, 1779, reported in Cook, *Journals*, 307.

37. Letter of Daniel Broadhead to Gen. George Washington, September 16, 1779, reported in Cook, *Journals*, 308.

38. Hurt, *Ohio Frontier*, 86.

39. Graymont, *The Iroquois*, 166.
40. See Watt, *Burning of the Valleys*.
41. Graymont, *The Iroquois*, 238–239.
42. Calloway, *American Revolution*, 48.

18

The Militia of the Seas

These people show a spirit and conduct against us they never showed against the French, and everyone has judged of them from their former appearance and behavior . . . which has led many into great mistakes.

—A British officer, 1775

THE AMERICAN PRIVATEERS

In the aftermath of Lexington and Concord, Congress provided for an army but doubted the practical value of forming a navy. It was inconceivable that the colonies could deploy a fleet with any chance of matching the Royal Navy. Nonetheless, enterprising Americans were not willing to miss an opportunity to profit from a little privateering. The bulk of the patriot naval force was made up of these commerce raiders, which operated under commissions issued by the individual states or the Congress. Loyalists also went to sea as privateers under licenses from the royal governors or from the British commander in America, but their number was very small and their effect was somewhat overshadowed by the presence of the Royal Navy.

The annals of armchair seamanship and fictional accounts of daring single-ship encounters have reinforced the myth that privateers were all inspired by patriotic motives. Simple economic self-interest spurred hundreds of patriots to serve in private warships from 1775 to 1783. Nonetheless, it is certain that in the Revolution, for "the first time in history

Table 18.1

Disposition of Royal Navy Warships in North American Waters, January, 1775

Vessel	Guns	Crew	Station
Boyne	70	520	Boston
Somerset	68	520	Boston
Asia	64	480	Boston
Preston	50	300	Boston
Mercury	20	130	Boston
Glasgow	20	130	Boston
Tartar	28	160	Halifax
Rose	20	130	Rhode Island
Swan	16	100	Rhode Island
Hope	6	30	Rhode Island
Fowey	20	130	Virginia
Lively	20	130	Salem
Scarborough	20	130	New Hampshire
Canceaux	8	45	New Hampshire
Kingfisher	16	100	New York
Tamer	14	100	South Carolina
Cruizer	8	60	North Carolina
Savage	8	60	East Florida
St. John	6	30	East Florida
Magdalen	6	30	Philadelphia
Halifax	6	30	Maine
Diligent	6	30	Maine
Gaspee	6	30	Maine
Diana	6	30	Unassigned

the privateer system assumed approximately the shape of a marine militia or volunteer navy."[1] Yet there was no guarantee that the licenses issued by the states or Congress would protect individuals from a charge of piracy while acting in rebellion against their rightful king. Throughout the rebellion the British held all captured patriot sailors under a bill of attainder charging them with piracy and treason.[2]

New England sailors took naturally to privateering, and many adventurous spirits served as part of the crew. However, most Americans participated from the safety of their own homes as mere investors and let the professional seamen take the risks. A great deal of money could be realized from a single captured vessel. Many patriots served in the army while at the same time hoping to realize a considerable profit from the timely capture of a single prize. Occasionally, a privateer would take a British prize loaded with hard-to-get fabric or wines, and a seaport might be animated by a supply of foreign finery for a day or so.

American shipbuilders and designers provided vessels that were generally superior to those of the British in terms of speed and ability to sail to windward. Yet even a small British frigate carried more guns and had a larger, better disciplined crew than a privateer. In a ship-to-ship engagement, a British man-of-war would simply blow most privateers out of the water. Consequently, the privateers relied upon their speed to make captures and to make good their escape from patrolling British warships. Privateers paid for this advantage by carrying fewer guns and sacrificing what little cargo capacity they had to essential stores. The usual plan was to overtake and attack unarmed or lightly armed merchant vessels; detach a few men as a prize crew; and make for a friendly American or foreign port where both ship and cargo would be condemned as a prize.

Patriot privateers also attacked unescorted supply ships sent to support the British land forces in America. A favorite hunting ground for privateers was at the entrance to the Gulf of St. Lawrence, where small fishing and trading vessels could be taken with little risk from the Royal Navy base at Halifax due to the fog and storms that ravaged the region. Another favorite spot was in the West Indies, but here the patriots had to deal with the West Indian Squadron based in Jamaica. The failure of the Royal Navy to stop the privateers from attacking British commerce in American waters was overshadowed only by its equally frustrating inability to drive them from the English Channel. British newspapers were filled with stories of the recurring appearance of rebel privateers in home waters. Their success served to fuel war weariness among the population in England.

Rebels Under Sail

A comparison of the Continental Navy and the privateer fleet is interesting and enlightening. A total of 47 vessels served as a regular naval force during the entire course of the Revolution. These vessels carried 1242 cannon and swivel guns (weapons larger than a musket and too heavy to fire unsupported). The Continental Navy captured a total of 196 vessels valued at about $6 million (Spanish). By comparison there were 792 privateers mounting more than 13,000 guns licensed during the rebellion. Many operated throughout the entire war. Admittedly, many of the vessels were small with lightweight armament, yet the privateers captured more than 1000 prizes valued at almost $18 million. Some patriot cruisers were formidable warships, carrying 150 crewmen and more than 20 guns.[3]

The successes of the citizen soldiers on land and the citizen sailors at sea took on an importance of legendary proportions in later American thinking that blocked out the realities of just how they were accomplished. The ships of the Continental Navy had some obligation to stand their ground and make a fight, while the privateers were free to choose their battles. Yet, the myth of American naval invincibility, taken together with a characteristic aversion to standing professional forces, caused the new United States to eschew a large army and a line of battleships for reliance on a citizen militia and a minuscule navy supported by a heavy dependence on privateers.

Private Warships

Both George Washington and Benjamin Franklin commissioned a number of vessels to act in the cause of American independence. In 1775 Washington authorized Nicholas Boughton to proceed to the port of Beverly, Massachusetts, where he was to take command of *Hannah*, a schooner fitted out with a few small cannon as a privateer. This was the first of six small vessels that ultimately formed "George Washington's navy." Each vessel sailed under a white ensign bearing a green pine tree with the words "An Appeal to Heaven" inscribed below it. In forming this force, Washington ignored Congress and acted solely on his own authority.[4] Benjamin Franklin, as a member of the Naval Committee of Congress, issued commissions to likely officers and provided funds for the arming and fitting of American warships in foreign ports. *Black Prince*, the *Black Princess*, and *Fearnot* were among the most successful of the vessels that Franklin commissioned. Many among the crews of these cruisers were Irish and English smugglers who patrolled European waters, where they captured 114 merchant vessels.[5]

Colonial consciousness of the military value of prosecuting a war at sea was fueled largely by the necessity to procure arms from the West Indies. In November 1775 Capt. John Manly, one of Washington's finest captains, intercepted a lightly armed Royal Navy storeship that had become separated from its convoy. *Nancy* carried military stores including 100,000 flints, 2000 muskets, and a 13-inch mortar—"the finest piece of ordnance ever landed in America."[6] British Vice Admiral Samuel Graves wrote: "It is much to be lamented that a cargo of such consequence should be sent from England in a vessel destitute of arms even so to protect her from a rowboat."[7]

In quick succession supplies and arms were also taken from the British storeship *Concord* and from four lightly armed troop ships (*Anne, George, Lord Howe,* and *Annabella*) carrying almost 400 Scottish Highlanders destined to serve in America. The *London Chronicle* reported that the ships were taken by privateers "within sight of the fleet in Boston."[8] Vice Admiral Samuel Graves so feared the American efforts in and around Boston that he "ordered the ships of war in the harbor to be secured with booms all around to prevent their being boarded and taken by rebel whaleboats."[9] Of 36 storeships and troop transports dispatched to New England during 1775, only 18 arrived safely.[10] British Admiral Shuldham wrote: "However numerous our cruisers may be or however attentive our Officers to their Duty, it has been found impossible to prevent some of our ordnance and other valuable stores, in small vessels, falling into the hands of the Rebels."[11]

Americans looked upon these successes with awe, and they celebrated each victory with enthusiasm. Celebrations were held in the streets, and illuminations and bonfires in the town squares accompanied speeches of praise for the intrepid sailors who had faced down the might of the Royal Navy. A tavern song was altered in favor of the captains of the privateer navy who were defying the British North American Squadron at sea:

> Then rouse up, all our Heroes, give MANLY now a cheer,
> Here's Health to hardy Sons of Mars who go in Privateers . . .
> They talk of Sixty Ships, Lads, to scourge our free-born Land,
> If they send out Six Hundred we'll bravely them withstand . . .
> Then rouse up all my Hearties, give Sailor Lads a Cheer,
> Brave MANLY . . . and [all] those Tars who go in Privateers.[12]

THE CONTINENTAL NAVY

Congress, elated by these successes, quickly appropriated $100,000 to buy four merchantmen that would immediately be converted into warships. The members also approved the construction of 13 warships to be built from the keel up in the overly optimistic time of just three months. Five ships of 32 guns, five of 28 guns, and three of 24 guns were authorized. The building contracts were spread among seven states having considerable shipbuilding facilities, but neither the materials to build the ships nor the crews to man them were available. Almost $1 million was appropriated to provide for the Continental Navy.

Order of Precedence

The Naval Committee also drew up an ordered list of officers to serve in the new navy. Unfortunately, the men on the list were given precedence mainly because of political or social patronage rather than ability. None of Washington's experienced captains was listed, except John Manly, who topped the list. Some months later, John Paul Jones (eighteenth) wrote to Robert Morris of the Naval Committee of Congress, "I cannot but lament that so little delicacy hath been observed in the appointment and promotion of officers in the sea service, many of whom are not only grossly illiterate, but want even the capacity of commanding

The shipbuilding program envisioned by Congress was somewhat optimistic. Many of the ships that were started were burned by the British before they were completed.

merchant vessels."[13] In 1781 a congressional committee, investigating how the list was generated, could not "fully ascertain the rule by which that arrangement was made."[14]

Esek Hopkins was named commander in chief of the navy, a purely political appointment made to please his brother, Stephen Hopkins of Rhode Island, who was chairman of the Naval Committee.[15] He was described by a contemporary as "an antiquated figure, shrewd and sensible . . . only he swore now and then." The Naval Committee gave Hopkins command over only those ships being fitting out in the Delaware River. Several other Continental vessels were at sea, but they clearly were not placed under his orders.[16]

The complement of American naval officers included the friends and relatives of the Naval Committee's chairman. John B. Hopkins (thirteenth), Esek's son, had taken part in the burning of the British revenue cutter *Gaspee*. Dudley Saltonstall (fourth), a Hopkins cousin, had been a privateer in the French wars. He was something of an enigma, being described by some of his contemporaries as morose, ill-natured, or narrow-minded, and by others as sensible and indefatigable. John Paul Jones, whose own temperament was cold-blooded and autocratic, disliked Saltonstall intensely, declaring that the man had "a rude unhappy temper."[17] Abraham Whipple (twelfth), a leader of the expedition that burned *Gaspee*, came to Philadelphia in the sloop *Katy*, which he turned over to the Continental service and renamed *Providence*. This vessel was fitted as a warship and given to the command of Capt. John Hazzard (unlisted), a New Yorker. There is little known of Hazzard except that he was described as "a stout man, very vain and ignorant."[18] Nicholas Biddle (fifth) of Pennsylvania, a most capable officer, had served in the Royal Navy. Appointed midshipman in 1771, he had served with another midshipman named Horatio Nelson.[19]

The First Cruise of the Continental Navy

By January 1776, the minimum needs of the tiny Continental squadron had been met, and the force was made operational. Commodore Hopkins ordered *Alfred*, *Columbus*, *Cabot*, and *Andrea Doria* to cast their moorings and move down the ice-filled Delaware toward the sea. By February, *Providence*, *Fly*, *Hornet*, and *Wasp* had joined the group at its anchorage opposite Philadelphia. The eight vessels of the Continental fleet mounted a total of only 114 guns—the largest being 9-pounders. Besides officers and 700 sailors, over 200 marines were added to the personnel of the fleet.[20]

The Naval Committee had given Hopkins specific instructions to proceed to "Chesapeake Bay in Virginia . . . enter said bay, search out and attack, take or destroy all the naval forces of our enemies that you may find there," and then to "the Southward and make yourself master of such forces as the enemy may have both in North and South Carolina." These orders acknowledged southern support for the creation of the navy in Congress, but they were hopelessly optimistic.[21]

On February 14, Hopkins called the commanders of all vessels in the fleet to the flagship, *Alfred*, to meet under his fine yellow flag emblazoned with a 13-segment serpent and inscribed with "Don't Tread On Me." Although his own brother was its chairman, Commodore Hopkins thought the Naval Committee "a pack of fools, ignorant as lawyers' clerks, who thought the navy could help pay for the war."[22] The commodore informed his captains that he would use his discretion to recast the mission entrusted to him by Congress, and raid New Providence (Nassau) to capture a store of gunpowder and arms said to be there. He issued orders to that effect and set the immediate destination of the fleet as Grand Abaco Island in the Bahamas.[23]

With a fresh wind, the fleet sailed later that day. By March 1 six of the eight vessels lay at anchor off Grand Abaco. *Hornet* and *Fly* had disappeared during the voyage. For two days the fleet waited, using the time to train their men and refill their water casks. Two small British merchantmen were taken, and from the prisoners Hopkins received intelligence about New Providence. From this information and his own knowledge of the place, Hopkins drew the specifics of his raid. Since the harbor was guarded by two forts, a direct assault by the fleet seemed ill-suited to the task at hand. Although he had made "no attempt to hide his presence or to take advantage of the speed and surprise that was his," Hopkins decided to employ a subterfuge and send in the marines.[24]

The Birth of the Marines

American marines, like their British counterparts in the Royal Navy, were carried aboard naval vessels for several reasons. Primarily they served as a force trained specifically in close combat and amphibious landings. Their station in an engagement was in the fighting tops or as boarders. They also served as a force, separate from the seamen who formed the nucleus of the crew, that the officers could count on to help control the men. With this purpose in mind, marines were kept separate from the seamen, sleeping and eating in an area between the ratings and the officers. They had their own officers.

The initial corps of American marines had been raised in the Tun Tavern in Philadelphia. Robert Mullan, owner of the tavern, and Samuel Nickolas were made captains of marines. The marines adopted a dark green uniform coat with white cuffs and facings. Their smallclothes—shirts, waistcoats, and breeches—were white. They wore black leather neck stocks, and their leather accouterments and crossbelts were white.

Packed into the two captured British vessels, two and a half companies of marines and 50 sailors—270 men in all—approached the harbor of New Providence. Although Hopkins's plans called for the fleet to remain over the horizon until the marines landed, the commodore misjudged his timing. The fleet came barreling into the port immediately in the wake of the marines' vessels. Nonetheless, the marines stormed ashore in their first amphibious landing and swept through the forts, which were abandoned after a nominal defense by the British garrison.[25]

The raid was a success marred only by the fact that the governor of New Providence had spirited 150 barrels of gunpowder off the island upon word of Hopkins's arrival at Grand Abaco. Seventeen large cannon (32-, 18-, and 12-pounders) were taken, as well as thousands of round shot and other ordnance supplies. Once the town was taken, the total number of guns and mortars removed rose to 88 of various sizes. The marines also recovered 24 barrels of powder that remained in the forts. While the fleet was lying in New Providence harbor, it was rejoined by *Fly*, which had collided with *Hornet* in a storm. *Hornet*, damaged in the collision, had made for the South Carolina coast, and later returned to Delaware Bay.

A Fleet Action

With sickness ravaging his crews, Hopkins had no thought of holding the town, and he ordered his captains to sail north to Block Island Channel, off Rhode Island. Here *Andrea Doria* and *Fly* captured an armed schooner, *Hawke*, and the bomb vessel *Bolton*. Both were taken with little trouble—*Hawke* was the first Royal Navy warship captured by the Continental Navy. Shortly thereafter the British frigate *Glasgow* of 22 guns, Capt. Tyringham Howe commanding, and its tender, a sloop, were sighted. Although all seven Continental vessels cleared for action, no orders came from Esek Hopkins. In fact, not one order was issued by the commodore during the engagement that followed. His son, Capt. John B. Hopkins, in *Cabot*, began the engagement.

As *Cabot* and *Glasgow* came within pistol shot of one another, both ships opened with broadsides. *Cabot*'s 6-pounders were no match for the 9-pounders aboard *Glasgow*, and as *Cabot* sheered away, it was hit with a devastating broadside that wounded Captain Hopkins. Nicholas Biddle in *Andrea Doria* was forced away from the battle in order to keep from colliding with *Cabot*. The flagship, *Alfred*, now joined the battle. *Alfred*'s 20 9-pounders were certainly a match for *Glasgow*, and Lt. John Paul Jones was below on the gundeck, urging on his crews. Suddenly *Cabot*'s wheel and tiller were struck, and the vessel broached (turned sideways). In this condition it could be raked at will.

However, *Andrea Doria* had come back into range of the British frigate, and *Columbus* was nearing. *Glasgow*'s captain, having acquitted himself brilliantly so far, decided that there was no future in taking on the entire patriot fleet, broke off the action, and fled using his stern chasers to ward off pursuit. *Columbus* had one last chance to rake the fleeing Britisher, but most of its shot went high. After four hours of fighting, Hopkins signaled a recall. This was the only direction he gave to his captains in the action. Five Americans had been killed and nine wounded. The British tender had been taken by the prize, *Hawke*.

The *Glasgow* was later reported to have sustained a good deal of punishment. She was "considerably damaged in her hull, had 10 shot through her mainmast, 52 through her mizzen stay sail, 110 through her main sail, 88 through her fore sail, had her spars carried away and her rigging shot to pieces." *Glasgow* had one man dead and three wounded. Each of these had been hit by American marines serving as sharpshooters. Although it was remarkable that any ship could escape after sustaining such extensive damage, American naval gunnery had been notably ineffective in not crippling the vessel.[26]

A Naval Court-Martial

The successes of the first American naval expedition quickly wore off as the details of the *Glasgow* action came to light. Captain Hazzard of *Providence* had made no attempt to join the battle, seeming content to sail back and forth out of range. He was hauled before a court-martial, and found guilty of neglecting his duty. Hazzard was cashiered, and John Paul Jones was given *Providence* as his own command. Numerous questions were raised of how a single British ship could do so much damage to an entire fleet and make good its escape. This failure was emphasized when Capt. John Barry, in command of the brigantine *Lexington*, captured the Royal Navy sloop of war *Edward* in a sharp single-ship encounter. Flag Capt. Abraham Whipple demanded and received a court-martial that found him to have been ineffective due only to an error in judgment and not from cowardice.

Although no Continental ship had been lost and several prizes had been taken, Commodore Hopkins quickly became the target of widespread criticism. Politics and preferment among his officers prevented the fleet from putting to sea again. The details of Hopkins's demise as commander in chief are complicated and unimportant. Ultimately, he was admonished by the Naval Committee for taking an initiative without the express orders of Congress in attacking New Providence, and he was censured for keeping the fleet inactive thereafter. The remainder of his career was marked by antagonism, hostility, and disaffection. On January 2, 1778, Congress found that it had "no further occasion for the service of Ezek [*sic*] Hopkins, Esquire," and it resolved that he "be dismissed from the service of the United States." Never again during the war was the rank of commander in chief given to another American naval officer.[27]

Saluting the Flag

On November 16, 1776, Capt. Isaiah Robinson, in *Andrea Doria*, approached the Dutch island of St. Eustatius in the eastern Caribbean.[28] As he entered the port, Robinson broke out an American flag. As was the custom when a friendly ship entered a foreign port, Robinson had the guns of the *Andrea Doria* fire a salute, which recognized the sovereignty of the Dutch government. The governor of the island, Johannes de Graaf, was used to seeing American vessels in his port. St. Eustatius had been a source of powder and arms for the American rebels for many months. However, never before had an American ship broken out a distinct set of national colors. De Graaf, who knew of the signing of the Declaration of Independence, resolved after several minutes of consultation with his advisers to answer the salute with one of his own. As the guns of Fort

Orange at the entrance to the harbor barked out a salute in response, Captain Robinson understood that the diplomatic status of the United States as an independent nation had for the first time been recognized by an official of a foreign power.[29]

The flag that received the salute was the Flag of Union sewed by a Philadelphia milliner, Margaret Manny. With thirteen red and white stripes, the Flag of Union had the crosses of St. George and St. Andrew in the corner, much like the all-red British naval ensign with its Union Jack in the upper quarter. Margaret Manny's flag, made of more than 45 yards of cloth, had been raised on board the flagship *Alfred* by John Paul Jones in January 1776.

Manny's design was the first for a national flag approved by Congress, and the same design was flown by Washington at the siege of Boston. The more famous Betsy Ross flag of thirteen stripes and a circle of thirteen stars on a blue quarter was not recognized by Congress until 1777. Other flags with red and white stripes sported a wide variety of patterns of thirteen stars on a blue field, including a very common 3-2-3-2-3 horizontal arrangement.

John Paul Jones

Eighteenth on the list in order of precedence for a naval command was John Paul Jones. Born in Scotland in 1747 as John Paul, this American naval officer is the best known single-ship commander to have served in the Continental Navy. Having brushed with the wrong side of British maritime law by killing the ringleader of a mutinous crew in the merchant service without a trial, John Paul quickly vanished from sight and changed his name. There is some evidence that before the Revolution he made his living as a smuggler and pirate in North Carolina. Nonetheless, when the war began, Jones was able to use the patronage of several influential colonial shipowners to receive a place near the end of the precedence list of the Continental Navy.

Jones was made the first lieutenant of Commodore Hopkins's flagship, *Alfred*. Having survived the political storm that surrounded Hopkins's fiasco in the Bahamas and having been given command of *Providence*, Jones quickly proceeded on a series of independent cruises, taking 16 prizes in short order. Although *Providence* mounted only a dozen 4-pounders and some swivel guns, Jones found the vessel fast and maneuverable and later wrote that the crew was the best he ever commanded.[30]

After leaving *Providence*, Jones traveled to France in a new command, the American sloop-of-war *Ranger*. Armed with 18 4-pounders, he ravaged the English Channel and the Irish Sea. Palpable fear overtook the British public when Jones attacked the home of Lord Selkirk on the west coast of Britain, stole his silver plate, and burned several vessels in the nearby port of Whitehaven. The alarm was sounded all along the coast, and several British cruisers were sent in pursuit of "the Yankee pirate." One of these was the *Drake* (20 6-pounders), built in an American ship-yard in Philadelphia before the war and taken into the Royal Navy as a sloop-of-war.[31]

Ranger vs. Drake. The American and British ships encountered one another an hour before sunset on April 24, 1778, in the Belfast Lough. Jones, with his yards set back, waited for *Drake* to approach. The British vessel sent a lieutenant to check *Ranger*'s paper's; he was immediately taken as a prisoner of war. *Drake* raised the red British naval ensign and was approaching *Ranger*'s stern when Jones broke out the American colors and opened a broadside. The British captain was caught unawares and allowed Jones to suddenly cross his bows, raking him from stem to stern. Wanting a prize, Jones stood off, blasting *Drake*'s rigging with chain and bar shot and the deck with grapeshot.

The British captain was killed in the first minutes of the battle. *Drake*'s first lieutenant was mortally wounded, and 42 of the crew were killed or wounded. Within an hour the British vessel became unmanageable, and the remaining crew surrendered. *Drake* was the first Royal Navy warship taken by an American in European waters. *Ranger* lost only three killed and five wounded. Jones sent his first officer, Lt. Thomas Simpson, to take over the prize.[32]

Jones disliked Simpson, a political appointee, and found fault with his handling of *Drake* on the return to France. In fact, Jones placed Simpson under arrest for insubordination at the end of the cruise. Jones also found himself at odds with a large segment of his crew over prize money, bad treatment, and his charges against Simpson (who was generally well-liked). Seventy-seven sailors and 28 warrant and petty officers complained to the American commissioners in Paris that Jones was arbitrary, bad-tempered, and insufferable. Supported only by Benjamin Franklin, who promised him command of a new powerful frigate, Jones dropped his charges against Simpson, who sailed away in *Ranger*. The frigate promised by Franklin never materialized, but late in 1778 a ship was found that could serve Jones's purpose.[33]

Duc de Duras was a tired East Indiaman of 900 tons built in 1766. The ship was sturdy, but ponderous and slow. It was armed with six 9-pounders on its upper deck, 28 12-pounders on its main gundeck, and six ancient 18-pound garrison guns mounted so close to the waterline that they could not be run out in any weather other than a flat calm. Jones handpicked his officers and personally approved the 380 men who served aboard, many of them British deserters or former prisoners of war. Before sailing, Jones renamed the ship *Bonhomme Richard*.

Bonhomme Richard vs. Serapis. Serving as the commodore of a small squadron including *Bonhomme Richard* (40 guns), the corvette *Pallas* (26 guns), the brig *Vengeance* (12 guns), the small cutter *Cerf* (18 guns), and the American-built frigate *Alliance* (36 guns), Jones sailed into the Atlantic from France in search of the enemy. Each of his companion vessels, except *Alliance*, was outfitted and maintained by France but sailed under American commissions. *Alliance* was commanded by a Frenchman, Capt. Pierre Landais, an honorary citizen of Massachusetts.

On September 23, 1779, *Bonhomme Richard* sighted a large number of sails, which turned out to be a Baltic convoy of 41 supply ships under the protection of the frigate *Serapis* and the sloop-of-war *Countess of Scarborough*. The sloop-of-war was armed with only 22 guns, but *Serapis* was a fast, new frigate rated at 44 guns but carrying 50. Captain Richard Pearson had added further armament (20 9-pounders and ten 6-pounders) to the frigate's massive main battery of 20 18-pounders.

Since the wind was light, it took more than three hours for Jones's squadron to make its approach to the supply fleet. *Pallas* made for the *Countess of Scarborough*, engaged, and quickly made the Britisher a prize. *Vengeance* inexplicably took no part in the action, and *Alliance*, though initially making to engage *Serapis*, sheered off at the last moment. With darkness falling, *Bonhomme Richard* and *Serapis* maneuvered for advantage.

With its first fire, two of the ancient 18-pounders on *Bonhomme Richard* blew up, killing most of the lower gundeck crews and blowing a hole in the gundeck above. The two vessels entangled, and with his guns unable to bear, Jones attempted to board *Serapis*. Jones was driven back, and at this point in the action, Pearson, feeling that he had demonstrated his superior firepower and tactics, called out to Jones, "Has your ship struck?" From the deck of *Bonhomme Richard* came the reply, "I have not yet begun to fight!"[34]

Bonhomme Richard backed off, and the two antagonists were again broadside to broadside. Now the pounding match began. So close did the ships come that they again became entangled. Grapples were thrown and made fast. Sharpshooters in the American fighting tops began clearing the British deck. Suddenly *Alliance* came out of the growing darkness, and the Americans gave a cheer, supposing that Captain Landais would put his vessel along *Serapis*'s unengaged side. To their horror, Landais swung to the other side and let go a broadside into *Bonhomme Richard*. He then put about and put another into the bow. Jones was astonished at the actions of his subordinate, who may have mistaken his ally for the enemy in the dark.

With *Bonhomme Richard* sinking under him, Jones was once again asked to surrender. "No, sir, I haven't as yet thought of it, but I'm determined to make you strike." At about this time, seaman William Hamilton, who had been fighting in the tops, inched his way out onto a yardarm with a basket of grenades, determined to drop one into one of the open hatches of *Serapis*. After several tries, a grenade fell through, exploding among a pile of loose cartridges on the British gundeck. A terrible roar followed the exploding ammunition as the flames passed from pile to pile. About 20 men were killed, and many more were terribly burned. When a final British attempt to board Jones's ship failed, Pearson struck his own colors. Fearful that *Alliance* might return, Pearson later wrote that further battle seemed "in vain and in short impracticable from the situation . . . [and] with the least prospect of success."[35]

One of the most bitter and famous ship-to-ship actions in naval history was over. It had lasted for more than three hours. Jones lost 150 killed and wounded; Pearson had 120 casualties. Although *Countess of Scarborough* was made a prize by *Pallas*, not one of the Baltic supply fleet had been taken. This was remarkable, since *Vengeance* and *Cerf* had remained totally unengaged. *Bonhomme Richard* was a total loss. No amount of effort could save her. When Jones transferred his command to *Serapis*, he found his prize a leaking wreck also. Only through the efforts of both surviving crews did the ship make harbor in Texel, Holland.

Captain Pearson later faced a court-martial before the Admiralty for losing two warships in a single action, but the safety of the convoy and the number of enemies ranged against *Serapis* saved him. He was later knighted, causing Jones to remark, "Let me fight him again . . . and I'll make him a lord!" Jones was immediately raised to the status of a legend in America. His victories stood in sharp contrast to the failures of the rest of the Continental navy. Jones went on after the Revolution to renovate the organization and practices of the U.S. Navy and to serve as an admiral in the Russian navy.[36]

THE FAILURE OF THE ROYAL NAVY

The belligerent patriots were certain that they could defeat the British army that they so depised, but the one great fear shared by all Americans was that they would not be able to overcome the presence of the Royal Navy. In fact, this was a reasonable concern. The Americans never attempted to defeat any of the large British warships. They took on only the least fearsome of British vessels known as sloops-of-war.

The unrated sloop-of-war was a particular class of warship carrying less than 20 guns. There were only 23 sloops-of-war on the Royal Navy lists between the 1770s and 1780s, and many of these were specifically built to serve in the American War of Independence. At least three were on North American station as early as January 1775. Each carried between 14 and 16 light cannon (6-to-9-pounders), formidable against lightly built privateers and smugglers but too few and of insufficient weight to take on the American frigates.

Royal Navy vessels bombarded or burned every seaport town of appreciable size during the course of the war with the exception of Baltimore and Salem. Aside from creating a good deal of local terror and propaganda for the patriots, the bombardment of towns had little positive effect on the British war effort. The real failure of the Royal Navy was not in that it failed to make its presence felt but in that it failed to close off American shores to the constant flow of war materials from Europe and the West Indies. It also failed to maintain an uninterrupted logistical lifeline for the support of its own troops by allowing America's minuscule navy to intercept vital shipments of war materials and fighting men.

NOTES

1. Francis R. Stark, *The Abolition of Privateering and the Declaration of Paris* (New York: Columbia University Press, 1897), 121.

2. Samuel W. Bryant, *The Sea and the States* (New York: Thomas Y. Crowell, 1967), 86.

3. James M. Volo, "The War at Sea," *Living History Journal* (January 1987). Also see William Bell Clarke, *Ben Franklin's Privateers: A Naval Epic of the American Revolution* (New York: Greenwood Press, 1969).

4. See William Bell Clarke, *George Washington's Navy: Being an Account of His Excellency's Fleet in New England Waters* (Baton Rouge: Louisiana State University Press, 1960).

5. See Clarke, *Ben Franklin's Privateers*.

6. Nathan Miller, *Sea of Glory: A Naval History of the American Revolution* (Annapolis: Naval Institute Press, 1974), 72.

7. Clarke, *George Washington's Navy*, 62–63.

8. The *London Chronicle* (December 30 1775–January 2, 1776), as reported by Clarke, *George Washington's Navy*, 61.

9. Clarke, *George Washington's Navy*, 63.

10. Arthur Bowler, *Logistics and the Failure of the British Army in America, 1775–1783* (Princeton, NJ: Princeton University Press, 1975), 53. Also see Robert W. Neeser, ed., *The Dispatches of Molyneux Shuldham, Vice Admiral of the Blue and Commander in Chief of His Britannic Majesty's Ships in North America: January–July, 1776* (New York: Naval Society Publications, 1913).

11. Gardner W. Allen, *A Naval History of the American Revolution*, vol. 1 (Williamstown, MA: Corner House, 1970), 83–84.

12. Clarke, *George Washington's Navy*, 228.

13. Miller, *Sea of Glory*, 214.

14. William M. Fowler, Jr., *Rebels Under Sail: The American Navy During the Revolution* (New York: Scribner's, 1976), 295n.

15. In what follows, the place of each officer will be given as an ordinal number, or be marked "unlisted," in parentheses.

16. Miller, *Sea of Glory*, 56.

17. Ibid., 118–119.

18. Ibid., 93.

19. Bryant, *Sea and the States*, 78–79.

20. See Miller, *Sea of Glory*, chapter 6, 84–99.

21. Ibid., 93–94.

22. Barabara W. Tuchman, *The First Salute: A View of the American Revolution* (New York: Alfred A. Knopf, 1988), 47.

23. Miller, *Sea of Glory*, 93. See also Fowler, *Rebels Under Sail*, 92.

24. Fowler, *Rebels Under Sail*, 92.

25. While this is celebrated as the birth of the U.S. Marines, Americans had made amphibious landings during the French Wars—in particular the landing at Louisburg under William Pepperrell, during the War of the Austrian Succession.

26. Miller, *Sea of Glory*, 115.

27. Ibid., 217.

28. Sometimes called the *Andrew Doria*.

29. Tuchman, *The First Salute*, 4–6.

30. Miller, *Sea of Glory*, 128.

31. Ibid.

32. Ibid., 365–366.

33. Ibid., 369–370.

34. Miller points out that this famous phrase was uttered much earlier in the battle than is normally thought.

35. Miller, *Sea of Glory*, 384–385.

36. See Dorothy Denneen Volo and James M. Volo, *Daily Life in the Age of Sail* (Westport, CT: Greenwood, 2002), chapter 13, 265–281.

19

Prisoners of War

It is better to be slain in battle, than to be taken prisoner by British brutes, whose tender mercies are cruelties.[1]
—A patriot held prisioner in New York City

There is no question that patriots held prisoner by the British suffered terribly, and that their treatment may have violated the accepted standards of treatment for war prisoners. The worst abuses seem to have been suffered by the 3000 patriots captured during the British invasion of New York in 1776. They were held in the city in warehouses, churches, and prison ships without facilities for humanely housing such a large number. However, the diaries and journals of these prisoners, published in the nineteenth century to document their sufferings, were largely anecdotal in nature and accompanied by no useful analysis. Unfortunately, many of the extravagant and inaccurate statements made by the editors of these works have been accepted at face value by later generations of historians.

The patriots threatened retaliation upon British soldiers held captive in consequence of any mistreatment received by Americans, and they used such persons as pawns in a political game surrounding the recognition of American sovereignty. Washington warned that he would not hesitate to treat the British prisoners in America with as much severity as his own countrymen received, and Franklin wrote, "We are determined to treat such prisoners precisely as our countrymen are treated in

England; to give them the same allowance of provisions and accommodations, and no other."[2] Certainly after the Saratoga Convention of 1778 the treatment of patriots held prisoner became "less susceptible" to abuses because the Crown retreated from its earliest draconian policies as an immediate consequence of Burgoyne's surrender of an army of 5000 men. Burgoyne's men were thereafter known as the Convention Army, and they were moved about the colonies en masse, in an attempt to secure them without repatriation.[3]

THE RIGHTS OF PRISONERS

Prisoners of war were entitled, by common practice between European nations, to certain rights and immunities. The peculiarities of eighteenth-century protocols regarding prisoners proved to be complex. As Edmund Burke declared in a session of Parliament dealing with the question of the status of American prisoners, "How difficult it is to apply these juridical ideas to our present case."[4] Although efforts to limit the brutality of war by the acceptance of conventions had been growing in the eighteenth century, the existing protocols remained fragile.[5] The rules applicable to the handling of war prisoners, unlike those of modern times, had simply not yet been "precisely defined or uniformly enforced."[6] It may be that the established conventions were earnestly applied, even in the face of rhetoric to the contrary.

There is evidence that certain protocols, at least with respect to sailors, had been codified. Published in 1763, *Traités des Prises Qui Se Font sur Mer*, a French treatise detailing the protocols regarding prisoners taken at sea, was cited by American diplomats in their letters to the Crown several times. In April 1777, Benjamin Franklin, Silas Deane, and Arthur Lee referred to them in a letter drafted to Lord Stormont, the British ambassador to France. The letter asked that his lordship alleviate the sufferings of the prisoners according to "the rules established, and generally observed by civilized nations."[7]

By common usage between sovereign nations, certain privileges had come to be expected with respect to prisoners. In most conflicts, prisoners of war proved only a minor annoyance. Soldiers and sailors could expect to save their lives by begging quarter and surrendering their arms to their captors in battle. The wounded could expect humane care. Captives commonly spent only a short time in prison or were allowed limited freedom to remain unconfined under their parole, or word of honor. Since it was uneconomical for both sides in a conflict to expend the resources needed to maintain and guard even a small number of prisoners for any length of time, captives usually were quickly exchanged by means of a formal arrangement known as a cartel. Such cartels normally applied to all ranks and were accomplished by exchanging men of equal rank, or by exchanging a man of superior rank for several of inferior rank following a previously negotiated scheme.

However, American prisoners of war were an embarrassment to the Crown. Since Britain did not recognize the existence of the American states as a sovereign nation, but rather as absolute subjects of the king, they could not officially hold patriots as prisoners of war. "Traitors were not afforded the protection owed under the international war code to soldiers and subjects of recognized governments."[8] In the early days of the war, the British resolved this difficulty to their own satisfaction by simply holding the patriots illegally. This was a direct violation of the habeas corpus provisions of the British constitution, under which some patriots in the West Indies, claiming the ancient rights of Englishmen, brought suit and actually obtained their release. This difficulty was overcome in 1776 by the temporary suspension of habeas corpus by Parliament, allowing the prisoners to be held on probable cause. Although this raised a storm of protest among those members of Parliament friendly to America, the suspension of habeas corpus was renewed in 1777, and captured patriots were thereafter held "at the pleasure of the King."[9]

The American captives were housed in various buildings in and about the city of New York, including several Nonconforming churches, a number of warehouses, and two sugar refineries. The overflow was placed on mastless prison hulks in Wallabout Bay, near the Flushing section of Queens.[10] Early patriot successes had embarrassed and humiliated the professionals of the British army. The redcoats had prosecuted a massive retaliatory campaign in November 1776. Thousands of patriot captives were taken, and instead of being confined by civil authorities, they were placed under the jurisdiction of the military, which was poorly equipped and ill-disposed to deal with them humanely.

American captives complained regularly about the amount of their ration, which should have been ten and one half pounds of bread per week instead of the seven and one half pounds they received. Contemporary sources fail to report how the prisoners came to believe that they were entitled to the greater quantity. The British claimed that this was what had been given to the Scottish rebels held prisoner in 1746, and that American rebels should expect no more. The prisoners also complained of a lack of firewood, clothing, and blankets in winter; severe discipline and the demand that they maintain silence; overcrowding; exposure to diseases, including smallpox; and inadequate ventilation in summer, caused by being closed down in the holds of ships or shut into buildings with few or no windows.[11]

NEGOTIATIONS

To their credit, the brothers Howe repeatedly corresponded with the patriots during the 1776 campaign concerning reconciliation and met with congressional delagates to discuss the disposition of prisoners. They extended offers of pardons to Washington as early as July 1776, but the congressional representatives at the meetings rejected their repeated entreaties.[12] As the campaign wore on, Lord Richard Howe became disgusted with these meetings because the Americans insisted on discussing prisoner exchanges. Ultimately General Howe presided at these conferences alone, always trying to bring the discussions back to the topic of pardons. He was met with an unvarying negative response. Washington aptly expressed the American position: "Those who have committed no crime, need no pardon."[13]

In light of the devastating defeat of the patriots in New York, General Howe may have expected a different response. Therefore, he patiently awaited the collapse of the rebel cause in the wake of his successful campaign through New Jersey. The collapse never occurred. Howe's guarded campaign against the patriots and the repeated attempts at reconciliation by both Howe brothers were a marked departure from the violent and unrelenting prosecution of the Scottish rebellion in 1746.

Edmund Burke expressed the moderate Whig view in Parliament against proceeding with a similar prosecution of the Americans. "Though rebellion is declared . . . modes of coercion have been adopted, [that] have much more resemblance to a sort of qualified hostility towards an independent power than the punishment of rebellious subjects." Burke suggested to Parliament that a lack of restraint in this regard would teach the colonials that "the government against which a claim of liberty is tantamount to high treason is a government to which submission is equivalent to slavery."[14]

In what may have been a crucial decision in establishing the status of Americans held as prisoners, General Howe relented with respect to pardons and arranged for the exchange of both Gen. John Sullivan and Gen. William Alexander (Lord Stirling) in November 1776. The offer to exchange two high-ranking rebels, one of whom was a member of the Irish peerage whose father had been a Jacobite, was an extremely sensitive issue. Lord George Germain, the colonial secretary, was sharply critical of the Howe brothers for their liberality during this period.[15]

Nonetheless, General Howe did little to change the immediate situation of the bulk of the prisoners. His actions may have been predicated on the belief that the war would soon end, and the problem would cease to exist. It was not until after the Saratoga surrender that the British came to the realization that the war was going to last longer than previously expected. This may have caused them to reform their thinking with regard to the captives. British officals predictably denied that the prisoners were being ill-used. Even so, the status of the captives remained unresolved, and the British maintained a confused attitude toward them until 1781.[16]

General Howe was replaced by Henry Clinton as the commander of New York in May 1778, thereby freeing him of some responsibility for the fate of the prisoners housed there after that date. Even if Howe was not directly responsible for the conditions in which the captives were confined, some of the subordinates he appointed were particularly loathsome fellows. Joshua Loring, the commissioner of prisoners in New York and the husband of Howe's mistress, admitted starving to death 300 men by appropriating two-thirds of their rations for his own use. Loring's provost marshal, William Cunningham, swore in a deathbed confession, "I shudder at the murders I have been accessory to, both with and without orders from the government, especially while in New York, during which time there were more than 2000 prisoners starved in the different churches, by stopping their rations, which I sold." The misdeeds testified to by these men are consistent with other contemporary evidence as to their nature and scope.[17]

War Crimes

British regulars sometimes strayed from a scrupulous adherence to prisoner of war policies. As many as 67 American dragoons may have been executed in a barbaric fashion after their surrender at Tappan, New York, by a detachment of regulars under Gen. Charles Grey. Witnesses to the massacre reported that the captives were herded into two large barns to be killed by bayonet and bludgeon in comparative silence. This atrocity, often considered rebel propaganda, has been confirmed by recent archaeological finds in the area, and the traditional details of the massacre have been verified by the scrutiny of modern forensic science on the remains of several hurriedly interred victims.[18] General Grey was also charged with the massacre of 54 Americans at Paoli during the Philadelphia campaign of 1778. At Waxhaws, the regulars of Tarleton's Legion slaughtered 113 Virginians of Colonel Buford's command who had already surrendered. This number included the wounded, who were bayonetted on the ground. This was one of several atrocities attributed to Lt. Col. Banastre Tarleton, giving rise to the derisive phrase "Tarleton's quarter."[19]

Although few other patriots were killed after surrender, many lost their lives due to prolonged periods of confinement. A survivor of the prisons estimated that 1500 American captives died in the first year of their confinement in New York. It must be remembered, however, that although the patriots took many of their wounded with them when they retreated from New York, they left behind those so seriously hurt that they could not be moved. Although records indicate the allocation of hospital staff to prison facilities, the large number of wounded and sick patriot prisoners taken in the New York campaign may account for the high rate of mortality in the first year of their prison confinement.[20]

NOTES

1. Frank Moore, *Documentary Account of the American Revolution*, 2 vols. (New York: Columbia University Press, 1972), vol. 1, 194; See also Danske Dandridge, *American Prisoners of the Revolution* (Baltimore: Genealogical Publishing, 1911).

2. Moore, *Documentary Account*, vol. 1, 329.

3. John Fiske, *The American Revolution*, 2 vols. (New York: Houghton, Mifflin, 1896), vol. 2, 3.

4. Edmund Burke, *Speeches on Conciliation with America* (Boston: Ginn, 1897), 34.

5. Russell F. Weigley, *The Age of Battles: The Quest for Decisive Warfare from Breitenfeld to Waterloo* (Bloomington: Indiana University Press, 1991), 211.

6. Larry Bowman, *Captive Americans: Prisoners During the American Revolution* (Athens: Ohio University Press, 1976), 3.

7. Edward Hale, *Franklin in France* (Boston: Roberts, 1887), 195.

8. Weigley, *Age of Battles*, 211.

9. William M. Fowler, Jr., *Rebels Under Sail: The American Navy During the Revolution* (New York: Scribner's, 1976), 257.

10. Thomas J. Wertenbaker, *Father Knickerbocker Rebels* (New York: Scribner's, 1948), 163.

11. Bowman, *Captive Americans*, 54.

12. Geoffrey Regan, *SNAFU* (New York: Avon Books, 1993), 25.

13. Wertenbaker, *Father Knickerbocker*, 153–154.

14. Burke, *Speeches on Conciliation*, 33–34.

15. Don Higginbotham, *The War of American Independence: Military Attitudes, Policies, and Practice, 1763–1789* (Boston: Northeastern University Press, 1983), 198.

16. Bowman, *Captive Americans*, 129–130.

17. Wertenbaker, *Father Knickerbocker*, 163.

18. Burt Garfield Loeschner, *Washington's Eyes* (Fort Collins, CO: Old Army Press, 1977), 74–75.

19. See Bruce Lancaster, *The History of the American Revolution* (New York: American Heritage/Bonanza, 1971).

20. Richard M. Ketchum "New War Letters of Banastre Tarleton—Edited," in *Narratives of the Revolution in New York* (New York: Kingsport Press, 1975), 180.

20

The French Allies

Admiral de Grasse's 1781 offensive was "the most important and most perfectly executed naval campaign of the age of sail."
—Jonathan R. Dull, Naval Historian

It is conceivable that the British colonies in America could have overcome the overwhelming military superiority of Great Britain in their struggle for independence without the help of some established foreign power. However, as British naval power closed off outside commerce with the Americans and prohibited the colonists from receiving or renewing their stocks of firearms and munitions, independence became increasingly unlikely. The victory of the patriots at Saratoga in 1777 has traditionally been cited as the impetus needed by the colonials to establish an alliance with France that would help to ensure their success.

However, by 1777 the French Council of State had already faced the necessity of entering the war. Through overt and clandestine efforts Charles Gravier Vergennes, French minister of state, pursued "an aggressively anti-British policy." His plan was to weaken Britain economically through the loss of its colonies and to reestablish the balance of power that had been lost in the Seven Years' War.[1] Initially, he had hoped to sustain the American war effort solely with military supplies and money. He secretly arranged for the patriots to receive aid through the services of Hortalez and Company, a front for the French government managed by the playwright Beaumarchais.

FRANCE ENTERS THE WAR

Fearing that a compromise Anglo-American peace was in the offing in 1777 and mistrusting the assertions of the American commissioners in Paris to the contrary, Vergennes suddenly sought a reason to actively enter the war. Only in this manner can the victory of the Americans over the British at Saratoga be said actually to have ensured the active participation of the French. When the French frigate *Belle-Poule* was fired upon by the British fleet of Admiral Kepple in 1778, Vergennes seized upon the incident to declare war on Britain.[2]

The immediate problem was to design a strategy that would assist the patriots while preserving French possessions in the Western Hemisphere. France's ships of the line were ready to take on those of the British, but at the same time, Vergennes attempted to attract Spain into the alliance. Spain, ruled by another Bourbon monarch, was of great potential help to France. While Vergennes claimed that French ships alone could "dominate the English Channel [and] force Britain to choose between peace and general bankruptcy," Spain had enough ships to add to the French fleet to function primarily as a distraction to the English. The superfluous ships of the line would crush the scattered British naval forces in North America.[3]

THE NAVAL WAR

In the years after the Seven Years' War, the British ruling classes became indifferent to the needs of the Royal Navy. Having won an empire and having humiliated their traditional enemies, they seemed to have misunderstood the perils that continued to exist. The failure to maintain the Royal Navy in fighting trim was to have devastating consequences. Many of the British vessels that fought in the Seven Years' War entered the American Revolution as overaged derelicts.

By contrast, the French continued building warships with greater resolve during the interwar years. By 1770, the French had 64 of the finest ships of the line and an additional 50 state-of-the-art frigates. These vessels were some of the swiftest warships in the world. Moreover, Spain had built or refitted another 50 ships of the line. The British viewed this buildup with a certain amount of disquiet. Nonetheless, much of the Royal Navy had been systematically sold off by 1775, with 97 warships struck from the Admiralty lists. Just 57 had been added, and they were of inferior size and weight of metal. There was also a severe shortage of timber, made worse by the loss of the great stands of oak and pine in North America.[4]

French entrance into the war transformed it from a ground engagement in the colonies into a multiocean naval war, spilling over into India and the Far East. The French alliance, and that of Spain and finally of Holland, forced the British to "severely modify [their] strategy for suppressing the American rebellion."[5] Initially the British planned to destroy the patriot army by crushing the rebellion in the urban centers, as in New York in 1776; but this strategy failed mainly because the rebel armies melted into the unrestricted colonial hinterland. Alternately, the British planned to wear down American resistance by detaching mobile forces from their urban bases, particularly New York, Philadelphia, Savannah, and Charleston. This strategy proved to be seriously deficient, especially in view of the need to detach forces to counter the French potential of invading the undermanned and economically important British possessions in the West Indies.

The British also failed to exploit a number of tactical opportunities offered to them by concentrating on countering French strategy rather than taking the naval initiative. The British navy missed over a dozen strategic opportunities by ignoring the realities of naval operations and repeatedly obtaining a meaningless naval superiority in autumn in Europe and in summer in the Caribbean, when adverse weather, particularly the hurricanes of the West Indies, made French incursions unlikely.[6] "For such strategic ineptitude the British could have no excuse."[7]

French Strategy

The general French strategy in the war was well-conceived, especially their ability to obtain a tactical superiority for Admiral De Grasse's 1781 Chesapeake campaign. Ironically French plans revolved around the use of sea power against the very nation that had so effectively used its navy to gain an empire in the previous conflict. The French used their ships to pour troops into the islands of the West Indies while the Spanish concentrated on reinforcing Louisiana and West Florida. French troops were also dispatched to India, Minorca, Gibraltar, Senegal, Dutch Guyana, Pensacola, and Hudson's Bay.

The first actions by French troops in support of the patriots were at the siege of Savannah in the fall of 1779, but this operation ended in failure. Meanwhile, the arrival in New England of a land army of 6000 troops under Gen. Jean Baptiste Comte de Rochambeau in 1780 had little to do with winning the war beyond supplying the patriots with artillery and muskets and depriving the British of the harbor at Newport, Rhode Island. The French allies brought to the patriot army the equivalent of nine battalions of infantry and artillery, and about 300 mounted hussars of the duke of Lauzun's Legion, composed of German, Polish, Hungarian, and Irish volunteers. The foot troops were from the Soissonois, Bourbonnois, Saintonge, and Royal-Deux-Ponts regiments, and the artillery was detached from the Metropolitan Royal Artillery Metz and Auxonne regiments.

The French found the patriots so weakened by five years of war that they could not contemplate a new campaign with the Main Army. General Rochambeau was "the soul of patience and diplomacy" in his dealings with Washington, under whom he placed himself. He quietly planned a joint operation with Washington in Westchester County and the Hudson Highlands to draw Sir Henry Clinton from his New York stronghold in 1781. However, Nathanael Greene had successfully bled the British army under Lord Cornwallis to the point that it needed to abandon its future operations if it did not receive supplies and reinforcements. As Cornwallis moved to Yorktown in Virginia, Rochambeau and Washington deftly moved their men south from New England without alerting the British in New York. The French made up about half of the troops and almost all of the artillery that besieged Cornwallis in Yorktown.

The French Navy Secures American Independence

In 1781, the British Atlantic Squadron was based in New York under Vice Admiral Lord Thomas Graves. From the great harbor in New York Bay, Graves kept a cautious eye on a small squadron of eight French warships based in Newport, Rhode Island. The more numerous British warships were more than a match for the French, and the distinguished admiral Lord Richard Howe had chased them back into Newport in a series of maneuvers in 1778 before leaving for England. However, Graves, although an able sea officer, lacked the flexibility and ingenuity of Howe. He tended to follow orders cautiously and deliberately. Nonetheless, in March 1781, Graves led a fleet of warships sufficiently well to drive a small French squadron back into Newport once again.

When Cornwallis entered Yorktown, he was confident that he had completed the most dangerous part of his operations. Though besieged to landward, he had a reasonable expectation that he would be relieved on the York River side of his position by Graves's fleet of 19 warships, which had sailed from New York. He was seemingly unaware that the French fleet campaigning in the Caribbean under Admiral De Grasse had stolen a march on the Royal Navy's West Indian Squadron under Admiral Sir George Rodney and had run north into the coastal waters off Virginia. While Rodney frantically tried to locate De Grasse's fleet in the Caribbean, Graves found the 24 French warships quietly sailing for the mouth of the Chesapeake.

The immediate relief of Cornwallis was impossible under these circumstances. Noting that the French were "in no sort of battle-order,"

Graves cautiously edged his well-formed battle line down upon the French fleet. De Grasse moved away from the bay, close-hauled to the wind to take up the challenge. What followed was little more than a long-range cannonade. Having engaged less than half of Graves's line, De Grasse cleverly maneuvered and sailed back into the mouth of the bay, where he dropped anchor. Joined shortly thereafter by the French Rhode Island squadron that had sailed to Virginia in the interim, De-Grasse's fleet now numbered 36 ships of the line.

Graves was left at sea with a substantially inferior fleet and unable to do anything but return to his base at New York. He had lost no engagement. No ships had been lost on either side, and few cannonballs had flown. Yet Graves's inability to bring the French fleet to heel had lost America. Left without relief, Cornwallis could do nothing but surrender. By most standards the battle of the Chesapeake, one of the most decisive sea battles in history, had been a somewhat boring affair.[8]

Lord Cornwallis was paroled and allowed to return to England, but it was not immediately evident that the war was over. The allied army was broken up, with some of the patriot units being detached to Greene's command and others to the Hudson Highlands to watch over the British in New York. The French troops went into winter quarters in Williamsburg, Virginia. Washington stayed in Philadelphia that winter. Yet the momentum of the successful allied war effort in 1781 led to an increasing likelihood of the war coming to a speedy conclusion.

This placed Vergennes under some stress to extricate France from the conflict with its war aims fulfilled just as events were turning against him. In 1782 Admiral De Grasse was captured and his fleet scattered by the Royal Navy at the battle of the Saintes. French forces found themselves beleaguered in India, and unilateral operations by the Spanish were muddying the diplomatic waters. The peace negotiations being held in Paris increasingly centered on Spanish, rather than French, war aims. Vergennes urged better allied coordination to avoid a bad peace, but he became convinced that the situation would continue to deteriorate if the war continued.[9]

Ultimately Vergennes found his policies being undermined by the unpredictable consequences of English politics, which he had enormous difficulty understanding. He was also hampered by a fear that the Americans would agree to any peace proposition that explicitly or implicitly recognized American Independence. On December 15, 1782, he wrote to Benjamin Franklin, who served on the peace treaty committee:

I am at a loss, Sir, to explain your conduct and that of your colleagues on this occasion. You have concluded your preliminary articles without any communication between us, although the instructions from Congress prescribe that nothing shall be done without the participation of the [French] King. You are about to hold out a certain hope of peace to America without informing yourself on the state of the negotiation on our part.[10]

Franklin returned an answer to the French foreign minister two days later that included an apology, a good deal of diplomatic deference, but very little in the way of substance on this issue: "It is not possible for any one to be more sensible than I of what I and every American owe to the [French] King for the many and great benefits and favors he has bestowed upon us."[11]

THE PEACE OF PARIS

In January 1783 a peace treaty was signed that recognized the independence of the former British colonies in America. France's participation in the war proved tragic for the French Crown. Vergennes had sought and won a war, which unfortunately failed "to bring about the rapprochement he sought, and which raised dangers from within the [French] monarchy far greater than those which threatened it from without."[12] Unwittingly the foreign minister had helped to prepare a financial and political crisis, which was to lead France into its own revolution in less than a decade. Nonetheless, Vergennes poses an impressive figure in the history of American independence. He successfully combined a "consistency of ends with a flexibility of means." However, he risked France's own empire by fighting such a damaging and costly war simply to reduce Britain to parity in the balance of European power.[13]

A VIEW OF AMERICA

One of the French officers who served with General Rochambeau recorded his impressions of the United States and of Americans as he prepared to return home from a long winter in Williamsburg, Virginia:

The Americans are generally large, strong and well made: the women are handsome, tapering in form, having very little bust, of a disposition the more gentle from the fact of their having among them many Anabaptists, known to be the most charitable of all sects. Hospitality is greatly practiced, as travellers in this extensive country are few, scarely any in fact.

The servants are negroes, certainly the least unhappy of their kind, being treated with more kindness than our lackeys in France; hence we never hear in this country of masters poisoned by their negroes, so common an occurrence in our West India islands. The Anglican is the dominant religion; yet all are suffered here; the language is English. I believe these two things may well make them [the Americans] give the English the preference over us in a few years.[14]

NOTES

1. Johnathan Dull, *The French Navy and American Independence: A Study of Arms and Diplomacy 1774–1787* (Princeton, NJ: Princeton University Press, 1975), 33.

2. Ibid., 118–120.

3. Ibid., 139.

4. Michael Lewis, *The History of the British Navy* (Fair Lawn, NJ: Essential Books, 1959), 140–141.

5. *The French Navy*, 105.

6. Ibid., 263.

7. For a wider discussion of naval strategy in this regard see ibid., 188–225.

8. Lewis, *History of the British Navy*, 145.

9. Dull, *The French Navy*, 239.

10. Richard B. Morris and James Woodress, eds., *Voices from America's Past: The Times That Tried Men's Souls, 1770–1783* (New York: McGraw-Hill, 1961), 56.

11. Ibid.

12. Dull, *The French Navy*, 11.

13. Ibid., 228.

14. William P. Cumming and Hugh Rankin, eds., *The Fate of a Nation: The American Revolution Through Contemporary Eyes* (London: Phaidon Press, 1975), 332.

Epilogue: Independence

INEVITABLE VICTORY

Americans entered the revolution with little hope of military victory over Britain. Only the intervention of France, Spain, and Holland allowed the war to end as it did. The many victories won by British arms on American soil prior to Yorktown should have proved decisive in ending the Revolution. The series of defeats suffered by Washington's army in New York alone should have ended the war in November 1776. The subsequent loss of Newport, Savannah, Charleston, and the nation's capital at Philadelphia should have ended the war by 1780. That they did not makes the War for Independence that much more remarkable.

The battles of the American Revolution were fought by relatively small armies, compared to the giant forces that swarmed across Europe during the eighteenth century. This is important to better understanding the nature of the conflict in North America. Decisive battles in Europe involved many more men, and the killed and wounded often numbered one-third of those on the field. In America not only were the armies smaller, but so was the number killed and wounded. Generally low casualty rates allowed both armies to survive repeated tactical defeats in order to fight again.

Small armies rely more on capable leadership and creative strategy than do larger ones. The patriots seem to have been blessed with both. A limited number of troops also emphasizes the importance of terrain, of unit morale and cohesion, and of the concentration of fire upon the enemy. Small unit operations, the interdiction of supply lines, the use of surprise and other stratagems, and a reliance on the effects of partisan warfare were never more important than they were in the Revolution.[1]

Washington quickly surmised that he could win the war only by keeping his army intact until Britain tired of fighting. Both he and his opponents considered the war one of outposts and ambuscades. The patriots won few pitched battles, but their victories came when they were most needed. The continuance of the war hinged on the successes at Trenton and Princeton in the winter of 1776–1777. Without these victories the patriot army might easily have dissolved into the footnotes of history. Likewise, an otherwise indecisive battle fought in the heat of late June 1778 at Monmouth, New Jersey, showed that the patriots could face adversity in a European-style engagement. The training and discipline acquired by the patriots during the Valley Forge winter were evident even to their opponents, making Monmouth the last major battle fought in the North. Thereafter, British strategy turned to the southern colonies.

INDECISIVE WARFARE

Much of America was never firmly controlled by either side through eight long years of warfare. Whole armies were surrendered, and strategic positions were taken and retaken, without a decisive determination of victory or defeat. It may be that decisiveness simply eluded military strategists throughout the struggle. Even after their defeat at Yorktown, the British retained undisputed control of many of America's major urban centers, and they had more than 30,000 troops on station in America. The Revolution was a war waged "upon territories already fought over, sometimes more than once, by the contestants in conflicts over and done with."[2] Nonetheless, many historians rank Saratoga and Yorktown among the dozen most decisive battles in military history.[3]

A COMMON CAUSE

It seems clear that the patriots were unprepared to found an entirely new form of government when the war ended. The immediate reaction to victory was one of sometimes violent retribution directed at the loyalist population. At least 100,000 loyalists fled to England or Canada during the course of the Revolution. Many waited until 1782 to take ship with the last of the redcoats to leave New York City, hoping in vain for a positive turn in British fortunes. One historian has noted, "The formation of the Tory or Loyalist party in the American Revolution; its persecution by the Whigs during a long and fratricidal war, and the banishment or death . . . of these most conservative and respectable Americans is a tragedy but rarely paralleled in the history of the world."[4]

**The last boatload of British soldiers to leave New York. The city was held
longer by the British than any other urban center in America.**

In March 1783, two seditious papers were circulated among the patriot
officers at the encampment at Newburgh, New York, suggesting that the
army overthrow Congress and the state governments, and set up a monarchy or dictatorship. The papers were unsigned. Washington was ap-
prised of the situation, and at a meeting in the Temple, a large building
used for church services, he quietly defused the potential disaster by
employing a simple piece of theatrics. As he rose to speak, he took out
his eyeglasses to scan the offending papers. He then said:

Gentlemen . . . I have not only grown gray, but almost blind in the service of my
country. . . . Let me plead with you . . . that you express your utmost horror and
detestation of the man who wishes to overturn the liberties of our country and
who wickedly attempts to open the floodgates of civil discord and deluge our
rising empire in blood.[5]

Washington took formal leave of his officers at Fraunces Tavern, at
the corner of Broad and Pearl streets in New York City, some months
later. It was a tear-filled scene as the former commander in Chief shook
the hand of every man in attendance. He said only a few words:

With a heart full of love and gratitude I now take leave of you. I most devoutly wish that your later days may be as prosperous as your former ones have been glorious and honorable.[6]

In forming a new national administration, there were many patriots with reservations about the exact limits of power to be given to the federal government and what authority should remain with the states and the individual citizen. A central government without proper limits to its power would result in trading a tyrannical monarch for a despotic congress. The founders, therefore, designed a government under the Articles of Confederation that would possess only those powers necessary to provide for the common needs of the thirteen states. In this regard Congress may initially have gone too far. The obvious weakness of the Articles quickly threatened the existence of the nation. Thus, less than five years from the end of the war, the entire problem of governance had to be revisited again by the Constitutional Convention.

The patriots were all volunteers—citizen soldiers—and they fought for independence under the specters of impoverishment, imprisonment, disability, or even death without resorting to European-style conscription. John Marshall, who served in the army and later became chief justice of the Supreme Court, wrote, "I found myself associated with brave men from different states who were risking life and everything valuable in a common cause."[7]

NOTES

1. Jeremy Black, *Warfare in the Eighteenth Century* (London: Cassell, 1999), 105.

2. John Keegan, *Fields of Battle: The Wars for North America* (New York: Vintage Press, 1997), 138.

3. See Russell F. Weigley, *The Age of Battles: The Quest for Decisive Warfare from Breitenfeld to Waterloo* (Bloomington: Indiana University Press, 1991); and Archer Jones, *The Art of War in the Western World* (New York: Oxford University Press, 1987), for a wider consideration of these concepts.

4. Claude Halstead van Tyne, *Loyalists in the American Revolution* (Ganesvoort, NY: Corner House Historical Publications, 1999), 182. Most Americans today, who believe in traditional American government, would probably find themselves loyalists if they lived in 1775.

5. Bertrand M. Wainger, Dorothy W. Furman, and Edith Brooks Oagley, *Exploring New York* (New York: Harcourt, Brace, 1956), 107.

6. Ibid., 108.

7. L. Edward Purcell and David F. Burg, eds., *The World Almanac of the American Revolution* (New York: Pharos Books, 1992), xi.

Selected Bibliography

Anderson, Fred W. "Why Did Colonial New Englanders Make Bad Soldiers? Contractual Principles and Military Conduct During the Seven Years' War." *William and Mary Quarterly* 3d ser., 38 (1981), 395–417.

Berkin, Carol. *First Generations: Women in Colonial America*. New York: Hill and Wang, 1996.

Blumenthal, Walter Hart. *Women Camp Followers of the Revolution*. Salem, NH: Ayer, 1992.

Bowman, Larry. *Captive Americans: Prisoners During the American Revolution*. Athens: Ohio University Press, 1976.

Callahan, North. *Royal Raiders: The Tories of the American Revolution*. NewYork: Bobbs-Merrill, 1963.

Calloway, Colin G. *The American Revolution in Indian Country: Crisis and Diversity in Native American Communities*. Cambridge: Cambridge University Press, 1999.

Caruana, Adrian. *The Light 6-pdr. Battalion Gun of 1776*. Bloomfield, ON: Museum Restoration Services, 1977.

Clarke, William B. *Ben Franklin's Privateers*. Baton Rouge: Louisiana State University Press, 1956.

———. *George Washington's Navy*. Baton Rouge: Louisiana State University Press, 1960.

Commager, Henry Steele, and Richard B. Morris. *The Spirit of Seventy-six: The Story of the American Revolution as Told by Participants*. New York: Harper & Row, 1975.

Crane, Elaine Forman, ed. *The Diary of Elizabeth Drinker: The Life Cycle of an Eighteenth Century Woman*. Boston: Northeastern University Press, 1994.

Cumming, William P., and Hugh Rankin, eds. *The Fate of a Nation: The American Revolution Through Contemporary Eyes*. London: Phaidon Press, 1975.

Dandridge, Danske. *American Prisoners of the Revolution*. Baltimore: Genealogical Publishing, 1967.

Davies, K. G. *Documents of the American Revolution 1770–1783, Colonial Office series*. 22 vol. London: Irish University Press, 1976.

DePauw, Linda Grant, and Conover Hunt. *Remember the Ladies: Women in America, 1750–1815*. New York: Viking Press, 1976.

Dring, Thomas. *Recollections of the Jersey Prison Ship*. New York: Arno Press, 1961.

Dull, Johnathan. *The French Navy and American Independence: A Study of Arms and Diplomacy 1774–1787*. Princeton, NJ: Princeton University Press, 1975.

Fischer, David Hackett. *Albion's Seed: Four British Folkways in America*. New York: Oxford University Press, 1989.

Flexner, J. T. *States Dyckman: American Loyalist*. Boston: Little, Brown, 1980.

Foote, Allan D. *Liberty March: The Battle of Oriskany*. Utica, NY: North Country Books, 1998.

Fowler, William M., Jr. *Rebels Under Sail: The American Navy During the Revolution*. New York: Scribner's, 1976.

George, M. Dorothy. *London Life in the Eighteenth Century*. Chicago: Academy Chicago Publishers, 1999.

Gibson, Marjorie H. *HMS Somerset, 1746–1778: The Life and Times of an Eighteenth Century British Man-O-War and Her Impact on North America*. Cotuit, MA: Abbey Gate House, 1992.

Graymont, Barbara. *The Iroquois in the American Revolution*. Syracuse, NY: Syracuse University Press, 1972.

Guthman, William, ed. *The Correspondence of Captain Nathan and Lois Peters*. Hartford: Connecticut Historical Society, 1980.

Harrington, Peter. *Culloden 1746: The Highland Clans' Last Charge*. London: Osprey, 1991.

Hawkins, Christopher. *The Adventures of Christopher Hawkins*. New York: Arno Press, 1968.

Herbert, Charles. *A Relic of the Revolution*. New York: Arno Press, 1968.

Hibbert, Christopher. *Redcoats and Rebels: The American Revolution Through British Eyes*. New York: Avon, 1991.

Higginbotham, Don. *The War of American Independence: Military Attitudes, Policies, and Practice, 1763–1789*. Boston: Northeastern University Press, 1983.

Holliday, Carl. *Women's Life in Colonial Days*. Williamstown, MA: Corner House, 1968.

Hurt, R. Douglas. *The Ohio Frontier: Crucible of the Old Northwest, 1720–1830*. Indianapolis: Indiana University Press, 1996.

Keegan, John. *Fields of Battle: The Wars for North America*. New York: Vintage Press, 1997.

Kerber, Linda K. *Women of the Republic: Intellect and Ideology in Revolutionary America*. Chapel Hill: University of North Carolina Press, 1980.

Ketchum, Richard M. *Decisive Day: The Battle for Bunker Hill*. New York: Doubleday, 1974.

———. "New War Letters of Banastre Tarleton—Edited." In *Narratives of the Revolution in New York*. New York: Kingsport Press, 1975.

Koebner, Richard. *Empire*. New York: Grosset and Dunlap, 1965.

Lancaster, Bruce. *The History of the American Revolution*. New York: American Heritage/Bonanza, 1971.

Leach, Douglas E. *Roots of Conflict: British Armed Forces and Colonial Americans, 1677–1775*. Chapel Hill: University of North Carolina Press, 1986.

Lewis, Michael. *The History of the British Navy*. Fair Lawn, NJ: Essential Books, 1959.

Loeschner, Burt Garfield. *Washington's Eyes*. Fort Collins, CO: Old Army Press, 1977.

Martin, James Kirby, and Mark Edward Lender. *A Respectable Army: The Military Origins of the Republic, 1763–1789*. Arlington Heights, IL. Harlan Davidson, 1982.

Martin, Joseph Plumb. *Private Yankee Doodle: Being a Narrative of Some of the Adventures, Dangers and Sufferings of a Revolutionary Soldier*. Boston: Little, Brown, 1962.

Mayer, Holly A. *Belongs to the Army*. Columbia: University of South Carolina Press, 1996.

Meltzer, Milton, ed. *The American Revolution: A History in Their Own Words 1750–1800*. New York: Thomas Y. Crowell, 1987.

Middleton, Arthur Pierce. *A Virginia Gentleman's Library*. Williamsburg, VA: Colonial Williamsburg Foundation, 1952.

Moore, Frank. *The Diary of the American Revolution, 1775–1781*. New York: Washington Square Press, 1967.

———. *Documentary Account of the American Revolution*. 2 Vols. New York: Columbia University Press, 1972.

Morison, Samuel Eliot. *Sources and Documents Illustrating the American Revolution 1764–1788 and the Formation of the Federal Constitution*. New York: Oxford University Press, 1965.

Morris, Richard B., and James Woodress, eds. *Voices from America's Past: The Times That Tried Men's Souls, 1770–1783*. New York: McGraw-Hill, 1961.

Norton, Mary Beth. *Liberty's Daughters: The Revolutionary Experience of American Women, 1750–1800*. Boston: Little, Brown, 1980.

Padfield, Peter. *Maritime Supremacy and the Opening of the Western Mind*. New York: Overlook Press, 2002.

Pearson, Michael. *Those Damned Rebels: The American Revolution as Seen Through British Eyes*. New York: DaCapo Press, 1972.

Peckham, Howard. *The Toll of Independence*. Chicago: University of Chicago Press, 1974.

Phillips, Kevin. *The Cousin's War: Religion, Politics & the Triumph of Anglo-America*. New York: Basic Books, 1999.

Purcell, L. Edward, and David F. Burg, eds. *The World Almanac of the American Revolution*. New York: Pharos Books, 1992.

Randall, W. S. *Benedict Arnold: Traitor and Patriot*. New York: William Morrow, 1990.

Raphael, Ray. *A People's History of the American Revolution*. New York: New Press, 1991.

Riedesel, Baroness Fredericke. *Letters and Journals*. New York: Arno Press, 1968.

Risch, Erna. *Supplying Washington's Army*. Washington, DC: U.S. Army Center of Military Studies, 1981.

Ritchie, Carson I. A. "A New York Diary of the Revolutionary War." In *Narratives of the Revolution in New York*. New York: Kingsport Press, 1975.

Robson, Eric. *The American Revolution in its Political and Military Aspects, 1763–1783*. New York: Norton, 1966.

Rossie, Jonathan Gregory. *The Politics of Command in the American Revolution*. Syracuse, NY: Syracuse University Press, 1975.

Scheer, George, and Russell F. Weigley, eds. *Morristown*. Washington, DC: U.S. National Park Service, Division of Publications, 1983.

Tucker, Louis L. " 'To My Inexpressible Astonishment': Admiral Sir George Collier's Observations on the Battle of Long Island." In *Narratives of the Revolution in New York*. New York: Kingsport Press, 1975.

Volo, Dorothy Denneen, and James M. Volo. *Daily Life in the Age of Sail*. Westport, CT: Greenwood, 2002.

Volo, James M., and Dorothy Denneen Volo. *Daily Life on the Old Colonial Frontier*. Westport, CT: Greenwood, 2002.

Wacker, Peter O. *The Musconetcong Valley of New Jersey: A Historical Geography*. New Brunswick, NJ: Rutgers University Press, 1968.

Wahll, Andrew J., ed. *The Braddock Road Chronicles, 1755*. Bowie, MD: Heritage Books, 1999.

Watt, Gavin K. *The Burning of the Valleys: Daring Raids from Canada Against the New York Frontier in the Fall of 1780*. Toronto: Dundurn Press, 1997.

Wertenbaker, Thomas Jefferson. *Father Knickerbocker Rebels*. New York: Scribner's, 1948.

Williams, Selma R. *Demeter's Daughters: The Women Who Founded America 1587–1787*. New York: Atheneum, 1976.

Wright, Louis B. *The Atlantic Frontier: Colonial American Civilization, 1607–1763*. New York: Alfred A. Knopf, 1951.

Index

About the Authors

DOROTHY DENNEEN VOLO is a teacher and historian. She has been an active living history reenactor for 20 years and has been involved in numerous community historical educational projects. With James M. Volo, she is co-author of *Daily Life on the Old Colonial Frontier* (Greenwood, 2002).

JAMES M. VOLO is a teacher, historian, and living history enthusiast. He has been an active historic reenactor for more than two decades, participating in a wide range of living history events, including television and screen performances. With Dorothy Denneen Volo, he is co-author of *Daily Life on the Old Colonial Frontier* (Greenwood, 2002).